MARRIAGE

To Carolyn

MARRIAGE

Sex in the service of God

Christopher Ash

Inter-Varsity Press

INTER-VARSITY PRESS
38 De Montfort Street, Leicester LEI 7GP, England
Email: ivp@uccf.org.uk
Website: www.ivpbooks.com

First published 2003

British Library Cataloguing in Publication Data
A catalogue record for this book is available from the British Library.

ISBN 0-85111-994-8

Set in Monotype Garamond 11/13pt
Typeset in Great Britain by Servis Filmsetting Ltd, Manchester
Printed in Great Britain by CPD (Wales), Ebbw Vale

Inter-Varsity Press is the publishing division of the Universities and Colleges Christian Fellowship (formerly the Inter-Varsity Fellowship), a student movement linking Christian Unions in universities and colleges throughout Great Britain, and a member movement of the International Fellowship of Evangelical Students. For more information about local and national activities write to UCCF, 38 De Montfort Street, Leicester LEI 7GP, email us at email@uccf.org.uk, or visit the UCCF website at www.uccf.org.uk.

CONTENTS

Foreword 7

Preface 9

Acknowledgments 10

Abbreviations 11

INTRODUCTION

1 God and Sex 15

2 Prejudice and Grace 24

3 The Churning of Partners 34

PART ONE: THE BIBLICAL AND THEOLOGICAL BASIS
FOR THE STUDY OF MARRIAGE

4 Marriage and the Created Order 63

5 Marriage and the Kingdom of God 83

PART TWO: THE PURPOSE OF MARRIAGE

6 Why Sex and Marriage? 103

7 Sex in the Service of God 112

8 Sex in the Place of God 133

9 Children in the Service of God 157

10 Intimacy and Order in the Service of God 185

PART THREE: THE DEFINITION OF MARRIAGE

11 Public Choice and Private Intimacy 211

12 One Man and One Woman 246

13 Guarding the Family Circle 256

14 God's Pattern for Marriage   272
15 The Heart of Marriage – Faithfulness   340
    Conclusion   368

    Bibliography   370

    Scripture Index   387

FOREWORD

In a sound-bite culture like ours, many complex areas of Christian belief and behaviour are increasingly difficult to discuss and explain. The instant information and quick responses of modern technology lead to a rapid exchange of ideas and opinions, but they do not automatically lead to deeper understanding, or to more rigorous thought and argument. Indeed, they often mitigate against both, and trivialization becomes the dominant order of things. Increasingly, we are being driven to realize that in all the issues which matter most to us as human beings, a skilfully spun sound-bite will not do. As Christians we need to learn again what it means to love the Lord our God with all our mind and to give time and attention to today's burning issues.

This book is not a sound-bite! Rather, it constitutes a major piece of Christian thinking on a highly complex and controversial area of human life and behaviour – marriage. As such, it is not only a superb resource for biblical understanding and pastoral practice in an area of widespread disagreement, but it also provides a model of the method by which thoughtful, Bible-believing Christians should approach any and all of the challenges presented by the modern world. It represents and calls for a thoroughly wholesome transformation of outlook, by taking seriously the inspired teaching of Scripture, and through its explanation and application, bringing God's light to bear upon the confusion and despair of the current situation.

The central strength of this book is its conviction that the debate 'needs to focus on the nature and ends (or purposes) of marriage'. Rather than collecting anecdotal symptoms of the disease and applying a few hasty and impractical platitudes by way of a remedy, this treatment establishes a definition of 'health', by exploring in depth and detail the biblical and theological roots of marriage. This approach produces a working definition, which then serves to guide and focus the extensive discussion of the many issues raised. As the title implies, the major thesis of this book is that marriage is about serving God in his world, and for many of us that will involve a major paradigm shift.

To accomplish this goal, Christopher Ash provides a thorough-going exegesis of all the major biblical texts on the subject, with careful examination and weighing of the conflicting interpretations and arguments, particularly those of recent debate. Neither the traditional positions of Christian sub-cultural orthodoxies, nor the radical dogmatism of contemporary secularism are allowed to override the text of Scripture. But those original texts are also carefully set in their own contexts – literary, historical and cultural. Equally illuminating are the evidences and penetrating analyses of where twenty-first century secular (and sometimes Christian) attitudes are in conflict with the Bible. These thoughtful and stimulating connections give the book's clear and penetrating arguments greater trenchancy and relevance. Always, there is a sensitivity and pastoral wisdom to help hurting people in real-life situations of immense need to grapple biblically with these complex issues, which so deeply affect the innermost core of our humanness.

The depth of these theological foundations is matched by the breadth of its almost encyclopaedic coverage of all the 'hot potatoes'. From the current secular laws on marriage to issues such as cohabitation, polygamy, the privatization of marriage, contraception and adultery (to mention a few), the same sure touch, detailed examination of the issues and wise pastoral advice provide a rich resource of biblical understanding and application. The tone is consistently wholesome and positive, uncompromisingly clear and yet unfailingly gracious. This book will prove itself indispensable to pastors and counsellors in its compelling wisdom and practical guidance.

Christopher Ash is deservedly known for his biblical teaching gifts, his pastoral skills and his sharp theological and cultural insights. This rare combination has produced a unique book of great benefit to all who value the authority of Scripture and its application to every area of life. In thanking him for this magnificent achievement, I want to commend the fruit of his labours to the widest possible audience in the warmest possible terms. I have learned so much myself in reading this manuscript, with equal measures of challenge, encouragement and deepened understanding. May God be pleased to use this exposition to bring many to understand, accept and practise the gift of marriage according to the Maker's instructions, and in his service.

David Jackman
London, May 2003

PREFACE

There are some topics upon which everybody is willing to venture an opinion. Sex is one such. We are all interested in sex and we all feel we know something about it. As a result the literature, ranging across the whole spectrum from the popular to the academic, is vast and burgeoning. However, this literature is too often skewed away from the central focus of marriage and towards the various margins of the subject, since these margins are the foci of both pain and controversy.

This study therefore has a strictly limited but central focus. It focuses on the purpose and definition of marriage. It concerns those who are married and it bears also on the many who are living together unmarried. It is for pastor-teachers, church leaders and all who are engaged in the patient work of marriage preparation and marriage nurture. It is for those who wish to think clearly and Christianly about marriage. It is a book of foundations upon which pastoral practice should be built, but it is not itself a book of pastoral practice. My aim in this volume is to re-examine the biblical and theological foundations for sex and marriage.

I do not address here the concerns of the very many who are neither married nor living together unmarried. The burning topics of singleness and of divorce and remarriage will be included, God willing, in a forthcoming study.

Christopher Ash
Little Shelford, May 2003

ACKNOWLEDGMENTS

I am grateful to the many who have supported and helped me in writing this study. I began while on the staff of St Andrew the Great in Cambridge and appreciated the encouragement of their vicar, Mark Ashton, and the PCC. Since 1997 I have served as minister of All Saints, Little Shelford, whose consistent warm fellowship and support have enabled me to complete the work at last. I am grateful to the trustees of The Jerusalem Trust who generously awarded a grant to research and write. This grant has funded our first parish assistants and I am indebted to them (Domini Lucas, Alistair Seabrook and Andy Bleach) for freeing me from some of the burdens of church administration; I could not have done it without them. I am grateful to the warden and librarian of Tyndale House for allowing me the privilege of a quiet desk and superb library facilities to work on the project. Of the many in Little Shelford who have helped me, Professor Bob White in particular has offered support, suggestions and encouragement throughout. I am grateful to him. I have had a number of opportunities to speak on these subjects; the invitations to give three talks at a Proclamation Trust conference and a seminar at the Evangelical Ministry Assembly were especially helpful to me. Some of the material on the purpose of marriage appeared in an earlier form as an article in *Churchman* and the substance of this is reproduced here with permission. I am grateful to those who have read and commented on some or all of the book in draft form, especially to Dr Markus Bockmuehl whose detailed and perceptive comments were invaluable. Needless to say, the final manuscript represents my own views with all their failings. My editor, Stephanie Heald, and the staff at IVP have been expertly and perceptively supportive, all that a theological publisher should be.

My children, John, Andy, Barnaby and Ellie, have been wonderfully long-suffering while Dad was tied up writing his seemingly interminable book. Above all I am grateful to God for the patient loving support and companionship of my wife Carolyn. She says I should record 'my gratitude to my wife and children without whom this book would have been finished a great deal more quickly'. This may be true, but more likely it would not have been written at all.

ABBREVIATIONS

I have used the author–date system system for citing references in this work. For full details of all works cited, see the Bibliography (pp. 372–389). Where no page reference is given the reference is to the place in the commentary dealing with the verse or passage in question.

b. Babylonian Talmud
BAGD W. Bauer, *A Greek-English Lexicon of the New Testament and Other Early Christian Literature*, 2nd ed. (University of Chicago Press, 1979)
BDB F. Brown, S. R. Driver and C. A. Briggs (eds.), *Hebrew and English Lexicon of the Old Testament* (Peabody, Mass.: Hendrickson; Oxford: Clarendon, 1979)
CBQ *Catholic Biblical Quarterly*
ICC *International Critical Commentary*
JBL *Journal of Biblical Literature*
JRE *Journal of Religious Ethics*
JSNT *Journal for the Study of the New Testament*
JSOT *Journal for the Study of the Old Testament*
JSS *Journal of Semitic Studies*
JTS *Journal of Theological Studies*
LXX Septuagint
m. Mishnah
NRSV New Revised Standard Version
NT *Novum Testamentum*
NTS *New Testament Studies*
t. Tosefta
TB *Tyndale Bulletin*
TDNT *Theological Dictionary of the New Testament*
TDOT *Theological Dictionary of the Old Testament*
VT *Vetus Testamentum*
WUNT *Wissenschaftliche Untersuchungen zum Neuen Testament*

INTRODUCTION

1. GOD AND SEX

God and sex

It is hard to keep God out of sex.

Carl Jung once remarked that when people brought sexual questions to him they invariably turned out to be religious, and when they brought religious questions to him they always turned out to be sexual (Nelson 1979:14). No doubt this is an exaggeration, but it is hard to keep God out of sex.

In Ian McEwan's harrowing novel *Atonement* (shortlisted for the Booker Prize in 2001), there is a defining moment in which the lovers Robbie and Cecilia first make love in the modern sense of sexual union and at the same time in the older sense of declaration in word. At this moment the author comments, '[Robbie] had no religious belief, but it was impossible not to think of an invisible presence or witness in the room, and that these words spoken aloud were like signatures on an unseen contract' (McEwan 2001:137). In a haunting novel almost devoid of grace and remote from true atonement, this 'religious' moment shines like a beacon from beyond. Sex with love and (in this novel) followed by costly faithfulness is imbued with a deep significance.

While it is one thing to recognize the significance of sex, however, it is quite another to agree on how marriage might fit into the moral picture. At a dramatic moment in Thomas Hardy's novel *Far from the Madding Crowd* Francis Troy stands by the open coffin of his lover Fanny and their infant child, in bearing whom she died. As he stands there, his wife Bathsheba comes up beside him. Troy kisses Fanny's cold lips. Bathsheba protests at this sign of affection to one who was merely his lover. Troy turns from her protest and speaks to Fanny's corpse: '"But never mind, darling," he said; "in the sight of Heaven you are my very, very wife!"' Bathsheba asks in desperation, 'If she's – that, – what – am I?' Troy replies, 'You are nothing to me – nothing. A ceremony before a priest doesn't make a marriage. I am not morally yours' (Hardy 1874:281–282).

We cannot think seriously about sex without the unseen presence of God. Whatever our histories we want to be able to feel that our actions have been justifiable, moral and defensible 'in the sight of heaven'. We are right to want this, for sex is significant. Sex cannot be understood as a self-contained topic of ethics, let alone of Christian ethics. It can be understood only as a part of the great story of men, women and God.

Why did the Creator God make humankind male and female? The ethics of sex are entirely predicated on the answer to that question. Contrary to contemporary culture we shall find that the answer is not in terms of 'what sex can do for me', nor even of what sex can do for a sexual partner or for a couple; rather, sex is to be used in the service of God. Only when sex is understood in this context of wider service will sexual ethics make transcendent sense.

A hard subject for the Christian ethicist

There is, however, a threefold reason why it is hard for a Christian ethicist to argue any thesis about sexual ethics today. We speak into a confused culture in which our paradigms for thinking about sex have shifted radically. We speak from a marginalized church. And we seek to root our ethics in a challenged Bible.

Our cultural behaviour is certainly confused. There are many questions. Does marriage matter? Does marriage differ in any significant way from just living together? How should we view alternative forms of nonmarital sexual relationship? What is the definition of marriage (always assuming there is such a thing as 'the' definition)? Here, for example, Troy's passionate claim strikes a chord. Is being married really an outward status, which may be created by a public ceremony (with or without a minister of the church), or is it rather an inward quality of relationship which may wax or wane, mature or shrivel, and must be nurtured and developed by both husband and wife over time? Again, is marriage defined by sexual consummation or through mutual consent or by public ceremony, or by some combination of these? What is the point of marriage, our purposes, perhaps even God's purposes? What attitude should we adopt to questions of permanence, of stability, of sequential relationships ('serial monogamy' or, perhaps more accurately, 'serial polygamy'), of divorce and remarriage?

At times of relative stability in family structure, such questions may perhaps be left on the back burner. They press themselves insistently upon us in times of change. Such changes ask pressing pastoral, theological and ethical questions of the Christian churches. The churches find themselves increasingly squeezed to the margins of social life and in few areas more than sex. One of the legacies of 'Christendom' has been the close association in the popular mind between marriage and the offices (and officers) of the church. Since about the twelfth century most marriage, at least in England, has been church marriage, conducted first at the church door and later inside the church building, in the presence of the church (*in facie ecclesiae*) and with 'benefit of clergy'. For centuries, to be married has usually meant to be married in church, conforming to the disciplines of the church and under the watchful eye of the ministers of the church. This is becoming less and less so.

> Three out of four marriages in England and Wales were solemnised with a religious ceremony during the years following the First World War, and the proportion remained at this level until the early 1960s. By the mid-1970s the proportion had fallen to about one in two and the ratio remained at about this level until the early 1990s. In 1999 around two in five marriages in Great Britain were solemnised with a religious ceremony.
>
> (*Social Trends 31*(2001):47)

Since the Marriage Act 1994 authorized a wide variety of venues in England and Wales to be used for the solemnization of marriage, the proportion of marriages which are civil rather than ecclesiastical has slowly risen from 52% in 1994 to 62% in 1999 (*Social Trends 31*(2001):47).[1]

One of the confusions this accentuates in the minds of many is the question of whether church marriage and civil marriage are essentially the same or different. Is the latter easily dissoluble, while the former is indissoluble, perhaps? At a popular level this perception is illustrated in Graham Greene's

---

1. An example of the move towards nonreligious ceremonies is *Sharing the Future: A practical guide to non-religious wedding ceremonies* (British Humanist Association, 47 Theobalds Road, London WC1X 8SP). The *Independent* (13 February 1995) featured three couples who invented their own 'wedding' ceremonies; these included vows to be faithful and 'to share our feelings' and circle dances; they were united in their rejection of all characteristically Christian features.

depressing novel *Brighton Rock*. The petty teenage gangster ('The Boy') wants
to get 'married' so that the girl who knows evidence against him will not be
able to use that evidence in court. He is speaking to his lawyer, Mr Prewitt:

> Prewitt: 'Do you want to be married in a church?'
> 'Of course I don't,' the Boy said. 'This won't be a real marriage.'
>   'Real enough.'
>   'Not real like when the priest says it.'
> (Greene 1938:89)[2]

This squalid little exchange masks a theological question about the nature of
'real' marriage: is there an entity called 'Christian marriage' which is governed
by different morality from mere 'marriage' so that the former is 'real' in some
distinctive way?

The perceived distinction between 'marriage' and 'Christian marriage'
touches also on a deep ethical question which affects the apologetics and
evangelism of any marginalized church: is Christian ethics for the church
alone, or does it have a moral call upon the world? Is it for 'us', or for all? Can
Jerusalem speak to Athens about sex and marriage? May we speak for ourselves only, making rules and encouraging certain behaviours within our own
little ecclesial societies, or may we speak also to the wider world?

Another major area in which traditional Christian teaching has been under
attack is that of gender and power. Trenchant dismissal of oppressive 'patriarchy' is ubiquitous in feminist theology, as in much contemporary scholarship about English literature. The 'liberation' of women, financially as much
as socially, has been one of the most deeply significant factors affecting sexual
ethics and the shape of family life.

If the churches are socially marginalized, they are also handicapped in their
apologetic by having as their book a challenged Bible. When Christian ethicists seek to bring the Bible to bear on sexual ethics they do so in churches
where the use of the Bible in ethics is challenged from within, to say nothing
of scepticism without.

If we believe the Bible to be the Word of God which speaks to each generation and speaks with a coherence that gives meaning to the concepts of 'biblical theology' and 'biblical ethics', we find many within the churches who
challenge these assumptions. Some say it is a book of yesterday, or a succession of yesterdays, and spoke only to, or of, those yesterdays. The cultural
gaps between the worlds of the Bible writers and our own are unbridgeable,

---

2. On p. 124 there is a grim description of the fraudulent register office ceremony.

they claim. Others say it is a book with many voices and that these voices do not cohere. Yet others say that the concept of a text 'speaking' at all is fraught with difficulty.

It is not surprising that Christians find themselves puzzled in the face of this unsettling trio. To address a confused culture from a marginalized church using a challenged Bible will daunt the boldest ethicist. It is perhaps not surprising that, for all the confidence displayed by some about the doctrine of salvation, when it comes to ethics too many of us are 'catatonic' in our thinking (Longenecker 1984:1). The prominent ethicist Stanley Hauerwas comments, 'Current reflection about sexual ethics by Christian ethicists is a mess' (Hauerwas 1981:175). The Anglican evangelical John Stott comments, 'One of the great weaknesses of contemporary evangelical Christianity is our comparative neglect of Christian ethics, in both our teaching and our practice' (Stott 1991:76f). The Roman Catholic writer Gareth Moore offers incisive criticism of traditional Roman Catholic arguments in sexual ethics. He concludes, 'The Church needs to do more thinking about sex' (Moore 1992:213).

It is important that we do not abandon the field. Although I disagree with Anthony Harvey's conclusions, he is right to warn that unless the Church of England addresses the ethical issues with more clarity its ministers may find themselves involved 'in a damaging pantomime of compromise and pretence', particularly with regard to nonmarital cohabitation (Harvey 1994:11). This warning applies beyond the Anglican churches.

Responses to the challenge

There are two easy and ultimately fruitless responses that Christians may be tempted to make: retreat or surrender. Retreat into the ghetto is the danger of the theological conservative, who may withdraw into a world of privatized piety reinforced by social conservatism. In this world 'change' and 'decay' are inseparable. In such a mindset theological foundations are eroded and we are left with tradition unquestioned and unexamined. We must remember the saying attributed to Cyprian to the effect that 'a custom without truth is but error grown old' (*Epistle* 74:9.2).

In the ghetto we need the warning of Ecclesiastes 7:10: 'Do not say, "Why were the former days better than these?" For it is not from wisdom that you ask this.' Often defensive conservatives lament their powerlessness to influence society and to save it from its headlong path to disaster. We forget that the Christian gospel, while weak in human terms, is God's power to save (1 Cor. 1:18 – 2:5; Rom. 1:16). Gospel messengers were reputed to be 'people who have been turning the world upside down' (Acts 17:6).

Surrender, by contrast, is to stay in the world by drifting with the flow of cultural change. This may happen consciously; we feel that we must go with the tide if we are not to be left behind. Or it may happen unconsciously as culture seeps into our theology and we drift, unaware of how far we have moved.

Neither unprincipled drift nor retrenchment into tradition is gospel Christianity. Against both these the way forward is to search the Scriptures again and then to teach with confidence the gospel of Jesus Christ with its outworking in life. The authority of the church in the world is not an authority of hierarchy, power, money or political influence: it is the authority of the gospel. This authority is mediated by teaching. The church does not browbeat, intimidate or threaten the world: the church speaks to the world. She speaks in the public preaching of the gospel and as individual Christians speak in the workplace, the community or the home.

In order to speak, however, we must understand. To speak the gospel in issues of sex we need to understand the gospel, the story of men, women and God. We need a proper biblical and theological ethics of marriage. We need to look to the foundations of what we say – which is the purpose of this book.

Thus, while our study is occasioned by cultural and ecclesial confusion, it is driven by biblical conviction. I attempt to formulate a biblical and theological framework for understanding marriage. Most of the Bible is not about sex or marriage, but the parts that are need to be related to the great swathes that are not. Christian sexual ethics needs to be properly integrated into the mainstream of biblical theology. We must begin neither with our experiences nor with our traditions, but with God and the great true story of his dealings with the men and women he has made and whom he loves. This book is an attempt to reintegrate Christian thinking about sex into the overarching story of creation and redemption.[3] This story (or metanarrative, as it is sometimes called) is the key to a proper understanding of sex.

My aim is similar to that of Geoffrey Bromiley in his excellent but brief work *God and Marriage*. In his introduction Bromiley writes,

> In itself a book on the theology of marriage will not solve every modern marital problem. Nor will it necessarily arrest the serious decline in the solidity of Christian marriage. It will, however, present what is for many people a new dimension by stressing the outlook and activity of God himself in the situation . . . Far too many people, Christians not excluded, are self-centeredly preoccupied with their own marital problems and their attempts to engineer solutions to them. A theology of marriage

---

3. cf. the critique of atomistic approaches to reading the Bible (by both conservatives and liberals) in Barton 2001:60–62.

can help them to achieve a God-centered look at the larger situation of which their marriages constitute a small, if by no means unimportant, part. In the long run a new look means a new understanding, and a new understanding means a new practice. (Bromiley 1980:xii–xiii)

This study is a systematic theological exegesis of the purpose and definition of marriage in Scripture. It is written on the understanding that Christians ought to be biblical, our theology governed by Scripture as normative, and that Christians ought to be theological, not stopping with the work of exegesis but using exegesis to open up what is revealed to us of the consistent mind of God. I try to integrate our thinking about marriage into some of the great theological, anthropological and soteriological themes of the Christian revelation.[4] It is neither a sociological analysis of trends nor a study whose agenda is written by the shallow concerns of 'relevance'. I have tried to allow the great Bible story of God and humankind to determine my priorities.

Considerations of space have meant that the great theme of God's marriage to his people has been touched on all too briefly. Divorce and remarriage have not been treated, and nor has the unmarried state. All these are the subjects of a forthcoming volume. Nor have I attempted to deal except in passing with the controversies about homosexual practice. This is the focus of deep and often acrimonious dispute. I omit the subject partly because there are already some excellent contributions (e.g. Schmidt 1995; Thiselton 1997; Wright 1994; Webb 1994; Gagnon 2001; Hays 1986), but mainly because from the perspective of sexual ethics in the wider Bible story this is, in the proper sense, an issue on the margins.

This is not a practical book of anecdotes or 'tips' about marriage, a 'how to' guide, full of wisdom-style pithy guidance on how, for example, to 'keep romance alive' (a favoured topic of some contemporary Christian literature). Rather it seeks to root pastoral practice in theological and biblical soil. It is written for pastor-teachers, for seminary and theological college students, for thinking Christians engaged in the patient work of marriage preparation, marriage support and marriage repair in a broken world.

Although it is not a 'practical' book, it is written to be translated into pastoral practice. Every pastor relates to those struggling with breaking or broken marriages and to unmarried cohabiting couples, decides what to teach about

---

4. This is not a descriptive work of the kind that analyses patterns of family life in different periods of the biblical literature and compares them to contemporary trends. Such work may be found in, e.g., Malina 1983; Osiek 1996; Osiek and Balch 1997. See the useful summary and critique of this approach in Barton 2001:41–43.

sexual ethics and administers some disciplines in church life. The clearer our grasp of the truths we teach, the fairer, more gracious and intelligible will be our practices. We must understand deeply that we may teach confidently.

Humility and hesitation

And yet we must hesitate. James warns, 'We who teach will be judged with greater strictness. For all of us make many mistakes' (Jas. 3:1–2). We must pause before addressing such a sensitive subject. I write conscious both of my fallibility and of the dangers of damage by deviating from grace and truth. I do not know for sure what the wise man meant when he included 'the way of a man with a girl' in his list of things 'too wonderful' for him to understand (Prov. 30:18–19), but the man-woman relationship is full of mystery. We all know something of the chemistry of desire and delight, or indeed the dynamic of aversion and estrangement; but what we do not know greatly exceeds what we do.

This book is not about abstract 'issues'; it is for real people often in pain. It is about our wider families, neighbours and friends, to whom we are deeply committed. For this reason I have more than once been close to abandoning the book: the potential for making the damage worse and the pain deeper by wrong teaching has seemed too great. Time will tell.

A further reason for hesitation relates to decency. There is a paradox: a subject of great wonder, intrinsic privacy and delicate fragility must some-times be spoken of indelicately. Roger Scruton, in the preface to his philo-sophical study *Sexual Desire*, writes,

> In this book I shall present a defence of decency; but in doing so I illustrate the truth
> of Bernard Shaw's remark, that it is impossible to explain decency without being
> indecent. I only hope that the benefit, in terms of moral understanding, will outweigh
> the moral cost.
> (Scruton 1986:viii)

This tension is evident in the Bible. On the one hand there is reticence; it is impossible to reconstruct what went on in the Canaanite fertility cults because the Old Testament texts, while scathing, generally omit descriptive detail. And yet there are times when shocking language does seem to be considered nec-essary.[5] In Ephesians 5:3 Paul insists that 'fornication and impurity of any

---

5. Ezek. 16, 23 are perhaps the most extreme examples of this.

kind, or greed, must not even be mentioned among you'; yet he cannot forbid 'mention' without making a mention.

The structure of this study

With hesitation, therefore, I embark on the study. Chapter 2 outlines the need for a properly evangelical approach to Christian sexual ethics. Chapter 3 sketches the background in contemporary culture, thought and practice. After these preliminaries the main study divides into three. Part One is a theological defence of marriage as a proper entity founded in creation and significant until the end of history; some may find this tiresomely theoretical and prefer to move straight to Part Two. Part Two addresses God's purpose for marriage. In many ways this is the kernel of the study; it argues for marriage to be pursued *in the service of God*. Chapter 7 is the key to this section. Part Three then attempts to delineate God's definition of marriage, culminating in Chapter 15 which addresses its heart.

2. PREJUDICE AND GRACE

The time is fulfilled, and the kingdom of God has come near; repent, and believe in the good news. (Mark 1:15)

If we are to embark with any prospect of profit on this study we must recognize prejudice and make room for grace.

To recognize prejudice is to adopt towards our study a degree of openness, a willingness to be changed. We must not impose upon the study our prior understandings; for if we do this we will simply end with cheers for the parts with which we already agreed and boos for the rest; we ourselves will be unchanged. To be ready to change our views and behaviour corresponds to the fundamental gospel challenge to repent.

We must also make room for grace, for the counterpart to repentance is belief in the good news of the grace of God. We must remember that the gospel is both law and grace. The world expects a Christian ethicist to lay down rules, prohibitions and regulations, to sit in judgment on others and to pronounce from on high. But while the gospel testifies to the goodness of the created order as an objective order given for our blessing (O'Donovan 1994: chs. 2 – 4), it ministers to us in our confused subjectivities the word of grace. At every stage of our study we must make room for grace.

Recognizing prejudice

In order to repent properly we must recognize both our individual fallenness and our embeddedness in fallen history and culture.

There is no such thing as a dispassionate ethicist. Writer and reader alike have histories of sexual experience or inexperience, of hopes realized or deferred, of longings or aversions, of fulfilment or frustration, of fears, anxieties, delights, regrets. Our histories condition our beliefs. Each of us has an inbuilt bias towards a belief system that justifies our history, like 'the adulteress . . . [who] says, "I have done no wrong"' (Prov. 30:20). 'Even individuals who do not enjoy or desire an experience or who feel that it is wrong, may develop more favourable attitudes as a way of rationalising their own previous choices or situation as an attempt at dissonance control' (Morgan 2000:67). Our interaction with a Christian ethic of sex is conditioned both by our personal histories and by the networks of corporate interpreted experience into which we are tied. Both our individual stories and the shared stories of our culture shout to drown our listening to the word of God.

Our fallen personal histories
It will be clear from the argument of this book that some contemporary Christian sexual ethics are considered unhelpfully weak and bland, crying 'Peace!' where there is no peace. But it is possible also for a treatment of sexual ethics to be inappropriately robust. We need to recognize that human sexual feelings and behaviour are fragile, a badly damaged part of our humanity. The media too often portray men and women as constantly overflowing with libido, waiting constantly for uninhibited passionate sex. A proper understanding of the fall helps us recognize that human sexuality, like human intellect or feeling, is deeply damaged and terribly fragile.

A recent newspaper report, for example, quotes from the *Journal of the American Medical Association* to the effect that, for more than a quarter of young women aged 18 to 29 in America, sex brings them more pain than pleasure. 'The survey', says the report, 'painted an unexpectedly bleak picture of sexual satisfaction. It suggested that two in every five women and about a third of men in all age groups experience some form of sexual dysfunction . . . The report suggests a reality that is at odds with the images of satisfying sex that saturate books, magazines, film and television' (*Independent*, 11 February 1999).

Our histories prejudice our responses to Christian sexual ethics. In *Sexual Desire* Roger Scruton claims to bypass faith commitments and to 'look on the human condition with the uncommitted gaze of the philosophical anthropologist' (Scruton 1986:14). This idea of the uncommitted spectator rests on a false objectivity. We may claim impartiality neither for the way we speak nor for the way we hear the ethics of the gospel. Any knowledge we may have of the created order is knowledge from within that order, an existential knowledge by subjects who participate in what they know. It is, of course, possible to know an object with a degree of relative distance, as in the natural sciences, but the greater and more encompassing the object (and the whole sexual sphere of human existence is very wide) the more difficult it is to transcend it and to speak from a position of even approximate objectivity (O'Donovan 1994:79).

Nor may we claim for Christian interpreters in the past the authority of the impartial. In his influential study *The Man-Woman Relation in Christian Thought*, Derek Sherwin Bailey makes much of the influence of their personal histories on the sexual ethics of Augustine, Jerome and Tertullian, and subsequent Christian tradition through them. So, for example, he argues that Tertullian's vehement reaction against his pre-conversion adultery led to his view that coitus even within marriage is sinful. Likewise, Jerome's pre-conversion sexual experiences and post-conversion reactions 'show that he never succeeded in coming to terms with his own sexuality . . . Both his confessions and his controversies proclaim a psychological unfitness to act as a guide in sexual matters . . .' (Bailey 1959:49).

We may admit this, and indeed press the problem one stage further: the way in which Bailey reads and understands the writings of Tertullian, Jerome and Augustine was itself conditioned by his own personal history (of which I know nothing) and culture; the very phrase 'coming to terms with his own sexuality' roots Bailey in the twentieth century. For Barth also, whose theology of marriage has been enormously influential, we must recognize that this theology was not forged in a hermetically sealed chamber untouched by his own troubled marital history. It is important to admit that the dynamic of the moral life is not a one-way process beginning with some faith commitment that is then worked out in acts of the moral agent, acts which are merely the outworking of prior commitment. The lines of influence flow both ways between behaviour and faith. Our actions and responses to moral choices form our character, and our character informs the development of our faith.

We may regard this as a problem. None the less, Christian ethics has never claimed to be an objective treatment of 'issues' by dispassionate observers; it has always been a transformative interaction between our 'stories' and the great story of God's dealings with humankind. What Bruce Birch writes of Old Testament narrative is true of all Scripture: it 'cannot become a resource for the moral shaping of our lives if its story is not allowed to intersect our own story' (Birch 1988:86).

Our fallen culture

There is a danger, however, in talking of 'my' history, as though 'my' history of sexual experience or inexperience is a purely personal and individual thing. It is not and cannot be. Even what I do or think on my own is habit-forming, character-building and comes to affect others. What others do affects me; and not only what they do, but how they *interpret* what they do, powerfully conditions my own thinking and practice. So when Bailey speaks of 'the Fathers and the Schoolmen' as 'children of their age whose thought was inevitably conditioned by current attitudes, and who simply moulded the tradition unconsciously, as it were, in conformity with the contemporary climate of opinion' (Bailey 1959:238), we need to remember that he too was recognizably conditioned by the cultural climate of post-1945 Britain in which he wrote. (Though whether either they or he 'simply moulded the tradition *unconsciously*' [my italics] is a moot point.)

The communal dimension of ethics is vital. Even the thinker in the hermit's cave is touched by memories and desires.[1] We can consider Christian sexual ethics neither by abstracting it from its biblical contexts, nor by isolating ourselves from our own social mores and cultural worldviews, nor yet by neglecting the church, which at its best can be 'a primary community for the nurturing of moral vision' (Birch 1988:101–104).

Making room for grace

This study is not 'descriptive ethics' but rather 'normative ethics', ethics that makes moral demands upon us (Baelz 1977:2–6). We cannot think clearly about this without a theological understanding of the relations of law and grace. We need to remember three aspects of the engagement of the gospel with us.

---

1. A vivid example of this is provided by Jerome. In a letter to Eustochium he wrote, 'How often when I was living in the desert, parched by a burning sun, did I fancy myself among the pleasures of Rome! Sackcloth disfigured my unshapely limbs, and my skin from long neglect had become as black as an Ethiopian's . . . And although in my fear of hell I had consigned myself to this prison, where I had no companions but scorpions and wild beasts, I often thought myself amid bevies of girls. My face was pale, and my frame chilled with fasting; yet my mind was burning with desire, and the fires of lust kept bubbling up before me when my flesh was as good as dead. Helpless, I cast myself at the feet of Jesus' (quoted in Loane 1968:29).

a. Christian sexual ethics is addressed to moral failures

The law of God, the moral obligation laid on every human being, is unitary and searching (Matt. 22:34–40).[2] Every human being ought to love the Creator with heart, mind, soul and strength. By nature we do not do this and one purpose of the law of God is forcefully to bring home to us our failure.[3] It does this not finally to condemn, but as 'disciplinarian' (Gal. 3:24, *paidagōgos*) to lead us to Christ.

This preliminary gospel truth is put very strongly (and in a context with a strong flavour of sexual sin) in 1 Corinthians 6:9–10: the wicked will not inherit the kingdom of God. There is a law of God which comes to us from beyond ourselves (in Bible language, from the mountain top of Sinai) and sets before us the order placed in creation by the Creator, in which order his creatures are morally bound to live. This is a necessary objective foundation of the gospel, for the gospel is addressed to those who have failed to keep the law (Rom. 3:19f.; 5:13f., 20).

It is vital to recognize that Christian sexual ethics is not addressed to the notional (and fictional) ideal family of the 1950s caricature. It is addressed to moral and sexual failures. In his book *Christian Marriage in Crisis* David Phypers observes, 'As a new generation begins to turn to Christ from non-church backgrounds, so a growing number of converts are bringing tangled sexual and marital relationships with them into the life of the Church' (Phypers 1985:2). Churches need to be communities of grace. We need to hear, for example, 'the plea' of Paula Clifford in her book *Divorced Christians and the Love of God* 'for more encouragement and better pastoral care to be given to Christians whose marriages have ended' (Clifford 1987:118).

The words 'this is what some of you used to be' (1 Cor. 6:11) ought to be burned into the desk of every Christian ethicist and emblazoned above the door of every Christian meeting place. A Christian ethic does not say, in the words of the old joke, 'I wouldn't start from here.' It says, 'We all begin from the wrong place; this gospel is precisely addressed to us who start in a mess.' The doctor came for the sick, not for those who reckon they are healthy (Matt. 9:12f.).

It will be necessary in our study to explore truths of created order against which we are all measured as failures. This recognition of the place of failure in

---

2. Mark 12:28–33; Luke 10:25–28; cf. Rom. 13:8–10. Ch. 11 of O'Donovan 1994 is an outstanding treatment of the fundamental unity of human moral obligation.

3. The 'right use' in 1 Tim. 1:8–11 seems to refer to this, possibly alongside the 'political' use whereby, when civil law is aligned with the law of God, it functions to restrain evil in human society.

Christian ethics is a vital precondition for hearing the word of God. Both writer and readers are failures. We must reject any sexual ethics purporting to be Christian yet which tends towards human self-justification.

There is no place in Christian sexual ethics for self-righteousness. We are not to sit in judgment on others, putting ourselves in the place of God to them, for three reasons. First, we cannot see the motives of another's heart, motives which will not be revealed until the Lord returns (1 Cor. 4:5). No human being can understand from the inside the sexual yearnings and temptations of another; no outsider can fully enter into the dynamics of another's marriage or unmarried state. Second, when we sit in judgment on another we are self-condemned (Matt. 7:1f.; Rom. 2:1f., 22) because we too are guilty of the sins we condemn. Third, even (relative) innocence of one commandment does not excuse us from the guilt of sin (Jas. 2:10f.). We have our private hierarchies of sins, and we all tend to place the sins we think we do not commit in the Premier League, relegating our pet sins to the lower divisions. The self-righteousness of the Pharisee (Luke 18:9–14) is a constant danger for the Christian ethicist, preacher or counsellor.

We must recognize and admit our failure in Christian sexual ethics. Failure is never good: it is failure not success. Yet there is a place for it, both at the start (recognizing where we begin) and throughout this life. Sinless perfection, being like Christ, is for when we see him, not for now (1 John 3:2).

b. The gospel offers grace to moral failures

We must never consider Christian ethics apart from the cross of Christ. The cross reveals to us the wrath of God against sin (Rom. 1:18) and at the same time the just means by which the Judge of all the earth can justify the wicked (Rom. 3:21–26; 4:5). In the cross we see that judgment is what Luther called God's 'strange work', the operation as it were of his 'left hand'. Further, it is in the cross that we see the fulfilment of the truth adumbrated in the Old Testament, that the Creator himself suffers when he sees human sin and its consequences. The Christian ethicist and pastor needs to speak in a spirit which shares the distress of those bringing with them sexual pain. Christian ethics is infused with redemption.

Specifically when we consider sexual ethics, the Bible is peppered with pointers to grace. The family lives of the patriarchs are far from unblemished, and yet the promised line passes through them. The great King David is forgiven after sexual sin and violence of great seriousness (2 Sam. 11f.; Ps. 51). The God of Israel is a God who washes away moral filth (e.g. Is. 4:4). We see hints of grace in Matthew's genealogy of the Messiah (Matt. 1:1–17) with its 'outsider' women: Tamar (Gen. 38:11–30), Ruth, Bathsheba (2 Sam. 11f., 1 Kgs. 1). We see it in the ministry of Jesus: the Samaritan woman in John

4:1–42, the woman caught in adultery in John 8:1–11, the prostitute of Luke 7:36–50. Forster rightly notes that in these three pastoral encounters Jesus is not primarily interested in exposing sinful pasts (though that is sometimes necessary) but in pointing by grace towards a better future (Forster 1995:57–60). We see grace at work in the multitude of doubtful reputation who keep on appearing in the ministries of John the Baptist and Jesus (Matt. 9:10–13; 21:31f.; Luke 5:30; 7:34; 15:2). The gospel is not for the sexually upright, but for the sexually fallen.

All consideration of sexual ethics must keep the grace of God and the cross of Christ in the forefront. It was the Pharisees and teachers of the law who tied up heavy loads, hard to bear, and put them on people's shoulders (Matt. 23:4; Luke 11:46). The Lord Jesus would not break a bruised reed or snuff out a scarcely smouldering wick (Matt. 12:20; Isaiah 42:1–4). His yoke is easy and his burden light (Matt. 11:29).

One feminist critic of traditional sexual ethics refers poignantly to 'a theology of marriage shattered by experience' (Thatcher 1999:10). Some theologies of marriage appear to have had a 'charisectomy' (an excision of grace), and any such will indeed be shattered by painful experience. My wife and I were seeking to help a dear friend who was struggling with the aftermath of a sad sexual failure in the past. Nothing we said seemed to help, until my wife turned her to the gospel promise of Joel 2:25, 'I will repay you for the years that the . . . locust has eaten.' No human being is to say, 'It is too late; my life is too spoiled by sin.' We must preach grace and believe in the power of a gracious God to heal. Some years ago I read a then-popular book of family psychology. I remember little of its content, but have never forgotten the comment of a friend who had also read it. 'The trouble with that book', he said, 'is that it leaves no room for the grace of God.'[4] This is the problem with deterministic psychology; it argues that if certain conditions have not been fulfilled (e.g. in childhood) certain deleterious effects are bound to follow. This leads all too often to despair, and despair leaves no room for the grace of God. The gospel, however, is first and foremost a gospel of grace.

c. The Spirit of God works in us, who are moral failures, to change us

Grace has a purpose that looks beyond a present change in legal status to a future Christlikeness of character (1 John 3:2; Rom. 8:29); it brings salvation and trains us 'to renounce impiety and worldly passions, and in the present age to live lives that are self-controlled, upright and godly' (Titus 2:11f.).

The moral distinctiveness of the people of God is a constant theme under

---

4. The Revd Roger Simpson, in conversation.

both the old covenant and the new.[5] If Titus 2:11–14 points us particularly to the goal and purpose of grace, which is purity (vv. 12, 14), it hints also at the confusion and tensions of our present existence. The motions of grace in the heart are competing with 'impiety and worldly passions . . . while we wait for the blessed hope . . .' A Christian ethics, and perhaps especially a Christian sexual ethics, is embedded in a situation of tension and conflict made bearable only by Christian hope.

We live in a world in which we are all both sinners and victims. The tragic theme in the Scriptures of 'the sins of the fathers' is worked out in family after family. A vivid example in Bible narrative is the family of David after his adultery with Bathsheba (2 Sam. 11ff.). It is possible to suffer the consequences of sin elsewhere in a family without ourselves being directly responsible. But lest we slip into a fatalist or determinist mindset, allowing that bad consequences always follow from bad actions, we need to remember the gospel caveat of John 9:1ff. In a context where a simplistic model of action and consequence was held in a way that denied the possibility of grace, the Lord Jesus spoke the word of grace.

The magnificent vision of Romans 8:18–27 sets before us a created order suffering in frustration, but in which those frustrations must be understood to be like the pains of a woman in labour, not fruitless but ready to issue in glorious life.

The gospel, however, does not simply give us a tension between the reality of our sin and a legal fiction of justification, nor between a sinful present and a glorious future. Our justification is at the same time a righteousness that is imputed to us, grounded on the propitiatory death of Jesus Christ, and also a righteousness that is being worked in us by the ministry of the Spirit. There is real ethical change in character and practice: 'This is what some of you *used to be*' (1 Cor. 6:11, my italics).

The gospel sets before us a work of the word and Spirit of God in the heart, which renders a measure of purity that is not easy but is none the less possible.[6] The change is not superficial, but one wrought by the Holy Spirit at the level of the human spirit. We cannot overstate the depth at which the Spirit works in the human person. It is easy to understate it. It is not (*pace* some proponents of natural theology) that God speaks to 'the natural potentialities of the individual' (Brown 1983:23) and draws out of him or her what is already there *in nuce* as a creature made in his image. Rather, he addresses

---

5. For example in Judg. 19:12, the force of the story is the horror that this should happen in a city of *Israel*.

6. Ps. 119:9; 1 John 2:13f.; 1 Tim. 5:2; 2 Tim. 2:22; 3:10; Titus 2:6.

those in whom the image of God is terribly defaced; every facet of their personhood is tainted by sin, so that (in Calvin's words) the things we consider good 'are but wine spoiled by the odour of the cask' (Calvin, *Genesis*:285). And at the deepest level of human personhood (the spirit) he changes us, so that the response of the believer to the gospel is a response not of the unredeemed heart stirred into penitence but of a newly created redeemed heart.

In the believer the law works as a blessing and a gift of grace, as it was ever intended to be. When the believer asks, 'How shall I now live to please the God I love?' the law points to the character of this God and the good order he has placed in his world.[7] Grace changes us, and we need law to show us the direction of change. We need to learn from the apostles 'how [we] ought to live and to please God' (1 Thess. 4:1). Ethics as a pattern for the believing life is a part of the gospel; we need to teach this. If ethics is a response to grace in its motivation, it is a response to created order in its shape and content.

This gospel truth is important in view of the primacy often accorded to 'nature', whereby we blame God for 'the nature he has given me'. The gospel bears testimony to a created order that is not transparently discerned in human experience. And James 1:13f. safeguards the goodness and the benevolence of the Creator, who may never be blamed for our moral failures.

To the believer, who has received the gift of the Spirit of God, law changes its character from condemnation to liberation. It is evangelical in the deep sense of being good news. In the absence of faith this is not so, for then morality is imposed upon us from outside: 'The burden of morality arises from its arbitrariness' (O'Donovan 1994:151). It comes to us from outside as an alien imposition, cutting across our desires and perceptions. It is therefore resented. But when, by the Spirit of God at the deepest level of human personhood, a man or woman begins to find his or her spirit's desire aligned with the will of God (Rom. 7:18f.), then the law of God becomes evangelical in character, pointing to the objective and liberating creation order. It ceases to be perceived as arbitrary and is at last recognized as bringing freedom.

There is a danger that we will be so frightened of self-righteousness or of sitting in judgment that we fail to preach law. Salvation, however, comes through the preaching of law and grace together. Grace is superfluous without law's condemnation, and it is purposeless and contentless without law's revelation of what pleases God. John the Baptist repeatedly told Herod that it was unlawful for him to have Herodias as his wife. Jesus said to the woman caught in adultery, 'Go and sin no more' (John 8:11). Freedom is not

---

7. See O'Donovan 1994:153f. for a nuanced critique of the Lutheran tradition in this regard.

found in free-floating autonomy but in 'free response to objective reality' (O'Donovan 1994:25).

Conclusion

We must make room in our sexual ethics for grace. This is not the thin gruel of counterfeit grace apart from law, the pseudo-grace that cries 'Peace!' when there is no peace. Nor is it the cheap grace that proclaims forgiveness without the dynamic of the Spirit to work a changed life. Rather, it is the grace of the gospel, grace to which law points and which in its turn works to the fulfilment of the law.

3. THE CHURNING OF PARTNERS

We live in the throes or aftermath of a sexual revolution. The 1960s and 1970s, as Haskey comments,

> marked a turning point in the pace of change and level in almost every demographic series, most particularly those on fertility – especially extra-marital childbearing – marriage, divorce, and family structure. These considerable changes, amounting to a structural shift in individuals' demographic behaviour and societal norms, occurred throughout many countries of Europe, and have been termed the 'Second Demographic Transition'.
>
> (Haskey 2001a:5)

This observation by a senior British government statistician could probably be echoed by observers in North America and much of northern Europe. Our theological study is set against a background of deep social change. The salient features of this change are now clear. They relate to the way men and women enter, leave and re-enter sexual relationships; and they affect childbearing and the nurture of children. We begin with behaviour and then move on to consider perception.[1]

---

1. Stafford 1993: chs. 1 and 2 give a vivid portrayal of some of the same ground from a North American perspective.

New patterns of behaviour

Not all sexual behaviour is amenable to accurate social analysis. We should be cautious with survey results,[2] for there is perhaps no area of life in which we are habitually less honest. However, phenomena such as cohabitation and childbirth have a public dimension that enables us to assess them with reasonable confidence.[3] Patterns and trends are never as simple as a summary suggests, but it will be helpful to draw attention to four salient features of contemporary practice as background to our theological study.[4]

a. Unmarried cohabitation

Easily the most significant feature we need to note in the contemporary Western scene is the custom of living together without being married. Such cohabitation[5] may be a youthful first-time living together, a living together that leads to marriage, or a cohabitation subsequent upon either a previous cohabitation or a previous marriage; there is wide variation of circumstance,

---

2. Statistics quoted refer to Great Britain, unless otherwise stated. Trends in Britain are in general shared by northern (but not yet southern) Europe. A clear and illuminating analysis covering much of Europe is to be found in Dormor 1992; more recent comprehensive analyses for Great Britain are to be found in Haskey 1999 (for Britain) and Kiernan 1999 (for Europe); also Haskey 2001a and *Social Trends 31* (2001): ch. 2. Subsequent editions of *Social Trends* and *Population Trends* will update the data; these may be found on the British government's Office for National Statistics website at statistics.gov.uk. There is a mine of useful information about the USA on the website of The National Marriage Project, Rutgers, The State University of New Jersey, http://marriage.rutgers.edu.

3. Data on cohabitation rely on voluntary surveys and are therefore not as accurate as data on marriages which are by definition registered in law (Haskey 1999:14).

4. The principal source of such information is the Family Information Section of the *General Household Survey*. There are also important studies that follow those surveyed over time; two of these are the *British Household Panel Survey* and the *National Child Development Study* (Haskey 2001a:6). Clear summaries may be found in the British government publications *Social Trends* and *Population Trends*.

5. I will usually use 'cohabitation' as shorthand for 'unmarried cohabitation'. Statisticians tend to use the phrase 'living together as a couple' in surveys. The first British census in which this was a possible answer was 1991 (Haskey 2001a:4). Haskey's article (2001a) gives a readable and comprehensive review of the demographics of cohabitation in Great Britain up to 2001. See also the comparisons of cohabitation and marriage in Taylor 1998 and the wealth of statistical and survey analysis in Morgan 2000.

duration and attitude (as with marriage itself). In every case, however, a man and a woman live together in a sexual and social relationship without being married in the eyes of the law. (We consider below the fact that law in increasing ways treats cohabitants as if they were married.) As a common social practice this is a recent development.[6]

The first year for which cohabitation statistics are available on a consistent basis is 1986, but there is information (especially about women) before this date (*Social Trends 31*(2001):45). It is clear that the number of couples in Great Britain living together without being married has risen greatly since the late 1960s and is set to rise further. For example,

> Among non-married women aged under 60 in Great Britain, the proportion
> cohabiting almost doubled between 1986 and 1998–99 from 13 per cent to 25 per
> cent. For men it more than doubled from 11 per cent to 26 per cent over the same
> period.
> (*Social Trends 31*(2001):45)

Unmarried cohabitation began to be a significant feature of British life in the 1960s, when the small cohabiting population consisted almost entirely of divorcees. In recent years, however, the major increase has been among single (never married) people (Dormor 1992:5, 13). For example, the percentage of never married women cohabiting roughly quadrupled from 1979 to 1998 (from 8% to 31%). Further, we should note that this rise is concentrated on the younger cohorts: of never married women between 25 and 29 years old in 1998, almost 40% were cohabiting (Haskey 2001a:9). It is now estimated that the majority of men born after the mid-1960s started their first union as a cohabitation rather than a marriage (Haskey 2001a:7). Government statisticians estimate that over the quarter-century from 1996 to 2021 the proportion of couples cohabiting will roughly double, from 12% of all couples in 1996 to 22% in 2021.[7]

Not surprisingly, public attitudes to cohabitation have changed in line with custom.

---

6. There have, of course, over history and in different cultures, been a wide variety of
   marriage customs, but the contemporary phenomenon of quasi-marriage that is *by*
   definition not marriage in the eyes of the law does seem to be new.
7. This was a 'combined estimation and projections exercise undertaken by the
   Government Actuary's Department and the Office for National Statistics' (*Social Trends*
   31 (2001):44f.; cf. Haskey 2001a:15).

It is widely accepted that the stigma associated with living together outside marriage . . .
has diminished considerably over the past three or four decades. Indeed, for a growing
majority, it has now all but disappeared.

(Haskey 2001a:4)[8]

For the never married, most cohabitation is premarital, although there has
been some growth in cohabitation as an alternative rather than a precursor to
marriage. Indeed, our culture worries less and less whether a couple living
together are married or not; when a woman keeps her maiden name on marriage, neighbours may not even know which is the case. Nevertheless, 'for
most people, cohabitation is part of the process of getting married and is not
a substitute for marriage' (*Social Trends 31*(2001):45).

Further, most marriage is now preceded by a period of premarital cohabitation, and the duration of this is slowly growing. The British Household
Panel Survey does long-term tracking on 10,000 people; this shows that two
thirds of those marrying between 1985 and 1992 had lived with someone
(often but not always their future marriage partner) before marriage. The
director of the study comments, 'For a lot of young people cohabitation is
replacing a long engagement' (*Independent*, 15 September 1994).

Haskey comments,

Increasingly, couples who have started living together do not place a high priority on
marrying, though they intend to do so; many view the cost of a 'proper wedding' as
very expensive, particularly in the early days of a partnership when setting up home,
and housing costs, can be demanding, even on two incomes. There perhaps has been
a tendency for couples to defer considering when to marry until they feel they can
afford it, when domestic arrangements have been settled and when they are ready for
the large social occasion they wish it to be.

(Haskey 2001a:11)

Various analyses of cohabitation and the reasons behind the decision to
cohabit rather than marry have been made (e.g. Dormor 1992:12–15; Forster
1988:7–8), but there can be no doubt of the scale and significance of the phenomenon. It seems clear that a wide spectrum of commitments is evidenced
in such cohabitations, from fairly casual and shallow at one extreme to significant (even publicly expressed) intentions of long-term faithfulness at the

---

8. See Fig. 2 for a clear indication that changing attitudes are strongly age dependent, the
   younger cohorts regarding premarital cohabitation as not merely acceptable but the
   recommended option.

other. All unmarried cohabitations, however, are symptomatic of a weakening social emphasis on the public commitment of marriage.

b. Children: fewer, later, not necessarily within marriage

The social climate in which cohabitation flourishes has also seen great changes in attitudes to children. It is often observed that from the 1960s effective and readily available contraception spearheaded a revolutionary separation between the activity of sexual intercourse and the expectation of pregnancy.[9] But as the increased ease and social acceptability of 'sleeping together' has led on to comparable acceptability of 'living together', so the desire to avoid pregnancy (when sleeping together) has metamorphosed into a significant ambivalence towards conception (both when living together and when married). If pregnancy is unwanted when merely sleeping together, it becomes a matter of lifestyle choice when living together or married. The contraceptive wedge continues to keep sex and procreation apart until a deliberate choice is made to try to bring them together. For various reasons (notably burgeoning prosperity and the growth in tertiary education since the 1960s) this choice has been made later (and therefore less) over recent years.

In Britain the birth rate was consistently above the replacement rate (the rate needed to keep the population constant without net immigration) until the mid-1970s, and has been consistently below since then. A British government statistical report says,

> The estimated average number of children that would be born to a woman if the 2000 pattern of fertility continued throughout her childbearing years is 1.66. This is well below the average completed family size of about 2.1 children needed for the population in the long term to replace itself if mortality rates are constant and there is no international migration.
> (Ghee 2001:12)

The birth-rate drop has been experienced elsewhere, including Sweden (down to about 1.5), Germany (about 1.3), Italy (about 1.2) and Spain (about 1.2) (Taylor and Taylor 2001:22).

This trend towards a lower birth rate seems to reflect a combination of later marriage[10] (and to a lesser extent later cohabitation, Haskey 2001a:11) and the reluctance of women in careers to have large families (Church of

---

9. The oral contraceptive pill first went on sale in 1961 (*Social Trends 31* (2001):49).

10. 'In 1971 the average age at first marriage was 24 for men and 22 for women; by 1999 these had risen to 29 and 27 respectively' (*Social Trends 31* (2001):47).

England 1995:30; cf. Haskey 2001a). The mean age of women at childbirth in England and Wales rose from 26.2 years in 1971 to 29.0 in 1999 (*Social Trends 31* (2001):50). 'The most noticeable shift in fertility in the last twenty years or so has been a shift towards later childbearing' (*Population Trends 106* (2001):70).

For a time it was assumed that premarital cohabitation would be followed by marriage as and when the first child was planned. This is no longer so. Even though few couples cohabit indefinitely (most either split or marry in the end), marriage now often does not take place until one or more children have been born. The large rise in conceptions and births outside marriage is almost all accounted for by cohabiting couples, even though a pregnancy in a cohabiting couple is about four times as likely to lead to an abortion as a pregnancy in a marriage (Morgan 2000:40). It is estimated that the proportion of conceptions that took place outside marriage[11] more than doubled between 1971 and 1990 (from 21% to 43%) (Dennis and Erdos 1993:109). Little of this increase is accounted for by teenage noncohabiting pregnancy, although where it is the consequences have changed sharply. In 1971 almost half of teenage pregnancies led to marriage before the birth of the child, and a quarter to abortion; a decade later these proportions had been reversed (Dormor 1992:8f.).[12]

Perhaps partly because of the large increase in abortion, the growth of births outside marriage reflects the growing practice of cohabitation rather than simply an increase in teenage sexual activity. The proportion of births outside marriage remained at a fairly steady 4–5% throughout the nineteenth century and the first half of the twentieth century, with minor peaks of 6% and 9% respectively during the two world wars. But from the late 1970s it began rising sharply, to 30% in 1991 and 39% in 2000 (Ghee 2001:9, 12). Unlike the two world wars, almost all this increase is accounted for by couples who jointly register the birth and live at the same address – that is, who are cohabiting.[13]

c. 'The churning of partners'

Relationship breakdown is both a sad and a salient feature of contemporary family life. An odd story on the eccentric fringe of social custom illustrates

---

11. Extramarital conception is reckoned either when the birth also occurs outside marriage or when the birth occurs less than seven months into marriage (Dormor 1992:2).

12. The figures were 45% and 26% in 1971, 20% and 41% in 1981, for marriage and abortion respectively.

13. *Population Trends 106* (2001):70–71 (Fig. 4 on p. 70 makes this very clear); *Social Trends 31* (2001):50f.; Dennis and Erdos 1993:109–110.

the pessimism of an age in which, while faithfulness is still esteemed,[14] the expectation of even fairly short-term faithfulness is badly diluted. It appears that an entrepreneurial jeweller in the USA has begun offering wedding rings for hire. Rent is paid weekly; if the couple survive the first year of marriage they are sent a congratulatory message and the rings become theirs to keep (*The Times*, 29 December 1995). An advertisement caption reads, 'Statistically, people change their marriage partner before they change their Miele washing machine.'[15] In Britain, for those married in the later 1980s, the proportion who separated within the first five years of marriage had doubled since twenty years before (*Social Trends 31* (2001):48). It has been estimated that 'the direct cost of family breakdown in the UK [is] £10b each year – around 1% of GNP.'[16]

Both married and unmarried sexual relationships are suffering breakdown. The former is easier to measure. For every 1,000 marriages the number divorcing each year has increased more than sixfold from about 2 in 1961 to 13 in 1999 (*Social Trends 31* (2001):48 table 2.10). Even though the absolute number of divorces peaked in 1993 and has fallen by about 12% since then, this reflects not greater stability but the decreasing number of marriages (*Social Trends 31* (2001):46, 48). It is estimated that of current marriages about 4 out of 10 will end in divorce (Church of England 1995:35; Cornes 1993:9; *Independent*, 15 September 1994). We do not have to look back on an imaginary golden age to see that this is a significant change.

The trend towards cohabitation before marriage is sometimes linked to the idea that cohabitation is a (supposedly wise) trial before entering the commitment of marriage. However, at least until recently, where a couple have cohabited before marriage the divorce rate has been significantly higher than for those who have not. Writing in 1992, Dormor says,

> Evidence from Sweden, Norway, Canada and the USA suggests a growing consensus that those who cohabit pre-maritally are more rather than less likely to experience marital dissolution. In Sweden women who cohabit pre-maritally have almost 80% higher marital dissolution, in Canada 50% and in the USA 33%.
> (Dormor 1992:28).

---

14. Haskey 2001a:6 reports a finding of the British Social Attitudes Survey that while premarital sex is increasingly accepted, *extra*marital infidelity is thought to be 'always or mostly wrong' by a steady and large majority of those surveyed.

15. e.g. *Sunday Times*, 24 March 2002.

16. Bulletin of *One Plus One*, Vol. 6 (2), May 2002:1.

Dormor carefully suggests that there is no evidence that 'the experience of cohabitation *per se* is destabilising', but concludes,

> It is probable that those who cohabit before marriage are more likely to divorce because as a group of people they hold different values about marriage as a lifelong commitment.
>
> (Dormor 1992:28)

Similarly, Patricia Morgan observes, 'One explanation for the higher divorce rate of prior cohabitants is that "escape" is perceived as the foremost answer to problems' (Morgan 2000:66).

The British government statistician John Haskey explains, however, that it was only with a more recent survey (the Omnibus Survey) that it was possible to analyse separately marriages whose premarital cohabitation had been the first union for the couple (that is, they had had no previous cohabitations with other partners). Previously all marriages with a premarital cohabitation had been lumped together, whether or not the partners had a history of other cohabitations. This new evidence suggests that where the cohabitation followed by marriage is the first union for both partners, the premarital cohabitation does not introduce a statistically significant increased risk of subsequent marital breakdown (Haskey 2001a:7).[17] Against this apparently encouraging indicator we would, however, need to set the increased risk that the initial cohabitation would break down before it led to marriage. This risk is several times as great as the risk that an initial marriage would break down. On balance the evidence suggests that premarital cohabitation is far from being a wise way to begin a sexual relationship (cf. Morgan 2000:26–29).

The statistical evidence is also unclear about how long cohabitations themselves last.[18] We need to distinguish cohabitations that end in marriage from those that break up. We must not confuse these very different endings. The contemporary phenomenon of cohabitation is, in demographic terms, relatively recent and it is too soon to make confident assertions about how its stability will develop.

None the less, there is considerable evidence that cohabitations (excluding those that lead to marriage) last on average less time than marriages. In 1992

---

17. The former evidence is from Haskey 1992; the recent evidence from the Omnibus Survey is analysed in Haskey 1999:19f. This conclusion for Britain is confirmed for Europe by Kiernan 1999.

18. Questions on cohabitations which ended in the past were first introduced into the *General Household Survey* only in 1998 (Haskey 2001a:25).

Dormor's very full European study concludes, 'Cohabiting unions are not as stable as marriage. This has been shown in almost every country for which we have available information. For example in Sweden in 1986 a cohabiting union was more than six times as likely to break up as a marriage' (Dormor 1992:28). This finding is confirmed in 1999 by Haskey, who compared first cohabitations with first marriages to see how many had broken down after different durations of the union. He concluded, 'At each duration of the union, the proportion of cohabiting unions which had broken down was several times that of marriages – whether those preceded, or not preceded, by pre-marital cohabitation' (Haskey 1999:18–21).

In general we may observe that cohabitors are at least as likely to return to singleness as they are to enter marriage. A 1985 study in Detroit analysed a cohort all born in 1961 and showed that,

> For men, nearly two-thirds of all cohabiting relationships were terminated within two years of the initiation of the cohabitation; 40 percent were terminated by union dissolution within two years and another 23 percent were terminated because the partners married.
> (Thatcher 2002:7)

It has also been observed that in cohabitations the men are less committed to their female partners, and much less committed to their children, than in marriage (Thatcher 2002:13).

Many young divorcees remarry; in 1999 about 2 in 5 marriages were remarriages for at least one of the partners (*Social Trends 31*(2001):47, table 2.9). Other divorcees choose to cohabit and then marry, or cohabit rather than marry again (Dormor 1992:4). Likewise, the break-up of a cohabitation is often followed by new cohabitations with different partners. The story does not therefore simply begin with a couple entering a sexual relationship and end if and when they break up; rather, there is what has been eloquently called a 'churning' of partners (Scase 2000:29), or what is more neutrally referred to as 'serial monogamy' (i.e. where there is sexual exclusivity while a relationship lasts). The picture is of a restless kaleidoscopic movement, of 'cut and shuffle' relationships.

d. Living alone or parenting alone

One of the side effects of the relational kaleidoscope is an increase in the number of people living alone. 'Almost three in ten households in Great Britain comprised one person living alone in Spring 2000, more than two and a half times the proportion in 1961' (*Social Trends 31*(2001):41–42). This large increase is the result of a complex mix of factors including the prosperity that allows people to choose to live alone, and the longevity that sometimes leads to long periods of widowhood. But the sharpest increase in living alone has not been among the elderly. 'In recent years, the largest increase in one-person households has been among men under the age of 65' (this almost trebled between 1971 and 1998). The proportion of women under 65 living alone has almost doubled in that period. Part of this increase reflects later marriage, but part of it the breakdown of relationships (*Social Trends 31* (2001):44).

The number of lone-parent households is also increasing. Of all households with dependent children, in 1971 8% were lone-mother families. By 1991 this had risen to 19%, and to 22% in 1995. Households with a lone father are less common; for every 9 lone-mother households, there is one with a lone father (Dennis and Erdos 1993:109; Church of England 1995:38).[19] The growth in lone-mother households has even led Dormor to suggest that the combined effect of extramarital childbearing and divorce may be to make European society matrilinear, in the sense that 'the mother-child relationship [may] become the only close relationship which is indissoluble' (Dormor 1992:29).

Summary

Western societies are witnessing sexual relationships characterized by lower (or at least more ambiguous) levels of public commitment than before, which are proving more transient than previously, with fewer children, and in which a succession of public sexual partners is increasingly common. Relationships are pictured more by the kaleidoscope than by the stably growing network.

It is easy enough to observe this pattern of instability and disintegration, a story in which committed lifelong marriage is becoming more difficult and in which there are many casualties (McAllister 1995). But how are we to respond?

One response is to say that we may be indifferent to these changes, that we observe them perhaps with interest but no deep concern. Michael Wilmott, a director of the Future Foundation, writes, 'There has never been a golden age of the family. It has never been any better or worse than it is now, just different. The family is very strong – it is simply adapting. And it will keep adapting' (*Observer*, 25 October 1998). After all, say some, we are living much longer and cannot reasonably expect lifelong marital faithfulness with a partner who will change a great deal over the duration of marriage. All that is happening is that the marriages which would previously have ended with bereavement (before the spouses

---

19. cf. *General Household Survey* 1995 (reported in *The Times*, 1 December 1995).

tired of one another) are now ending with divorce. The conclusion of Lawrence Stone is often quoted, that 'it looks very much as if modern divorce is little more than a functional substitute for death' (Stone 1979:46). This comparison is also noted in the report *Something to Celebrate*, which observes that in the 1820s about 36% of marriages lasted less than twenty years because of the death of one partner and in the 1990s the figure is about 33%, although the marriage is now more often terminated by divorce (Church of England 1995:23).

There is, however, a deep difference between a relationship severed by death and one broken by divorce or separation. Two studies in particular point to the seriousness of the current breakdown in family structures. Dennis and Erdos argue that absent or uncommitted fatherhood is deeply detrimental to the educational, financial and social prospects of children. And the report from the One plus One project, *Marital Breakdown and the Health of the Nation*, provides a sobering analysis of the deleterious effects of marital breakdown on the physical and mental health of both adults and children (Dennis and Erdos 1993; McAllister 1995).

For cohabitation, although 'age for age, cohabiting couples have fewer children than married couples', none the less current statistics show that

> the increased risk of union breakdown amongst cohabiting couples compared with married couples means that children in cohabiting couple families are more likely to experience family breakdown and new parental partnerships. Recent research has shown that children born to cohabiting couples are twice as likely to see their parents separate as children born within marriage. Hence children born to cohabiting couples rather than to married parents are likely to be at relatively greater risk of subsequently living in a lone parent family or in a stepfamily.
> (Haskey 2001a:5)

Further, it must be clear to all with pastoral responsibility that the breakdown of a marriage by divorce (or indeed the failure of a cohabitation) is a very different phenomenon from the ending of a relationship by death. Both involve pain, but the shape and flavour of the pain are not the same. Ethically, humanly and affectively, we are guilty of culpable imprecision if we speak as though the two may even approximately be equated.

When a man or woman is widowed, their years of marriage are a part of their personal history that is visited and revisited not only in private memory but in shared memory with wider family, and indeed with new acquaintances and friends. It is a segment of their integrity as a person for which to be grateful, a time characterized more often by gratitude than by regret, a part of their story to be retold with gladness. The sorrow of widowhood is sharp and deep, but it is a sorrow in which regret has no integral part. Of course there may be regrets, but these are not written into the moral structure of widowhood in the way in which they are for divorce. There may be anger in a widow or widower, anger against those who caused the death, anger against God, even anger against the spouse for dying – but even as the anger is felt against the dead spouse, the survivor knows it is irrational. Personal guilt has no intrinsic part in bereavement.

For divorce it is very different. Divorce does not happen without fault. When two people who have pledged lifelong faithfulness split, it is logically necessary that one at least has, for whatever reason, failed to honour the pledge. No divorce happens without moral failure and a measure of guilt, however distributed. In at least one direction there is almost certainly anger that may be entirely rational. Regret for the failure of a love which might have remained faithful but did not is written into the structure of marriage break-down. The memory of the marriage that has ended does continue, but it tends to continue either just in painful private memory or in a shared remembering which focuses more on recrimination than on gratitude. The widowed put smiling photographs of their late spouse on the mantelpiece; the divorcee does not do this for an ex-spouse.

These observed changes in public behaviour must therefore be a cause of deep concern if we love our fellow human beings. Here in our society is a pain, sharp, deep and sour, whose wounds fester from generation to generation. And, unlike the pain of death, it is a pain not imposed upon us by circumstances beyond ourselves. It is brought on neither by disease nor by natural disaster, but by human failure. It is necessary, therefore, to understand these changes and then to endeavour to apply the astringent balm of the Christian gospel. There are many political and sociological causes for our changing patterns of relationship, but there is also – and for our study this is important – a changing paradigm of the way we think about sex and marriage.

A new paradigm of thought

When Dormor uses the phrase 'major historical transformation' and the word 'revolutionary' to describe the demographic transition we have just outlined, he recognizes that he needs to defend these descriptions against the charge of being melodramatic. Is it simply that sensationalist commentators lack historical perspective? 'It could be argued', he writes, 'that we may be seeing the return of many trends commonplace in the nineteenth century.' In defence of these strong descriptions of change, he argues first that the changes in the last three decades are on a far greater scale than a century ago, and second that, whereas a century ago the changes were largely the result of 'societal constraints on marriage and family formation, and death . . . Today's plurality is the consequence of *personal lifestyle decisions*.' What we are living through is not just altered behaviour, but 'a major transformation of (European) *attitudes* and behaviour in the area of marriage and family' (Dormor 1992:3f., 8, my italics).

In his essay 'Sex These Days, Sex Those Days' Jon Davies makes his major theme that, 'whereas "sex" – historically centred in the family and in procreation – once expressed and symbolized the stability of relations between the sexes and the generations, it now – freed from both its familial and procreational purposes – expresses the triumphant individualized freedom of the sexual market'. With 'the triumphant voracity of the sexual market' we see that 'society as a whole is embarked on a huge experiment with sexual fragmentation and sexual fission' (Davies 1997:18).

We may, with much simplification and probably some exaggeration, sketch the new paradigm in four stages.

a. Sex is primarily about one-to-one relationship

The major focus of most serious contemporary commentators is on how sex can build what Jack Dominian has called 'companionate love', rather than on the procreation of children. Stanley Hauerwas comments on this view that 'the quality of the interpersonal relation between a couple is the primary issue for considering sexual involvement' (Hauerwas 1981:178f.). Anthony Giddens has popularized the concept of sexuality realized in 'pure relationships'; such relationships are 'sustained primarily from within themselves, unsupported, unregulated and unconstrained by any external social standards, laws, conventions or rules. Entered into for their own sake, they are continued only in so far as the relationship is thought by each individual to deliver enough satisfaction' (Morgan 2000:3). In Giddens' words, what 'holds the pure relationship together is the acceptance on the part of each partner, "until further notice", that each gains sufficient benefit from the relationship to make its continuance worthwhile' (Giddens 1992:63, quoted in Morgan 2000:3).

In discussing this, we may dismiss the shallow assertion that affective love within marriage is a recent discovery unheard of amongst benighted premoderns. Affective love within marriage has long been valued. In the twelfth century, for example, Hugh of St Victor wrote eloquently of the benefits of marital companionship:

> See now the nature of the contract by which they [sc. the married couple] bind
> themselves in consented marriage. Henceforth, and forever, each shall be to the other
> as a same self in all sincere love, all careful solicitude, every kindness of affection, in

constant compassion, unflagging consolation, and faithful devotedness. And this in
such a way that each shall assist the other as being one's own self in every good or
evil tiding, the companion and partner of consolation, thus proving that they are
united in trial and tribulation.

(Brooke 1989:278f.)

We may also view with scepticism the view that affective love has been present
at the start of marriage only in recent times: 'Before the period of
Romanticism people married (or were married) and looked forward to the
individual love that would arise within this bond. After the period of
Romanticism people married on the basis of love already experienced'
(Thielicke 1979:102). Marriage arranged purely for purposes of family property or political alliance has only ever been the sad preserve of the wealthy or
well connected. Most people have probably always married at least partly
because of prior affection (Bridger 1995:12).

Thus there is nothing new about a high valuation of marital affection as an
integral part of the sexual relationship. What is new is the crowning of this
with unquestioned primacy over the objective 'good' of procreation, with its
entailment of years of sacrificial nurture. Popular portrayals of couples with
supposedly 'good' sex lives are not always superficial; they may major on deep
and fulfilling personal relationship as the context for sex. They do not,
however, commonly associate sexual relationship with the project of procreation and nurture of children as a joyful task integral to the sexual relationship.
And while it is true that romance generally comes before parenthood, the portrayal of the former outside the wider context of the latter builds up a powerful and misleading picture of the purpose of sex.

Those familiar with the liturgy of the Church of England may have noted
an implicit shift of emphasis from procreation to relationship by comparing
the *Book of Common Prayer* (*BCP*) with the *Alternative Service Book* (*ASB* 1980,
now superseded by *Common Worship*). The *BCP* lists the three 'causes for
which Matrimony was ordained' as,

First . . . for the procreation of children, to be brought up in the fear and nurture of
the Lord . . .

Secondly . . . for a remedy against sin, and to avoid fornication . . .

Thirdly . . . for the mutual society, help, and comfort, that the one ought to have
of the other . . .

The *ASB* introduction says,

Marriage is given, that husband and wife may comfort and help each other . . .

It is given, that with delight and tenderness they may know each other in love, and, through the joy of their bodily union, may strengthen the union of their hearts and lives.

It is given, that they may have children . . .

So in place of: (a) children; (b) avoidance of fornication; (c) companionship; we now have: (a) mutual comfort; (b) sexual joy; (c) children.

We must not read too much into this; after all, the *ASB* did not explicitly number the 'goods' of marriage. However, there does seem to be a change of emphasis. (The introduction to the *Common Worship* Marriage Service is more nuanced.)

In 1999 the Joint Liturgical Group of Great Britain published *An Order of Marriage* intended for couples belonging to different Christian denominations. Paragraph 6 is a 'Statement of Marriage' which includes the statement, 'God has given us marriage *so that* . . .' (my italics). This leads us to expect that what follows will summarize the Creator's purpose in instituting marriage for humankind. The only purpose explicitly stated, however, is 'so that husband and wife may live faithfully together'. Five lines later there is reference to children, but this reference is in parentheses and begins, 'In marriage, children *may* be born and nurtured . . .' The parentheses are presumably to be omitted in the case of an elderly couple, and perhaps the word 'may' is present in recognition of the possibility of involuntary childlessness. But taken together this falls far short of the traditional statement that children are part of the Creator's *purpose* for marriage. They have been demoted from purpose to accident, albeit sometimes welcome accident.

A more extreme example of this paradigm shift also comes from within the Christian church. In his book *Liberating Sex* Adrian Thatcher argues that when the intention of sex is procreation this *diminishes* the fully personal and relational element and leads to what he dismissively calls 'the genitalization of sex'. He writes with some scorn of the procreational emphasis, associating it with asceticism that denies the fundamental 'playfulness' of sexual intimacy (Thatcher 1993:38f.). He goes on to emphasize the relational purpose to the extent that 'loving intimacy [is] itself a justification for marriage' (Thatcher 1993:51). Children do not feature prominently in this study; we get the impression that they are optional, accidental and peripheral to sexual relations (Thatcher 1993:91).

The shift from the procreational to the relational is, I suggest, central to the paradigm shift in the perception of sex and marriage in Western society. It is a shift that is theologically characteristic of Protestantism, and it would be an interesting project for a social historian to explore the links between this cultural shift and the influence of Western Protestant thinkers. We shall examine later the influential teaching of Karl Barth, who argues passionately that the supreme good of marriage is not children but rather the 'innocent eroticism' of the Song of Songs and the delight of Genesis 2:23.

The path upon which Barth embarked has been travelled further than he can have imagined. From a focus on covenant relationship has grown an insistent pressure of relational expectations within marriage – for if sex is primarily about relationship, then the microscope must regularly be set to enquire into the quality of that relationship. A number of writers have noted this pressure. Brooke notes perceptively, 'While faced with the spectacle of broken marriages, we have come (by a strange paradox which however goes very deep into the roots of our subject) to expect far more from a happy marriage' (Brooke 1989:8). The paradox does indeed go deep into the roots of our subject.

b. Sexual relationship is in the private domain

If sex is primarily about relationship, that relationship is one-on-one, set firmly in the private domain of personal lifestyle choice. Before long any wider intergenerational and public dimensions fade from view; they drift unnoticed to the margins of the soft-focus image of romantic coupledom. Sex is firmly in the private domain (at least when it is consensual).[20] Indeed, the concept of an individual having an endowment called his or her 'sexuality' is itself an individualistic notion at odds with 'sex in a wider context' (Woodhead 1997:99).

The privatization of sex goes hand in hand with the privatization of the nuclear family. In a North American context, Robert Bellah writes,

> The family is no longer an integral part of a larger moral ecology tying the individual to community, church and nation. The family is the core of the private sphere, whose aim is not to link individuals to the public world but to avoid it as far as possible. (Bellah 1985:112)

The family ceases to be functional, public and political (an integral part of the wider polis). The sociologist Talcott Parsons puts it like this:

> The family has become, on the 'macroscopic' levels, almost completely functionless. It does not itself, except here and there, engage in much economic production; it is not a significant unit in the political power system; it is not a major direct agency of integration in the larger society. Its individual

---

20. An example is the journalist Matthew Parris (*The Times*, 30 October 1995), who argues that the state should leave marriage completely alone and allow couples to formulate and legalize their own individual contracts in their own ways.

members participate in all these functions, but they do so as 'individuals' not in
their roles as family members.
(Schluter and Lee 1993:137)

Before long the family becomes an introspective sphere whose purpose may
be reduced to offering the benefits of narcissistic relationships. This is dressed
up in language of 'giving a person self-esteem and a sense of identity', but the
reality is an imploding maelstrom of psychologically impossible demands.
The Orthodox writer Vigen Guroian comments that Americans overload 'the
nuclear family with too great a responsibility for providing persons with a
sense of identity and significance in life'. As a result, 'Under this moral weight
marriage cracks, and the family is incinerated from within by the intense
psychological demands placed upon it' (Guroian 1987:107).

In their book *The R Factor*, Michael Schluter and David Lee link the im-
plosive breakdown of marriages to the isolation, rootlessness and endless
mobility which are now institutionalized in much of Western society. It is not
only that

> mobility breaks up social networks, but . . . Western culture tends to idealise romantic
> love and to dream that in the beloved all needs are met and all passions consumed.
> Patently they are not. Most of us need to be relationally proximate to other people
> besides our spouse, and if these supporting relationships are weak, the result may be
> a loading by each partner on to the other of more roles and expectations than one
> individual can reasonably be expected to bear. Next stop: implosion.
> (Schluter and Lee 1993:90)[21]

They write vividly of the isolated nuclear family ('mum, dad, kids') and its
'death': 'It is a social quark, a subatomic particle that materialises in courtship,
whizzes through marriage and child-rearing, and dissolves in divorce or old
age. It comes together, divides, and vanishes' (Schluter and Lee 1993:138).

This sense of rootlessness is expressed in extreme form in the cult book
Generation X. In the first chapter we are introduced to the three main charac-
ters: 'Dag is from Toronto, Canada . . . Claire is from Los Angeles, California.
I, for that matter, am from Portland, Oregon, but where you're from feels
sort of irrelevant these days ("Since everyone has the same stores in their
mini-malls," according to my younger brother Tyler)' (Coupland 1992:4). The
chapter ends with Claire 'saying that it's not healthy to live life as a succession
of isolated little cool moments. "Either our lives become stories, or there's

---

21. See Schluter and Lee 1993: ch. 3 for a full explanation of what they mean by
'relationally proximate'.

just no way to get through them." I agree. Dag agrees. We know that this is why the three of us left our lives behind us and came to the desert – to tell stories and to make our own lives worthwhile tales in the process' (Coupland 1992:8). Such despairing comments are pregnant with theological themes. They contrast strikingly with the Old Testament vision of blessing as harmonious connectedness in the people of God.

If the nuclear family becomes introspective, how much more the nuclear couple. Children fit uneasily within the worldview of a privatized family, except as objects of sentimental gratification. It is logically and at heart a religion of 'coupledom', an intracouple relational focus at the expense of a wider social perspective.

Clapp associates this with the economic exchange theory of marriage, with persons as rootless consumers choosing in the supermarket of life, perhaps trading up to a better 'partner', seeking novelty above fidelity. In this context family may become private in the sense of trivial and sentimental (Clapp 1993:60–66).

c. Sex is for self-fulfilment

It is a short step from 'loving you' to 'loving me and wanting you'. By a profound paradox, a focus on relational quality as the primary aim of marriage destroys relationship. It is a deeply fissiparous dynamic. We have considered the privatization of the isolated nuclear family and argued that this is at heart a focus on the isolated nuclear couple. But all too often the couple who are nuclear in the sense of isolated become nuclear in the sense of explosive.

The problem with introspective relational intimacy is precisely that it has no outward goal. We are left with the goal of self-fulfilment through the relationship. So, for example, one speaker in a Church of England General Synod debate spoke of her desire for her sons to find 'a marriage of openness, intimacy, sexual fulfilment and the pursuit of personal significance' (Collingwood 1994:15). The value of sex is still in the relationship, but the value of the relationship now focuses on what it can do for my personal development, my self-esteem, and my sense of worth and significance.

One of the introductory questions in the report *Something to Celebrate* asks, 'What will best support these people [i.e. people in the wide variety of what they call 'family' forms] in the stages of their lives and *enable them to be happy and fulfilled*?' (Church of England 1995:13, my italics). This is not far from the consumer ethic so roundly castigated by Clapp. If we subscribe wholeheartedly to this ethic, he suggests, 'I have a *moral obligation* to divorce and seek a new mate if my original wife can no longer promote my growth and self-actualization' (Clapp 1993:63). I owe it to myself, using the language of self-debt which is now commonplace.

Guroian says we have moved from thinking of love as a permanent commitment with obligations to considering it to be a spontaneous personal choice, the expression of our inner freedom for our gratification. This is subjective, romantic and narcissistic. We have slipped into thinking of marriage as 'a norm of separateness together for the sake of personal psychic satisfaction, self-fulfilment and autonomous activity' (Guroian 1987:88).

d. Sex becomes our saviour

Our paradigm shift began with relationship as the primary focus of sex. This relationship became privatized, isolated from wider dimensions of public service. And then, by a cruel boomerang deception, it turned back on itself; the focus of each, which began so exclusively on the other, turned back on the one in a desire for self-fulfilment. When all this has happened to sex, there is no alternative but to deify it. Sex as source of self-fulfilment is sex as saviour.

When the privatization of sexual relationship is taken to its extreme, sex becomes a substitute religion. Germaine Greer writes with prophetic scorn of the pathological addiction of what she calls *homo occidentalis* to the 'religion' of orgasmic sex. She claims that Western society has become 'anti child', except as a soft target for profit.[22] Of the spread of this culture throughout the world she writes,

> Young grinning couples grace hoardings among the intricate polycellular structures of
> villages full of families and their message is intensely seductive to the young and
> restless. The lineaments of gratified desire they see there will be theirs if they
> abandon the land, abandon the old, earn their own money and have fun. Having fun
> means having recreational sex: recreational sex means no fear of pregnancy, a wife
> who is always available and who is content with orgasms in place of land, family, and
> children – orgasms and consumer durables.
> (Greer 1985:217)

To be self-fulfilled I must be free to express 'my sexuality'; so contemporary thought would have it. As a participant in the sexual free market the only question is which forms of sexual self-expression will promote my fulfilment as a sexual being (Wright 1994:11). There are deeply theological forces at work here. Our culture sees self-fulfilment and sexual fulfilment as inseparable. Taken to its logical conclusion, such thinking is a return to a nature religion, for 'the underlying motif . . . is that sex is an act of nature-worship in

---

22. As I write, the pre-Christmas television advertising is under way, with mouth-watering
   pictures of expensive toys shown in the commercial breaks in children's programmes.

which the participant experiences the ultimate reality of the wider universe and also of his or her own nature. It is both self-discovery and the discovery of the other' (Storkey 1994:96f., cf. 94–100).

This is a paradoxical metamorphosis of pagan fertility rites, for it is now studiedly sterile and obsessively unnatural in its fear of the 'risk' of pregnancy. But as in nature religion, sex is perceived at a deep level as a necessity in life, even a substitute for communion with the transcendent God (Stafford 1993: ch. 6). Thatcher openly admits this, writing of that 'deep pleasure in our bodies [which] is a *precondition* of that deep gratitude to God for our sexuality which is itself the key to responsible and passionate loving' (Thatcher 1993:3, my italics). The sequence is clear: no orgasms, no gratitude; no gratitude, no responsible love. Nelson is even clearer on the religious dimension. For him, 'Sexual communion furnishes more than an analogy for the human commun-ion with God. If God is the in-betweenness of self and self, the occasion itself *(i.e. sexual intercourse) is* the communion with God' (Nelson 1979, my italics, quoted in Banner 1992:104; cf. Nelson 1983). Michael Banner com-ments, 'This confusion of a created good with the Creator is what is known as idolatry' (Banner 1992:104). This will be explored in Chapter 8.

Marriage in the new paradigm

Marriage as relational process above public status

As a result of this paradigm shift, marriage in the public perception of those born since the 1960s is not the same as marriage understood by those born before that watershed. The word now carries a different popular meaning. If we are to engage in theological debate that engages with our culture, we must understand the change that marriage has undergone.

The change in perception is vividly illustrated by the age-dependent answers to a question in the *British Social Attitudes Survey* of 1990. Those sur-veyed (in 1989) were asked what advice they would give to a young woman. There were some non-responses; and a few (well under 10% each) advised living alone without a steady partner or living with a steady partner without marrying. The major answers were 'marry without living together first' and 'live together with a steady partner, then marry'. What is of interest is the dra-matic switch-over between these two answers depending on the age of the respondent. About 60% of those aged 55 and over advised marriage with no prior cohabitation, with 20% advising prior cohabitation; the majority advice was reversed from those aged 35 to 54, and the percentages were almost exactly reversed from those aged 18 to 34 (Haskey 2001a:6, fig. 2).

To live together as a preparation for marriage is now both the majority practice and (even more) the majority morality of those born since the 1960s. Marriage is no longer regarded as the right place to begin a steady sexual relationship, but as a relational process with no public expression, or as a subsequent stage (often linked to reaching some agreed level of stability, shared expectations or maturity in the relationship), or as a relational ideal.

I suggest that this is at least partly a result of the focus we have observed on sex being primarily for relationship. Quality of interpersonal relationship is a continuous and multifaceted variable, not a simple 'on or off' status. At least since Barth, there has been a tendency in Protestantism to focus on the relational qualities or interior 'goods' of marriage, as opposed to what is seen (at least by Barth, in whom there is much anti-Roman Catholic polemic) as the coldly formal and juridical approach of the Roman Catholic Church, with its emphasis on procreation (Barth, *CD* III/4:129ff.). Barth is insistent that a formal marriage-bond is on its own morally inadequate. So, 'Coitus without co-existence is demonic. And we have to realise that this is true even when it is supported by the apparent sanctification of a formal and legitimate marriage bond' (Barth, *CD* III/4:133). He stresses the need for total giving of body, mind and soul to the other in marriage. He follows this focus on inner reality to the logical conclusion that there may be degrees of marriage: 'Marriage ceases to be true marriage in proportion as this fulness is lacking and there is not achieved that which is really at issue, namely, that the two should become one body' (Barth, *CD* III/4:189f.).

The idea that 'there may be degrees of marriage' certainly subverts traditional usage. We may imagine the Barthian answer to the question, 'Are you married?' 'Well, I estimate that I am about 87% married just now, although a month ago it was only 65%. We are working at it.' We might imagine a marital equivalent of Jeremy Bentham's felicific calculus, a kind of relational quality calculus, perhaps with divorce allowed if the figure falls below some threshold for six months or more. But although we may mock, the idea that marriage is fundamentally a relational process rather than a public status has taken deep hold on our thinking. Negatively, this expresses itself in a culture that marginalizes marriage and ceases to mind whether or not a couple are married or cohabiting: if marriage is still defined in language as a status, then it must be ignored if the theological reality is that of process.

Barth himself did not take the logical false step of saying that because formal marriage was insufficient it was therefore unnecessary. That step has been taken by others. In Thatcher it is taken in rather confusing ways. He argues against a clear punctiliar definition of marriage on two contradictory grounds. The first is that consummation is not simultaneous with ceremony, so we cannot say when marriage begins. Marriage has no clear punctiliar genesis. The second is that the ceremony presupposes prior mutual consent, so that at any time after this prior consent, 'Any sex [a couple] have will be pre-ceremonial but not pre-marital' (Thatcher 1993:84). On this second basis marriage does appear to have a genesis, otherwise 'pre-marital' has no meaning. Thatcher appears to be asserting that the genesis may be private rather than public consent. This also begs the important question of the distinction between consent to marry in the future (*per verba de futuro*), which is engagement, and consent in the present tense (*per verba de praesenti*). On balance, however, he seems to prefer the absence of any clear definition, when he says that 'a couple grow into a marriage, without any decisive before and after on a temporal scale' (Thatcher 1993:85).

From a more careful and conservative perspective, Jenkins likewise is critical of black-and-white categorizations of relationships into 'married' and 'not married'. He says that this preoccupation with status 'pays little attention to the dynamics of the relationship'. What, for example, cohabiting couples need from the church is a focus on 'the inner workings of their relationship' (Jenkins 1993:7f.). He argues that black-and-white categorizations are 'pastorally crude' as a way of evaluating relationships. All relationships, 'married' and 'unmarried' alike, are mixtures of good and bad. The preoccupation with status is perceived as unhelpful.[23]

One of the results of speaking in terms of process rather than event or status is that marriage ceases to be viewed as an objective benchmark against which all sexual relationships are to be viewed. It becomes instead some kind of 'biblical norm' or ideal to which all sexual relationships are 'responses' with differing degrees of success (Jenkins 1993:8).[24] Marriage functions either as an ideal to which we aspire or as the process of aspiring to the ideal, but not as a status to be entered.

Uncertain church attitudes to cohabitation

As we generally acknowledge the primacy of relational process (the 'realities' as opposed to the 'formalities' of a relationship), we are not at all sure how to respond to the phenomenon of unmarried cohabitation. We observe that there are marriages in which the inner reality is poor, cold, strife-ridden, even abusive; and there are cohabitations in which the inner reality is rich, warm, harmonious and caring. As a result we are not sure how to respond to this

---

23. In response to the critique of Pratt 1994, Jenkins (1993:9) does agree in his 2nd ed. that 'in the Bible people are either married or not, and sex outside marriage is immoral'; also that 'cohabitation is wrong'.

24. The evaluation of all sexual relationships as 'responses to the biblical norms of marriage' is at the heart of Jenkins' approach.

cultural revolution. It is perhaps in this area supremely that a clear biblical ethics needs to be applied to the contemporary phenomenon of cohabitation.

Perhaps one of the most revealing statements of confusion comes from Harvey: 'Though I must strongly urge marriage as the right option, I cannot regard the alternative as sinful, any more than I can think it is sinful not to accept the gospel' (Harvey 1994:88). So marriage is *the* right option' (I take it the definite article here is not a misprint), but the alternatives are not wrong. This may be called postmodern, or just confusing.

In different ways and with varied nuances qualified moral acceptance of cohabitation has been voiced by various Christian commentators in Britain.[25] Acceptance is nearly always restricted to certain forms of cohabitation, typically those which exhibit relational qualities of faithfulness and love and some stability through time. Different arguments are adduced in favour. Some major on sympathetic understanding of the reasons for not marrying, or not marrying yet. Forster, Jenkins and Collingwood all sympathize with those who are frightened off by the perceived necessity for an expensive ceremony and reception. Some point to the failings of marriages and argue that some cohabitations are closer to the biblical ideal than some marriages. Debate focuses on the definition of marriage, and in particular on the place of publicly attested vows in this. All admit that cohabitations lack some at least of the wider public, familial and societal dimensions of marriage. The statistics which show widespread instability of cohabiting relationships are admitted. Some argue that this means the church should put more energy into supporting such couples in their struggle to stay together, rather than simply telling them they are wrong to try.

Broadly, those sympathetic to cohabitation may be divided into those who say some cohabitations are in fact marriages by another name and so should be recognized as such, and those who say they are less good than marriage but for various reasons this does not much matter.[26] An example of the former is Forster:

> My main argument [is] that society has institutionalized cohabitation even if the law has not yet caught up with social practice. [This] implies that a stable cohabitation is as legitimate as marriage because *social custom*, whether codified in law or not, *is what defines marriage*.
> (Forster 1994:83f., my italics).

---

25. e.g. Harvey 1994; Forster 1988 and 1994; Jenkins 1993; Thatcher 1993 and 1999; Avis 1989; Collingwood 1994; Church of England 1995.
26. This seems to be the position of Avis 1989 and Harvey 1994.

So Collingwood argues that many cohabitations may be 'biblical' without being 'legal'.

> In addition to these publicly registered and recognized common law marriages (*which there will be if his proposals are followed*), it is probable that a fairly high proportion of cohabiting unions would be unregistered and unrecognized. However provided that such unions fulfilled the criteria of stability and commitment within an exclusive sexual relationship, they ought to be recognized by the Church as *biblical marriages*, even if not *legal marriages* under the law of the country. This is important because such cohabiting unions are likely to present themselves to clergy where couples are seeking to use the services of the church for the occasional offices of baptisms, marriages and funerals.
>
> (Collingwood 1994:19, his italics).

The report *Something to Celebrate* is also uncertain. On the one hand it claims that 'some forms of cohabitation are marriages already in all but name'. In the next sentence, however, it admits, 'Theologically and morally, what makes a marriage is the freely given consent and commitment in public of both partners to live together for life.' It ends up with a compromise: we are to recognize that 'cohabitation is, for many people, *a step along the way* towards [marriage]' (Church of England 1995:115–116).

One argument for viewing cohabitation sympathetically is that to do otherwise is to 'stand like Canute against the irresistible social tide' (Collingwood 1994:20). Since evidence suggests that 'in Western Europe living together before marriage will soon become a majority practice' (Dormor 1992:31), this argument may seem to have some force. As an *ethical* argument, however, it will not bear Christian scrutiny. One trembles to think how easily it would have transferred, for example, to Nazi Germany. And quite apart from the depressing lack of gospel nerve in such a statement, it suggests ignorance of Christian history. It is hard to see that this 'social tide' is any stronger than first-century Graeco-Roman promiscuity or the centuries of the institution of slavery. This is hardly the spirit of those who were once reputed to have 'turned the world upside-down' (Acts 17:6). *Something to Celebrate* goes a little further. For them the retreat from the incoming tide is a welcome thing. They point out that 'another reason for regarding cohabitation sympathetically has to do with changes and developments in modern life', these including the fact that the advent of contraception makes optional the link between intercourse and procreation. The changes are noted and described as 'significant and positive' without any attempt to subject them to critical scrutiny (Church of England 1995:116f.).

The acceptance or advocacy of premarital (and precohabitational) sex

Once entry to marriage ceases to be the moral boundary of sex, there appears to be no good reason for allowing cohabitation to become a replacement boundary. Instead the boundary fades into a blur of relational subjectivity. Stanley Hauerwas quotes James Nelson in his book *Embodiment*, where Nelson argues that any one act of 'genital sexual expression should be evaluated in regard to motivations, intentions, the nature of the act itself, and the consequences of the act, each of these informed and shaped by love'. But as Hauerwas trenchantly comments, while all of this may be true up to a point, it 'is a lot for the teenagers in the back seat of a car to remember' (Hauerwas 1981:182).

Societal norms are now such that Germaine Greer can appear radical when she writes an article expressing both astonishment and approval for a young male hitch-hiker who appeared entirely normal, focused, motivated, and yet was a self-confessed virgin with no intention of engaging in sexual intercourse before marriage (*Independent*, 27 October 1995). This, to her, surprising behaviour is now usually considered evidence of abnormality.

Christian responses to premarital (and precohabitational) sex have been as varied as those to cohabitation. At one extreme there are advocates of premarital sexual experience. Thatcher writes (with curious logic),

> Since sexual desire is God-given, those who are in a hurry for sexual experience and eager for sexual experiment do not place themselves outside the community of faith. Their sexual activity already provides them with precious experience within which the Christian vision for sex within love can take root.
> (Thatcher 1993:75)[27]

Thatcher warmly affirms what he calls 'intentional' sex, that is to say preceremonial sex where there is already private mutual consent to future marriage. He also treats with 'sympathy' (an interesting word) what he calls the 'appropriateness' view of sex; this leaves the decision whether or not to have sex to the couple, whether or not marriage is in prospect. And in chapter 11 on 'Sexual Friendships' he argues that while 'procreative sex' should be kept for marriage, 'There will be countless other contexts where sexual activity is an appropriate expression of love. That love will not have as its intended outcome children or be a commitment until death. These contexts are sexual friendships' (Thatcher 1993:172).

Countryman likewise advocates premarital sex as valuable experience: 'Even among young adults, the first choice of a sexual partner is not likely to

---

27. The argument could equally be applied to paedophilia. 'Since X finds himself with a God-given desire for sex with children . . . precious experience . . .'

be the best . . . If marriage is treated in society simply as license to have sex,' then people will make bad marriages. 'If the decision [to marry] is not merely about first sexual experience but about life-partners, it will be easier for people to make it in a realistic way' (Countryman 1989:259).

In similar vein but with more caution, Harvey suggests that just as we have moved from the procreative to the relational as the primary purpose of sex within marriage, so we may move from sex as relational within marriage to sex as 'exploratory and preparatory' before marriage. He says this must be done 'seriously' and not as 'a ticket for trying one partner after another until one finds the right one' (which sounds rather like Countryman's approach). None the less, the experience may be valuable, Harvey suggests, and ministers preparing cohabiting couples for marriage 'could actually give some positive encouragement to them to use that intimacy as a serious way of preparing for . . . marriage'. He suggest 'a simple ceremony of betrothal' to 'enable the couple to live together with a good conscience (if that is what they intend to do anyway)' (Harvey 1994:73–75).

Conclusion

We live in an age of revolution. Sexual relationships are visibly unstable. marriage is more and more preceded, and sometimes supplanted, by cohabitation. Fewer children are being born, they are being born within cohabitations as well as within marriages, and they are being born later. More and more people are living alone or parenting alone. We cannot ignore or minimize the pain these changes bring.

I have suggested that these changes of behaviour correspond to a new paradigm governing the way we think about sex. The primary purpose of sex is perceived to be the building of one-on-one relationship. This relationship is essentially in the private domain; it is not, except tangentially, connected with a wider framework of public function or service. In this privatized world of 'coupledom' a tragic transition occurs by which concern for the other is metamorphosed into self-fulfilment through sex; to fulfil this grand destiny of bringing personal salvation sex must be deified. Its failure to respond to such high expectations when worshipped – for, when worshipped, it becomes an idol and is bound to disappoint – carries in its train a tragic entailment of relationship breakdown. I have therefore suggested that a paradigm in which the primary purpose of sex is to build one-on-one relationship has itself contributed to the breakdown of relationships. If this claim is true it is deeply paradoxical. At the heart of our study will therefore be a theological enquiry into the purpose of sex (Part Two).

PART ONE

THE BIBLICAL AND THEOLOGICAL BASIS FOR THE STUDY OF MARRIAGE

4. MARRIAGE AND THE CREATED ORDER

In Part Three (Chapters 11 to 15) I shall discuss the shape of marriage using the following working definition.

Marriage is
the voluntary sexual and public social union (Chapter 11)
of one man and one woman (Chapter 12)
from different families (Chapter 13).
This union is patterned upon the union of God with his people his bride,
the Christ with his church (Chapter 14).
Intrinsic to this union is God's calling to lifelong exclusive sexual faithfulness
(Chapter 15).

I shall examine each element of definition, and consider the scriptural evidence and the theological questions. Before that, in Part Two (Chapters 6 to 10), I shall ask the question 'Why did the Creator make humankind male and female so that we marry?' I shall suggest that this question of divine purpose is foundational to the subject.

Before we consider either purpose or definition, however, we need to address the first two words, '*marriage is* . . .' I need to defend my suggestion that a (even 'the') definition *exists*. This chapter therefore defends the objective existence of marriage as part of the created order. The next defends its continuing significance in the light of the kingdom of God. It is acutely necessary to make these defences in the light of the changes noted in Chapter 3.

The words 'marriage is . . .' mask a theological foundation which must be examined. There are two ways of understanding the relationship of an ethics to the world. On the one hand we may understand that ethics has an inherent fit with the world, like the skin on an animal; on the other, we may claim that different ethics are like suits of clothes worn by a model, which may be changed at will.[1] Or we may use an analogy of the writer Will Self, describing his father's vain attempts to interest him in Christianity in childhood.

> Try as he might to enthuse us with the sonorous beauties of the King James Bible, as declaimed by middle-class, middle-aged men in dresses, it was far too late. We had already been claimed by the split infinitives of *Star Trek*, were already preparing to boldly go into a world where ethics *so far from inhering in the very structure of the cosmos, was a matter of personal taste akin to a designer label, sewn into the inside lining of conscience.*
> (*Independent*, 12 April 1999, my italics)

In the hope that it is not too late, this study believes that ethics does 'inhere in the very structure of the cosmos'; there is a moral order placed in creation by the Creator, however imperfectly we perceive it and however much we need the grace of redemption to open our eyes to it in its fullness. The moral structure of the world and the core anthropology of the human person, although flawed and spoiled, yet bear this order of creation, to which we must attend if we are wise. Marriage is a part of this moral order.

The concept of creation order ought not to be neglected by Christian ethicists. In an incisive critique of the searches of five Christian denominations for a contemporary sexual ethic, Michael Banner notes,

> The concept of the order of creation [is] a theme in Christian ethics which the present era is inclined to forget. For a Christian ethics which takes seriously the fact that the Gospel of Jesus Christ is a gospel of the world's redemption, and not of escape from it, cannot but inquire with the utmost seriousness as to the nature and form of the order of creation which it was God's will not only to create but also to redeem. And it cannot but treat this order as morally significant.
> (Banner 1999:258f.)

Banner rightly acknowledges, 'The most important contemporary treatment of this theme and of its significance for Christian ethics in general is found in Oliver O'Donovan's *Resurrection and Moral Order*' (Banner 1999:258f.). I too am deeply indebted to O'Donovan's magisterial study. It is worth quoting O'Donovan:

---

1. I borrow and adapt an illustration quoted by Soskice 1985:3 in another context.

In the ordinance of marriage there was *given* an end for human relationships, *a teleological structure which was a fact of creation and therefore not negotiable*. The dimorphic organization of human sexuality, the particular attraction of two adults of the opposite sex and of different parents, the setting up of a home distinct from the parental home and the uniting of their lives in a shared life . . . these form a pattern of human fulfilment which serves the wider end of enabling procreation to occur in a context of affection and loyalty. Whatever happens in history, Christians have wished to say, *this is what marriage really is*. Particular cultures may have distorted it; individuals may fall short of it. It is to their cost in either case; for it reasserts itself as God's creative intention for human relationships on earth; and it will be with us, in one form or another, as our natural good until (but not after) the kingdom of God shall appear. (O'Donovan 1994:69, my italics)

Such confidence is alien to contemporary culture. There are two dimensions to our claim, the ontological (that this order exists) and the epistemological (that it may be known). Although it is not here possible to embark on a full-scale defence of either, it is necessary to make some attempt to delineate (and in some modest measure defend) what I understand the answers to be. I do this by considering five assertions.

1. Creation order is moral and not just material

The order of creation extends beyond simply the material and physical world, and includes within its scope the moral, psychological, anthropological and social dimensions of human existence. It is an extensive order from which no facet of human personhood or relationship is exempt. It extends to actions and character (the sphere of morality) as much as to materiality (the sphere of the physical sciences). In particular it extends to the sexual dimension of human existence.

The magnificent drama of Genesis 1 begins with the earth as 'a formless void' (Gen. 1:2), the emphasis being not on disorder (the negation of order) but on the absence of order. The universe is empty, waiting to be filled, or embryonic, waiting to be developed.[2] The drama, as it unfolds, emphasizes

---

2. I am grateful to Derek Kidner (personal correspondence) for distinguishing this biblical concept from the pagan one of a hostile and actively chaotic world waiting to be subdued. This pagan concept would not make sense after Gen. 1:1; indeed, in the pagan myths there is no unitary concept of one Creator creating 'in the beginning'; there are always some powers and entities already 'on stage' when the curtain rises, to use an analogy from Lewis 1961b:68.

order, structure, boundaries and appropriate relationships. There is light and darkness and they are ordered to one another with boundaries. The waters above the firmament, the waters below the firmament, the dry land – each has its place. Living creatures appropriate to each fill each.

Each is also implicitly ordered not simply to its fellow creatures and to the inanimate world, but to the Creator. The order is generic (there are 'kinds') and it is teleological (it is 'good' in the eyes of its Maker, each kind being suited to its purpose). There is both structure and purpose. This order is the foundation of creation (cf. Prov. 3:19). We tend to consider the 'foundation' in terms of the physical, material and biological world on which Genesis 1 focuses, but to restrict creation order to these dimensions would be absurd. What kind of a cosmos would it be in which the physical sciences were a worthwhile enterprise – because they look for structure that is there to be found – but in which the fields of personal relationships and morality were undifferentiated chaos? This would be a world in which personhood was still 'a formless void', waiting to be given shape by the subjective whims of each person or each succeeding culture. No, the moral order which Old Testament law and New Testament ethical instruction attest is rooted in the moral order inherent in creation – just as, in the physical sciences, what we call 'laws of nature' are objectively there to be discovered (however approximately, by us); they are not the free creation of the scientist's will or imagination.

This assertion that the created order is extensive is ontological, but it has an epistemological correlate. Any knowledge we may have of this order must be knowledge not just of a part but of a part as it relates to the whole. Since the whole universe is ordered (including its moral dimensions) we can only properly understand, for example, the sexual dimension when we endeavour to grasp its place within the whole; and in particular its purpose within the whole (for it is inconsistent to allow merely generic order while ruling out teleology). It is the proper work of Christian theology (and in particular creation theology) to place sexuality within the metanarrative of God's purpose for humankind (O'Donovan 1994:77f.).

2. Creation order is created not constructed

Marriage is an institution given by God, not a project fashioned by culture

It may seem obvious to say that creation order is created, but it is important to tease out some of the implications of this. The concept of autonomy is always pushing to the surface in ethical thought, and must be resisted (Hebblethwaite 1981: ch. 1). We human beings are not self-sufficient in our physical existence; we have many dependencies upon others and upon the world in which we live.

Since we cannot be physically autonomous, it is implausible to suppose that we may be ethically autonomous, for these multiple physical dependencies point us to our original and total (including ethical) dependency upon the Creator. As we rejoice in the created order, we are to 'Know that the LORD is God. It is he that made us, and we are his . . .' (Ps. 100:3).

We are placed in the created order in a position of unique authority over it, and, within it, of uniquely privileged responsibility to the Creator. But neither human beings (individually or corporately) nor 'nature' as an independent concept enjoy the autonomous right to create ethics. We must not speak of 'nature' as if 'she' enjoyed an existence independent of the mind and purpose of God. 'The laws of the universe are not the independent edicts of autonomous Nature but the direct corollary of God's sending forth his word to the earth' (Bockmuehl 2000:90). When we say loosely, 'This is how the world *is*,' we mean, 'This is how the personal Creator has made it, and it is how he personally sustains it moment by moment; our response to it is inseparable from our response to him.'

This is a necessary safeguard against idolatry, for it is a commonplace to understand ethics as a social construct. In Michel Foucault's three-volume work *The History of Sexuality*, for example, the assumption is that sexual identity is a sociocultural and psychological construct rather than a given (Foucault 1978).

James Nelson is a prominent proponent of sexuality as a cultural construct. In his book *Embodiment* he argues that sexuality is formed by 'patterns of meaning which are more socially constructed than biologically determined'. Sexuality is a highly symbolic dimension of human existence, and the symbolism may vary. The assertion of this freedom, he argues, frees us from 'the heavily biological emphasis typical of traditional natural law theory in ethics'. Instead, as we grow we 'become sexual' less by 'a natural unfolding of biological tendencies' and more by 'a social learning process through which we come to affirm certain sexual meanings in our interaction with significant others'. And these 'sexual meanings are not absolute but rather are historically and culturally relative' (Nelson 1979:25–30).

One of the more influential angles on construing ethics as a human volitional creation comes from biblical scholars who discuss ethics in terms of the boundary markers for communities of faith. Wayne Meeks is a prominent example of this approach. In his comprehensive surveys of the early Christian communities set in their cultural contexts, it seems that his underlying understanding of Christian morality is that it is at root a collection of arbitrary boundary markers that serve to delimit the fence around the believing communities.[3]

---

3. E.g., Meeks 1983:84–110 (esp. 97–103); Meeks 1987:125–130.

The primary motivation in the construction of these ethics is the social cohesiveness of the communities, rather than any sense that these behaviours might be absolutely right or wrong. Hence, very revealingly, in a postscript to his book *The Origins of Christian Morality* he writes that 'the process of *inventing* Christian – and human – morality will continue' (Meeks 1993:219, my italics).

If we reject a voluntarist concept of ethics (by which I mean one in which the *content* of the ethics is grounded in the will and choice of humankind), we must reject also a historicist view, that understands ethics as swept along by historical processes, cut free from its anchor in the givenness of creation. In this view marriage is 'an item of cultural history' (O'Donovan 1994:70) in a process of constant metamorphosis. The statement 'Marriage is . . .', if it is possible at all in this framework, must be heavily circumscribed: 'Marriage *in our culture and our time* is . . . but of course it will not always be so and we watch with interest to see how it will develop.' In such a framework of thought, biblical ethics is evacuated of integrity. Of course we must admit that marriage has been dressed with a wide variety of ceremonies and customs in different places and at different times. And this observation holds also for marriage customs in the various cultures of the biblical texts (Perdue 1997; Osiek and Balch 1997), for no culture is normative simply by virtue of appearing in a biblical text. We are not so naïve as to think that marriage practices of biblical periods can have normative significance, but nor therefore are we vulnerable to the accusation that the variety of marital custom evidenced in biblical cultures renders normative marriage untenable. The normative structure of marriage is revealed in creation, not recorded in transit by snapshots from short-exposure film of fast-moving historical moments.

Brigitte and Peter Berger, in their book *The War over the Family*, observe that in all these kinds of humanly constructed ethics, 'the family ceases to be an institution, an objective given, and becomes a project of individuals, thus always susceptible to redefinition, reconstruction and termination' (in Guroian 1987:87). Against such uncontrolled fluidity we must seek to argue that the order of creation is precisely not the product of the human mind or will; that ethics cannot be voluntarist in the sense of deriving from the will of humankind imposing order on a chaotic moral field. If it were simply the commitment of one observing mind, it would be evacuated of any metaphysical claim on us, since the commitment of another observing mind would have an equal claim and neither could lay claim to correspond to a transcendent reality. Ethics derives from metaphysics and theology. Ethics is the exposition of order placed in creation by God; it is not the imposition of order arising from the human will imposing itself upon an originally disordered moral field.

Christians ought confidently to affirm this, for it is a source of joy. This order is 'given' to us in a double sense: it is freely received and it is not negotiable.[4] Givenness as good gift depends on recognizing givenness as transcendent order. As O'Donovan puts it, created order is 'not negotiable within the course of history' and is part of 'that which neither the terrors of chance nor the ingenuity of art can overthrow. It defines the scope of our freedom and the limits of our fears' (O'Donovan 1994:61). The joy of Psalm 8 is the wonder of man, 'set within an order which he did not make, joyfully accepting his privileged place within it' (O'Donovan 1994:38). It is the dignity of human beings not to usurp the authority of God but joyfully to enter into the responsibility under God of understanding the created order and governing that order by lives informed by that understanding (that is, by wisdom).

The alternative is terrible indeed, for it means that morality must of necessity fracture into shards of local, cultural or individual code. Such moral scattering is, like Babel, a sign of the judgment of God, a descent from cosmos to ethical chaos. On the contrary, the Christian joyfully proclaims, morality does have integrity and it is to be perceived and understood, not invented (cf. Baelz 1977: ch. 1).

The objection that truth claims are masked power claims

It is important to raise an objection here. Any claim to access objective truth (as here, an ethics rooted in creation) is vulnerable to the objection that such a claim is really a masked bid for power. This issue is peculiarly acute in sexual ethics, and particularly in the question of gender relations (Thiselton 1997:154–157). Much contemporary theological debate is no longer carried on in terms of truth, but of power. Moltmann has observed, 'The modern critique of religion no longer makes any critique of the content of faith, but is a purely functional critique of the psychological, political and social effects of the faith. It no longer asks whether it is true or false, but only whether it has the function of oppression or liberation, alienation or humanization' (in Tomlin 1999:1; cf. Thatcher 1999: ch. 1).

The accusation is simple: 'Beneath the façade of reason there is the crude conflict of competing interests' (Baelz 1977:12). In particular Christian ethics may, it is said, be a masked instrument for communitarian regulation (Countryman 1989:138–143). This motif of ecclesial control is taken up by Graham Shaw in his book *The Cost of Authority*, where he writes, 'In historical terms, conformity to a pattern of sexual behaviour has given the Church its social visibility and identity. In blessing, regulating and policing that conformity the clergy have exercised control at the most intimate level of human experience' (Shaw 1983, quoted in *Church Times*, 11 June 1993).

---

4. The ordinance of the one in seven Sabbath rest has this same double character.

In answer to this we may note first that – paradoxically – there is nothing so authoritarian as autonomous human ethics. Both the historicist and the voluntarist lack any possibility of prophetic critique from beyond history or from outside their particular group, to challenge the mores of the strong and to announce salvation for the oppressed. For autonomous ethics any contemporary orthodoxy is bound to be the imposition upon the weak (for the historicist, 'the outdated' or those not in tune with the age) of the mores of the strong. There is none so illiberal as the consistent historicist or voluntarist in ethics.

A proper understanding of human creatureliness safeguards against this abuse of authority. Only if we maintain that purpose is not inherent in the natural order may we assume to ourselves the liberty to devise ethics guided by technology. It is then up to us to *devise* the uses to which we will put humankind (or the animal world or the inanimate creation). We can no longer allow the argument that there is a Creator's purpose to which our stewardship must respond, and that sets limits to our exercise of technology. If we find we can turn our 'sexuality' to some purpose which we find 'fulfilling', who is to say we should not follow this path? Far from creation ethics being a mask for oppression, it is the necessary safeguard against human oppression (O'Donovan 1994:52).

The second answer we must give is that authentic Christian ethics, like the Christian gospel, is shaped by the cross – and the cross is the negation of the human search for power. No ethic that promotes the power of the strong over the weak can be Christian. The gospel proclamation of truth, that includes the revelation of the order of creation, is a word of foolishness and weakness. It can never be a word of manipulation or power play (cf. Paul's classic exposition of this in 1 Cor. 1:18–2:5). It may be timely that this study coincides with a period when the Western churches are increasingly marginalized as regards sexual ethics. Only as the churches eschew the trappings of power can the authentic gospel weapons be wielded, weapons of open persuasion not clever manipulation (2 Cor. 4:2; 10:3–5). We must never mistake the order of creation for an instrument of social control.

Marriage is a status that is entered, not a project that is enterprised[5]

If marriage in creation order is given, above culture and history, so that it is neither the result of historical process nor the outcome of social construction, this truth of grace must also be focused on the individual couple. When a couple marry, they enter marriage; they neither invent the particular terms of their relationship, nor do they gradually create the status as a relational project

---

5. See the related discussion in Chapter 15, pp. 345–348.

over time. This observation is of great significance in contemporary debate in which marriage is either regarded as a negotiable contract or as a developmental process.

Alan Storkey writes that 'the Judaeo-Christian view is one which identifies marriage, not as an ideal, but as an institution within which couples are called to live' (Storkey 1996:4). The difference between an ideal and an institution is important. A couple may have in their minds some ideal and strive to move towards that in their relationship. This is deceptively similar to marriage but actually radically different. To get married is to enter a status of relationship *within which* the growth and maturity are to develop. Marriage must first have a *stasis* before it can have a proper *dynamis*. A couple are instantiated into a status. That status has a moral structure within which the Creator calls them to live. To understand this is a necessary precursor to stability and security within marriage; the alternative is the terrifying possibility that each couple must generate the terms and qualities of their particular relationship as they see fit.

It is not possible, however, for a couple to define by their own choice the terms of their relationship and for that relationship to be marriage. Marriage is not a humanly constructed contract whose terms may be negotiated (and perhaps renegotiated at a later date). 'This is not a relationship which can be cobbled together as we see fit' (Storkey 1996:38). Marriage is a status of relationship whose terms, structure and calling are given by the Creator.

Thus it is misleading to consider marriage simply or primarily in terms of the process of relational growth embarked upon by the couple, important though this is. To do this is to confuse living up to the calling of marriage with the given institution of marriage within which this divine calling is heard. This is the fallacy of some contemporary commentators when they argue against what they regard as a static institutional concept in favour of a warm pastoral emphasis on relational realities. One of the most influential thinkers in this area was D. S. Bailey. In *The Man-Woman Relation in Christian Thought* he makes much of what he sees as the unhelpful preoccupation of the medieval church with 'the formal and legal aspects of matrimony' (Bailey 1959:154). The church devoted its thinking to the kinds of issues of interest to the ecclesiastical courts (such as what constituted proper consent or legal impediments to marriage), thus addressing juridical or forensic categories and taking 'little account of the metaphysical and personal aspects of the relationship between husband and wife' (Bailey 1959:154). This alienated church thinking from both scriptural and patristic concerns and prevented the medieval church from having a proper theology of sex and marriage.[6] In this connection

---

6. Bailey returns to this at the start of his final chapter VII, 'Towards a Theology of Sex'.

Bailey twice quotes with approval Barth's scathing dissociation of himself from the medieval schoolmen's 'doctrine of marriage which is essentially a doctrine of the wedding ceremony' (Barth, *CD* III/4:226; Bailey 1959:156, 260).

Bailey has correctly understood the structure of Barth's emphasis on the inner relational realities as being the heart of marriage. Partly in the context of anti-Roman Catholic polemic, Barth has a deep prejudice against what he calls 'the equation of marriage with the wedding ceremony', which he calls 'a dreadful and deep-rooted error'. Indeed,

> Two people may be formally married and fail to live a life which can seriously be regarded as married life. And it may happen that two people are not married and yet in their precarious way live under the law of marriage. A wedding is only the regulative confirmation and legitimation of a marriage before and by society. It does not constitute marriage.
> (Barth, *CD* III/4:225)

Now at one level we may agree with Barth. A preoccupation with 'correct' forms of wedding ceremony or (even worse) with the perceived necessity of church involvement is a misleading distraction from the true nature of marriage (which is why in our definition at the start of this chapter no mention was made either of a wedding ceremony or of the church).

Barth, however, does not simply mean this. When he stresses the inner relational dynamic of love within a 'real' marriage, he slips too far towards questioning the *'real marriedness'* of disappointing or 'loveless' (often used in an emotional sense) marriages. This becomes clear in his discussion of indissolubility. In discussing the saying of Jesus that man must not tear apart those whom God has joined, he writes,

> We cannot sufficiently seriously realise that by no means every human striving, coming and being together of two partners in love and marriage automatically implies and indicates that God has joined them together and that permanence and indissolubility attach to their union. It would be wanton to apply that saying of Jesus to every such couple merely because it has actually discovered itself as such and spoken its human Yes before the civil authorities or the priestly altar and perhaps lived long in conjugal fellowship . . . It may be that [God] has not called a specific couple to marriage, that the divine basis and constitution are lacking from the very outset, that in the judgement of God and according to His will and command, *it has never become a married couple* and lived as such. In this case the partnership is radically dissoluble because there has been no real union in the judgement of God.
> (Barth *CD* III/4:208f., my italics)

Barth here is not addressing the traditional grounds for nullity such as defective consent or forbidden degrees of kinship or affinity; he is arguing that sometimes the relational realities fall so far short of real love that a couple must conclude that they are not really married.[7] Such thinking evacuates Jesus' saying of all moral force, since it opens the way to the easy evasion of claiming that 'in our case' incompatibility shows that 'God never had really joined us'. And it thereby introduces into marriage the most catastrophic insecurity. Essentially it removes the security of entering the institution of marriage *within which* we are called to live lives of mutual love and faithfulness, and replaces it with a terrifying concept of marriage as the project of each couple and the precarious process of growth in love. It is not a long step from this to being able to caricature a couple as reporting, 'Our love is growing well; we are considerably *more married* this year than last,' or, 'We are having relational problems and are rather *less married* now than we used to be.' And if our 'coefficient of marriedness' falls below some critical benchmark, divorce proceedings are triggered. This is the logical consequence of confusing the status of being married with the quality of the married relationship. Both status and relationship are important, but if the latter is confused with the former it removes the stability, the necessary foundation.

Adrian Thatcher also espouses a processive view of marriage which sees the 'marriedness' of a couple as contingent on the relational realities of their love. In his book *Liberating Sex* he argues against any clear punctiliar definition of when marriage is entered. Marriage is a process of growth in relationship, not a legal change of status. 'A couple grow into a marriage, without any decisive before and after on a temporal scale' (Thatcher 1993:85). Although the book is entitled *Liberating Sex*, the irony is that an understanding of marriage as process rather than 'given' introduces into marriage the most enslaving insecurities. A man and woman cannot grow in love in the security of knowing the divine origin of the relationship in which they live;

---

7. Cf. the argument of Macquarrie 1975:230–236. Macquarrie wishes to argue for an indissolubilist line on the inadmissibility of divorce. But in order to make this discipline 'pastorally more effective and compassionate' he suggests a liberalization of the nullity rules so that in cases where the continuation of the marriage proves impossible we 'recognize that in fact a marriage has not taken place. Some strand in the bond has been missing, some hidden impediment has been present, consummation (understood not merely in a physical way) has failed to come about' (p. 236). This *a posteriori* form of indissolubility is very close to Barth's position (cf. the position of Thielicke 1979: 108–124, 163–195).

instead they must try precariously to build their own. In his more recent book *marriage after Modernity*, Thatcher adopts an essentially Barthian view of indissolubility, which correlates very naturally with the concept of marriage as process:

> Once the notion that indissolubility is something conferred on marriages at the beginning is replaced with the notion that it is something to be attained through the marriage, through the deepening love of the spouses, a more dynamic understanding of marriage will have been reached. On this view the more Christian a marriage becomes, the more indissoluble it actually is.
> (Thatcher 1999:37)

We may also note the parallel legal observation of H. B. Vaisey:

> It is an important principle that to be married 'gradually' is impossible. If a man be not validly married on a particular day and at a particular hour and place he can never become married by mere lapse of time, or by virtue of mere acquiescence in a union supposed to be a valid one. This is by no means restricted to Christian marriages, but is true of all monogamous unions recognised in civilised countries.
> (Church of England 1935:71)

The distinction between marriage perceived as a status following an event and marriage perceived as relational process is of great pastoral importance. The marriage 'one flesh' union is an ethical imperative (we ought to grow in it),[8] but it is first a divine gift (Guroian 1987:88). There is a parallel here to the New Testament ethical calling to the Christian to 'become what you are'; the status and security of being adopted into the family of God is the foundation upon which the ethical life of the Christian is built. This safeguards grace as the principle that infuses all Christian living. It is the same in marriage: we enter a state in which security has been pledged without conditions, and in this safe state we live out the calling to which we are called, to build a relationship of growing sacrificial love. But when we focus on the gradually deepening (or evaporating) relational intimacy as the locus of marriage, paradoxically a terrible insecurity is engendered. This is how it is with an extramarital affair; it all rests on the current condition of an ever-fluctuating relationship. Graham Greene conjures up this insecurity in *The End of the Affair* as his 'hero' ruminates about the way that passionate desire when the lovers were

---

8. See the sensitive treatment in Atkinson 1979:77–82 of the dimensions of growing personal union.

together can go hand in hand with fear when they were apart. He speaks of loving her obsessively, 'And yet I could feel no trust: in the act of love I could be arrogant, but alone I had only to look in the mirror to see doubt . . .' (Greene 1951:208). Sceptics speak mockingly of 'living in an institution' and of a mere 'piece of paper', but those who engage in sexual relations outside this institution often yearn for the security it brings. To live outside is to live by works, to be constantly on best behaviour, to be only as good as the last time. To live inside is to live in grace, responding freely to unconditional pledged love, not to have failure and personal inadequacies drive us to paralysing despair.

3. Creation order is universal

The created order inheres precisely in all creation. It is not the preserve of any locality, any period of history or any culture. Nor is it applicable only to the people of God. This is important in view of the confusion surrounding the supposed differences between 'marriage' and 'Christian marriage'. Marriage is an ordinance of creation not a regulation of the church; it may be entered outside the sphere of faith, and when entered from within the sphere of faith it does not change its essential character. Couples may have different levels of understanding of the purposes for which marriage was ordained, but those who know neither the creation origins nor the redemptive significance of marriage may yet marry. And when they marry, they marry; they do not partially marry because they are outside the boundaries of the church, and they do not marry in some superior way if they are within (cf. Thielicke 1979:139f.).

In the light of this we must regard with some circumspection the claim of David Torrance:

> Whereas there is a recognisable form of marriage that is created and ordained by
> God for everyone in the world, [the Reformers] held that in Christ God has sanctified
> and redeemed marriage from its state in the fallen world and restored it to its original
> character and purpose as taught by Jesus himself. In its deepest sense true marriage,
> Christian marriage, is *altogether different* from an unchristian marriage. It is of a
> different order, for, it is 'in Christ'.
> (Torrance 1997:31, my italics)

There is not space here to discuss all the issues relating to marriage as it has been regarded as a sacrament of grace, or Christian marriage as essentially different from secular marriage, but the creation basis for marriage at least calls into question the strong difference posited by Torrance.

This universality of scope also means that Christian sexual ethics addresses the world. It is public ethics. An ethics of creation ensures that Christian ethics can never be 'esoteric, opted into by those who so choose, irrelevant to those who do not choose'. Rather, 'Christian moral judgments in principle address every man' (O'Donovan 1994:16f.; cf. Atkinson 1979:144f.).[9]

We must admit, however, that the world does not in general listen. The creation ethic of sex is worked out in the context of the community of faith. We need to take seriously the argument of Stanley Hauerwas that all sexual ethics are 'political' in the sense that they cannot be separated from the purpose of a 'polis' (here, a church community) in which they are lived out. This is so; we ought to see (at least partially) the sexual order of creation lived out in the community of the new creation, the church.

But when Hauerwas goes on to argue that 'a Christian ethic of sex cannot be an ethic for all people, but only for those who share the purposes of the community gathered by God and the subsequent understanding of marriage' (Hauerwas 1981:176), we cannot agree. An ethics of creation makes a moral demand on every human being. Rooted in creation, the ethics of the church are not the ethics of a conventicle but of an open and prophetic community,[10] a light to the nations. Because an ethics of creation is above cultural relativity and historical transience, it is ethics for all people and all time; it enables the church to speak to the world.

4. Creation order is revealed in Scripture

The ontological and epistemological poles of our enquiry are distinct and yet inseparable. For every statement about how things *are* we need to address the question of how we may *know* that they are thus. The Christian ethicist believes not only that the order of creation exists (it has an ontology), but also that it may be known through the revelation of God in the Bible (it has an epistemology). A full engagement with all the issues this raises about the proper use of the Bible in ethics is beyond the scope of this study. Two of the most important issues, however, are the coherence (or otherwise) of biblical sexual ethics and their contemporary relevance. There are plenty of critics who assert that the Bible is a very limited resource for ethics, both because it

----

9. 'By referring back to Genesis and the creation narratives in his dialogue with the Pharisees on divorce, Jesus demonstrates that his teaching applies . . . to human marriage in its totality' (Atkinson 1979:144f.).

10. Schrage 1988:5, 'Community ethics is not conventicle ethics.'

is incoherent (it attests many different sexual ethics)[11] and because it is irrelevant (it spoke only to a past age, or succession of ages)(e.g. Nineham 1976).

This study proceeds on the assumption that the Scriptures are not a resource from which to pick and choose such parts as may seem to us inspiring, but rather one grand revealed story in which human sexuality is judged by a consistent (and essentially simple) standard of sexual ethics. Further, it builds on the premise that the ethics of sexuality to which Scripture witnessed 'then' (in its own days) is the ethics of sexuality binding on us today.

None the less, there is a difficulty in any defence of biblical coherence. On the one hand, no defence will be convincing until it is applied to particular texts. On the other, the question of coherence is not profitably approached by means of a few examples of (supposed) incoherence. Even if we were successfully to show that in each such example the texts might be reconciled, we would never get beyond what seems to be an arbitrary command here, an individual's moral viewpoint there. It would all appear a merely eclectic and indeed adventitious use of Scripture. We could never point credibly to any overall coherence. We must remember that sexual ethics is a part of ethics which is in turn subservient to theology. So we need to begin with the metanarrative of Scripture, and in particular the two great poles of creation and redemption.

Naturally we need to read the scriptural texts with sensitivity to their genres and their historical and canonical contexts. Above all we must read them theologically. The creation of male and female and their sexual union is set before us as integral to the original created order. All moral assessments of sex must have in the background this transcendent order and humankind's position within and yet over it. The Scriptures of both Old and New Testaments testify to this order, first in its institution, second in its breaking (the fall), and third (and this is most of the Bible story) in its redemption and transformation through Christ at the end. If there is a biblical sexual ethics it must be considered both under the doctrine of creation and under the doctrine of the new creation. Every moral text, whether relating to sex or otherwise, is to be understood not simply in the context of its time, but in relation both to creation order and to the consummation of that order in the kingdom. We are to consider scriptural texts not in isolation or even simply in their immediate contexts (of text or culture or time), but in the overarching context of creation and redemption.

---

11. For example Birch and Rasmussen 1976:192f. speak of the Bible containing 'the widest diversity of material' in which there is 'no single view of human sexuality'. Thatcher 1999: ch. 2 similarly argues for irreconcilable diversity in the Bible's teachings.

If it is objected that the Bible cultures (for it would be misleading to speak of one 'Bible culture') are far removed from us and therefore the Bible cannot speak with authority today, we must make two replies. First (and more generally), our critic has neglected the great human continuities between Scripture and ourselves. It is a mistake so to major on differences of perception and varied constructions of reality that we forget it is perfectly possible for us to read all manner of ancient texts with a significant measure of understanding simply by virtue that we, the readers, share with the writers a common humanity. We know what it is to hunger and thirst, to experience sexual desires, to be satisfied or deprived, to be secure or in fear, to be selfish or sacrificial. Further, the more we so read, the deeper are the continuities between ourselves and other cultures. Our understanding is not limited by our personal experience – unless, that is, we never read or talk to other human beings. Indeed, the more we mix (in conversation and by reading) with those of different cultures and ages, the stronger are the ties of comprehensibility. Ironically, the more we soak ourselves in the Bible texts our critic says are so remote, the smaller the cultural distance between us and them. As O'Donovan wisely concludes, 'Cultural foreignness . . . is not a final barrier to understanding, but a warning against shallow understandings' (O'Donovan 1994:161).

Second, we answer even more emphatically that Scripture speaks to a community of believing readers who share not only one humanity but also membership in one church through the ages. Those who read Paul or Matthew today are the *same* community of faith who read Paul or Matthew in any other century. As Robert Jenson has perceptively pointed out, 'The error of most modern biblical exegesis is a subliminal assumption that the church in and for which Matthew or Paul wrote, or in which Irenaeus shaped the canon, and the church in which we now read what they put together, are historically distant from one another.' Indeed, *'The initiating error of standard modern exegesis is that it presumes a sectarian ecclesiology'* (Jenson 1999:98, his italics).[12]

This continuity of the people of God is recognized in texts such as Deuteronomy 5:2f. and by biblical authors when they made ethical and theological application of texts over very long intrabiblical periods of time. Whoever wrote the postscript to the book of Hosea certainly expected those prophecies to be of enduring relevance ('Those who are wise understand these things; those who are discerning know them . . .' Hos. 14:9). And Paul asserts in 1 Corinthians 10:1–13 that varied events from long before were recorded precisely 'to instruct us'.

---

12. I am grateful to Markus Bockmuehl for drawing my attention to this perceptive article.

It is important also to insist that in order to avoid the abuse of the Bible we must become attentive and obedient listeners to Scripture, willing always to find it uncomfortable with its persistent challenge to repentance. The spirit in which we read the Bible reveals our fundamental attitude to its authority. We must not turn the text into a ventriloquist's dummy, so that we hear from it what we want to hear. In his essay 'Can Hermeneutics Ease the Deadlock?' (Thiselton 1997) Anthony Thiselton helpfully summarizes the importance of a hermeneutic of attentive listening. This applies to sexual ethics more widely than the homosexuality debate of which he writes there. He outlines the important contribution of Hans-Georg Gadamer (Gadamer 1975) in stressing 'the priority of the question', by which he means the importance of appropriate openness in hermeneutics, so that, 'It would be a poor hermeneuticist who thought he could have, or had to have, the last word' (Thiselton 1997:146). Indeed, to think this is to move the supposed locus of true authority from the text to ourselves; the authoritative hermeneuticist is an oxymoron and contradicts the authoritative text. When we read the Bible we need to recognize its 'otherness' and guard against seeing in it a pale reflection of our own ideas.

Yet hermeneutics is more than simple open-mindedness. It has been said that the purpose of opening the mind, as of opening the mouth at a meal, is in order to close it on something. So Thiselton adds the perceptive observation of Paul Ricoeur that hermeneutics must involve a double dynamic: on the one hand, the interpreter must be inherently suspicious, particularly of himself and his presuppositions, but on the other, he must be willing to listen to the text and to obey as he understands. 'Hermeneutics seems to me to be animated by this double motivation: willingness to suspect, willingness to listen; vow of rigor, vow of obedience.' Jurgen Habermas has also spelled out more fully the meaning of hermeneutical suspicion in terms of the 'interests' (including vested interests) of the interpreters (Thiselton 1997:147). To sit under the text of Scripture is to be uncomfortable; we ought to be suspicious of any hermeneutic which renders us more comfortable. The command to *repent* and believe is fundamental to the gospel and we never move beyond its stringent discipline.

5. Creation order is significant

We ask finally in what way the order of creation *matters* to us, given that it has been spoiled and distorted in the frustration to which it has been subjected (albeit in hope, Rom. 8:20). How much does it matter for the human moral agent to live in accordance with the created order?

The general truth may be simply stated: 'The well-being of man is grounded in the good will of God' (Baelz 1977:87). This well-being is both individual and social. God has given man a uniquely privileged place in the universe. He has the dignity that his moral actions have consequences (Gen. 3:17, 'To Adam he said, "*Because* you have listened . . . cursed is the ground because of you"'). The Bible relates human moral agency to the created order by the language of blessing and curse.

The created order is an ontological given, an objective reality. Our subjective freedom is to respond to that objective reality by conforming to it or rejecting it. When a society conforms to that order, the general truth is that blessing follows. For example, when a society honours parents, its days will be long in the land. When a society chooses to live out of harmony with that order, curse follows, and we see in family life acutely how the sins of the fathers are visited on the children down the generations.

This is the teaching of the wisdom literature at its most confident. The present significance of creation ethics lies in this: conformity with creation order involves conformity with the will of the Creator, and this means blessing. Nonconformity means rebellion against the Creator, and this means curse. There is a correspondence between human flourishing and conformity to the created order.

This act-consequence relationship is viewed equally in terms of the blessing or curse of God and of the consequences that are observed to follow in life. The disobedient will be cursed because God says so (Deut. 27:15–26). But we may observe this curse in action in the normal laws of act and consequence; this is the appeal of, for example, Proverbs 6:20–35 in dissuading a man from adultery. The argument here is not that it is wrong (though it is), but that it is stupid. Just as we all know we cannot scoop fire into our laps without being burned (v. 27), so the adulterous man is bound to bring disaster upon himself, because this is how the world is.

This is the general truth. But within the wisdom literature itself there is the clear recognition that life is not as simple as this. Much of the book of Job wrestles with precisely this difficulty. For example, we may place Proverbs 6:20–35 (to which we have referred above) alongside Job 31:9–12. Here Job admits (as one of a succession of hypothetical sins) that if he had allowed himself to be enticed into an adulterous relationship this would have been 'a heinous crime . . . a criminal offence'. But in fact he is sure that he has not done this, which renders the more sharp and puzzling the suffering he endures.

What can we say in the light of such moral and consequential complexity? First, we may observe that in the wisdom literature itself and in the Psalms (e.g. Psalm 73) there is repeated recognition of the problem. The consequences of blessing and curse must therefore be understood in this life as a general rather than a universal truth. But a general truth with exceptions is not a worthless truth. At the beginning of this chapter we spoke of ethics as fitting the structure of creation like its skin to an animal. We might do better to consider the case of a well-ordered town that has suffered an earthquake. The main lines of the streets are still usually the best way to travel, even though we know we may encounter obstacles that ought not to be there, and indeed there may sometimes open up through a former building an apparently clear path that ought not to be there. Although there is disorder in the ruins, it is disorder superimposed upon underlying order. It is like this with the created order in this age.

Then we must note that there is an indissoluble future-directedness about even the simplest wisdom-style act-consequence teaching. Such and such a behaviour *will* lead to blessing. It is true that the blessing may be envisaged with some immediacy, as, for example, when a soft answer turns away wrath. But it is always future. This prepares us for the theological understanding that ultimately all talk of blessing and curse applies only provisionally in this age and will be fulfilled only eschatologically. The rock-solid quality of the life of obedient faith becomes evident only finally when the rain comes, the streams rise and the wind blows (Matt. 7:24–27). Until then it may seem with Job to attract curse rather than blessing.[13]

Finally, we must be clear that the categories of blessing and curse are not impersonal and deterministic but fiercely personal; they draw our eyes away from the processes of human history and towards the final question of the love of God. Blessing is not the same as profit; curse is deeper than simple loss. Profit and loss are related to the individual alone, but blessing and curse are related to the access to, or exclusion from, the personal presence of God. Blessing is thus a radically different category from human achievement or ambition.

Having said all this about the fallen ambiguities of blessing and curse as they relate to the created order in this age, we must reaffirm the strong general corporate truth: that a society living in line with the created order in the realm of sexual ethics will in general be a happier and more fulfilled society than one that does not.

This reminds us that marriage (as a part of the created order) exists as a significant institution in the world whether or not societies conform to its free constraints. So when as Christians we seek to persuade society about this

---

13. See also Psalms 37, 49 and 73 with their emphasis on what happens at 'the end'; cf. Von Rad 1972a:203–206.

moral order, we are not *defending* the institution of marriage, as though the God-given institution of marriage were under ontological threat. If ethical systems were voluntarist constructs, that is indeed what we would be doing, engaging in a power struggle for the convictions of people. But it is not within the power of humankind finally to destroy created order. It was given to humankind in creation, it stands above human history and the human will, and finally it will be restored and transformed in the new heavens and earth. No institution that is part of the created order can be destroyed by human disobedience. Human nonconformity leads not to the destruction of the order, but to judgment on human beings. No Christian movement needs to defend marriage: rather we seek to protect human beings against the damage done to them by cutting across the grain of the order of marriage. That knowledge takes a burden off our shoulders. When teaching ethics we are engaged in proclamation of a given order and appeal to men and women to live in believing obedience to that order in Christ; we are not engaged in a desperate attempt, like King Canute, to turn back the tides of social affairs.[14]

We conclude that marriage is a part of the moral fabric of creation, given in grace by God to men and women as a non-negotiable shape for sexual relations, given for our blessing, within whose free constraints a man and a woman may respond to God's calling to serve him in love.

---

14. The analogy of Canute is used by Collingwood 1994:20 when he argues that Christians who seek to turn the tide towards nonmarital cohabitation are bound to fight a losing battle.

5. MARRIAGE AND THE KINGDOM OF GOD

We have argued that marriage exists as a part of the created order; but no theology that calls itself Christian can rest on creation alone. Intrinsic to the story of salvation is a bipolarity of focus, both backward to beginnings and forwards in hope – and the whole centred in Christ. In this chapter, therefore, we consider sex and marriage under the broad and extensive light of beginning and end together, that is, under the order of the redeemed creation or the kingdom of God. We need to consider three questions. The first is theological and concerns the impact of redemption on creation ethics in general. The second addresses a particular problem in this which concerns marriage. The third is exegetical and concerns the ethical framework underlying New Testament sexual ethics.

1. The general eschatological objection to creation ethics

The value of creation theology is that it speaks to all people without exception and for all time. It is neither sectarian (the ethics of the ghetto), nor cultural (to be swept away by the waves of history); rather, it is universal in its scope and eternal in its significance. But what do we mean by 'for all time'? Scripture envisages a time when this world will be, in the vivid language of 2 Peter 3:7–13, dissolved and burned up with fire – so how can we claim for the present created order a moral significance that will endure? Do we not await 'an inheritance . . . imperishable, undefiled, and unfading, kept *in heaven*' for us

(1 Pet. 1:3, my italics)? The grand story of salvation is not a line that begins with creation and continues indefinitely on an unbounded trajectory. It begins with creation, centres in Christ, and ends with the consummation of the kingdom of God and of his Christ.

It is important in any context where creation theology is attempted to consider how the beginning relates to the centre and the end, for unless it does, creation theology and ethics will be merely antiquarian, even antediluvian. What does it mean to live in this age in the light not only of its beginnings (creation) but also of the age to come (redemption)? What does redemption have to say to creation, or what we may call 'kingdom ethics' to 'creation ethics'? We do not live simply in the age that is passing away; we live in the overlap of the ages. Do not loyalty to Christ and his kingdom radically relativize our obligations to the created order?

Christian ethics must be founded on Christ. But how does Christ relate to the created order? Perhaps the most illuminating New Testament treatment of this is in Hebrews 2:5–9, where the writer makes use of Psalm 8. Psalm 8 is about creation and man's task within creation of exercising dominion; it images with limpid clarity the unique position of man, entrusted by the Creator to whom he is responsible with authority to govern. Here is the fundamental matrix for creation ethics. By contrast, it might seem, the writer to the Hebrews is speaking (2:5) about 'the coming world' (*tēn oikoumenēn tēn mellousan*), that is to say about the kingdom of God, or the eschaton. And yet he immediately quotes from Psalm 8. In the world to come the rule of man purposed by God over creation will be fulfilled, as the human one, the Son of Man, exercises man's dominion aright at last. The world to come is not a sphere severed from the created order. It is the fulfilment, redemption and transformation of the created order. At its head is the man Christ Jesus. The rule of humankind over God's world is already anticipated by this truly human figure, so that, although we do not as yet see the created order ruled by humankind as a whole, 'we do see Jesus . . . crowned with glory and honour' (Heb. 2:9).

This is the great vision of Ephesians 1:9f. and Colossians 1:15–20. The universe is held together and prevented from moral and material disintegration in Christ, in whom all things hold together (*ta panta en autō sunestēken*, Col. 1:17). It is 'in the Christ' that God has purposed to 'gather up all things' (*anakephalaiōsasthai ta panta*, Eph. 1:10) at the fulfilment of the ages. It follows that, 'We cannot . . . separate or seek to understand creation apart from redemption in Christ, nor yet redemption apart from creation' (Torrance 1997:ix). 'The wholeness of the universe depends on its being a created universe, and thereafter on its being reconciled, brought back into the order of its creation' (O'Donovan 1994:32).

Thus a Christocentric ethics will at the same time be creation ethics and kingdom ethics in him. If we wish to understand the relationship between this age and the age to come, we need to consider the relationship between the Jesus of history and the risen Christ. The relationship is not one of spiritual discontinuity (such that his body died but his spirit lives on), but rather of bodily continuity in bodily resurrection. This resurrection is God's 'Yes' to the created order, his cry of triumph that sin will not finally ruin the good world he has made. The 'sons of God' who will one day be revealed to the waiting and groaning creation (Rom. 8:19) will be those with resurrection *bodies* (1 Cor. 15:35 ff.), living not in some ethereal 'heaven', a gnostic realm discontinuous with this evil world, but in the new heavens and the new earth (Is. 65:17; 66:22; cf. Rev. 21, 22). Far from being a denial of creation, Christian eschatology is a resounding 'Yes' to creation (Ware 1997; Louth 1997).

For this reason, even the most realistic assessment of human sin in the human bodily appetites must be held alongside the recognition of the human body as destined for redemption and resurrection. We may take as an example of this tension the agonized questions of John Climacus, the seventh-century Abbot of Sinai. Writing of his body, he says,

> He is my helper and my enemy, my assistant and my opponent, a protector and a traitor . . .
>> How can I break away from him when I am bound to him for ever?
>> How can I escape from him when he will rise with me?
> (Ware 1997:90)

Even with the strong negative language about this age in 1 and 2 Peter (noted above), it would be a complete misunderstanding to think that Peter had a gnostic concept of salvation. Indeed, 1 Peter 1:4f. makes it clear (a) that the new birth is ours through the resurrection of Christ (which in scriptural thought is always bodily resurrection), and (b) that the inheritance presently 'kept in heaven' is not kept there so that the believer may 'go up to heaven' to claim it, but rather that it is kept safe 'there', 'ready to be *revealed* in the last time'. It is kept safe 'in heaven' (where the corruption and threat of this age cannot touch it), so that one day it will be revealed when the new heavens and the new earth are inaugurated. And in 2 Peter 3:7–13 it is clear that the very strong language of burning and dissolution speaks not of the final casting of the created order on the scrap heap of God's judgment, but rather of the most searching and radical cleansing preparatory to its restoration or new birth in the new heavens and new earth.

It is for this reason (and not only for reasons of intelligibility) that the language used to describe 'the age to come' in Scripture is so earthy and real. We may take, for example, the vista held out in Hosea 14:5–8. Here is dew to make physical beauty flourish (the lily), sitting under the olive tree conjuring up intense physical well-being, fragrance like a cedar, comforting shade. As has been noted by commentators, this is the language of the love poem, imagery found in the Song of Songs – the shade of the lover, his fragrance like a forest, the lily, the budding vine (Wolff 1974, ad loc.). Here is a vision of real and intense physical (including sexual) well-being. This is not a misleading or exaggerated picture of the age to come, but rather, if anything, an understatement of a world that will be intensely real and physical.

This strong continuity, between a good creation at the beginning and the kingdom in which the spoiled creation is restored and transformed, is the reason Peter can root his ethical challenge (2 Pet. 3:11, 'what sort of persons ought you to be in leading lives of holiness and godliness . . .?') in eschatological hope. Were the new order to be discontinuous with the present order, it is hard to see how life in this age could have moral seriousness or enduring significance. We 'wait for new heavens and a new earth, where righteousness is at home' (*en hois dikaiosunē katoikei*, 2 Pet. 3:13). The 'righteousness' which dwells in the new creation is not a different righteousness from that which infuses the first created order; it is the same righteousness, which is why it is incumbent on us to live holy and godly lives in this age as we await the coming of the next.

It is striking how often New Testament ethical exhortation is closely linked to eschatological hope. For example, the practical outworkings of faith in Ephesians 4 – 6 are prefaced by the plea 'to lead a life worthy of the *calling* [*klēsis*] to which you have been called' (Eph. 4:1, my italics). And the practical admonitions to (specifically sexual) holiness in 1 Thessalonians 4:1 ff. are in the context of a letter strongly emphasizing the eschatological hope of the church.

There are two weaknesses in ethics based solely on a concept of natural law. One is the deep epistemological confusion introduced by the fall, which renders the proper order of creation opaque to our eyes. The other is the absence of the future from its gaze; the tension between what we are and what we ought to be (and may become) is a religious and eschatological question (Baelz 1977:54). For if the created order is opened to us by divine revelation, it is given enduring significance by the eschatology of hope. 'The task of actualising God's eschatological purposes – God's future "is" – comprises the "ought" of our present' (Grenz 1997b:224). Or, to put it more simply, the reason we 'ought' in this age is because we 'will be' in the next.

As O'Donovan puts it in a helpful postscript to his discussion of authority, language of 'ought' (deontic language) usually has its roots in a voluntarist conception of divine command; we ought to do such and such because God tells us we should (O'Donovan 1994:137–139). We need this framework of obedience because of the fall; our lives are disordered and the command of God cuts across our fallen wills and calls to repentance. Properly understood, this command is not arbitrary, a heteronomous burden intrinsically alien to human flourishing. On the contrary, when understood in the light of the end, it will be seen to be rational in the sense that it coheres with the proper (and to be restored) order of creation.

Since the new creation coheres deeply with the original created order, a coherence rooted in the faithfulness and triumph of God, creation theology is the foundation of kingdom theology. The kingdom is the fulfilment, redemption and transformation of the created order. This is, in outline, the answer to the general eschatological objection, but we now have to address an acute objection specific to marriage.

2. The particular eschatological objection to considering marriage under creation ethics

The argument from created moral order rests on the thesis that this same order is to be restored in the eschaton. Its present significance is predicated on its future restoration. And yet Jesus appears explicitly to exclude marriage from that restoration.

> Jesus said to them, 'Those who belong to this age marry and are given in marriage; but those who are considered worthy of a place in that age and in the resurrection from the dead neither marry nor are given in marriage. Indeed they cannot die anymore, because they are like angels and are children of God, being children of the resurrection.' (Luke 20:34–36; cf. Matt. 22:29f.; Mark 12:24f.)[1]

Paul might seem to echo this in 1 Corinthians 7:29: '. . . the appointed time has grown short; from now on, let even those who have wives be as though they had none'.

Even if we grant the general continuity between creation and kingdom, therefore, there is this particular problem pertaining to the ethics of marriage. It is all very well saying that in general the new heavens and new earth will

---

1. We may leave to one side the extraordinary exegesis of Thatcher 1999:84f., that Luke 20:34–36 has Jesus 'say that married people place themselves beyond the resurrection altogether' and that 'People who marry are citizens of this world, not of the world to come, and their married status actually endangers their partaking in the resurrection.' Were this so, poor Lazarus would come 'to Abraham's bosom' (Luke 16:22) to find Abraham himself absent!

fulfil the created order, but what if the transformation of that order explicitly excludes marriage? If marriage is not to be part of the order in the resurrection age, how can we claim that it has enduring ethical significance in this age? Has it not been radically relativized by the resurrection of Christ?

We may perhaps agree with Meilander, who suggests that despite Luke 20:34–36 our created maleness and femaleness continues in the resurrection, that 'we have no warrant to suppose that the bodily resurrection will be anything other than a resurrection of those who continue to exist within the differentiation of male and female' (Meilander 1995:71).[2] But even if this is so (and certainly there is no suggestion that the risen Lord appeared to the disciples in some new androgyne body), it does not answer the objection that marriage and sexual intercourse are not *per se* a part of the order of the new creation.

The reason this is so appears clear from Jesus' explanation (Luke 20:36) that to be a child of the resurrection means no longer to be subject to death. And where there is no death there is no more need for procreation and nurture of future generations, *and therefore no more need for marriage.* This connection between death and the need for procreation could hardly be clearer than in the drum-beat repetition in the genealogy of Genesis 5 of the refrain 'and he died' (*wayyāmōt*, vv. 5, 8, 11, 14, 17, 20, 27, 31, interrupted only by the proleptic non-death of Enoch, and then concluding after the flood with the death of Noah himself in 9:31). But where death is no more, all this procreation is unnecessary. In Hebrews 7:3 the mysterious Melchizedek is described in a typological sense as having no mother, no father, no genealogy, no beginning and no end, like 'the Son of God'; here is an anticipation in the primeval history of life in the resurrection age, where marriage and its function for human continuity is superseded by 'the power of an indestructible life' (Heb. 7:16).

None the less, alongside this negative teaching about the temporary nature of marriage in its procreative aspect, we have to place a rich and strongly flowing theme that runs irresistibly through the story of salvation right to the end and gives to marriage a significance which is not merely temporary but actually proleptic and anticipatory of the very highest and deepest aspect of the consummation of the kingdom. That word 'consummation' contains exactly the semantic elasticity we need. Just as sexual consummation at its best is a distillation of passionate joy and deeply delightful fulfilment, so it will be at the end. The consummation of all things is a marriage, a *gamos*, in which the people of God are the bride and the Christ is the bridegroom. In a sense Genesis 2:24

---

2. Augustine (*City of God*, XXII.17) argued that both sexes will exist in heaven since Jesus' words 'They shall not be given in marriage' can apply only to females, and 'They shall not marry' only to males (quoted in Jewett 1975:41).

is the proleptic preaching of the gospel, for the first marriage foreshadows the climactic marriage of the Lord with his people. This end, which is also a new beginning, is the consummation of a theme that runs through Scripture,[3] of the Lord as the husband or future husband of his people his bride, the Christ of his people the church. (New Testament texts do not invent a new theme, but apply to the Christ and his church Old Testament imagery of the Lord and his people.) How this divine marriage provides a matchless pattern for human marriage in this age will be the subject of Chapter 14.

There is a strong marriage motif in Scripture of the covenant love between God and his people. This theme gives to human marriage a theological and eschatological significance such that we cannot simply regard it as temporary and of this age alone. Perhaps even more than other dimensions of the created order, marriage will be transformed and renewed.[4]

This eschatological dimension to sexual ethics sheds light on an important debate. It is sometimes claimed that when Christian people restrict sex to marriage they are simply choosing to 'invest' something which has no inherent significance (in terms of 'natural law') with an imparted (and perhaps adventitious) significance. For example, Moore argues that since degrees of intimacy are expressed in different ways in different cultures (e.g. the varying significance of a kiss) we cannot argue *from nature* that sex has an intrinsic significance such that it ought to be confined to marriage (Moore 1992:140–142). However, the theological reason we claim it does have such significance is not simply arbitrary divine command, but rather that in 'the marriage supper of the Lamb' we see revealed – as the culmination of a great prophetic theme – a significance of sexual union that is indeed intrinsic to the order of creation and whose full significance will be revealed only when that created order is finally redeemed.

Marriage is indeed a part of the created order. Its enduring significance lies not in its simple continuance in the new creation, as if marriages were for eternity (as is sometimes wrongly thought); rather, it is to be fulfilled and transformed at the marriage supper of the Lamb. The fundamental reason why marriage is to be honoured in this life is that it corresponds to the covenant relationship at the heart of the new creation between Christ and his people, the relationship which is itself the fulfilment of the creation covenant of pledged faithful love between Creator and created order.

---

3. Relevant texts include Hos. 1 – 3; Jer. 2 – 4; Is. 50:1; 54:1–10; 62:4f.; Ezek. 16, 23; Matt. 9:14f.; 22:1–14; 25:1–13; 2 Cor. 11:2; Eph. 5:22–33; Rev. 18 – 22.

4. It is worth noting that the Sabbath rest principle, another creation ordinance, seems also to be quite radically transformed in the new age, cf. Heb. 4:1–11.

3. The continuity between Old and New Testament sexual ethics

If marriage is rooted in the order of creation, and that order will be fulfilled and consummated at the end of the age, then the framework of New Testament sexual ethics ought to be the same as that of the Old. If Old Testament sexual ethics was different in substance from that of the New, our case for marriage to be rooted in creation is weakened. We must therefore consider the claim that the sexual ethics of the New Testament stands in strong continuity with the sexual ethics of the Old, and that both apply in principle to the whole world. There is a revealing indicator of this continuity in the inclusion of sexual immorality (*porneia*) in the requirements laid upon Gentile converts by the Council of Jerusalem (Acts 15). We therefore consider the background of this requirement and see what it suggests of old to new covenant ethical continuity.

Jewish public ethical discourse in the diaspora

We begin by asking how the Jewish diaspora approached the problem of public ethical discourse in the Graeco-Roman world (Bockmuehl 2000: chs. 5–7, 9). What 'ought' the Gentile to be and do? A Gentile could not become a member of the people of God without taking upon himself the obligations of the law of Moses, including male circumcision, Sabbaths and food laws. But Gentiles outside the people of God are still bound by moral obligation, that they *ought* to do certain things and not do others. What things? This must have been a question asked by the Gentile 'God-fearers' on the fringes of the diaspora synagogues.

On searching Scripture for Gentile moral obligation, three kinds of material were seen by the rabbis to be relevant.

(i) Ethical material from Genesis 1 – 11

The most important observation is that moral obligation explicit or implicit before Abraham was presumed to be universal in its scope, since it was only with Abraham that the family and people of the covenant came into being; Genesis 1 – 11 was therefore mined for universal moral order. This is the created order, and even though it is spoiled by the fall, it remains the moral substructure of how the universe is. We ignore or reject it to our cost.

Rabbinic exegesis noted that in Genesis 2:16, for the first time in Scripture, we are explicitly told that God gave a *command* to man. From this and other passages in Genesis 1 – 11 it was argued that in principle the Creator gave to Adam six commandments, prohibiting idolatry and blasphemy, regulating justice, prohibiting homicide, illicit sex and theft (Bockmuehl 1995a:80f. and references there). The question came to be discussed under the umbrella heading of 'the

Noachide commandments', finding its primary locus in the universal covenant made by the LORD with Noah in Genesis 9 after the flood. Here we find three moral foci. First comes a heavy emphasis on the evil of homicide, to which the blood prohibition in meat is related (Gen. 9:4–6). This is bracketed by a renewal of the foundation of sexual ethics in Genesis 1 and 2 (Gen. 9:1, 7), and immediately followed by a misuse of sexuality (Gen. 9:18–23), and the idea of covenant faithfulness between the Creator and his creatures (Gen. 9:8–17). We may see in these the origins of a core of universal morality with three balanced foci: relationship with the Creator (no idolatry), peaceful relations between creatures (no homicide), and sexual relations between creatures (no sexual immorality).

(ii) Laws in Torah binding on the resident alien
In the Torah itself, despite its primary focus on the redeemed community, we may note a distinction between law binding only on the member of the covenant community and law binding also on the 'resident alien' (*gēr*), the non-Israelite living amongst Israel in the land; again, presumably the latter points to universal moral obligation. If a law is binding on all, it cannot be in any sense simply a 'boundary marker' for the people of the covenant; it must point to a universal principle. In particular, therefore, they looked for laws binding on the resident aliens (and occasionally on the foreigners). Most of these are found in the so-called 'holiness code' of Leviticus 17 – 26,[5] and specifically in Leviticus 18 – 20. The laws they found pertain to three basic categories:

1. laws relating to God – improper sacrifice, including sacrifices to idols (17:8f., 20:2–5), as well as blasphemy (24:10–16);
2. laws relating to homicide and injury (24:17–22), the killing of animals (24:18), as well as the eating of animals' blood (17:10–16);
3. illicit sexual relations (Lev. 18) (Bockmuehl 1995a:82).

In later Judaism the *gēr* came to be considered sometimes as a convert or partial convert to Judaism, but more often as a 'Gentile adherent of the Synagogue' (Callan 1993:290–295), probably the kinds of people loosely referred to by Luke either as 'God-fearers' (Acts 10:2, 22, 35; 13:16, 26) or 'God-worshippers' (Acts 13:50; 16:14; 17:4, 17; 18:7). These were the sympathetic and spiritually hungry Gentiles with whom the synagogue had the most fruitful contact; they were also the Gentiles from whom the earliest Christian converts were drawn.

---

5. E.g., in Lev. 17, of the legal cases listed, the first (v. 3) applies to Israelites, while the others (vv. 8, 10, 13, 15) apply also to 'the aliens who reside among them'; cf. Lev. 20:1 et al.

The creation basis for the specifically sexual laws of Leviticus is correctly noted by Mary Douglas in her perceptive anthropological and theological treatment. She notes, 'Holiness requires that individuals shall conform to the class to which they belong . . . Holiness means keeping distinct *the categories of creation* . . . Under this head all the rules of sexual morality exemplify the holy' (Douglas 1984:53, my italics).

The universal scope of Leviticus 18 is emphasized by the motif of the land 'vomiting out' the pre-Israelite inhabitants, who should have known better even without the benefit of the spoken or written Torah (see Chapter 13).

(iii) Prophetic moral condemnation of 'the nations'
The theme that 'they ought to have known better' appears in a third category of relevant Scripture, which is moral castigation in the Prophets of 'the nations' who are to be judged because they have contravened laws they ought to have known even without the knowledge of Torah. Amos 1 and 2 is the most important of these passages.

There is also a striking example of this motif in Ezekiel 33:23–26. Just after the fall of Jerusalem (v. 21) Ezekiel, in exile in Babylon, hears of people back in the land (called 'waste places', v. 24) who are falsely optimistic. They do not seem to have taken into account that they are doing what the pre-Israelite inhabitants of the land did, and for which, according to Leviticus 18, the *land* vomited them out. So he castigates them because their moral standards have fallen below even the minimum standard required of the resident aliens. And the 'constellation of sins' of which they are accused includes, not accidentally, violence and blood offences, idolatry and adultery (Bockmuehl 1995a:84). Both verses 25 and 26 end with the ironic question, 'Shall you then possess the land?' These sins are universal sins, for which the land will vomit them out, as it vomited out the Canaanites. That is the import of Ezekiel's prophecy. We find the same fundamental moral trio again in Ezekiel 23:36–49.

The conclusions to which the rabbis came were not always formulated in the same way. The history of Jewish thought about what we may call 'the Noachide question' (the moral obligation of Gentiles) is complex (Moore 1927:274f., 338f.; Davies 1970: 113–117; Bockmuehl 1995a). But after a carefully nuanced discussion of the sources,[6] including more liberal and more rigorist strands, Bockmuehl concludes, 'The core of the Noachide Commandments is explicitly

---

6. The book of Jubilees (7:20ff.) dated no later than 100 BC (Charlesworth 1985:43f.) provides 'the earliest extant text in which Genesis 9:3–6 is expanded into a body of Noachic law' (Aune 1997:187). See b.Sanhedrin 56b, where seven commands are listed. See also Bockmuehl 1995a:85.

made up of the three offences which constitute capital crimes, viz. fornication, bloodshed, and blasphemy or idolatry' (Bockmuehl 1995:90). This trio may be thought of as (a) essentially religious sins against God, primarily idolatry and practices associated with idolatry; (b) social sins focusing on harm or violence done to the neighbour; and (c) sexual sins. In a nutshell, universal morality was perceived to have three core components: sex, violence and idolatry.

For the purposes of our study, it is significant to note that sexual ethics was consistently part of the universal moral core of Jewish ethics and was never relegated to what might be considered the cultural margin. This universal moral core was defended by Jewish apologists on the grounds that it cohered with creation: 'The Law of the Lord is in accordance with creation, and the perceptible pattern of creation is a pattern of moral meaning and significance' (Bockmuehl 1995b:33f., commenting on t.Naphtali iii.2–5). As Torah and creation sit easily side by side in Psalm 19, so in Jewish apologetic. Sexual ethics is part of creation ethics.

Early Christian public ethics

There is strong continuity between the public ethics of the diaspora synagogue and the public ethics of the early church. The problem facing the early Christian churches in the Graeco-Roman world paralleled closely the problem of public ethics that faced the diaspora synagogue. They addressed the same religiously pluralist world in which moral consensus had broken down. This is a strong point of continuity with the position of the churches in the Western world today.[7] Like us, they spoke into a context of ethical chaos.

In the Gentile mission Christians met two questions. The primary one concerned salvation, the subsequent one the saved lifestyle, how to 'walk' (halakhah). Negatively, as regards salvation, it was soon established that the full law of Moses was not to be expected of the Gentile convert (Acts 15, Gal. 1, 2);[8] Gentiles could be saved as Gentiles. But when a Gentile was converted and asked in gratitude, 'How should I now live so as to please God?'

---

7. Bockmuehl 1995a:73 quotes from Alasdair MacIntyre *After Virtue*. 'The most striking feature of contemporary moral utterance is that so much of it is used to express disagreements; and the most striking feature of the debates in which these disagreements are expressed is their interminable character . . . There seems to be no rational way of securing moral agreement in our culture' (MacIntyre 1981:6).

8. My view is that the disagreement recorded in Gal. 2 occurred during the Jerusalem visit recorded by Luke in Acts 11:27–30, but that the question rumbled on until the public resolution recorded in Acts 15. Detailed arguments in support of this harmonization are given by Longenecker 1990:lxxii–lxxxviii.

(the question implicitly referred to in 1 Thess. 4:1) careful thought had to be given to the answer. 'Both historically and conceptually, the key problem of New Testament ethics is this: while the exalted Jesus is both its motivation and highest authority, the historical Jesus in fact had little or nothing to say about the *content* of an ethic for Gentiles' (Bockmuehl 1995a:91). The teaching of Jesus was never intended to be a new ethical guide; in fulfilling the law Jesus introduces no ethical novelty. To posit ethical novelty under the new covenant is to slip into a neo-Marcionite understanding of the relationship of Old and New Testaments.

When the issues were debated in Jerusalem (Acts 15), a clear answer was given to the question about salvation.[9] The men who had gone down from Judea to Antioch saying that circumcision was essential to salvation (v. 1) were firmly contradicted by Peter. Salvation for Jew and Gentile is by faith alone (v. 9) through the grace of the Lord Jesus alone (v. 11; cf. Gal. 2:15f.). The Pharisaic believers are not to test God (who has made his choice known by the gift of the Spirit to the uncircumcised Gentiles, v. 7f.) 'by placing on the neck of the disciples a yoke that neither our ancestors nor we have been able to bear' (v. 10; cf. Matt. 23:4). The law of Moses is not to be loaded onto the backs of the Gentile converts.

After contributions from Barnabas and Paul, James the Lord's brother gives an authoritative summing up. He understands the Gentile mission as a fulfilment of the restoration from exile promise of Amos 9:11f. and then gives his judgment in verses 19–21. The apostles and elders should write a letter. This letter will have two motivations and four points of content. The first motivation is in verse 19, 'We should not trouble those Gentiles who are turning to God.' This appears much the same as Peter's concern (v. 10) that the unbearable burden of the law should not be imposed on them.

The second motivation is in verse 21: 'For in every city, for generations past, Moses has had those who proclaim him, for he has been read aloud every sabbath in the synagogues.' It is not clear what this second motivation means. Three main lines of interpretation have been suggested. Some read it as meaning that 'Moses' will not suffer by the Gentiles not submitting to his law, since there are plenty of Jews in the diaspora synagogues who do pay attention to him, so the release of Gentile converts from this requirement is not damaging to 'Moses' (references in Bruce 1990, ad loc.). This is possible, but it seems a little tangential.

It is common to regard this as a practical recognition of the difficulty of

---

9. Table fellowship was clearly the presenting issue in Gal. 2 and the letter of Acts 15:24–29 has implications for such fellowship, including as it does such clear statements about meat. But table fellowship as such is never mentioned in Acts 15.

Gentile mission in cities with substantial Jewish populations, if the Gentile converts do not at least pay outward courtesy to some of the more obvious Jewish sensibilities. If the Gentile Christians will have the generosity of spirit to avoid needless offence to the Jewish Christians (and indeed to the synagogue), this cannot but help the cause of the gospel. Again, this is possible, although the condition is not presented as a request, but as a requirement; and anyway the abrogation of the massively significant laws of circumcision, food and Sabbaths would render the compromise of limited use in facilitating good relations with the Pharisaic party, whether inside or outside the church. The Pharisaic party have lost the battle on every issue that matters to them.

It is more convincing to read verse 21 as indicating a much stronger causal link in the word 'for' (*gar*). The rationale underlying the four prohibitions of verse 20 is precisely *derived from* the law of Moses preached so regularly and for so long in every city. These are not arbitrary injunctions settled on by some process of synodical compromise, making the best of a difficult job; they are injunctions whose logic inheres in some profound way in the law of Moses itself. The logic is in its essentials the same logic we have examined above in our discussion of the Noachide commandments. There is a threefold core to ethics that is binding on all people in all places at all times. This core is the prohibition of idolatry, sexual immorality and violence against fellow human beings.

We may support this line of exegesis by considering the four prohibitions.[10] These are given by James in verse 20, repeated with minor changes in the report of the letter in verse 29, and reiterated in 21:25.

1. 'things polluted by idols' (*tōn alisgēmatōn tōn eidōlōn*; repeated in v. 29 and 21:25 as 'what has been sacrificed to idols', *eidōlothutōn*)
2. 'sexual immorality' (*porneia*; repeated fourth in v. 29 and 21:25)
3. 'the meat of strangled animals' (*pniktōn*; repeated in the same place and using the same word in v. 29 and 21:25)
4. 'blood' (repeated in second place in v. 29 and 21:25)

Scholarly discussion of these focuses on where they lie on an axis from the ethical at one end (enduring ethical principles) to the ceremonial at the other

---

10. Callan 1993:285–289 discusses in detail all the passages in Torah that refer both to Israel and to the *Ger*. He notes that they cover more than the issues addressed in Acts 15, but that if we add the further restrictions of the phrase *'îš 'îš* ('any man') and that the offender should be cut off from the people, we end up with a fairly good correspondence between the elements of the apostolic letter and Lev. 17 and 18.

(temporary Jewish ceremonial regulations). We may argue that all four are purely ethical (Simon 1981:414–416), that all four are purely ceremonial, or that some are ethical and some ceremonial. None of these is without its problems.

The complex textual issues suggest that the church has struggled with these from very early days. The Western Text of Acts removes 'the meat of strangled animals' and adds a negative form of the golden rule ('whatever you do not wish they would do to you, do not to them'), thus enabling the whole to be read in a purely ethical light, with 'blood' understood to mean homicide and 'food offered to idols' to refer to idolatry (Metzger 1971:429–434; cf. Barrett 1987, ad loc.). So three ethical prohibitions are given: idolatry, sexual immorality and homicide. These are summed up in the negative golden rule. The textual evidence, however, strongly supports the omission of the negative golden rule and the inclusion of 'the meat of strangled animals'. This would seem to preclude reading all four in a purely ethical and nonceremonial sense.

Those who wish to read all four in a Jewish ceremonial sense have to grapple with the inclusion of 'sexual immorality'. In what sense may this be understood to be a Jewish ceremonial prohibition? The answer is sometimes given that *porneia* here refers not to sexual immorality in general but specifically to the contravention of the prohibited degrees of kinship and affinity listed in Leviticus 18.[11] The prohibition is thus not of a general ethical principle but of contravening the purely Jewish scruples arising from Leviticus 18. This is not entirely convincing, partly because the *porn-* word group is not used in the LXX of Leviticus 18 and generally has a wider scope of meaning unless the context requires it to refer specifically to incest (as it does in 1 Cor. 5:1). Also it is highly unlikely that Gentile readers (to whom the letter was addressed) would have understood *porneia* in this way (Simon 1981). Others argue that here *porneia* refers only to sex with a temple prostitute (see Barrett 1987); again, this is unduly narrow and not suggested by the context.

Some therefore argue that the four are a curious mixture of Jewish ceremonial and enduring ethical prohibitions (e.g. Barrett 1987). If sexual immorality is the only clearly ethical prohibition, it leaves open the puzzling question as to why it alone was selected. Why must a special letter be written to forbid fornication while not mentioning, for example, murder? Such an arbitrary mixed reading is a counsel of hermeneutical despair.

A more holistic reading may be adopted by linking the ceremonial with the

---

11. Bruce 1990 suggests that *porneia* may also be read in this sense in Matt. 5:32 and 19:9. Certainly in *b.Sanhedrin* 56b the sexual element in the seven Noachide commandments is incest rather than sexual immorality more broadly defined. See also Heth and Wenham 1984:153–168.

ethical in each of the four. Each ceremonial has an ethical significance. This is most easily done in the case of 'food polluted by idols' or 'food sacrificed to idols'. In Acts 15:29 and 21:25 the word *eidōlothuta* is used, which simply refers to food sacrificed to idols. In Acts 15:20 it is described as *tōn alisgēmatōn tōn eidōlōn* ('the pollution of idols'). The word *alisgēma* is a New Testament hapax legomenon, but occurs six times in the LXX, always related to food pollution (Bruce 1990:342). The phrase points in the first instance to meat which has been sacrificed to idols, but it does so in such a way as to point us to the significance of this ceremonial regulation, which is the ethical and religious prohibition of idolatry itself. Here is an element in the ritual law of Moses which points to an enduring ethical/religious principle.

Leviticus 17 contains the prohibition of idolatry in the context of meat offerings. Verses 1–7 address this to the Israelite, and then verse 8f. extends the same principle to the resident alien, who is always to offer sacrifice at 'the entrance of the tent of meeting', as a safeguard against idolatrous practices. The religious principle underlying the ceremonial prohibition is very clear. It is even clearer in Ezekiel 14:7f., where both Israelite and resident alien are warned not to 'separate' themselves from the LORD by setting up idols in their hearts; here there is no explicit mention of meat at all.

Sexual immorality (*porneia*) suggests most obviously the ethical injunction against sexual immorality broadly defined. But even if it does refer here also to the specific incest (and other sexual) prohibitions of Leviticus 18, it does so in such a way as to point beyond the specifically Jewish and towards the enduringly ethical. We are mistaken if we allow ourselves to think that the regulations of Leviticus 18 were ever considered to be purely Jewish in the scope of their moral demand; the strong motif that the pre-Israelite inhabitants of the land were 'vomited out' for flouting them implies that they point to an ethical demand on all people at all times.

It is most likely that we should take 'the meat of strangled animals' and 'blood' together (whether they are placed second and third, as in James's speech, or third and fourth, as in the letter, they are always together) as a prohibition of eating meat with the blood still in it, since a strangled animal has not been drained of blood. There are puzzling problems as to how we relate strangling to other forbidden methods of killing and in particular how closely we may relate these laws to Leviticus 17:10–16 (Callan 1993:288f.), but the central point in both seems to be the blood prohibition of Genesis 9:4–6 with its clear ethical significance in terms of homicide. The dietary prohibition of blood carries with it *a fortiori* the prohibition of homicide, just as the idol meat prohibition carries with it *a fortiori* the prohibition of idolatry. Again, these are ceremonial laws, but they point to the value of human life, the enduring ethical issue of homicide. If *porneia* does refer to incest here, perhaps it also does so in such a way as to prohibit *a fortiori* all forms of extramarital sexual behaviour.

In the letters from the risen Jesus to the churches in Pergamum and Thyatira there are three allusions to the apostolic decree (Aune 1997:187). In Revelation 2:14 the church in Pergamum is told the Lord has a few things against them: they have some who hold the teaching of Balaam, who taught Balak to put a stumbling block in front of the sons of Israel, to eat idol food (*eidōlothuta*) and to commit sexual immorality (*porneusai*). Again, a few verses later in 2:20, the church in Thyatira is told the Lord has against them that they tolerate the woman Jezebel, who calls herself a prophetess and by her teaching misleads the Lord's servants into sexual immorality (*porneusai*) and the eating of food sacrificed to idols (*eidōlothuta*). And in verse 24 there is a suggestive allusion in the word *baros* to the fact that the Lord does not overburden his people; just as in Acts 15:28 the apostles and elders refuse to lay upon the Gentile believers a burden (*baros*) beyond the requirements of their letter. The repeated association of idol food and sexual immorality is certainly suggestive of the apostolic letter of Acts 15, although it echoes a long theme of association between idolatry and sexual immorality (cf. Rev. 9:20f.; 21:8; see also Chapter 8).

It is hard to avoid the conclusion that lying behind the selection of these prohibitions is the thinking that later lay behind the formulation of the so-called Noachide commandments. Torah ceremonial is never arbitrary but always points to and signifies some truth beyond itself. And the ceremonials selected here are precisely the ones that point us to the enduring trio of idolatry, sexual immorality and violence against human beings. Excluded are the ceremonials whose function was to point to Jewish distinctiveness: circumcision, food laws and Sabbaths. Also excluded is the sacrificial system of temple worship understood by the early Christians to be fulfilled in Christ.

The apostolic decree of Acts 15 supports the conclusion that when Gentiles were accepted into full fellowship with the Jewish believers in Christ, they were accepted on the basis that they were bound by essentially the same ethical boundaries as guided the Gentile 'God-fearer' on the fringes of the synagogue, broadly the boundaries that later came to be formulated in terms of the Noachide commandments.[12] The convert was saved by grace through

---

12. We must note Callan's caution (Callan 1993:293) against too close an identification. He notes that there is no clear-cut one-to-one correspondence between the Noachide formulations and the apostolic decree. Rather, we follow Bockmuehl in seeing the correspondence between the threefold ethical core of the Noachide debates and the ethical core to which the apostolic decree points. It is worth noting also the argument of Carrington 1940:14–21 that early Christian catechesis drew heavily on levitical material.

faith, but he or she was saved into a life in the Spirit whose moral form was given in creation as attested by the law of Moses. The motivation, authority and example are that of Jesus Christ; the shape is that of created order. The ethical core of the New Testament is the ethical core of the Old, rooted in creation, an ethics for all people at all times. And sexual ethics is part of this enduring core. In the face of scholars who argue otherwise,[13] we conclude that the sexual laws of the Old Testament point to a sexual ethics that is binding on all human beings at all times. This explains why the New Testament writers consistently regard Old Testament sexual ethics as binding. Attitudinally the life that pleases God is, and has always been, a life of faith; but in terms of its shape and order it is a life lived in harmony with created order as revealed in the Old Testament and restored and redeemed in Christ.

Conclusion

We conclude that both the biblical testimony to creation and the biblical theology of the kingdom of God support the thesis that sexual ethics should be centred upon the objective existence of marriage as a divine ordering. We turn now to explore the purpose (Part Two) and shape (Part Three) of that ordering.

---

13. Notably Countryman 1989: chs. 2 and 3; Meeks 1983:100f.

PART TWO

THE PURPOSE OF MARRIAGE

PART 3

6. WHY SEX AND MARRIAGE?

Why does 'Why?' come before 'What?'

Sexual relationships break down because of disappointment. This is a generalization, of course; there are other reasons. But whenever a man and a woman enter a sexual relationship or marriage they do so with hopes, expectations and goals. Whether these are openly expressed or secretly cherished, each enters the relationship for reasons. And very often a relationship ends because, for one or both, these expectations have not been adequately fulfilled. For this pragmatic reason alone the question of purpose is important. We begin our study with this before we ask how marriage might be defined. This may seem to be the wrong order.

We are used to asking three questions: 'What?' 'How?' 'Why?' The first focuses on definition: what is marriage? what is moral or right? The second addresses resources needed to build or repair sexual relationships; it raises issues of individual moral capacity and of social moral capital. Both definition and resources are given attention in our society and in the churches.

'Why?' is the Cinderella of the three. Yet this last question ought to be the first, and not only for the pragmatic reason of preserving against disillusion. There is a deeper, theological reason why we must consider purpose first. We must accord it this primacy not only as a matter of practical policy but also of theological principle. Every human being is called, by virtue of being human, to love God; this is our primary human obligation. To love God involves aligning our desires with his will and purpose. We cannot therefore begin to understand sex and marriage until we have considered the Creator's will. This is fundamental. To be godly is to enter sexual relationship willing the same goals for which the Creator made humankind male and female.

Before we delineate *what* marriage is we must therefore ask *why* the Creator instituted marriage at all – what we may call 'Purpose with a capital P'. If we consider definition first, we will be vulnerable to the accusation that our definition is arbitrary, lacking an inner logic. The definition of marriage follows theologically and logically from the purpose of marriage.

The purpose into which we must enquire is the purpose of God. We might, on purely pragmatic grounds, enquire into the different purposes of particular couples in entering their relationships and observe how things work out. We might then generalize to say that certain goals tend to lead to disillusion and certain other goals to fulfilment. But, as Richard Hays has shrewdly observed, the New Testament is 'strikingly indifferent' to this kind of 'what happens if?' reasoning, asking consistently instead, 'What is the will of God?' (Hays 1996:455).

To begin with the purpose or will of God is deliberately to push questions of definition, of permissions and prohibitions, away from the centre. Definitions, permissions and prohibitions are, as we shall see, necessary and logical consequences of purpose, but when they are considered as central we inadvertently remove sexual ethics from the sphere of the love of God and the moral call to live a life in harmony with his will. It is the privilege of the human calling gladly to embrace the task and to align our wills with his will. Just as it was said of King David that he 'served the purpose [*boulē*] of God in his own generation' (Acts 13:36), so we wish to see how marriages may serve the purpose of God. Marriage lived in the light of the purpose of God will be dynamic and actively teleological; marriage considered only in terms of rules and definitions may be coldly static.

To ask the purpose question is not fundamentally to ask of any particular man or woman, or any couple, what were *their* purposes in marriage. People enter, or seek to enter, or continue in marriage with widely differing goals, ends or hopes. Nor is it to ask of a particular social culture for what purposes it 'constructs' what it calls marriage, and what benefits it perceives in any particular sexual social arrangement. These too may differ. Both individual and social purposes may vary widely and are certainly culturally relative. Nor is it simply to look at how human beings 'are', or even how the human body 'is', and to try to deduce from 'nature' what the purpose of sex might be. These would be inadequate foundations.[1]

---

1. Cf. Moore 1992: ch. 5 for an incisive analysis of the weakness of traditional Roman Catholic 'natural law' arguments in sexual ethics.

The order the Creator has placed in creation is – at least in part – teleological order, order that serves a purpose. We seek therefore in this part of the book to elucidate the purpose of the Creator in instituting marriage as a part of the good created order. This search will seem doomed to those who locate purpose only in human beings. So, for example, one newspaper columnist insists, 'The purpose of marriage is personal to each couple' (*The Times*, 19 June 2000). Such subjectivism fails to address the question why sexual differentiation and sexual attraction exist at all. The Christian theologian must insist that these things exist because the Creator made them; and he did so for purposes of his own, purposes which transcend our varied hopes or fears.

The question of purpose is foundational also to the understanding of law, the regulation of sexual relations in societies. Biblical laws, like other laws, can be related to ethics only by way of an overarching grasp of goal. We need to gain insight, from a particular legal formulation at a particular time in a specific culture, to the purpose for which that law was formulated and which it was designed to serve. Purpose alone gives a pathway from law to ethics.

Purpose is also a necessary theological undergirding to the interpretation of the Bible as a whole in its teaching about sexual ethics. It is easy but misleading to read Scripture as though it were primarily concerned with matters of law and definition, peppered with seemingly arbitrary permissions and prohibitions. Definitions and regulations are necessary consequences of an ordering with an aim; they cannot be understood without first grasping the aim.

Consideration of the Creator's purpose serves another function. This is to bring precision and perspective to the rather hazy humanist ethics of sex, which is often conditioned by some concept of human 'flourishing' or fulfilment. It is a truism in sexual ethics, as in much other contemporary ethics, to speak of what does or does not promote the flourishing of human beings, and to consider the promotion of human flourishing as a criterion for ethical analysis. For example, *Something to Celebrate* asks, 'What will best support . . . people . . . and enable them to be *happy and fulfilled*?' (Church of England 1995:13, my italics).[2] Such ethics asks primarily, 'What will be good for men and women?' This is a laudable aim, and a proper doctrine of creation will lead us to expect that the creation ethics we propose will indeed promote human flourishing rather than human frustration. But we will not reliably

---

2. Likewise Thatcher 1999:15 argues that when in doubt, we need to settle 'for the interpretation (of scripture) which *enhances people's lives*' (my italics); but where 'life-enhancement' comes from as a criterion, or how it is to be delimited, is not clear.

discover what promotes human flourishing simply by consulting human beings. The criterion is almost infinitely elastic.

To adopt human flourishing as the fundamental criterion in ethical analysis is to build on sand; the foundation is too soft. It will not do to ask what some human beings feel makes for their fulfilment; the answers would be muddied by culture, confused by personal histories and obscured by sin. Either we end up with what O'Donovan calls the endless 'balkanisation' of knowledge, or one group imposes its will by cultural and ethical imperialism on others (O'Donovan 1994:50–52). We must ask of the Creator his purpose (transcending culture) for all men and women. For what reason does the Creator make humankind male and female and so order human affairs that a man leaves his father and mother and cleaves to his wife? What purpose of the Creator ought this union to serve?

One of the most rigorous recent attempts to ground a sexual ethic philosophically without reference to a Creator is by Roger Scruton in his book *Sexual Desire*. As a philosopher who values teleology, Scruton leans on Aristotle's *Nicomachean Ethics* and argues that human fulfilment necessarily involves development from simple self-awareness in the present moment (understanding the meaning of 'I' or 'me') to awareness of myself as a person with a history and a future, who 'lives according to the logic of a human biography' (Scruton 1986:332), who expresses moral intentionality (towards the future) and accepts responsibility (for the past). Continuity through time is integral to fulfilled personhood, and it is for this reason that sexual fidelity is a virtue. This analysis is penetrating and yet insufficient. For we need ethics that goes beyond a focus on self, which reaches out to an intentionality that transcends that of the human individual: we need theological ethics.

The candidates for 'Why sex and marriage?': procreation, relationship and public order

In the history of Christian thought the major candidates for the purpose of sex and marriage have been procreation, relationship and what we may call public order. These are sometimes referred to as the 'goods' of marriage. They have been formulated and related to one another in various ways. In each case the reason for teaching these 'goods' is that the particular couple entering marriage may, at least approximately, align their own individual purposes with the purposes for which the Creator ordained marriage; they are pointers to the intentions that inhere in creation order.

I will not here review how these 'goods' have been considered throughout

Christian history.[3] They are introduced only briefly as background to the next chapter, in which I endeavour an ethical analysis from Genesis that will enable us to assess them.

a. The procreational good

The procreational good is, in principle, the simplest. Sexual union leads naturally to children and this is to be valued. Did God not command or bless humankind in Genesis 1:28, and repeat this in Genesis 9:1, to be fruitful and multiply? So it has been argued, and continues to be the mainstream position of the Roman Catholic Church, that the intention to have children is the *primary* purpose of sexual relationship. This position is increasingly alien in a Western culture like the UK, where more than one in five pregnancies is deliberately terminated with an abortion.[4] Chapter 7 is devoted to consideration of this traditional 'good'; we need to test it, to see if there is a logic, and in particular an authentically Christian theologic, that underlies it.

We should also note that the procreational good does not itself answer the question of why God chose to make humankind reproduce sexually rather than asexually. Asexual reproduction (or cloning, for that matter) would 'produce' more human beings, albeit without the creative variety that results from gene mixing in sexual reproduction. Perhaps this variety is a pointer to the purpose of a creative God in making procreation image the rich variety of creation.

b. The relational good

'It is not good that the man should be alone' (Gen. 2:18). This saying is often taken to mean that it is not good for man to be 'solitary' (Barth *CD* III/1:289 and elsewhere). Man is a social creature, made for relationship, and the creation of woman is – it is said – God's primary provision for his social need. So the relational good focuses on the good inherent in the marriage relationship, irrespective of whether or not there are children.

The perceived relational benefits are described in a number of ways. These may include the comfort each gives the other, the companionship, the psychological benefits of mutual affirmation and acceptance, loving sexual relations and the experience of unconditional love. The relationship meets deep felt

---

3. The classic formulations are often sought in Augustine, *On the Good of Marriage* (esp. §32), *On Original Sin* (ch. 39) and *On Marriage* (§19). See also brief discussions in Bailey 1959:197–199; Forster 1995: ch. 2; and in many other places.

4. *Social Trends 31* (2001):49 (table 2.12) gives the figure for legal terminations as 22% of all conceptions in 1998.

needs and may contribute to the healing of past hurts. So, for example, the influential Church of England report *marriage, Divorce and the Church* has a section on 'the needs which marriage meets', these needs being the personal needs of the couple concerned.

> Marriage, considered not merely sexually, but also in its psychological aspects, can meet the deepest human needs because it contains the basic ingredients of a relationship within which each partner can discover himself or herself through the other, and each can offer to the other the opportunity for healing and growth on the basis of progressive mutual completion.
> (Church of England 1971:109f.)

This report includes the recommendation that when the church explains the meaning and purpose of marriage, primacy should be accorded to this kind of relational good. The Roman Catholic writer Jack Dominian has written eloquently on the healing power of a good marriage.[5]

Some press the relational aspect further and use it as a kind of generalized locus for the experience of human togetherness or fellowship. So Barth writes of 'humanity, the characteristic and essential mode of man's being' as 'in its root fellow-humanity. Humanity which is not fellow-humanity is inhumanity' (Barth, *CD* III/1:117). There is a purpose of relationship inherent in man as the image of God. Because God is not a solitary God, but rather 'the deus triunus', a solitary human being would not be a fitting goal of creation. According to Barth the relational nature of humankind is focused on the man-woman encounter, so that, 'Whatever may take place between man and man and woman and woman is only as it were a preliminary and accompaniment for this true encounter between man and fellow-man, for this true being in fellow-humanity.' Even in male-female relationships it is marriage that is primary, so that in relationships such as father-daughter, mother-son, or brother-sister, the male-female element is 'the subterranean motive'; in marriage it has its 'proper locus' (Barth, *CD* III/1:288f.).

Similarly, Helmut Thielicke describes the mutual independence of the sexes as having a symbolic meaning in terms of man's existence as a 'being in fellow-humanity' (*Mitmenschlichkeit*), 'the representative expression of which is that man and woman belong together' (Thielicke 1979:4). The 'I-Thou' of person to person is above the mere 'I-It' of person to thing; and the duality of the sexes points to this primacy of interpersonal relationship in true humanness.

---

5. See, for example, Dominian 1981: ch. 4 (Sustaining) and ch. 5 (Healing). See also the section of Church of England 1995:57–59 on families as 'therapy'.

Such thinking can burden marriage with a heavy weight of symbolic importance. In paganism such a transcendent significance may readily be justified by attaching to the sexual relationship a mystical or religious value. Among philosophers and some pagan religions sexual union is esteemed because in this (literally) climactic relational experience the couple are given an entrance into the presence of the divine. We might dignify this with a fourth heading, 'the mystical good of sexual union', but it is probably best considered as a subset of the relational good. In some way the relational act of sexual union itself mystically joins the worshipper/lover to the divine.

In his most recent book, *Let's Make Love*, Jack Dominian appears to stray over the line into such a mystical view, in his enthusiasm for sexual intercourse. For him, 'The whole procedure of intercourse is a divine liturgy of love . . . In marriage, the couple has their own domestic church and at the centre of this church is the enactment of sexual intercourse,' which is 'the channel of the divine', for it 'reflects the inner world of the Trinity in that the Trinity expresses the relationship of the love of persons . . . The Father loves the Son, and the fruit of this love is the Spirit . . .' (Dominian 2001:79f.).

At their best, Christian theologians have been very wary of such extensions of the relational 'good' of marriage. Barth criticizes Schleiermacher's romanticism for speaking of marriage as 'a work of eternal love which is itself eternal', thus trying 'to exalt this dialectic (*i.e. sexual encounter*) to a metaphysical absolute' (Barth, *CD* III/4:122). He is also scathing about Schubart's work *Religion und Eros* for arguing for the integration of Eros into religion, thus blurring the line between Christianity and nature religion (Barth, *CD* III/4:125–127).

Throwing such caution to the winds, James Nelson in his book *Embodiment* writes of the blessing of sexual sensuality in reuniting the self formerly sundered by a body-spirit dualism. He makes it clear that this reunification is to be understood as a deeply religious experience when he goes on to write, 'This sensuality is God's invitation to reunion – with both self and the loved companion. And in this reunion *God is experienced*, whether there is consciousness of the divine name or not' (Nelson 1979:90). It would appear that through sexual union there is a way to experience God which bypasses Jesus Christ; we may have salvation through Christ or salvation by coitus.

The Bible consistently abhors such sex-mysticism. And yet it does give to the marriage *relationship* a deep and uniquely theological significance, for marriage mirrors the covenant love of God for his people, and their answering love. The theologian who has expounded this theme most influentially in modern times is Karl Barth. Barth therefore sees in marriage a strong apologetic value, for the human experience of marriage points beyond itself to the

God-man relationship. The possibility and indeed the need for man to be in relationship with God is already imprinted on man by virtue of his nature as male and female. 'In virtue of his nature man must be formally prepared for grace' (Barth, *CD* III/2:290). So, 'If God comes to man, he comes to his possession which he has already marked as such in creating it' (Barth, *CD* III/2:321–323). For Barth, this fundamental anthropological marker is human sexual differentiation.

According to Barth, it is this covenant meaning of marriage which forms the theological summit of sexual ethics. He argues passionately that 'the Old Testament Magna Carta of humanity' is to be found not in the high Old Testament valuation of procreation but rather in the relational delight of Genesis 2:18–25, echoed in the Song of Songs and validated by the motif of the covenant relationship of Yahweh with Israel, of Christ and his church (with a major emphasis on Ephesians 5) (Barth, *CD* III/2:291f.; cf. III/1:312–321).

Developing this Barthian approach, David Atkinson argues from the covenant nature of the marriage relationship that, 'The *primary purpose* of marriage is to be found in the acceptance of God's will that the covenant relationship of man and wife, both made in the image of God, shall be an image of his covenant relationship with his people' (Atkinson 1979:75, my italics).

At its strongest, proponents of the relational good insist that the purpose of marriage is to be located *wholly* in terms of the relationship of the couple to one another. Although Barth elsewhere balances this, in one passage of the *Church Dogmatics* he writes uncompromisingly of working at marriage 'in and for itself as an end in itself'. The marriage task is 'not a means to an end, but a life-form *sui generis* to be maintained and developed according to its own inherent meaning and claims' (Barth, *CD* III/4:189). We shall need to reassess these relational emphases in the light of our study of Genesis in Chapter 7.

c. The public good

What I call the public or institutional good is different in kind both from the procreational good and the relational good. It encompasses the benefits of ordered and regulated sexual relationships in human society. Undisciplined and disordered sexual behaviour must be restrained, for it carries with it a high social and personal cost in family breakdown, destructive jealousies, resentments, bitterness and hurt. Ordered behaviour is to be encouraged because this has benefits that extend beyond the couple to children, neighbours and the wider networks of relational society.

We find this wider dimension of order and disorder referred to, for example, in Proverbs 6:20–35 with its reference to the destructive jealousy of the husband and his fury at his wife's lover; also in 1 Corinthians 7:2 with its commendation of stable man-woman pairings as a safeguard against the disorder of 'cases of sexual immorality', and in 1 Thessalonians 4:6 where immorality is noted in its aspect as doing wrong to a brother. The public good refers, there-fore, to the wider dimension of sexual order or disorder, looking outwards beyond the couple.

Each of these three candidates for purpose may, when carefully formu-lated, lay claim to a certain weight of theology, some biblical basis and histor-ical antecedents in the Christian tradition. Each is sometimes also argued in terms of 'natural law' and commended in this way as a basis for public sexual ethics. But the whole edifice of divine marriage purpose so construed is vul-nerable to the charge of being an amalgam of three disconnected purposes that lack theological unity. In Chapter 7 we therefore seek in Genesis an underlying ethics that coheres with the big story of scripture, and in relation to which the procreational, relational and public dimensions of marriage purpose may be evaluated.

7. SEX IN THE SERVICE OF GOD

Why begin with Genesis?

If we want to know why God made humankind male and female, we must begin with Genesis 1 and 2. When Jesus was asked about divorce, he spoke first about marriage; he rooted his ethic in 'the beginning of creation' (Mark 10:6f.; cf. Matt. 19:4f.), quoting from Genesis 1 and 2. Paul also quotes and alludes to Genesis 2:24 (Eph. 5:31; 1 Cor. 6:16). In Genesis 1 – 2 we have the most fundamental presentation in Scripture of the structure of creation before the fall. In this chapter we study Genesis 1 – 2 to discern the Creator's purpose in making humankind male and female. This leads us to challenge and qualify the contemporary paradigm that gives primacy to relationship in sex.

Genesis 1:1 – 2:3

The creation of man[1] (Gen. 1:26–31) is a crucial and unique part of the placing of order in creation. Man is made in the image and likeness of God so as to exercise 'dominion' over the created order, while being in his own nature a part of that order. The reason why man is given this unique dignity of being

---

1. I shall sometimes use 'man' rather than 'human' to reflect the tension in the Genesis accounts between 'man' (*'āḏām*) as male and 'man' as humankind; it would be misleading to dissolve this tension completely by using gender-neutral terminology throughout.

created in the image of God is that he may fulfil the task of responsible dominion (vv. 26, 28). *In this context* of task, man is created (v. 27) 'male and female'. And *in this context* (v. 28) man is blessed with the possibility of pro-creation, to 'fill the earth *and subdue it*'. Human sexuality is to be understood within this matrix of meaning, encompassing human dignity (in the image of God) and human task (exercising dominion).

Within the order of creation, humankind is placed uniquely with a dual orientation. On the one hand, towards the Creator, humankind is given moral *responsibility*; on the other, towards creation, he is entrusted with a *task*. The coordination of both aspects of this orientation is the key to the ethics of sex. The understanding of sex is not simply a matter of arbitrary moral response to the command of God, as though God spoke and we obey simply because he says so (ours 'not to reason why'); nor is it a matter of constructing our own sovereign ethics as the absolute masters of creation, subjecting the cosmos (including its bodily sexual dimensions) to our tyrannical will and whim. In order to delineate with understanding a proper sexual ethics, we need to understand both the character of the Creator, to whom we are responsible, and the nature of the creation, over which he has set us as stewards.

We need to tread carefully in relating four aspects of the human condition: the task of dominion, the human responsibility to the Creator, our sexual differentiation as male and female, and our human dignity in the image of God. We are not justified in dissolving any one of these into another. Barth, for example, goes too far when he seeks virtually to *equate* 'the image of God' with human sexual differentiation.[2] This is not justified by the text, and Barth fails convincingly to address the objection that animals too have sexual differentiation, indeed that sexual differentiation is one of the most obvious features shared with non-human living creatures.[3] He is correct, however, to distinguish 'the image of God' from the task of dominion, so that human lordship over creation is 'not the essence but the accessory' (Barth, *CD* III/1:186) of man's determination as the image of God. We shall return to this distinction between ontology and function. None the less, man's ontology as the image of God and man's function as God's vicegerent over creation are

---

2. For a concise and sympathetic summary of Barth's view, see Jewett 1975:33–48.

3. Barth argues that in man alone sexual differentiation is the unique and only distinction (*CD* III/1:186), since 'Man is not said to be created or to exist in groups or species, in races and peoples, etc.' But the same may surely also be said about dogs, for example. It is an argument that relies on contrasting 'man' on the one hand with 'non-human living creatures' on the other. If, for example, we were to compare 'dogs' with 'non-canine living creatures', we could turn the argument on its head.

intimately coordinated. Human sexual differentiation is set in the same context.

It is sufficient for our purposes to note the close relationships between these four elements of the fundamental matrix of human meaning. Man is given sexual differentiation as a basic and unique distinction; this is 'the only structural differentiation in which [man] exists' (Barth, *CD* III/1:45), unlike, for example, race, which is miscible, or class, which may change. There is no such thing as an androgynous human person; there is only the human male and the human female.

For what purpose has the Creator made humankind this way? In the context of Genesis 1 humans are made to rule a world that is already teeming with living creatures, a world which is abundantly fecund, but which will be out of control unless it is ruled. How may we fulfil this task? We also, like the subhuman living creatures, need to 'be fruitful and multiply' so that there will be sufficient human beings to exercise responsible dominion.

There is also a suggestive link between image and procreation in Genesis 5:3, immediately after a reminder of human sexuality. 'When Adam had lived one hundred thirty years, he became the father of a son *in his likeness, according to his image*, and named him Seth' (my italics). This might simply mean that Seth had a physical resemblance to Adam, sharing his father's anatomical structure. But coming immediately after the reminder in verse 1 that Adam (NRSV 'humankind') was made 'in the likeness of God', it would seem to suggest that, even after the fall, the work of procreation echoes the work of creation. It passes on image and likeness. In the wider perspective of the Bible's theology, we know that this likeness is now flawed. As Calvin observed, Adam cannot now avoid passing on his corruption, 'because Adam, who had fallen from his original state, could beget none but such as were like himself' (Calvin, *Genesis*:229). None the less, the implicit connection between image and procreation has powerful ethical implications for marriage. We shall discuss later the entailment that godly nurture is integral to procreation, which – when understood in the context of task – can never be minimized as just 'making babies'.

We note also that this close association of procreation and task is repeated after the flood in Genesis 9:1–7, where the blessing 'be fruitful and multiply' (vv. 1,7) brackets a renewed (albeit modified) teaching both of image (v. 6) and of dominion (v. 2f.).

In Genesis 1, echoed in 5:1–3 and 9:1–7, the procreational good of sexual union is set in the context of the task of exercising responsible dominion.[4]

---

4. Stafford 1993:70 touches on this when he says that procreation lifts the eyes of a couple beyond themselves to the task of raising children, which is their part in subduing the earth.

Genesis 2:4–25

There is a tendency to consider Genesis 2:18–25 in isolation from the context. Verse 24 (and its quotation by Jesus and Paul) suggests that this passage is foundational to the ethics of sex, showing us something of the nature, purpose and meaning of marriage. In Genesis 2:18 we hear the Creator speaking with himself about something 'not good' in creation, something that is remedied only by the creation of the woman. If we can discern what was 'not good' before this remedy, we shall understand theologically the true 'good' of marriage. Genesis 2:18 is therefore the key text when we ask the purpose question.

If the procreational emphasis of Genesis 1 ('be fruitful and multiply') appears too coldly functional, we may turn with relief to the warm delight of Genesis 2:23 ('This *at last* is bone of my bones . . .'). Here, we say, in Genesis 2 is a passage that does justice to the passion and power of sex, one that understands what men and women actually experience in desire and delight. In particular we often read verse 18 as an eloquent pointer to man's nature as a relational being who cannot live without love. 'It is not good that the man should be alone.' 'Ah,' we say, 'poor Adam was lonely. A pet dog, cat, ox, budgerigar or goldfish did not meet his *needs*. God will give him a wife so that he will not be lonely any more.' From this we deduce that the primary function of sex is not procreation but the unity of fulfilling relationship; sex is to bring healing and fulfilment to the sexual partners.

The forceful exposition of this theme by Karl Barth has been immensely influential: it is not God's purpose that the man should be alone, and the creation of the woman is God's remedy for his loneliness. From this it is deduced that the institution of marriage and sexual union is *in principle* God's remedy for human aloneness or loneliness (though these are not quite the same). That is to say, if Genesis 1:26–28 points to the procreational good of marriage, Genesis 2:18–25 points with equal vigour to its relational meaning. And while Barth himself maintains a rigorous theological insistence on the covenant structure of marriage as a pointer towards the God-human covenant, in popular perception and Protestant piety this has dissolved into a focus on marriage as God's remedy for human loneliness.

It is very common in popular Protestant writing to understand Genesis 2:18 in this way. M. Blaine Smith, for example, writes on this verse,

> Only one reason is mentioned for God's bringing Eve into Adam's life – the fact that Adam needed companionship. Nothing is said about Adam deserving a wife, nor is it even suggested that Adam would serve God better with a spouse. It's simply said that Adam had a personal need, and this was basis enough for God to fill the void.
> (Blaine Smith 2000:22)

Jay Adams deduces from this verse that 'the reason for marriage is *to solve the problem of loneliness*' (Adams 1980:8, my italics).

This idea has seeped deep into the substructure of our thought, both in Western society and in the church. If I may be forgiven a personal anecdote, at the end of a day when I was thinking about these questions, I was reading to our young daughter at bedtime from a (generally excellent) children's story Bible. We had come to Genesis 24 (supposedly) and I found myself reading the words, 'Abraham was very old. His wife Sarah had died. He said to himself, "I must make sure that Isaac has a wife to love him. *I don't want him to be on his own when I die*"' (my italics). Re-reading Genesis 24, I could not find this motivation in the text, and it was not clear how the storybook author claimed this intriguing insight into Abraham's mind; it reads more like a revealing imposition of contemporary Western culture onto the Genesis account (Lion 1985:4).

Although the homosexuality debate is not the focus of this study, it is worth noting that the assumption that celibacy and loneliness are inevitable partners is widespread here also. In Paul Avis's book *Eros and the Sacred*, for example, he suggests that homosexual partnership may be 'the lesser of two evils, the greater evil being enforced celibacy *and the accompanying loneliness*' (Avis 1989:147). But as Thomas Schmidt points out, this 'objection to celibacy rests on a false assumption that the homosexual person is thereby consigned to relational loneliness' (Schmidt 1995:167). We must question this assumption.

Protestants especially have read Genesis 2:18 in the context of what follows to the neglect of what precedes. Like a form critic treating a Gospel pericope as an isolated pearl only loosely connected to the other pearls on the string,[5] we have failed to read Genesis 2:18 as part of a continuous narrative. The effects of this have been very significant.

Two arguments may be used to show that a simple 'loneliness' reading, or even a covenant relationship reading, of Genesis 2:18 does not do justice to the text in context. The first is the wider context of Scripture, the second the immediate context in Genesis 2.

Loneliness in the wider context of Scripture

We begin with the wider argument, from the rest of Scripture. First, we should note that the theological superstructure erected on this reading of Genesis 2:18 is weighty and sometimes only slightly linked to the text. Here is

---

5. To borrow Morna Hooker's caricature of some form-critical treatments of Mark's Gospel.

one example from Barth, who writes of human sexual differentiation that 'here at the heart of creation there is a gap which must be filled if man is really to be man and not in some sense only so potentially, and in the presence of which, even though surrounded by the superabundance of the rest of creation, man would always be solitary, always in a vacuum and not among his equals' (Barth, *CD* III/1:292). But if solitude is the problem we must ask why this gap must be filled with *woman* and not by a second human male. The need for relationality could have been achieved by unisexual humans in whom was planted a universal homosexual urge, for example, if we must have sex at all; it is not obvious that human relationship needs sex in order to flourish. Those who rely on purely relational arguments are driven to rather speculative comments about the 'otherness' of woman which in some way 'answers' to man's cry; it is sometimes hard to know what this means.

If it is true that in some profound way marriage is – in principle and in general – God's gracious provision for human loneliness, the answer to man's heart cry, and if it points to and signifies also in itself the satisfaction of the religious longings of the human heart for its Creator, we might reasonably expect to find support for this elsewhere in Scripture.

The theme, so central in Barth's thought, of the God-man covenant is indeed intimately linked with marriage language. But when we look to find this theme reflected back into the supposed benefits of human marriage for man or woman, we draw something of a blank.

The Bible has a great deal to say about the longings of the human heart. This is more pronounced in some places than in others, but there is much about love, friendship and fellowship. It is very striking, however, that almost never are these longings and their satisfaction placed in the context of sexual relationship. If Genesis 2:18 does indeed indicate that marriage is God's provision *in principle* for human loneliness, this scriptural lacuna is surprising. Some examples may be considered.

The passage 1 John 4:7–21 is eloquent about love, the love of God for his people, the love of his people for God and the love of his people for one another. There is reference to love driving out fear (v. 18), which is exactly where we might expect a reference to the healing power of unconditional acceptance in a marriage. Yet there is no hint of sexual relationship anywhere within the horizons of this passage. And if we ask how the presence of God is *signified*, the answer in verse 12 (in language which is reminiscent of the incarnation language of John 1:18) is found not by looking at marriages, but rather at the church: 'if we love one another . . .' This is about love found in the fellowship of a Christian church.

In 1 Thessalonians 2:6–8 Paul employs language of great warmth to describe the love he has for this church, the sharing of his life with them, his gentleness in dealing with them. Again, there is no hint of sexual relationship or even sexual imagery.

In spite of the common association of 1 Corinthians 13 with wedding services, the context is again the life of a church (although in this case in ironic contrast to a church which conspicuously fails to show such love). There is no allusion to marriage, but rather to the fellowship of the church.

In John 13 – 16 Jesus speaks with great love and intimacy to the inner circle of disciples, at a time of great stress, about his love for them and the love they must have for one another. There is much about the Father's love for the Son, the Son's love for the disciples, the disciples' love for one another, but again, there is no hint of sexual relationship or sexual imagery. One of the highest things he can call them is not his (sexual) lovers (this is nowhere in sight or thought) but his friends (15:15).

In Paul's letter to Philemon we find 'the hearts of the saints' being 'refreshed' by the love of Philemon (v. 7). Again, sex and marriage are nowhere in sight.

Friendship again is described with great warmth in the love of David and Jonathan (1 Sam. 18 – 20; cf. 2 Sam. 1:26, 'passing the love of women'). The context is loyalty (including political loyalty, Ackroyd 1975; Thompson 1974) and friendship, and sexual relationship is nowhere in sight. Indeed, it is a sad symptom of an obsessively sexualized society that some feel we must read sex into any relationship of warm trust, whether between David and Jonathan or between Jesus and his disciples.

Perhaps supremely in Scripture it is the Psalms which express and address the deep longings of the human heart, longings deep and urgent like a deer for water (Ps. 42:1) or all-absorbing bodily longings of 'heart and flesh' crying out (Ps. 84:2). There is in the Psalms healing for the broken-hearted in many deep ways. And yet (apart from the royal marriage, Ps. 45) sexual relationship and marriage are conspicuous by their absence. Indeed, when the 'lonely' are specifically mentioned in Psalm 68:6 (NIV), the Lord's remedy is to put them in families or a home, not necessarily in sexual relationships; the cure is belonging, security, trustworthy relationships, but not necessarily the marriage bed. There is a fundamental exclusivity that distinguishes sexual relationship from friendship and strongly suggests that the former cannot be the Creator's general remedy for loneliness.

This evidence suggests to us that God has remedies other than marriage for human loneliness. I must be careful, however, not to overstate my case. When the wise men note, 'Hope deferred makes the heart sick, but a desire fulfilled is a tree of life' (or 'sweet to the soul', Prov. 13:12,19), we must not exclude sexual desire and fulfilment from this observation. Likewise when the psalmist sings of being satisfied with good things (Ps. 103:5). We would place ourselves clean contrary to human experience if we arbitrarily excluded sex from God's remedy for loneliness, and there is no theological reason to attempt this strange exclusion. None the less, we must maintain that, while sexual fulfilment may be one of the ways in which God remedies human loneliness, the Bible does not teach that it is the only, or even the major, remedy.

The Creator understands the human heart with its longings for fellowship, but it is not at all clear that sexual relationship is his general provision to meet these yearnings. On the contrary, God's general provision for human loneliness appears to be friendship and fellowship, both with God and with fellow believers, rather than marriage necessarily.

Loneliness in the context of Genesis 2

Armed with these wider grounds for doubt, we return to Genesis 2:18 in its immediate context. Again we shall find the 'loneliness' reading of verse 18 to be inadequate. 'Then the LORD God said, "It is not good that the man should be alone; I will make him a helper as his partner"' (Gen. 2:18). We need to ask where the man is and what he is doing there at this point in the narrative. The word 'helper' (*'ēzer*) means 'one who helps or comes to the aid of someone needing help'. It is often observed that the word usually refers in the Old Testament to divine assistance and on three occasions to the bringing of military aid (BDB 740b), and therefore carries with it no necessary connotations of inferiority. It is less often asked, however, why the man needs help in the first place. With what does he need assistance? This can be answered only by reading the story so far.

The story begins with a picture of incompleteness, 'when no plant of the field was yet in the earth and no herb of the field had yet sprung up' (v. 5). Perhaps this is not as dramatically wild as the 'formless void and darkness' (*tōhû wābōhû*) of 1:2, but it is none the less an unsatisfactory scenario. There are no plants. The reason seems to be not shortage of water (v. 6) but the absence of man (v. 5, 'there was no one [lit. no man] to till the ground'). It is man who will bring the water to the ground by irrigation and 'work' the ground.

It should therefore come as no surprise to read in verse 7 of the formation of the man. He is not an arbitrary irruption into the story, but the logical meeting of creation's need. Only then does the 'garden in Eden' appear (v. 8), into which the man is put. We are not told at this stage why the man is placed in the garden. Indeed, it is often assumed that man is there for his own pleasure, given the plethora of pleasant trees (v. 9). We need to remember, however, that the incompleteness of creation is connected with the need for man to be a 'worker' or 'servant'. Man is not in the garden for sensual enjoyment, despite what Von Rad scathingly calls 'the commonly accepted fantastic ideas of "Paradise"' (Von Rad 1972b, ad loc.). This is confirmed in verse 15: 'The LORD God took the man and put him in the garden of Eden to till it [*'āḇaḏ*, work or serve it] and keep it [*šāmar*, watch or guard].' Man's task is to serve and to guard, so if in Genesis 1 man's calling is described with reference to creation as one of dominion, in Genesis 2 any thought that this dominion is self-serving is corrected by its description in terms of service and work. This is not a burdensome or miserable calling; it is service in the context of abundant goodness (vv. 9, 16f.). But it is service none the less. Where Genesis 1 speaks with grandeur of the dignity of responsible dominion and rule, Genesis 2 speaks with homely warmth of the need for gardeners in God's garden or parkland. Ethically, both point beyond humankind (and certainly beyond the horizons of any given couple in marriage) to work that needs to be done.

The natural thought from the flow of the text, therefore, when we are told that Adam needs a 'helper', is that this is connected with the work he has been given to do.[6] He needs someone to come to his aid, for he cannot do this work 'alone'. We know the end of the story, and it is hard to read it as though for the first time, but in verse 18 there is only the slightest hint about the nature of this necessary helper. The word *kᵉneḡdô* ('as his partner', literally 'like opposite him') suggests 'both likeness and difference or complementarity' (Perriman 1998:180), but not identity. It is not just that the man needs another pair of hands, for which another male would suffice. Wenham 1987 (ad loc.) cites in this context Ecclesiastes 4:9–10: 'Two are better than one, because they have a good reward for their toil. For if they fall, one will lift up the other; but woe to one who is alone and falls and does not have another to help.' Purely on the level of statistical averages of strength, and at the risk of seeming pedestrian, we might say that a second male is likely to be more useful for this. And yet, in some unexplained way, he cannot carry out his calling without one who is complementary to him.

This calls into question reading verse 18 in terms *purely* of the social nature of

---

6. Perriman 1998:179 is one of very few commentators to make this connection when he writes of Gen. 2:18, 'In the first place, this has to do with the work of cultivating the garden in which the man has been placed (2:15; cf 2:5).' However, he fails to integrate this observation with the passage that follows when he continues, '*But* verse 24 makes it clear that the story of the creation of the woman is also, and perhaps primarily, an explanation of the institution of marriage' (my italics). The point, however, is not that marriage is a *separate* focus of the text, but rather that this text in the context of v. 15 contains an important pointer to the purpose for which marriage was ordained.

man. So when Von Rad says it teaches that 'man is created for *sociability*' (Von Rad 1972b, ad loc.) or Wenham that 'it alerts the reader to the importance of *companionship* for man' (Wenham 1987, ad loc.) or Kidner that it 'poignantly reveals [man] as a social being, made for *fellowship*' (Kidner 1967, ad loc.), we need to ask whether there is something missing, something unique to relationship between men and women. As soon as we have said this, we have to admit that same-sex friendship is and has always been a fruitful and valid context for companionship, fellowship and sociability. So why, in the terms of the story, does it *have* to be the woman?

For woman it has to be. We follow the drama of initial disappointment, followed by seemingly endless further disappointment (v. 19f.), followed at last by delight (v. 23): 'And the man said, "*This one* – at last! Bone of my bones, and Flesh of my flesh. I shall call *this one* Woman for from Man she was taken, *this one!*"'[7] Here is a natural and innocent affirmation of sexual desire and delight, of nakedness untouched by shame.

Yet we must not conclude that the final *goal* of this delightful and intimate companionship is to be found in the delight, the intimacy or the companionship. This is delight with a shared purpose, intimacy with a common goal, and companionship in a task beyond the boundaries of the couple themselves. As we rejoice with the lovers in the garden, we must not forget that there is work to be done. The garden still needs tilling and watching. The purpose of the man-woman match is not their mutual delight, wonderful though that is. It is that the woman should be just the helper the man needs, so that together they may serve and watch.

At this point in the narrative we are left to surmise just how the woman is to be this helper. Against many commentators (who protest too much that procreation is not mentioned in Gen. 2:18–25), we must insist that it is arbitrary to exclude procreation from our thoughts at this point, for Genesis 2 follows Genesis 1. We may also note, however, the very strong explicit emphasis in verse 24 on the strong bond formed by the man and the woman. This secure relationship also relates to the task in hand, for as a kingdom divided against itself cannot stand, so the task of keeping the garden will fail unless the man and the woman work together in faithful union.

When we read Genesis 2:18 in the context that precedes (both from 2:4 and also 1:1 – 2:3) and in the wider context of all Scripture, we are therefore led to recognize that both the procreational and the relational benefits of marriage are set before the fall in the context of an overarching purpose, the achievement of a task calling humankind into an awesome dignity. Any

---

7. My rather literal translation.

creation ethics of marriage must set it in this outward-looking context of task, and not simply (or even predominantly) as God's answer to human loneliness.

In arguing this we will seem to many to be tilting at windmills. The perception and indeed the experience of so many, that sexual union is indeed the answer to loneliness, is so widespread and deep that it will take more than one study to change it. It is therefore important to be clear what we mean. The phrase 'in principle' is crucial. In the life of an individual, God may indeed – and often does – use the companionship of a loving husband or wife as a significant, if not overwhelming, factor in remedying his or her loneliness. This is obvious from the deep loneliness experienced by the recently widowed, or indeed many recently divorced.[8] It would be absurd to deny this. In these cases the pain is not only (or even mainly, depending on age) the sexual frustration that accompanies bereavement or divorce; it is the deprivation of valued companionship.

The argument of this book is that marriage is not *in principle* God's remedy for human loneliness. This remedy, in general, in principle and for all men and women, is fellowship and friendship. If in our society the unmarried (or those who are not in what are revealingly called 'relationships') do experience loneliness (as they undoubtedly do), we are not therefore to point their hopes inevitably in the direction of a sexual relationship, but rather to human relationships of friendship and fellowship. This is a challenge to churches to be the kinds of loving communities in which real relationship is not coterminous with sexual relationship.

We conclude that marriage ought to be considered under the umbrella of the governing ethic of human responsibility (to the Creator) and of the human task (over the creation). This bifocal ethical foundation is central to the argument of this book. It will therefore be worth pausing at this stage to consider the liberating effects of such ethics and by contrast the disastrous outcomes of the tendency in contemporary Protestantism towards unbridled relational primacy.

The need for a task and the damaging effects of introverted relational primacy

We have already noted (in Chapter 3) some of the damaging effects of considering sexual relationship wholly or mainly in terms of the relational benefit to

---

8. Cf. Is. 62:4, where the desolation of the divorced is contrasted with the joy of the married.

the couple themselves. In the categories used in scriptural exhortation this may easily lead to sin (in the language of law) and to foolishness (in the language of wisdom); it is both wrong and stupid.

It is wrong because it promotes a selfish perception of sexual relations. 'If you love those who love you, what credit is that to you?' asks Jesus (Luke 6:32). Any relationship of mutual love, which looks only inwards in mutuality, fails this critical moral test. It is not a loving relationship unless its charity extends beyond the bounds of reciprocity. In Jesus' parable of the rich man and Lazarus, the rich man in Hades does have a care for his five brothers in danger (Luke 16:27f.); perhaps he had always been a good family man with concern for his family circle. But his 'charity' never extended to Lazarus at his gate; and so it is not accounted as true charity at all. We must remember that 'the family can easily become no more than a licensed form of selfishness' (Woodhead 1996:41).

Although I am critical of aspects of Barth's treatment of sex and marriage, he does recognize that 'marriage is not permission to establish an egoistic partnership of two persons'.[9] After all, we have in Ananias and Sapphira (Acts 5:1–11) a model of what today's world might consider a 'successful', because intimate, marriage. So far as we can judge this couple are at one; it may be they communicated admirably, understood one another perfectly and shared deep agreement as regards their goals in life. And yet they come under terrible judgment. Intimacy is not a moral goal for marriage, for it may be intimacy in selfishness.

Unbridled relational primacy is not only wrong, it is also foolish and self-destructive. This has been noted by a number of writers and social commentators. It is unstable because it reinforces social trends that already isolate the couple from the supportive influences of wider society.

The effect of social mobility on relational depth has been perceptively observed by Rodney Clapp in his book *Families at the Crossroads*. Contrasting the American small town with the suburb, Clapp comments, 'If the image of small-town life is a sturdy, intricately rooted tree, the image of suburban life is the hydroponic plant that floats on the water's surface and easily adapts when

---

9. Barth, *CD* III/4:225. Also, there is a very positive point in III/2:45 section 1 about how Jesus is the 'Man for other men': theological anthropology should look to Christology. We begin with the humanity of the man Jesus, and 'only on this basis extend our enquiry to the form and nature of humanity generally' (p. 207). True humanness, just as in Jesus, is not a private thing, but an outward-looking, serving character. This foundational anthropological insight needs to be extended into our consideration of marriage.

moved to another pond or tank' (Clapp 1993:49). As a result relationships are generally shallower, briefer and destructively intense. In their essay 'Confluent Love and the Cult of the Dyad' Mellor and Shilling speak of 'patterns of courtship where the couples are structurally isolated, becoming intensely focussed on each other' (Mellor and Shilling 1997:54).

This has an impact both on the perception and the practice of sexual relationships. The couple think of themselves as a unit in a manner that differs from before. In the older paradigm, the couple are a social unit intimately tied by links of wider family, neighbourhood and history to others. Now they are a mobile unit that moves from shallow suburban 'community' to another shallow suburban 'community'. The effect on their relationship is profound, for it critically weakens the positive effect of communal expectations and neighbourly support, so that if the two of them decide their relationship has outlived its usefulness, others have little option but to shrug their shoulders and nod resignedly to this diktat of blind fate. Neighbours in what passes for suburban 'community' do not expect them to stay together and encourage and help them when they do. Certainly they would not dream of attaching any wider social cost or disapproval to them if they do not. The whole project moves from being a social unit integrated within a wider social matrix towards being an insular and floating project of coupledom. In the face of these social changes, a theology of marriage that gives unbridled primacy to the man-woman relationship in marriage has little theological leverage to exercise on behalf of lasting faithfulness.

The couple working at the project of coupledom for its own sake face also the problem that introspection is stifling and self-destructive. 'Even the smallest cottage of the happiest of lovers cannot be habitable unless it has at least a door and a few windows opening outwards' (Barth, *CD* III/4:224). Much might be said about the therapeutic impact of an outward-looking focus on dynamics such as anger and forgiveness. The idea of a couple 'staying together for the sake of the children' is sometimes ridiculed; on the contrary it should be extended, so that a couple accept a strong moral obligation to stay together not just for the children (if any) but for the sake of neighbours and wider society.

There is only a short step between marriage as coupledom and marriage as self-actualization. And once the relationship is self-actualization, all extrinsic motivation for faithfulness 'for better or worse' has evaporated. Indeed, our motive in marrying will be the same as our motive in staying married or in ending a marriage; in each case my motive will be that I should become all that I can become as a person. 'So in fact I have a *moral obligation* to divorce and seek a new mate if my original wife can no longer promote my growth and self-actualisation' (Clapp 1993:63).

John Shelby Spong fully accepts that the motive for sexual relationship is self-actualization. He cites the analysis in Alvin Toffler's influential book *Future Shock* that there are typically three stages in a relationship. There is young love, perhaps the stage of 'trial marriage' in which there is the limited commitment to live together for the present; there is the stage of building a home and bringing up children (from conception to maturity); and there are the mature years after the children have left home. Since the needs we have are different in these three stages, it is perfectly in order (says Spong) to choose different sexual partners for each stage (Spong 1988:179, citing Toffler 1971). In a similar vein, in his influential book *The Transformation of Intimacy* Anthony Giddens has coined the phrase 'confluent love' for the inherently transient way in which 'lives can run parallel only for a time before they diverge again as the individuals concerned pursue new life-courses and seek to fulfil new needs' (Giddens 1992, cited in Mellor and Shilling 1997:56).

One consequence of relational primacy has been the concept of 'compatibility' as a prerequisite for 'intimacy'. Stafford analyses this under the heading of 'The Ethic of Intimacy'. He comments ironically, 'Few favour divorce or adultery, but against incompatibility, who can stand?' (Stafford 1993:44, and all of ch. 4).

The problem is heightened because of the unrealistic expectations thus loaded onto the man-woman relationship. Not only do I slip easily into seeking my own self-actualization, I also look primarily to my marriage partner to promote and be the major instrument to provide or at least catalyse this result. We noted in Chapter 3 the perceptive comment of Christopher Brooke: 'While faced with the spectacle of broken marriages, we have come (by a strange paradox which however goes very deep into the roots of our subject) to expect far more from a happy marriage' (Brooke 1989:8). Lawrence Stone likewise observes, 'It is an ironic thought that just at the moment when some thinkers are heralding the advent of the perfect marriage based on full satisfaction of the sexual, emotional and creative needs of both husband and wife, the proportion of marital breakdowns . . . is rising rapidly' (Stone 1979:427).

It is the problem of what each *expects* that makes an introspective religion of coupledom so destructive. 'The leech has two daughers; "Give, give," they cry' (Prov. 30:15). Couple-centred marriage dissolves into self-centred marriage, and self-centred marriage is like a leech. Or, to put it another way, it is like a pair of parasites trying to feed off one another. In his best-selling book *The Road Less Travelled*, Scott Peck suggests that we can shape other people into host organisms on which we are parasites.

People say, 'I do not want to live, I cannot live without my husband (wife, girlfriend, boyfriend), I love him (or her) so much.' And when I respond, as I frequently do,

'You are mistaken; you do not love your husband (wife, girlfriend, boyfriend)', 'What
do you mean?' is the angry question. 'I just told you I can't live without him (or her).'
I try to explain. 'What you describe is parasitism, not love.'
(Peck 1978:98)

Marriage that is primarily 'companionate' is dangerous, for in such marriage,
'each becomes not only a lover, but companion, friend and confidant, with
whom most or all leisure time is spent', and such a pressure of relational
expectation creates a marriage that 'is in itself unstable, and . . . contains the
roots of its own destruction' (Richards 1995:57). In contemporary Western
marriage, 'the marriage partner has been culturally defined as *the most significant
other* in adult life . . . This has given to marriage an altogether new weight . . .
which . . . has created an emotional burden of its own: There are very high
expectations, and tensions and dissatisfactions are likely in consequence'
(Berger and Berger 1984:180, my italics).

Our contemporary ideals of personal autonomy sit uneasily with goals of
life-partnership or 'a merged intimacy' (Richards 1995:63), for there is an
inherent conflict between 'companionate marriage [as] a shared life' and 'the
desire for individual autonomy' (Richards 1995:60). Martin Richards is right to
point out this conflict. In the Bible's perspective the way forward is neither via
individual autonomy nor in introspective companionship, but in the joyful
shared service of God.

The therapist Susie Orbach, writing about the weight of expectation loaded
onto marriage and family, comments, 'The image of the family unit is the gos-
samer over which we stretch our needs for attachment, for intimacy and autonomy' (*The Times*, 27 March 1996). Michael Banner notes that Schliermacher
pictured 'the privacy of the family as a haven from the vicissitudes of the public
sphere' (Banner 1996:17). We noted in Chapter 3 the observation of Vigen
Guroian that Americans overload 'the nuclear family with too great a responsibility for providing persons with a sense of identity and significance in life . . .
Under this moral weight marriage cracks, and the family is incinerated from
within by the intense psychological demands placed upon it' (Guroian 1987:107).
Guroian goes on to contrast intimacy, which he defines as expansive,[10] reaching
out to wider spheres of activity and association, with privatism, which is reflex-
ive, withdrawing from a world in which it cannot find value. (In contemporary
Protestant piety, the word 'intimacy' means much what Guroian means by 'privatism'.) The cult of privacy thrives where there is 'a gnostic distrust of the

---

10. Contrast the negative characterization of 'intimacy' in Stafford 1993: ch. 4, 'The Ethic
of Intimacy'.

world outside the self' (Guroian 1987:107f.).[11] At the conclusion of his argument Guroian says that families need a *transcendent purpose* for 'coming together, remaining together, and raising children' (Guroian 1987:114). This transcendent purpose we find in Genesis 1 and 2 in the task the Creator has given to humankind.

There is a paradox here. The Protestant (and particularly Barthian) emphasis on the marriage *relationship* is predicated on the theme of the covenant relationship in Scripture. Marriage is to be a visible and lived-out image of the love of the Lord for his people, and this relationship is so central to reality that the project of imaging it is seen as the primary purpose of marriage. The paradox is that when we begin to think of the marriage relationship as an end in itself, or even as an end that serves the public signification of the love of God, we slip very easily into a privatization of love that contradicts the open, outward-looking and gracious character of covenant love. By this I mean that the covenant love of the Creator for his people is a love that has the world, the whole created order, as its proper object; in loving his people with a jealous love he has in mind that this people should be a light to the nations and that through them blessing should spread more and more widely. The moment we begin unquestioningly to treat marital intimacy as the primary goal of marriage, however, we contradict this outward-looking focus and the project becomes self-defeating.[12]

It is worth exploring more deeply and theologically why merely couple-focused marriage is self-defeating. The theological theme that suggests itself here is idolatry. When the relationship of the couple is considered as an end in itself it becomes an idol, and idols are empty nothings whose worshippers become like them (e.g. Ps. 135:15–19; cf. 1 Cor. 8:4). To make anything or anyone other than the Creator God the object and goal of a human project is to worship an idol and to place oneself on the path towards ever-increasing lightness and vacuity. It is dangerously possible for Christians to do this with regard to marriage while seeming to be pious. Rodney Clapp comments,

> With the private-public separation and the idealization of the home as a haven, I am afraid Christian families today often live for themselves. They think the church exists to serve them. They buy books that make spiritual disciplines important *because* they

---

11. Guroian also observes, 'Privacy becomes the clarion justification for abortion in our society. Intimacy values human presence and welcomes unknown others into a common world.'

12. See also Thielicke 1979:97 on the creative nature of the love of God as contrasted with the stifling nature of self-serving love. The former creates value in the beloved, the latter asks of the beloved his or her value 'for me'.

will strengthen the family, that tell them to go to church *because* going to church will make the family happier. But this gets it all backwards.
(Clapp 1993:162)

We end up making church, prayer and the Christian life a means to the idolatrous end of strengthening family.

It is also dangerously possible to speak of marriage as if it were a discipleship-free zone. We hear in other contexts the hard words of the Lord Jesus about the cost of discipleship and the vital need to give absolute primacy and loyalty to him, but somehow, when it comes to the supposedly private sphere of marriage and family, we do not really believe these challenges to be pertinent. One of the most helpful emphases in Richard Hays' treatment of divorce and remarriage (Hays 1996: ch. 15) is that marriage is to be understood as one aspect of discipleship for those who are called to the married state. So, when listening to Mark 10:2–12 for teaching about marriage, Hays rightly notes that it falls in the middle of a challenging section of Mark (8:31–10:45) about discipleship (Hays 1996:349). The disciple follows the Lord who found his 'food' in doing the will of him who sent him (John 4:34). If the married disciple begins to seek fulfilment and satisfaction in his or her married relationship, this is not walking in the footsteps of the master. The stringent demands and the inspiring vision of discipleship must not be removed from view within the theatre of the marriage relationship.

There is a real danger that popular church-based courses or literature about marriage will fall into this trap. When a practical book about marriage is subtitled 'Achieve a happy and more fulfilling relationship' (Lawson 1998; I do not know if this subtitle was the author's or the publisher's)[13] we ought to ask whether this is an appropriate motivational appeal. When a course is entitled 'Developing Closeness in marriage',[14] again we must ask whether this goal is really the best. I received publicity for a marriage course entitled 'You, Me and Us: The Relationship Course You Cannot Afford to Miss'. The leaflet claims, 'The course offers a blueprint for happiness with your partner.' The first of the four main themes is described as 'Love' in the words, 'Relationships begin when you fall in love. Relationships end when you no longer feel in love. So love is central, but it is rarely fully understood. The course will show how you can each give and receive the love you need. It will show you how to keep romance permanently alive.' The other themes are 'Communication',

---

13. Cf. the subtitle of John Gray's *Men are from Mars, Women are from Venus* (Gray 1993), which is *A practical guide to getting what you want in your relationships*.
14. Run by 'Rapport' on behalf of Care for the Family.

'Understanding Yourselves', and 'Handling your Conflicts'. Much in these books and courses is practical and wholesome, but it is too needs centred, too couple centred and too feelings centred; we ought rather to be asking how we may *serve God* in our marriages.

Supposedly Christian responses to marriage breakdown may have majored too much on trying to help people build and sustain relationships without giving them the outward-looking focus of serving God. In so doing we are buying unwittingly into the spirit of the age; we appear to accept much of the implicit relational primacy of our culture and just try to show our readers how to do it better than the world outside. Instead the whole paradigm needs to be challenged.

At the very simplest level, it does not take a Christian commentator to observe that our society is endlessly preoccupied with 'loving relationships', so much so that to watch many soap operas we might easily forget that anyone ever had work to do. (The same might perhaps also be said of a novel such as *Pride and Prejudice*.) In an intriguing column in *The Times* (26 February 1996) Matthew Parris laments the excess of 'love' on television and ends by waxing eloquent about work:

> Leave love with its slippers by the fire; put on your boots. Lift your gaze from your lover's eyes and see the sky behind, and all the stars! There are mountains and forests and rivers, whole wide oceans to cross. There are furrows to plough, rocks to shift, streams to dam. There is work, so much work – that happiest of pursuits – to be done.

The Christian may give qualified applause to this, qualified because in the vision of Genesis 1 and 2 it is both lover and beloved who together put on their boots to go into the garden to work.

Our need is not to turn *from* marriage *to* work, but rather to remember that marriage is instituted by the Creator in the context of meaningful work. In Ecclesiastes 1:12–2:26 the tragedy of the human condition is vividly portrayed in terms of meaninglessness. It is interesting to note that both sexual pleasure (2:8, the harem) and human achievement (e.g. 2:4, great projects) are rendered empty together in the absence of the Creator. When work becomes meaningless, sexual union also evaporates into transient pleasure. There is a deep link between meaningful work and meaningful sex.

The dislocation introduced by the fall

It is important at this point to anticipate an objection. Surely, says a Christian, we cannot simply draw a straight line from the Genesis creation mandate (to exercise stewardship over God's world) to today, as though we can understand marriage as if humankind had never rebelled against God. This is true. We must not forget the dislocation introduced by the fall. Indeed, biblical theology addresses this problem precisely in terms of the marriage relationship and of the procreation of children.

We cannot simply argue that marriage must serve the purpose of humankind ruling God's world. This would be theologically naïve. The fall of man has catastrophically altered the conditions under which the mandate given to Adam is to be obeyed. Adam abdicated and since he has passed on to his heirs his own flawed nature, they too abdicate and are unable to do what Adam was commanded to do.

The task of humankind is transformed into a new key after the fall. It must now be a work of rescue before it can be one of stewardship. Before, it would have answered the need for Adam, God's vicegerent, to have built up a people with Eve so that together they might rule God's world or keep God's garden. But when the rulers place themselves out of relationship with the Creator they are no longer fit to rule. Fallen human beings, excluded from the garden by flaming swords, must not seek to rule autonomously (which is what happens when the created order is thought of as 'nature' rather than 'creation', and which informs so much of the non-Christian 'green' movement). Before there can be stewards to rule God's world there must be surrenders of rebels who at present claim autonomy to rule that world for themselves. The creation mandate and the Great Commission are not alternatives; the former is deeply compromised without the latter.

What is needed is a work of grace, whereby one man – Abraham – is justified by grace through faith, and through him there comes fruitfulness and multiplication, not of all humankind (this happens too, but is not significant in the same way), but of the people of God. The creation mandate language of multiplication is now transferred in the Bible narrative to the people of God. Instead of a longing that there should be a multiplication simply of humanity, now there must be a multiplication within the people of God, in order that they may rule the nations and thus order God's world aright. It is in this redemptive context that the Old Testament procreational blessings are now placed.

This is why, from Genesis 12 onwards, the blessings of fruitfulness and multiplication focus not on humankind as a (fallen) whole, but on Israel as God's remedy for fallen humankind. Israel is called now to rule God's world as the community of those reconciled to the Creator by faith. This is her vocation. There need to be many who will respond in joy to their Creator and, because they live in right relationship with him, steward his world aright.

The creation mandate is fulfilled only in Jesus Christ. Indeed, it is only 'the

Second Adam' who fulfils the mandate given to the first and handed on to Israel, as the writer to the Hebrews implies when he comments on Psalm 8, 'As it is, we do not yet see everything subject to him,[15] but we do see Jesus . . . now crowned with glory and honour' (Heb. 2:8–9). Creation still groans and yearns for the day when 'the sons of God' will be revealed in all their glory to order and rule creation as the Creator intended (Rom. 8:19–21).

In the interim, therefore, the task to which God calls men and women focuses on the proclamation of the gospel. It is only by the gospel that men and women are called into the family of God and take upon themselves the dignity 'in Christ' of exercising responsible stewardship over creation. The task of kingdom proclamation is the necessary precursor to creation steward-ship. When we say that marriage must serve the creation mandate, this implies that the primary and urgent present task is the proclamation and heralding of the kingdom. The creation mandate must be read in the light of the Great Commission.

This is why Rodney Clapp (Clapp 1993: ch. 4) and Stanley Hauerwas (Hauerwas 1981)[16] are right to point to the missionary primacy and the social significance of the church as the proper focus of discipleship. The church is to be God's new society in which the proper relations between humankind and the created order are to be lived out.

It is very striking in the Bible how little there is explicitly about marriage and sex, and how much about God's purposes to rescue a lost world. Paul's brief mention in Romans 16:3–5 of Priscilla and Aquila illustrates this; the emphasis is neither on their intimacy, nor on their children (if any), but on the way they as a couple served the cause of the gospel. Our culture is obsessed with 'relationships'. Similarly, in Acts 9:36ff. we are not even told whether Dorcas was single, widowed or divorced; it is hard to imagine a contemporary drama or film omitting this 'essential' personal information. Instead we are told of her virtue and godly character.

We turn therefore to what I believe to be a health-giving ethics of marriage in the context of image and dominion. There is a garden to be tended, a world to be stewarded – and marriage is instituted with the purpose of contributing to that great task and vision of human responsible dominion over the created order. Marriage is *given* to enable humankind to exercise responsible dominion over God's world, a dominion only entered into in Christ. It is in this context

---

15. NRSV confusingly has 'in subjection to *them*'; the singular 'man/him' is important here.

16. See especially p. 186ff. Hauerwas criticizes the liberal ecclesiology which 'assumes that the church is a voluntary association which exists for the spiritual enrichment of the individuals comprising it' (188).

of task that we must consider the traditional 'goods' of marriage. We shall
relate each of the three 'goods' of marriage to this coherent ethical foundation. Before doing so, however, we consider a significant and sobering biblical
theme that plays in counterpoint to that of 'sex in the service of God'. This is
the link between sexual immorality and idolatry, or what we may call 'sex in the
place of God'.

8. SEX IN THE PLACE OF GOD

Perhaps the deepest manifestation of human sin is the replacement of the Creator by some created good. The more emphatically the created good bears the Creator's imprint, the greater the danger, and sex bears the hallmark of the Creator with great clarity. Although sex is created to be used in the service of God, it powerfully seeks promotion from servant to master. There is a deep and persistent biblical nexus between sexual immorality and idolatry. This is the negative counterpart to that which associates the service of God with marriage.

Sexual immorality is an expression of idolatry

Sexual immorality would not exist if it did not promise so much: pleasure, fulfilment, release, satisfaction, fruitfulness, life, escape from frustration. But what it promises it cannot perform; always in the end it disappoints and leads to emptiness. It has about it this fraudulent quality because it is idolatry. Only in the sexual faithfulness of one man to one woman, one woman to one man, is substantial love to be found; infidelity is inherently empty and disappointing.

An idol is a nothing, a vanity, an emptiness. This is a paradox: an idol has an existence (such that it must be opposed), and yet that existence is itself vacuous. It exists, and yet it is not really real (1 Cor. 8:4–6; 10:14–22). To combat sexual immorality, in ourselves and others, it is never sufficient to command or forbid, but if we can unmask the idolatrous (and therefore empty) nature of sexual immorality, we will undermine the foundations of its appeal. Only fools run after an 'oasis' when they know it to be a mirage.

The essence of idolatry is subjectivism. An idol is an object of worship that is no object, for it owes its existence to the subjective imagination of its worshipper, who is also its creator. I make an idol in my image to reflect my preferences and reinforce my choices. The moment I describe my choices as valid 'for me', and abandon any claim that values may be true for all, my ethics sinks from being theistic to being idolatrous. Any sexual ethics that owes its existence to my subjectivity (as ethics must, in a pluralist worldview) will be idolatrous. Only a transcendent Creator who has placed objective order in creation and revealed that order can rescue us from subjective ethics.

The Bible repeatedly associates sexual immorality with idolatry. This association is principled, not accidental. Idolatry is the fundamental human sin; sexual immorality is one of the persistent entailments of idolatry.[1] Humankind was made male and female that we might use our sexuality in the service of God; those who marry are to direct their marriages to the stewardship of God's created order. Sex ought to be an expression of the worship of God. Just as right sex is part of the worship of the true God, so wrong sex is allegiance to false gods.

When any part of the created order is sought for its own sake, divorced from the service of God, it becomes an idol. This is true of sex. It should not surprise us that the Bible associates sexual immorality with idolatry. This association gives an ontological basis for sexual ethics; the right use of sex is real, wrong uses are empty and insubstantial.

This chapter explores the sustained and profound biblical nexus of sexual immorality with idolatry. Idolatry is repeatedly described as spiritual adultery or sexual immorality (Ortlund 1996). At the least this means there is a likeness of moral structure between the turning away from God that is idolatry and the turning away from a covenant partner that is sexual immorality. Much Old Testament sexual immorality language is in this spiritual sense,[2] and this is carried over into the New Testament.[3]

---

1. Idolatry has other entailments, notably greed (e.g. Babylon in Rev. 18); cf. Wisdom 14:12ff.

2. It is not always certain whether or not there are physical rites of 'sacred' sex behind a text; references that have no explicit reference to such rites include Lev. 17:7; 20:4–6; Num. 15:37–40; Deut. 31:16; 32:20f.; 2 Chr. 21:13; Judg. 2:16f.; 8:27, 33; Is. 1:21; Jer. 23:13f.; 31:21f.; 49:4 (of Ammon); Lam. 1:2; Ezek. 6:9; 14:13; 43:7–9; Amos 5:2 (and other references to 'Virgin Israel'); Mic. 1:7; Nah. 3:4 (of Nineveh); Zech. 8:2 (and other references to the Lord's jealousy for his people).

3. Matt. 12:39; 16:4 ('a wicked and adulterous generation'); 2 Cor. 11:1–3 (the church presented as a pure virgin to Christ); Jas. 4:4; Rev. 14:8 and much of 17:1–19:8 (the adulteries of Babylon).

The connection is more than parallelism or simple likeness, however, for again and again we find that physical sexual immorality is practised in the context of idolatry. It is not just that the two are alike; the former is an endemic expression of the latter. In this chapter we study this theme of idolatry expressed in physical sexual immorality.

Some important texts

1 Corinthians 10:1–13

We begin with the 'typical' Old Testament episodes referred to by Paul in 1 Corinthians 10:1–13. These events in the history of Israel serve as examples (*tupoi*, v. 6) to warn us against idolatry. The wider context in 1 Corinthians (from chapter 8) is eating food sacrificed to idols (*eidōlothuta*, 8:1). This 'does not refer primarily to marketplace food, but to the eating of sacrificial food at the cultic meals in the pagan temples' (Fee 1987:359f.). The whole section 10:1–22 is strongly directed to the prohibition of idolatry. The events alluded to in verses 7–13 are bracketed by references to idolatry in verse 7 and verse 14 (the latter strongly linked to the preceding passage by 'therefore', *dioper*).

Paul selects four incidents from Israel's history: verse 7, the golden calf (Exod. 32); verse 8, the event at Baal-Peor (Num. 25:1ff.); verse 9, the complaining against God that led to attack by snakes (Num. 21:4–9); and verse 10, grumbling in the wilderness (Num. 14:1–38 or possibly Num. 16:41). In each case disobedience led to disaster. It is not simple disobedience, however, it is disobedience driven by inordinate *desire* (typically for sex or food): verse 6, 'These things occurred as examples for us, so that we might not *desire evil* [*epithumētas kakōn*][4] as they did' (my italics). Inordinate desire, or lust (*epithumia*), is so closely woven into idolatry that one scholar even considers it to be the theme here rather than idolatry (Perrot, in Fee 1987:453, n.13). Lust and idolatry are distinct but inseparable. A yearning becomes a lust when it is not subordinated to the purpose for which it was given by God. When the satisfaction of the desire becomes a goal in its own right, it becomes an idol. Collins comments that the word group *epithum-* 'suggests a strong desire *to satisfy a felt need*, often in excessive fashion' (Collins 1999:370, my italics).[5]

In three of Paul's examples the appetite for food seems to be present, and

---

4. The only New Testament use of the noun *epithumētēs*. Also used in LXX Num. 11:34 of the people craving other food.

5. Collins suggests a strong connection between this passage in 1 Cor. 10 and the 'craving' (*epithumia*) motif in Num. 11, in the tradition of Pss. 78 and 106.

in two sexual immorality. Both the episode of the golden calf (v. 7) and the events at Peor (v. 8) are associated with food or feasts; the testing of God in Numbers 21:4–9 related to the desire for better food to replace 'this miserable food' (i.e. manna). Indeed, whenever the New Testament mentions 'idol food' (*eidōlothuta*) it associates idolatry with sexual immorality (Acts 15:29; Rev. 2:14, 20). It is interesting how craving for food seems to be associated with sexual immorality. Perhaps there is a suggestion that sexual desire has been reduced to merely a bodily appetite. To 'lustfully desire' or 'crave' means to set the heart on something, in a way that contradicts receiving with thanksgiving. This is the difference between enjoying a created good as it was meant to be enjoyed and worshipping an idol.

The strong craving inherent in idolatry is sometimes expressed in sexual immorality, which has always been associated with idolatry. This association is also suggested by the 'jealousy' to which the Lord is provoked by idolatry (v. 22), since jealousy is often associated with the image of the Lord's marriage to his people.

In the old Corinth (destroyed by the Romans in 146 BC) the Temple of Aphrodite had been 'so rich that it owned more than a thousand temple-slaves (hierodules), courtesans (hetairai), whom both men and women had dedicated to the goddess' (Strabo, *Geography* 8.6.20). Sexual immorality had in that age been an expression of idolatry. It is likely that the same connection persisted in the Graeco-Roman world of New Testament times. Libertine sex associated with pagan feasts was probably common. In cities like Corinth, 'There were peripatetic brothel keepers who supplied prostitutes for grand occasions and it may have been that they provided services at dinners on such great festive gatherings as the (Isthmian) Games. The concern, then, about immorality at feasts on the part of Paul was not unfounded' (Winter 1994:173f.; cf. Rosner 1998).

It seems likely that in Corinth religious idolatry went hand in hand with physical sexual immorality. In his first two Old Testament 'types' Paul suggests that this association stands in a long and unworthy tradition.

Exodus 32:6

'Do not become idolaters as some of them did; as it is written, "The people sat down to eat and drink, and they rose up to play [*paizein*]"' (1 Cor. 10:7). As his first example of idolatry, Paul looks back to the episode of the golden calf, and quotes from Exodus 32:6b (LXX). The eating and drinking are in connection with sacrifices to the golden calf. 'To play' (*paizein*, LXX) translates the Hebrew verb *ṣāḥaq* (NRSV 'to revel'). This revelry is associated with shouting (v. 17), dancing (v. 19) and 'running wild' (v. 25). Both Hebrew *ṣāḥaq* and Greek *paizein* may have sexual connotations here. The word *ṣāḥaq* occurs thirteen times in the Old Testament. Apart from Exodus 32:6, it is used six times of Abraham's and Sarah's laughter in connection with the birth of Isaac (Gen. 17:17; 18:12f.,15; 21:6), of Lot seeming to his family to jest (Gen. 19:14), of Ishmael playing with Isaac (Gen. 21:9), and of Samson performing for the Philistines (Judg. 16:25). In none of these is there any sexual connotation. But it is also used in Genesis 26:8 of Isaac 'fondling' or playing sexually with Rebekah in such a way that Abimelech concludes she must be his wife. And it is used twice by Potiphar's wife in her protestations about the (supposed) improper advances of Joseph (Gen. 39:14, 17).[6] Although the verb *paizein* is more common in the LXX than *ṣāḥaq* in the Hebrew text,[7] it overlaps with the use of *ṣāḥaq* on only five occasions other than Exodus 32:6 (Gen. 21:9; 26:8; 39:14, 17; Judg. 16:25), three of which are sexual. Partly for this reason, there is a long tradition in both Jewish and Christian exegesis of understanding the golden calf event as having a dimension of disorderly sexual misconduct.[8] While sexual delight properly has a dimension of playfulness, the presence of delight and playfulness do not render such intercourse moral.[9]

Numbers 22 – 25

'We must not indulge in sexual immorality as some of them did, and twenty-three thousand[10] fell in a single day' (1 Cor. 10:8). The association of idolatry with sexual immorality is most clearly present in Paul's next example, the

---

6. Although NRSV translates 'insult' in this context of (supposed) unwelcome advances.

7. *Paizein* is used to translate other Hebrew words; only a minority of its uses translate *ṣāḥaq*.

8. E.g. In the t. Sotah 6.6 Rabbi Eliezer says, '*Playing* stated here refers only to fornication, as it is said, *The Hebrew servant whom you have brought among us came in to me to play with me*'; Tertullian, *Fasting*:105 argues that 'nothing is so proximately supersequent (sc. to eating) as the savouring of lasciviousness' and further that the word 'play', 'unless it had been immodest . . . would not have been reprehended'; recently Fee 1987, ad loc. suggests that the word 'almost certainly carries overtones of sexual play'; and Durham 1987:422 says that although the primary meaning of *ṣāḥaq* is 'to laugh, make fun', in this context it 'has a connotation also of sexual play'; also Cassuto 1967:414, '*and the people sat down to eat and drink, and rose up to play,* in accordance with the custom obtaining at the feasts of the peoples addicted to the worship of the gods of fertility and the inchastity connected therewith'; also Rosner 1999:24, 'The verb "to play" in Hebrew is clearly a euphemism for sexual activities.'

9. Against Thatcher 1993:38f., who seems to elevate sexual playfulness almost to an ethical value in its own right.

10. No satisfactory explanation has yet been given for Paul's 'twenty-three thousand' where Numbers 25:9 has twenty-four thousand.

event at Peor. On the verge of the Promised Land, there took place an event which seared itself into the memory of Israel. This was the sexual immorality of the Israelite men with the women of Moab, recounted in Numbers 25. George Steiner has said that civilization is 'the cultivation of trained, shared remembrance' (Lycett 1999:4). In Israel that remembrance was a foundation for her communal life. Again and again Israel is recalled to a shared remembrance of events in her salvation history. Seminal events in her history shed light on the ethics of the present.

This anamnesis included painful events of apostasy. If redemption could be understood only by retelling the exodus, sin could be avoided only by remembering Israel's faithlessness. As with redemption, so with apostasy, some of those events took on a paradigmatic significance; they could not be laid to rest, but had to be re-remembered. The event at Peor is one such. It seems to have fixed itself in Israel's corporate memory and become for her almost a defining event for the sinful nexus of idolatry and sexual immorality. 'There can be no doubt that the episode became a *paradigmatic example in perpetuity*' (Mendenhall 1973:106, my italics). In this tradition Paul recalls the same event.

Israel is near the end of her wilderness wanderings, on the borders of the Promised Land. Balak, king of Moab, is frightened of the hordes of Israel and he allies himself with the Midianites. They seek to persuade the 'magic man' Balaam to curse Israel; instead Balaam blesses Israel repeatedly and goes home. Then the men of Israel engage in sexual immorality with Moabite women and join in their idolatrous worship,[11] resulting in a plague of judgment.

The events narrated in Numbers 22 – 25 are referred to within the Bible in Numbers 31:1–18; Deuteronomy 4:3f.; 23:3–6; Joshua 22:17; Nehemiah 13:2; Psalm 106:28–31; Micah 6:5; Hosea 9:10–13; 1 Corinthians 10:8; 2 Peter 2:13–16; Jude 11 and Revelation 2:14. They also form a significant motif within the rabbinic traditions (Vermes 1961:127–177; Green 1992:148–154).

In Moses' sermon in Deuteronomy 4, with its appeal for wholehearted love for the Lord, of all the episodes of backsliding he could have chosen for illustration, he chooses Peor (v. 3f.); even in the context of remembering Horeb/Sinai he chooses Peor above the golden calf. In Joshua 22:17 the ten cis-Jordan tribes appeal to the trans-Jordan tribes not to apostasize. Of all the events in Israel's history they choose to appeal to Peor as the seminal event of apostasy, whose consequences are with them still.[12] In Hosea 9:10 Peor is used

---

11. In Num. 25:2 LXX translates the Hebrew *ʾelōhêhen* (their gods) by *tōn eidōlōn autou* (their idols) to make this clear.

12. Mendenhall 1973:106f. links this with continuing bubonic plague, but this is hypothetical.

as the defining event of Israel's first apostasy. These citations give to the events at Peor a striking prominence.

Other facets of the event, notably the avarice and malice of Balaam and the malice of Israel's enemies, are highlighted in some scriptures (e.g. Num. 31:1–18; Deut. 23:3–6; Neh. 13:2; Mic. 6:5; 2 Pet. 2:13–16; Jude 11), but the theme that concerns us is the association of idolatry and sexual immorality. At Peor for the first time, it seems, the people came face to face with the nature religion of Canaan. The effect is disastrous. In Numbers 22 – 24 we have read 'essentially a celebration of the powerlessness of enemies to hinder Israel . . . In summary the story is a powerful celebration of the certainty of Israel's success. Her triumphant progress to the land of promise cannot be halted or even hindered by the stratagems of adversaries' (Budd 1984:271, 273). And yet now, quite suddenly and unexpectedly, where powerful foes, enemy money and strong magic cannot avail, seduction does. In Balaam's first blessing we read of Israel as 'a people living alone, and not reckoning itself among the nations' (Num. 23:9); they are large in number (23:10) and free from misfortune (23:21). Before chapter 25 is finished, 24,000 are dead.

Sexual immorality has become a gateway to idolatry. Where attack from outside has failed, sexual seduction succeeds. The seduction was at the same time sexual and religious. Some critics play down the element of physical sexual immorality and regard the sin as consisting primarily or exclusively in the idolatry. On this reading, the problem with the sexual liaisons was not that they were intrinsically immoral, but that they happened to be with non-Israelite women who did not worship Yahweh. Such an account is not persuasive.

The liaisons of Numbers 25:1 do not seem to have been intermarriages. The women did not stay with their Israelite men; at the conclusion of the Midianite war (Num. 31:13ff.) they are back with the Midianites, not with Israel. Even without the strong reaction of Moses it is doubtful they had intended staying with the men in marriage. Nor, I suggest, was Zimri bringing the Midianite maiden Cozbi into his tent (Num. 25:6–8, 14f.) to marry her (*pace* Budd 1984:281, who assumes that, 'a marriage appears to have been arranged'). What Zimri did is presented as a particularly blatant example of what was recounted more generally in 25:1. These were passing unions. The use of the verb *zānâ* in verse 1 is appropriate precisely because of the transient nature of the unions. Even had the women been pure-blooded Israelites, such practices would have been immoral. This is sex detached from public committed relationship in the service of God.

To what purpose, then, were these unions entered? And how were they connected with the idol feasts of 25:2? Mendenhall (1973:115) suggests that a bubonic plague had broken out; some had died while still virgins and this was a disaster until their unfulfilled spirits could be put to rest, and they could only

be put to rest if they could experience sex vicariously through the ritual intercourse of the survivors with foreigners. This is a speculative reconstruction. It
is simpler to assume (in line with fertility rituals more widely) that the aim of
the unions was the promotion of fertility, as part of the worship of the idols.

Whether the object of the liaisons was the prevention of plague or the promotion of fertility, what the Moabite women offered was a kind of twisted pro-
life religion. So, it is suggested, the Israelite men may have been well meaning
but happened to be misguided. We are to be sympathetic with Zimri who, faced
with the choice between Yahwistic separatism and the traditional Moabite
methods, thought he would try the latter. The poor Israelite men had to steel
themselves to the unpleasant but necessary task of this ritual intercourse. Such
a cool analysis is curiously detached from the earthy realities of male sexual
arousal. This was not a question of one dispassionate religious practice
(Yahwism) against another dispassionate religious practice (ritual intercourse
with Moabite maidens).

Critical attention has focused on the translation of 25:8. The interpretation
of this verse is important in discerning whether the focus of the passage is
purely cultic (worshipping a god or gods other than Yahweh) or also moral
(sexual immorality). Two phrases need to be considered: Phinehas 'went after
the Israelite man into the tent (*'el-haqqubbâ*) and pierced the two of them, the
Israelite and the woman, through the belly (*'el-q°bâṭāh*)'. In most English translations the noun *qubbâ* is translated 'tent' and the noun *qēbâ* as 'woman's body',
'belly' (NRSV), womb or even genitals (Reif 1971:202, n.14). Reif has argued that
the word *qubbâ* does not signify just an ordinary tent but rather a cultic tent
shrine; and that the crime of Zimri was not that he had (necessarily) had sexual
relations with the woman, but rather that he had installed her in a Midianite tent
shrine next to his own tent. Reif's suggestion has not been found persuasive.
The sexual interpretation accords with the most natural reading of *zānâ* in verse
1; verse 6 records a particularly blatant example of what had been happening
more generally in verse 1. It also accords with widespread archaeological evidence of sexually exaggerated figurines associated with popular Ancient Near
East religions. And, while the text is not explicit, the supposition that Zimri and
Cozbi were *in flagrante delicto* may well be supported by the description of what
seems to have been a single spearing.[13]

What happened at Peor had a strong religious dimension. This is clear in

---

13. This is the interpretation of Philo, *Vit.Mos.*1.302 (who calls the woman a *hetaira*). Note
    also with grotesque explicitness, b.Sanhedrin 82b, '[Phinehas] succeeded in driving his
    spear exactly through the sexual organs of the man and the woman' (ET London:
    Soncino Press, 1969).

verse 2 (the Moabite women 'invited the people to the sacrifices of their gods, and the people ate and bowed down to their gods'). But it is equally clear that the sexual immorality was physical, actual and flagrant, and that it featured large both in the event and in its subsequent memory. It stands in biblical memory as a signpost to the intrinsic association of physical sexual immorality with idolatry.

The sexual dimension of the event at Peor is suggested in Psalm 106:28–31 by the language of attachment or yoking ('they attached themselves', v. 28, as used in Num. 25:3). The verb 'to attach' (*sāmad*) almost certainly 'has sexual connotations'; indeed, 'Roots with the normal meaning "to yoke together" have sexual meanings in virtually all the Semitic and Mediterranean languages' (Mendenhall 1973:111). It is significant that the attachment, while physically with the Moabite women, is described spiritually here as being with 'the Baal of Peor', so closely are sexual immorality and idolatry linked.

The sexual dimension is less prominent in Hosea 9:10–13, where the verb 'consecrated' (*nāzar*) emphasizes the religious dimension of the union with the Baal of Peor. But even here the staccato judgment of verse 11 ('no birth, no pregnancy, no conception!') probably connects this with the fertility rites of the nature religions.

In Revelation 2:14 the risen Jesus says to the church in Pergamum, 'But I have a few things against you: you have some there who hold to the teaching of Balaam, who taught[14] Balak to put a stumbling block before the people of Israel, so that they would eat food sacrificed to idols and practice fornication.' The same association of eating idol meat and sexual immorality is found in Revelation 2:20 in the letter to Thyatira,[15] and both echo the apostolic letter of Acts 15. Again and again, though sexual immorality and idolatry are distinct, they are closely connected. Although many uses of sexual immorality (*porneia*) in Revelation are metaphorical (notably those concerning 'Babylon'), it is more likely that 2:14, 20 are literal (cf. the close association of literal sexual immorality with idolatry in Rev. 9:20f.). That this connection should appear yet again, more than a millennium after the event at Peor, suggests a deep and intrinsic connection between the two.

The incident at Peor is effectively the worship of sex, a religion of sexual

---

14. The reader of Num. 22 – 24 is puzzled that this advice is not recorded until it is remembered in Num. 31:16. Rabbinic tradition plausibly assumes it followed his warning to Balak of 'what this people will do to your people in days to come' (Num. 24:14). So the warning was followed by, 'You will not overcome them by force. But there might be a chance if you try seduction.' See Vermes 1961:170.

15. See Hemer 1986:117–123 for background on 'Jezebel'.

pleasure in response to sexual desire. The essential nature of this sex is self-satisfaction. It is the exact reverse of sex and marriage for the sake of serving God in his world. Indeed, it is sex as self-gratification in contrast to sex for service; the whole episode functions as a diversion from the task in hand, which was to take the land for God. Part of the wonder of sex in marriage is that it turns a pleasure outwards towards the service of God in his world.

It seems that this licentious religious sex continued to plague the purity of Yahwistic religion in Israel for centuries to come, at least up to the time of the Babylonian exile. We find references and allusions to it throughout the law and the pre-exilic prophets (and also Ezekiel). In his commentary on one passage that uses language of whoredom about Israel's infidelity to the Lord (Jer. 3), McKane observes,

> The sexual imagery seems to be more than a metaphor for idolatry and to have a special appropriateness to the nature of Israel's unfaithfulness. Her involvement in sexual rites associated with the Canaanite cult lends such a particular appositeness to the sexual imagery that it is more than a metaphor for idolatry which could be replaced without loss by another metaphor not involving sexual imagery.
> (McKane 1986, vol. I:63)

Some of the prophetic texts draw our attention to the fact that spiritual infidelity to the Lord was tied up with physical sexual immorality. To illustrate this we may consider Jeremiah 5:7–8.

Jeremiah 5:7–8

'How can I pardon you? Your children have forsaken me, and have sworn by those who are no gods. When I fed them to the full, they committed adultery and trooped to the houses of prostitutes. They were well-fed lusty stallions, each neighing for his neighbour's wife.' Forsaking the Lord (i.e. spiritual adultery, v. 7a) is expressed in committing adultery (v. 7b). This adultery or sexual immorality seems here to be not just spiritual but also physical. This seems to be indicated by the clause 'trooped to the houses of prostitutes [*bêṭ zônâh*]'.[16] There is a tension here 'between images for literal sexual misconduct and images for the religious orientation of the people' (Holladay 1986:180). Although the primary prophetic burden is to condemn the religious sin of idolatry, physical sexual immorality was a visible expression of this apostasy.

The words translated 'well-fed lusty' are uncertain. Carroll suggests that it

---

16. The nearest parallel to this phrase elsewhere in the Old Testament is Josh. 6:22 (*bêṭ hā'iššâ hazzônâ*).

may mean 'well hung', that these are stallions with large genitalia (Carroll 1986:178). Whatever the precise allusion, Carroll helpfully observes that we have here 'disparagement of *male* activity in the community' (my italics).

> Contrary to modern feminist rhetoric, biblical condemnation of sexual activity, whether real or metaphorical, is a balanced matter of condemning male as well as female behaviour (epitomised in Hosea 4:14). If feminine images of sexuality appear to be more numerous, that is because it is masculine behaviour which is being condemned: 'whoring after . . .' is a male activity. The figure of 'well-hung stallions' denigrates males, not females.
> (Carroll 1986:180)

It is clear that what Israel did 'on every high hill and under every green tree'[17] was not 'just' to follow a religion that happened not to be Yahwism; it was a religion that involved, as an integral part of worship, actual physical sexual immorality. Such religion is the background to much of the Old Testament. Intrinsic to it is the understanding that sex is a part of deity – that is to say, in the pantheon there are both male gods (usually the baals) and female goddesses. We consider some of these below.

Goddesses and prostitutes

Asherah

(See Reed 1962:250; Day 2000). There are about forty references in the Old Testament to Asherah (*'ašērâ*) or 'an Asherah'. In the law (Exod. 34:13; Deut. 7:5; 12:3) the Israelites are told to tear down the Asherim when they enter the Promised Land. The worship of Asherah, or the presence or absence of an Asherah, or of Asherim is referred to in general in Judges 3:7; in connection with Gideon's family in Judges 6:25–30; in 1 Kings 14:15, 23; 15:13; 16:32f.; 18:19 (the 400 prophets of Asherah who ate at Jezebel's table); in 2 Kings 13:6 (the Asherah remained in Samaria); 17:10, 16 (the condemnation of the northern kingdom Israel including their Asherim); 18:4 (Hezekiah's reforms included the destruction of the Asherahs); 21:3, 7 (Manasseh reinstating one and putting it in the Lord's temple); 23:4–15 (Josiah's reforms); in Isaiah 17:8; 27:9; Jeremiah 17:2; Micah 5:13 and frequently in 2 Chronicles.

---

17. Jer. 3:6 and often elsewhere. Note also Is. 57:3–10 and the allusion to the trees in Is. 1:29. Also Jer. 13:26f. ('your shameless prostitutions on the hills of the countryside') and Ezek. 6:13; 20:27–31.

Like Astarte (see below), Asherah is known from ancient Ugaritic texts, although the precise association seems to vary from place to place and from age to age. She is distinct from Astarte and figures prominently in the Ras Shamra[18] texts as the mother-goddess, the consort of the supreme god El, and the mother of seventy gods including Baal. In the Old Testament texts there is a very close association between Asherah (the goddess) and 'an Asherah' (the symbolic representation of the goddess). The latter (NRSV 'sacred pole') seems to have been some kind of wooden representation of the goddess. Although Deuteronomy 16:21 prohibits the Israelites from planting 'a tree as an Asherah', it seems from the use of the verbs 'to make' (e.g. 1 Kgs. 14:15), 'to build' (e.g. 1 Kgs. 14:23) and to 'erect' (e.g. 2 Kgs. 17:10) that this was not a living tree but some kind of stylized wooden pole (Olyan 1988:1). That it was wooden is also suggested by the reference of the chronicler to an Asherah being burned (1 Kgs. 15:13; 2 Chr. 15:16; 2 Kgs. 23:6). It is called a *pesel* (image) in 2 Kings 21:7. Reed observes, 'No object has been found thus far in any excavation which could be called with certainty an Asherah . . . [but] . . . Since the Old Testament shows it to have been constructed of wood, this is not surprising' (Reed 1962:251).

The association of Asherah with fertility rites is strong in extrabiblical sources and supported by the connection with the high places and sacred trees (e.g. Jer. 17:2; 1 Kgs. 14:23; 2 Kgs. 17:10). Furthermore, in Josiah's reforms we read that 'he broke down the houses of the male temple prostitutes that were in the house of the LORD, where the women did weaving for Asherah', strongly suggesting sexual activity associated with her cult.

Usually 'an Asherah' seems to have been erected alongside an altar to Baal (e.g. Judg. 6:25–30; 1 Kgs. 16:32f.; 2 Kgs. 21:3; Is. 17:8), suggesting that Asherah functioned in popular religion as the consort of Baal (despite being his mother in the Ras Shamra texts). The boundaries between fertility and eroticism do not seem to have been clear. In his thorough study of the extra-biblical evidence Maier concludes that Asherah functioned both as a goddess of fertility and of eroticism (Maier 1986:193f.).

There was, however, a constant danger not only that the Israelites would be drawn to the cultic sexual worship of the Baals and Asherahs, but that they would place an Asherah beside the altar of the Lord, presumably regarding her as the Lord's consort. This association of the Lord's altar with Asherah is specifically prohibited in Deuteronomy 16:21. In 2 Kings 21:7 we read that Manasseh put an image of Asherah in the temple, although since he

---

18. Barton 1934 translates the relevant section of the Ras Shamra texts describing the intercourse of the female cult prostitutes.

also introduced two altars to the host of heaven it is not clear whether this Asherah was beside the altar of the Lord. Olyan suggests that in popular piety Asherah may well have been accepted as Yahweh's consort (Olyan 1988). There is some extrabiblical evidence to support this. One inscription seems to say, 'I bless you by Yahweh of Samaria and his Asherah'; another reads, 'May Uryahu be blessed by Yahweh my guardian and by his Asherah' (Maier 1986: ch. 2; cf. Block 1997:281). The evidence for this is scarce, but it is entirely plausible that, once sexual activity had been popularly accepted in connection with religion, it should be introduced into a debased syncretistic Yahwism.

Astarte

There are nine references in the Old Testament to the goddess Astarte (Hebrew *'aštōret*, plural *'aštārôt*; written in the Greek translations as *Astartē*, plural *Astarōth*). There are general plural references to worship of 'Baal (or the Baals) and the Astartes' in Judges 2:13; 10:6; 1 Samuel 12:10; also in 1 Samuel 7:3f., where she is also bracketed with a general reference to 'the foreign gods'. In 1 Samuel 31:10 the Philistines put Saul's armour in 'the temple of the Astartes'.

By the time of Solomon she seems to have been spoken of in the singular, at least in 1 Kings 11:5, 33, where she is called 'the goddess of the Sidonians' and is one of the foreign deities followed by Solomon. Her worship seems to have continued at least up to the reforms of Josiah, who defiled the high places Solomon had made for her (2 Kgs. 23:13).

The precise nature of Astarte (or the Astartes) is lost in the mists of history. By the time the Greek translations (loosely called the 'Septuagint') were being made, she seems not always to have been clearly distinguished. In 2 Chronicles 15:16, for example, the LXX translates Astarte where the MT has Asherah. And in 1 Samuel 12:10 the LXX translates the Hebrew Astarte by *alsos* (probably a glade or grove, the usual LXX translation of Asherah).

John Gray suggests that Hebrew scribes took the Canaanite fertility goddess *athtarath* (known from the Ras Shamra texts) and deliberately misvocalized the last two syllables with the vowels of *bōšet* (shame), to get *athtoreth* and hence *ashtoreth*, and used it to refer to 'various local manifestations of the fertility-goddess' (Gray 1962:255). In 1 Kings 11:5, 33 and 2 Kings 23:13 connection is made with Milcom, the god of Ammon (cf. Molech) and in the latter with Chemosh, the god of Moab. Both Milcom and Chemosh were probably local forms of the one astral deity, the Venus Star, Athtar. It may therefore be that Ashtoreth had also been an astral deity, the female counterpart of Athtar. Gray notes that her Babylonian counterpart Ishtar retained her character as an astral deity, while being at the same time the goddess of love and fertility.

Gray observes, 'Generally related to the fertility cult in Palestine are figurines usually molded of clay representing nude females with breasts and
pudenda emphasised' (Gray 1962:256).[19] Sometimes these seemed to be associated with Asherah and sometimes with Astarte. Great numbers of these
have been found, suggesting their use in popular piety in the home rather than
exclusively in temples.[20] Maier argues that the evidence suggests 'a goddess of
... the erotic, sexual vigor, love, grace and beauty, and fertility' (Maier 1986:85,
and cf. 81–96).

The queen of heaven

In Jeremiah 7:17f.; 44:15–25 there is reference to worship of 'the queen of
heaven' ($m^e leket$ $ha\check{s}\check{s}\bar{a}mayim$). The context strongly suggests that this worship
was associated with fertility; the women claim that when they worshipped her
they 'used to have plenty of food, and prospered, and saw no misfortune'
(44:17). While 'the precise identity of the queen in this context cannot be
determined' (Craigie 1991:123), and many suggestions have been made, the
most plausible is that she is linked to Astarte or her Babylonian equivalent
Ishtar, who is called in Babylonian literature by this title (Bright 1965:56;
Holladay 1986:255). Gray suggests that the most likely identification is with
'Ishtar, the goddess of love and fertility, who was identified with the Venus
Star and is entitled "Mistress of Heaven" in the Amarna tablets' (Gray
1962:975). D. R. Jones suggests that the worship of Ishtar was introduced into
Judah during the reign of Manasseh and enjoyed a resurgence after the death
of Josiah. He notes, 'After the first attack on Jerusalem in 597, the related cult
of Tammuz, brother-consort of Ishtar, is to be found practised, again by the
women, in the heart of the Temple precincts (see Ezekiel 8:14f.).' He goes on,
'No doubt, whatever the precise Babylonian or Canaanite origin of this cult,
the queen of heaven was understood as the consort of Yahweh.' The setting
of Jeremiah 44 is Egypt and Jones asks, 'Can there be a connection between
these Jews and the later military colony at Elephantine, who worshipped
Yahweh's consort Anath, and referred to her without batting an eyelid?'
(Jones 1992:151f., 481).

---

19. Cf. Holladay 1986:255, 'A great number of clay figurines of a nude goddess have been
    excavated from Israelite sites, and it is clear that practices associated with a fertility
    goddess were widespread in this period.' For examples from archaeology see Pritchard
    1954:162, fig. 469; Wright 1962:118.
20. Wright 1962:118 comments on the lack of male gods in Israelite homes but the 'large
    numbers of figurines representing the mother-goddess ... found in every excavation
    into Israelite houses'.

The identification with Ishtar is supported by Laetsch, who comments, 'The cult of the Queen of Heaven, or the Mother Goddess, was an ancient custom extending throughout the Orient in various forms and under various names, but of the same nature. We meet with it throughout the centuries of antiquity.' He quotes Kittel: 'Her primary, although not exclusive, province was physical fertility in man and beast . . . She was the goddess of sensuous love and the patroness of the generative and growing life' (Laetsch 1952:98f.).

As Carroll observes, this phenomenon of the goddess of fertility and eroticism may appear under 'different names', but these names 'tend to describe the one goddess, whatever her particular cultural manifestation' (Carroll 1986:213).

Ezekiel 8 and Tammuz

On the face of it Ezekiel 8 has nothing to do with sexual immorality, but on closer inspection it turns out that, yet again, it is not far beneath the surface. After Ezekiel's vision of the glory of the God of Israel (vv. 1–4) the first thing he sees is the 'image of jealousy' (v. 5), which has the sense of an image which provokes God to jealousy. The word used for 'image' here (*semel*) is rare in the Old Testament. Apart from Ezekiel 8:3, 5 it appears only in 2 Chronicles 33:7, 15 and Deuteronomy 4:16. In 2 Chronicles 33:7, 15 Manasseh's abominable image is called a *pesel hassemel*. In 2 Kings 21:7 this same image is referred to as a *pesel hā'ašērâ*. This parallel suggests that the *semel* may be a sculptured form of Asherah with all her associations of religious sex. What Ezekiel sees is reminiscent of the events of Manasseh's reign. Although Josiah's reform removed Manasseh's Asherah/Pesel (2 Kgs. 23:6), either Ezekiel considers that in private and in the heart of Judah such idolatry is continuing, or it ceased and since has been replaced.

If this image is indeed some kind of Asherah, it explains the strong emphasis in verse 3 on the jealousy this provokes in the Lord. Jealousy is God's consistent response to human idolatry, since the Lord desires and deserves the single-hearted love of his people. And in their sexual behaviour the single loyalty of one man for one woman and one woman for one man is to image this single love of the Creator for human beings and human beings towards him. Idolatry provokes God and makes him jealous and zealous for his name. This is the context of the chapter (and of much of Ezekiel, see Block 1997:13f.). It picks up a significant biblical theme, epitomized in Exodus 34:14 ('for you shall worship no other god, because the LORD, whose name is Jealous, is a jealous God').

It is worth noting here the extraordinary psychological readings of Ezekiel's sexual imagery by David J. Halperin (Halperin 1993), who regards this theme as an indication of Ezekiel's own sexual inadequacy. According to

Halperin, Ezekiel's description of divine anger and jealousy is an expression of his own sexual frustration and desire to conquer through the sex act. This is, as Block points out, completely to misunderstand the word *qin'â* (jealousy). Halperin writes, 'In common parlance jealousy tends to be associated either with envy and covetousness, the desire to own what someone else possesses, or exaggerated possessiveness over what one already owns, that is, an unwillingness to share it with others. In psychiatric terms, jealousy amounts to "vindictiveness born of sexual frustration"' (Halperin 1993:121). But the 'jealous' love of God described by Ezekiel 'is fueled not by an exploitative need to dominate but by ardor for the well-being of the object. In the OT *qin'â* is aroused when a legitimate and wholesome relationship is threatened by interference from a third party. Thus the word expresses an entirely appropriate response by a husband or wife when another "lover" enters the picture' (Block 1997, ad loc.).

In our reflection on sexual immorality and idolatry we may connect this important theme of jealousy with the new covenant promise of the 'undivided heart' (NIV) in Ezekiel 11:18–21. A man's or woman's heart that knows undivided loyalty to his or her spouse is an image of the undivided heart the Creator has in his love for those who are his bride and for his redeemed people's undivided love for him.

In Ezekiel 8:14–15 we meet women 'weeping for [the] Tammuz' (*m^{e}bakkôt 'et-hattammûz*). The background seems to be Dumu-zi (literally 'proper son'), the Sumerian name for Tammuz, a young virile male deity whose traditions go back to the fourth millennium BC. In the legends he becomes the husband of Inanna (the Sumerian name for Ishtar) and is *par excellence* through his procreative powers the giver of fertility (Block 1997:295 n.64, 65; Jacobsen 1976:39). The legends also include the laments of the women in his life when he dies.

Sir James Frazer popularized the view that Tammuz (like Adonis, Attis or Osiris) was a dying and rising fertility god whose death and resurrection corresponded to the yearly cycles of winter and spring (Gurney 1962:147). There is, however, no sure evidence of Tammuz rising again (Yamauchi 1965). T. H. Gaster connects the Tammuz rituals with a 'sacred marriage' ritual in the Ras Shamra texts, in which a priest and priestess have intercourse to represent the intercourse of the god and goddess (Gaster 1941). Whatever the details (and they are lost to us), it may be that the women 'weeping for Tammuz' are playing out in liturgical drama something of these legendary events.[21] The combined evidence we have considered for 'the image of jealousy' (vv. 3, 5)

---

21. Brooks 1941:240 suggests that the 'women sitting' were the living Astartes, sexual cult functionaries. Zimmerli 1979, ad loc., thinks this is 'very doubtful'.

and Tammuz (v. 14) suggests a background of religion in which sacral sex played a part.

Cultic prostitutes

In a helpful review article Beatrice Brooks surveyed what she called 'Fertility Cult Functionaries in the Old Testament' (Brooks 1941; cf. Ringgren 1973:25–30, 163–165). Writing in 1941, she comments,

> During the past decade much of the OT has been interpreted in terms of the fertility cult. Excavation of thousands of nude, plump female figurines from sites scattered widely over the Near East, as well as the translation of hundreds of liturgical texts and legal codes indicate that the Isis-Osiris, Ininni-Dumuzi, Ishtar-Tammuz, Astarte-Adonis cults had essentially common elements which went far back into the hoary past of Hamito-Semitic culture.
> (Brooks 1941:227)

The kinds of people who were involved (in an official capacity, as opposed to the participating 'worshippers') are usually described in the Old Testament as the qāḏēš (male) and qᵉḏēšâ (female) cult prostitutes (e.g. Deut. 23:18). Brooks also suggests that the women ministering at the entrance of the Tent of Meeting (Exod. 38:8) sometimes (though not in orthodox Yahwism) functioned in this way; it seems the sons of Eli treated them as such (1 Sam. 2:22).

> A characteristic of fertility cult ideology has been the belief that the propagation of human life, under certain conditions supposed to be controlled by the gods, will bring greater productivity of fields and flocks and hence prosperity to the social group. This idea, translated into action by sympathetic magic, is at least one of the fundamental factors which brought about the prevalence of sacred harlotry.

They really believed that by intercourse with a representative of the god, sterility would be cured in humans, animals and plants, 'and that by actual union with the human representatives of the deity one could assist the gods in bringing prosperity to mankind' (Brooks 1941:243).

Salvation by sex

The picture of the sexual worship of gods and goddesses in the ancient world is not clear in detail, but there is a persistent substratum of a religion different in substance from the worship of the God of the Bible. We may not be clear about the details, but the concept of emphatically male gods and emphatically female goddesses lies in the background throughout the Old Testament. This idea that male and female sexuality is intrinsic to divinity is not limited to Old Testament times. At the end of his comprehensive study of extrabiblical evidence for Asherah, Walter Maier concludes, 'In the end, one is impressed by two aspects of *ᵃšērâ's* worship seen throughout this study. The first is its diffusion (from Hierapolis in the Near East to Spain) and endurance (from the second millennium BC to the Christian era); the second, its basic consistency over the centuries' (Maier 1986:195).

We have seen repeatedly through the Old Testament how religion with deities imaged as male and female sexual beings is associated with idolatrous sexual behaviour by human beings. Human sexual behaviour is properly understood as a created good to be used in the loving service of the Creator. Remove those creation moorings and it becomes a desirable end in its own right and thus an empty idol. The corollary of all god-goddess religions is that sex itself may have salvific significance.

Schillebeeckx is correct to observe that in Genesis 1 and 2 Israel is given a fundamentally different understanding from the Canaanites of the relationship between sexuality and God (Schillebeeckx 1965:12–15). Whereas the Canaanites knew sexual intercourse as the human image of a divine prototype, Israel knew it as a 'secular reality' whose prototype was 'the first marriage of history' (Schillebeeckx 1965:15) rather than some mystical divine union between a god and a goddess. For the Canaanites and their religious successors, sex had about it the character of divinity; for Israel sex was a part of the good created order, something that 'though it comes from God, is not a way *to* God' (Stafford 1993:31). The consequences of this are great.

Whenever romanticism in any form exalts sex or marriage and speaks of it as if it were some kind of metaphysical absolute, idolatry enters.[22] All kinds of contemporary sex-mysticism or overexalted romanticism fall under the Bible's condemnation of idolatry. We may take as one example this passage from Walter Schubart:

> The essence of redeeming love is a breaking out of one's solitariness, a return to the divine whole . . . The beloved embodies for the lover this unity or offers himself as an instrument to mediate it. When two lovers come together, at one point in the cosmos the wound of individuation is healed . . . The whole extra-personal world has gathered shape and can now be embraced in the person of the beloved . . . As the distant roar of the ocean in the sea shell, so the whole of nature is felt in the breath of the

---

22. In similar vein Barth criticizes the romanticism of Schliermacher for 'trying to exalt this dialectic [i.e. *sexual encounter*] to a metaphysical absolute' (Barth, *CD* III/4:122).

beloved. This echo whispers: Thou shalt be released from thy solitariness. Thou shalt go out and meet thy Thou, who will help thee to God . . . In the end sexual life drives man into the arms of God and effaces the dividing line between I and Thou, I and the world, the world and the Godhead. Genuine sexual love is a *testimonium Spiritus sancti*. It makes possible the interpenetration of life by heavenly powers.

(from *Religion und Eros*, quoted in Barth, *CD* III/4:126)

We have here a fundamentally different concept of salvation from the Christian one; here the mediator between human beings and God is not Jesus Christ but rather sexual union. This is salvation by sex.

We may link this alternative soteriology with the work of Anders Nygren in *Agape and Eros* (Nygren 1982). Nygren claims that at the root of salvation by Eros is the idea that man is a being with a 'divine spark' which needs to be liberated from its bondage to the earthly. He connects this with the myth of Zagreus in Orphism, in which Zagreus, the son of Zeus, is killed and eaten by Titans while he was a child. Zeus smites the Titans with a thunderbolt and out of their ashes forms the race of men. This explains man's double nature: titanic (evil, hostile to God) and at the same time with a spark of the divine nature within. Whatever we make of this supposed origin of salvation by Eros, such a concept denies the seriousness of sin. Whereas the Christian religion understands salvation as built upon atonement for sin, salvation by sex is a religion that conceives salvation in terms of 'spiritual' release or finding the 'real me inside'.

In his book *Sexual Chaos* Tim Stafford writes perceptively of how the so-called sexual revolution has a strong religious dimension. If our Victorian ancestors showed their obsessive interest in sex by *not* talking about it, we show our obsessive interest in it by speaking of little else. All this amounts to a religious revolution where sex replaces Christian faith. 'If in the past sex was unrealistically regarded as demonic, it is now viewed as messianic. We study sex as a savior: it will tell us our true nature and save us from meaninglessness' (Stafford 1993:61). Sex has become a sacrament. It is a return to fertility religion, albeit in a studiedly unfertile form.

The study of how salvation by sex has re-invaded contemporary culture would take us well beyond the scope of this book. Elaine Storkey has documented some of the New Age concepts and practices of tantric sex that functions as a means of (re-)unifying the individual with the cosmos (Storkey 1997:144–148). She observes, 'The contemporary obsession with sex is part of a bigger search, for personal identity, meaning and spiritual integration' (Storkey 1997:152).

In his book *The Four Loves* (especially chapter 5), C. S. Lewis recognizes that Eros is at its most dangerous (and demonic or idolatrous) when it is at its most powerful and therefore most near (in resemblance) to God. Just as we may be only a few short yards from home on the map, and yet be at the bottom of a huge cliff with home at the top, so Eros may (through sex-mysticism) bring us apparently close to God while leaving us far distant in reality. So Lewis recognizes that there is something God-like in Eros, the total prodigal suprarational giving of self, not counting the cost. This total commitment 'is a paradigm or example, built into our natures, of the love we ought to exercise towards God and man' (Lewis 1960:101). And so Eros has an inbuilt tendency to become a religion of love, in which it is not usually the lovers who worship one another (that, as Lewis wryly observes, would generally be too ridiculous), but they worship the concept of Eros itself. Thus they act as though there were a 'law of love (i.e. Eros)' which has a claim on the two of them (who were 'made for each other'), a claim that overrides the claims of duty, justice or pledged loyalty. They 'hear' Eros speak to them with the voice of eternal authority. And yet the paradox is that Eros itself is fickle. Whenever lovers are in love, they make vows of eternal love, but they fail to recognize the folly, that they are making the same vows they made last year to a different lover. Always the delusion is that '*this* time it's the real thing'. In a sense, Eros is right to promise eternal fidelity. Eros is an image or foretaste of the eternal fidelity of the Bridegroom in his relations with the bride, and must therefore point in the direction of eternal fidelity. But 'Eros is driven to promise what Eros of himself cannot perform.' This will only destroy the marriage of the couple who have idolized Eros, who thought he had 'the power and truthfulness of a god'. Instead, it is we who have to bring our lives into line with the truths of which Eros has managed to give us a momentary glimpse. 'We must do the works of Eros when Eros is not present' (Lewis 1960:105).

The later Jewish and New Testament associations of idolatry and sexual immorality

We have seen (Chapter 5, pp. 90–99) that sexual immorality is persistently linked to idolatry in both Old and New Testaments (for the New, see Acts 15:19f., 28f.; 21:25; Rev. 2:14, 20; Rom. 1:23–25; Gal. 5:19–21; 1 Cor. 6:9–11; Rev. 9:20f.; 22:15) (Barrett 1965).

In making this connection, the New Testament writers are heirs also to a strong tradition of intertestamental Judaism, which emphasizes idolatry (in the composite sense of the contravention of both the first and second commandments) as the core of human sin, which leads to all other sins, including in particular the misuse of sex. This idea of the vicious primacy of idolatry appears clearly in Wisdom of Solomon 14:12f. Verse 12 begins, 'For the idea of making idols was the beginning of fornication [*archē gar porneias epinoia eidōlōn*].' Reading on, it seems at first as though the writer has here used *porneia* in a metaphorical sense. But the depressing entailment of idolatry that follows includes not keeping marriages pure (v. 24), disorderliness in marriages, and adultery (v. 26), all of which are literal. This should not surprise us, for 'the worship of idols . . . is the beginning and cause and end of every evil' (v. 27).

In the pseudonymous *Testament of Reuben* 4:6,[23] in the context of deep regret for his actions in going in to Bilhah his father's concubine (Gen. 35:22), Reuben warns that 'the sin of promiscuity is the pitfall of life, separating man from God and leading on towards idolatry' (cf. 3 Baruch 8:5). We find the association of idolatry and sexual immorality also in the rabbinic literature, although some of the contexts are obscure to modern readers (e.g. b.Sanhedrin 82a; b.Šabbat 17b; b.Megilla 25a; b.Ketubbot 13b; Sipre [on Deut.] 171).

Idolatry, sexual immorality and greed

It is easy to feel, as we wade through the complexities of gods and goddesses, that we have come a long way from contemporary sexual ethics. It is time therefore to explore the theological foundations for the nexus we have observed between sexual immorality and idolatry. This link touches on the first, second, seventh and tenth commandments.[24] The connection between the tenth and seventh commandments is already suggested by the inclusion in the tenth of the prohibition (addressed to a man) of coveting 'your neighbour's wife' (Exod. 20:17; Deut. 5:21). Misdirected sexual desire is covetous desire.

The association of greed with idolatry is made explicit by Paul in Ephesians 5:3–5 and Colossians 3:5.

> But fornication and impurity of any kind, or greed, must not even be mentioned among you, as is proper among saints. Entirely out of place is obscene, silly, and vulgar talk; but instead, let there be thanksgiving. Be sure of this, that no fornicator or impure person, or *one who is greedy (that is, an idolater),* has any inheritance in the kingdom of Christ and of God.
>
> (Eph. 5:3–5, my italics)

---

23. Part of *The Testaments of the Twelve Patriarchs*, probably second century BC.
24. See the useful discussion in Durham 1987:286f. about the distinction between the first and second commandments.

Put to death, therefore, whatever in you is earthly: fornication, impurity, passion, evil
desire, and *greed (which is idolatry)*.
(Col. 3:5, my italics)

The explicit connection made here is between greed (*pleonexia*) and idolatry.
Grammatically it is clear in Colossians 3:5 that 'idolatry' is equated simply with
'greed' rather than also with the four preceding nouns. In Ephesians 5:5 there
is a grammatical possibility that the phrase 'that is, an idolater' (*ho estin
eidōlolatrēs*), following *pas* at the beginning of a trio of nouns, refers back comprehensively to the person who is at the same time a fornicator (*pornos*), an
unclean person (*akathartos*) and a greedy person (*pleonektos*); this would then be
translated as in NIV, 'No immoral, impure or greedy person – such a man is an
idolater . . .' However, the simple equation of greed and idolatry in Colossians
3:5, allied to the two Mammon sayings in the Gospels (Matt. 6:24; Luke 16:13),
suggests that the primary reference is simply to greed as idolatry.

Having said this, both Colossians 3:5 and Ephesians 5:5 are surrounded by
passages with a strong sexual 'atmosphere' (Best 1998:476). This at least suggests that sexual misconduct ought to be considered within the same matrix
of thought as greed and idolatry. Before we explore this, it is necessary to ask
why greed itself is considered to be idolatry, for only when we have insight
into this can we hope to see where, if anywhere, sexual misconduct fits into
this theological nexus.

In his thorough study of the theme Rosner draws attention to three dimensions of greed which link it to idolatry. All are to be found in Matthew 6:24 in
context. 'No one can serve two masters; for a slave will either hate the one and
love the other, or be devoted to the one and despise the other. You cannot
serve God and wealth.' Greed shows itself in the service (*douleuō*) of
Mammon, in loving (*agapaō*) Mammon and (as vv. 25–34 show) in trusting in
Mammon for security. As Rosner shows, forbidden service, inordinate love
and misplaced trust are all characteristics of the idolater in Scripture. 'Greed is
idolatry because the greedy contravene God's exclusive rights to human love,
trust and obedience' (Rosner 1999:27f.).

If this is why greed is idolatry, we must now ask why these sayings (Col. 3:5;
Eph. 5:5) are set in contexts so redolent of sexual misconduct.[25] In Colossians
3:5 'greed' comes at the end of the list, preceded by 'fornication' (*porneia*),
'impurity' (*akatharsia*, a word which 'is usually associated with sexual sin',

---

25. Best 1998:481 is unconvincing when he seeks to draw a clear conceptual line between
    the admittedly sexual 'atmosphere' and the greed/idolatry saying in Eph. 5:5 ('It is best
    . . . to associate idolatry only with covetousness').

Lincoln 1990:321), 'passion' (*pathos* – 'passion, especially of a sexual nature' BAGD; 'shameful passion which leads to sexual excesses', O'Brien 1982:182), and 'evil desire' (*epithumian kakēn*). In Ephesians 5:3–5 we find three of the same abstract nouns with their concrete equivalents: *porneia/pornos, akatharsia/akathartos* and *pleonexia/pleonektēs*. We also have reference to 'obscene talk' (*aischrōtēs*),[26] 'silly talk' (*mōrologia*, foolish and especially impious talk), and 'vulgar talk' (*eutrapelia*, probably smutty talk, suggestive double-entendres, etc.).

While it is possible that in both Ephesians 5 and Colossians 3 the thought changes suddenly away from sexual misconduct to greed for money or possessions, it seems to me implausible to place a clear conceptual disjunction here between greed and sex. Best denies that 'greed' in Ephesians 5 has sexual overtones and comments, 'The furthest we can go is to say that wealth permits sexual indulgence' (Best 1998:476). This, however, is unpersuasive. Sexual misconduct is not particularly or exclusively the province of the rich. Lincoln is more sensitive to the wider context when he interprets covetousness here 'as the sort of unrestrained sexual greed whereby a person assumes that others exist for his or her own gratification' (Lincoln 1990:322).

The theological key may be found in the word 'thanksgiving' (*eucharistia*) in Ephesians 5:4 as the wholesome alternative to 'obscene, silly and vulgar talk'. In the context of sex, this word points (as in 1 Tim. 4:3f.) to the recognition that sex is a gift given by the Creator as part of the created order. It has about it the double character of gift and instrument. It is a gift to be received with thanksgiving and enjoyed, and it is an instrument to be used as the Giver intends. The reason why idolatry and sexual immorality are linked in biblical thought is that when true worship is replaced by idolatry the worshipper loses his or her moorings in creation order.

> The important idolatries have always centered on those forces which have enough specious power to be truly counterfeit, and therefore truly dangerous: sexuality (fertility), riches, and power (glory) . . . All idolatry is a form of covetousness, for by refusing to acknowledge life and worth as a gift from the Creator, it seeks *to seize them from the creation as a booty.*
>
> (Johnson 1981:52–55, my italics)

Sex (as other created goods) changes from being a gift to be received with thanksgiving to being a desirable goal to be grasped. Instead of understanding how this gift is to be used in the service of God (by faithful loyalty of one to

---

26. This usually means 'shameful behaviour', but in this context seems to refer particularly to obscene talk. See Best 1998 and Lincoln 1990, ad loc.

one for life), it becomes an instrument to promote the worshipper's pleasure, security and fulfilment. It will therefore be the concern of inordinate love, the object of inappropriate trust, and the subject of fruitless service.

Conclusion

By virtue of creation every human being inescapably has a moral obligation to love the Creator with heart, mind, soul and strength, just as he loves us. This love is to be exclusive (for no other god) and enduring (a matter of jealous faithfulness over time). God has so made the world that the context of procreation should mirror that of creation, in an exclusive and permanent loyalty, which we call marriage. Those who are called to marriage are to receive the gift with joy and to understand that it has been given to be used for the Creator's loving purposes of care for his world. Idolatry replaces this single integrity of loving worship with a multiplicity of competing gods. One corollary of idolatry is that we cease to receive sex as a gift. The autonomous ethic of sex claims, like all idolatry, to offer great and wonderful possibilities; but, again like all idolatry, it proves in the end to be empty and its claims vacuous. It substitutes emptiness where there might be substance, danger where there could be safety, and disintegration where there should be integrity.

One of the major Old Testament weapons against idolatry is unsparing mockery and derision. Idols are so pathetic; they cannot speak, act, hear or perform any of their promises. How foolish it is to worship them! We should learn from this that an important weapon in the Christian arsenal with regard to sexual ethics is mockery and derision at the sheer stupidity of sex outside marriage. We should point to the allure of pleasure, fulfilment, satisfaction and fruitfulness outside marriage and show them up for the hollow vanities they are.

9. CHILDREN IN THE SERVICE OF GOD

In Chapter 7 we argued that God made humankind male and female that we might the better care for his world. In this chapter and the next we revisit the traditional 'goods' of marriage to see how each of them should be considered under this governing ethic of the service of God. We begin with procreation.

It is God's general will and purpose that when a man and a woman come together in marriage they should have children. The project (if we may call it that) of the conception, birth and nurture of children is a natural and integral part of their service of God in marriage. They have children not for their own sakes as parents, nor for the children's sakes, but for the sake of contributing to the great task entrusted to humankind. These bald and provocative statements will be examined in this chapter.

In the history of Christian thought the good of procreation has often been argued from some concept of natural order or law. The way the bodies of male and female are made, it is argued, shows that sexual union is naturally ordered towards the end of procreation.[1] We can, however, place the procreational good on a firmer footing than this. We shall argue from Scripture that the end or goal of sexual union, in so far as it leads to procreation, lies beyond having children

---

1. See e.g. O'Donovan 1994:37 for a concise allusion to this argument. Even Thatcher 1999:161 recognizes, 'The separation of sexual pleasure from sexual reproduction is set to become a new secular dualism as damaging as any of the old religious dualisms between mind and body, spirit and flesh...'

and points to the dignity of human dominion. We do this initially by recalling our discussion of Genesis 1 and 2 in Chapter 7. We have seen in Genesis 1:26–28 that the blessing[2] of fruitfulness and multiplication is given to male and female in the context of the creation mandate to govern God's world. We have argued that although procreation is not explicitly mentioned in Genesis 2:18–25, the placing of this passage both as part of the narrative of Genesis 2:4–25, with the man given a task in the garden, and after Genesis 1:1–2:3, points to the procreation of children as an integral part of the Creator's purpose in making male and female and bringing them together in marriage. Adam alone cannot tend and watch over the garden; he needs the woman as his helper. And he needs her not only because in some psychosomatic way she 'answers' to his need, but also because she and he together may be given the blessing of children, who will extend and develop the project of the garden.[3] The procreational good of marriage is therefore to be considered under the governing ethic of the service of God in stewarding his world. Procreation is not a goal of marriage in its own right; it is a subservient or interim goal, which points to the greater goal of the service of God.

Procreation before and after the fall

We should note briefly at this point an unhelpful debate about a possible distinction between procreation before and after the fall. Augustine argued (*On the Good of Marriage* §2) that there would not have been sexual reproduction before the fall, since sexual intercourse presupposes *mortal* bodies. It is true that the argument of Jesus in Luke 20:27ff. and Matthew 22:23–32 against marriage in heaven is closely linked to the fact that 'they will no longer die'; in the fallen world the ongoing need for succeeding generations is because the older generation will die. None the less, the argument that before the fall, 'in the time of man's innocency', there would have been no sexual intercourse and no procreation is unwarranted speculation and also goes against the grain of Genesis 1:28, where human fruitfulness and multiplication is included in the 'very good' created order before the fall (v. 31). To ask what function procreation would have served before death entered the world is to ask the kind of hypothetical question Scripture does not address. In the narrative terms of

2. Meilander 1995:73 is right to observe that this is 'not precisely a command'. Arguments against voluntary childlessness based on the claim that this is a command to be obeyed are exegetically tenuous and ethically slight.

3. Cf. the observation of Meilander 1995:73 that children are needed 'to preserve humankind towards the end [God] has appointed'.

Genesis 2 it is still easy enough to see how the generation of a family of gardeners is a good and necessary thing, without which the aloneness of Adam would not be good. Beyond that we are in the realm of surmise, fruitless speculation far removed from the purpose of Genesis 1 and 2.

Ambiguities introduced by the fall

What is more important is that the fall of man introduced terrible ambiguities into the project of procreation. The woman is given pain in childbearing (Gen. 3:16), and both man and woman are expelled from the garden. Both procreation and task are thus called into question – and yet in Genesis 5:1–5 it is clear that even after the fall, Adam as a (still) God-like creature may beget other God-like (and yet Adam-like) creatures.

As the sad litany of Genesis 5 makes clear ('. . . and he died'), however, these human beings are born mortal. And in the strange story of Genesis 6:1–4 (however this is understood) our attention is drawn to the deep alienation of the procreative project from the task of God-like dominion. Although the children in this passage grow to be very strong ('warriors of renown'), they are deeply flawed and fill the earth with evil and violence (vv. 5, 11f.). And yet, even though man is alienated from the garden, the calling to dominion is reiterated in Genesis 9:1–7 after the flood (albeit with a sharp hint of violent domination) and is celebrated by the psalmist (Psalm 8).

These post-fall ambiguities force on us the conclusion that it is not procreation *per se* which is a 'good' of sexual union, but procreation of godly offspring (Mal. 2:15), who will be in God's world what Adam and Eve ought to have been. Procreation of sinful men and women can only approximately and ambiguously be the good that it was originally meant to be.

The tower of Babel (Gen. 11:1–9) is the pathetic culmination of humankind's twisting of the project of responsible dominion into the technology of autonomous rule. Although humankind is still proliferating (as the genealogy that follows suggests, Gen. 11:10ff.), they are now a 'scattered' people (Gen. 11:9) lacking harmony, integrity or unity in task.

Procreational blessing transposed from humanity to the people of God

The call of Abraham begins the rescue and restoration of the created order. It is noteworthy how the universal blessings of fruitfulness and multiplication are now transposed into a new and particular key in the context of the

Abrahamic promise (Gen. 12:2; 15:5; 17:5f. and onwards in the Old Testament). Before the fall it was a simple good for humankind to multiply, because by so doing they would fulfil the creation mandate. After the fall the proliferation of humankind is a deeply ambiguous 'good'. From the call of Abraham onwards there is a sharp distinction between the fruitfulness of Abraham's people and the multiplication of their enemies. Here are a people called to Adam's dignity, to be a light to the nations. Blessing is now linked precisely with the multiplication of God's people so that they can rule over their enemies and bring God's righteous rule to his world.

We see this in the growth of 'the sons of Israel' from a family to a people in Exodus 1:1–7, where the language of fruitfulness and multiplication is prominent. The same theme governs Exodus 2, where it is particularized in the birth and preservation of one baby, Moses the saviour. We see the context of a fruitful people in a hostile world in Psalm 105:24; during Israel's sojourn in Egypt, 'The LORD made his people very fruitful; and made them stronger [NIV 'more numerous'] than their foes.' Always the reason why God's people must multiply is to bring blessing to the world, as in Genesis 12:3. 'In days to come Jacob shall take root, Israel shall blossom and put forth shoots, and fill the whole world with fruit' (Is. 27:6). The Abrahamic multiplication promise is repeatedly echoed of Israel (e.g. Is. 48:18f.; 51:1f.; 54:1–3).

The partial parallel with the calling of Adam and Eve is clear. Adam and Eve were to be blessed with multiplication so that their family might bring order to the abundant creation; Abraham's people are to be blessed with multiplication so that they may rightly rule in the context of disorderly enemies. The ethical point to notice is that, when an Israelite couple had children, God's purpose was that these children should carry on and extend the task of bringing God's rule to his world. Procreation within marriage is an outward-looking project. Israel is to be a light to the nations.[4]

The pro-life orientation of Old Testament thought

In all this we cannot fail to observe that the Old Testament has a strong and consistent pro-life orientation. To grow in number is a blessing for God's people, to diminish is judgment (e.g. Lev. 26:9, 22; Deut. 1:10; 7:13; 10:22; 13:17). And if this is so for the people of God as a whole, it is true also for

---

4. Tom Wright illustrates the corruption of this into introspection by imagining a light-house in which the mirrors are all turned to reflect the light back inwards. As with Israel's calling, so with marriage, the purpose of God is outward-looking service.

individuals. It is a blessing to contribute to the multiplication of the people, a sadness to be deprived of such participation (e.g. Judg. 11:34–40, the tragedy of Jephthah's daughter, and the general blessings of procreation celebrated in Pss. 127:3–5; 128:3; cf. Exod. 23:26; Hos. 9:14). Wombs that bear children and breasts that suckle them are signs of blessing (e.g. 'blessings of the breasts and of the womb', Gen. 49:25). Indeed, judgment may be spoken of in terms of the awful contradiction of the death of a new life (cf. Amos 1:13; Matt. 24:19).

This pro-life orientation values as blessing what God declares to be blessing; it is in stark contrast to some contemporary worldviews in which a new life may (because of its inconvenience) be regarded as a curse.[5]

Procreation correlated with fruitful work

It is not often noted how strongly the Old Testament texts of blessing link the blessing of procreation with the task of fruitful work. This connection is important, for it connects on a small scale the ethics of marriage with the task of serving God in his world. To have children is not a blessing in Old Testament thought for sentimental reasons, but rather because, in the wider context of prosperity, they contribute to a growing and well-ordered people living in God's land as humankind ought to live.

Negatively, for example, we see this in Deuteronomy 28:30. One of the curses on covenant disobedience is described in the following terms:

> You shall become engaged to a woman, but another man shall lie with her.
> You shall build a house, but not live in it.
> You shall plant a vineyard, but not enjoy its fruit.

The three sadnesses here are not unconnected. The sadness of the unoccupied house and the not-enjoyed vineyard is the sadness of frustrated work; the man has worked but his projects have been in vain, fruitless and empty. The sadness of the man who fails to marry his woman is also, in a sense, the sadness of frustration. He had hoped not merely for sexual fulfilment, but

---

5. As a symptom of this we may cite the court case in Scotland in 1999 in which a couple sued the health authority after the husband's vasectomy failed and the wife conceived their fifth child. The child was born and the couple sued the health authority for substantial damages for the pain suffered during pregnancy and for the financial costs of bringing up their (healthy and normal) daughter (*Guardian*, 6 July 1999).

more deeply for the joy of a fruitful project of building a home, of fathering and nurturing children. The wife, the house and the vineyard are all of a piece. Of course, the sadness of his lost wife is personal and relational, whereas the house and vineyard are not. This link between marriage and task does not reduce the woman to a merely functional status, let alone a chattel, but the hopes and goals of the man are connected, the vision of building a home and a family partnership in which fruitful work would be achieved. We should probably read the military permissions of Deuteronomy 20:7 and 24:5 in the same light. A newly married soldier is given 'extended honeymoon leave' so that (with God's blessing) he may at least give his wife a child with whom to build a family.

Positively we may note the connection between work and procreation in Psalm 127, which begins (vv. 1–2) with fruitful work (house-building, city-guarding, toiling for food), and this leads straight on to the blessing of children (or, here, specifically 'sons', vv. 3–5). Here again the sons are not a blessing for sentimental reasons, but because they are 'like arrows in the hand of a warrior' – that is to say, they have work to do in fighting God's enemies and ruling God's world, just as in Isaiah 49:2 the Lord's Servant is 'a polished arrow' in the Lord's quiver. The figure of an arrow is related to the task of necessary warfare. The project of procreation is integral to that of fulfilling the creation mandate, transposed as it now is into the calling of the people of God to multiply and rule.

This correlation of work and procreation continues in an eschatological context. We may note in Isaiah 56 – 66 how the blessings of restoration are couched in terms that include both fruitful work and a multitude of people. The original pro-life language of Old Testament thought extends to future hope. In Isaiah 65:17–25, for example, we read of the new heavens and new earth, 'No more shall there be in it an infant that lives but a few days, or an old person who does not live out a lifetime' (v. 20). Then we read what these long-lived people will be doing: building houses, planting vineyards and eating their fruit (v. 21). Blessing will see many people doing fruitful work (v. 23, 'They shall not labour in vain, or bear children for calamity'). The scriptural theme linking procreation with fruitful work is strong and suggestive; children are to be born and nurtured to contribute to the task of ruling God's world.

Procreation and nurture

We have spoken deliberately of the project of procreation *and nurture*. We must now expand on the necessity of nurture, for it has wide ethical implications. It is not enough simply to bring new human beings into the world; it is not enough even to care for their physical protection in infancy and their material needs for food and shelter as they grow. Since the goal of their lives is to participate in the glorious task of ruling God's world, it is also necessary for them to grow into a relationship of glad response to the call of God so that they can exercise the dignity of responsible dominion. In the language of the garden, it is not enough that baby potential gardeners should be born; they must be taught to garden, to relate to the Creator, to learn his will and thus to till the garden in accordance with that will. It is deceptively easy to allow the costly project of nurture to slip from view in discussion of the procreative good of marriage. It is in one sense almost too obvious to mention, but it is part of the traditional understanding. For example, in another context Thomas Aquinas writes, 'The end of matrimony is the begetting *and upbringing* of children: the first of which is attained by conjugal intercourse; *the second by the other duties of husband and wife, by which they help one another in rearing their offspring*' (Summa III:39, my italics; cf. Hill 1986:429–466 for the Puritan ideal of the home as domestic church).

For a contemporary commentary on what happens in a society where nurture (and particularly here nurture by fathers) is neglected, we may refer to the study by Dennis and Erdos in which the authors refer to the traditional tightly knit bundle of 'sex, procreation, *child rearing*, and non-commercial, personal and permanent adult mutual-aid' (Dennis and Erdos 1993:73, my italics).[6] Stephen Barton has penetratingly observed that in the age of the isolated nuclear family (isolated, that is, from the wider context of service in the world), 'children . . . as we are learning to our cost, tend to be either idolized or abused' (Barton 2001:47).

Nurture in scriptural perspective

The importance of the theme of nurture is highlighted throughout Scripture. In Genesis 18:19 we are told the will of God for Abraham, 'that he may charge his children and his household after him to keep the way of the LORD by doing righteousness and justice'. It is not enough to father the children; he must nurture them in godliness. This is a pervasive theme in the book of Proverbs, with its constantly reiterated appeal from father and mother to their son to listen to the wisdom they impart (e.g. Prov. 1:8).[7] We find it also in

---

6. Chapter 3 is instructive on the need for parental socialization of the next generation, and chapter 4 gives devastating statistics from social studies of uncommitted fatherhood.

7. Even if the parenthood here may be figurative, perhaps for the teachers in the posited wisdom 'school', the point about the importance of nurture stands.

Ephesians 6:1–4, with the exhortation to fathers to bring their children up 'in the discipline and instruction of the Lord'.[8]

Ephesians 6:2 also draws attention to the promise attached to the commandment to honour parents, 'so that . . . you may live long on the earth' (cf. Deut. 11:18–21). Negatively, this issue of intergenerational harmony is also addressed in Malachi 4:5f., where the promised future Elijah 'will turn the hearts of parents to their children and the hearts of children to their parents, so that I will not come and strike the land with a curse'. The raising of subsequent generations to follow in footsteps of faith and godliness is of the utmost importance. When godly generation is followed by godly generation, the people's days will be long in the land; the alternative is to bring on the land a curse.

The content of nurture: creation and redemption

The nurture of children must include both creation (the order within which we are to live) and redemption (the restored relationship with the Creator), both law and gospel. On the one hand, the children need to be told the statutes and laws of the Lord, the Creator of the earth, so they may know how to live in harmony with created order; on the other, they need to remember the great deeds of redemption, so that they may understand what it is to be a people called to live in the land in restored relationship with the Creator.

Redemption is remembered, for example, in Exodus 10:2; 12:26f.; and 13:14, where the events of the exodus and Passover are the subject, so that future generations will know what it is to belong to the redeemed people of God. Likewise, in Joshua 4:4–7, 21f., stones are raised as a reminder to their children of the crossing of the Jordan.

None the less, it is never redemption simply for the sake of being redeemed. The children need not only to understand that they belong to a redeemed people, but also to what end or goal they are redeemed. This is where the reminders of Sinai/Horeb become significant. In Deuteronomy 4:9 they are told, 'But take care and watch yourselves closely, so as neither to forget the things that your eyes have seen nor to let them slip from your mind all the days of your life; make them known to your children and your children's children.' But here the things their 'eyes have seen' are not the events of redemption, but (v. 10) 'how you once stood before the LORD your God at Horeb, when the LORD said to me, "Assemble the people for me, and I will let them hear my words, so that they may learn to fear me as long as they live on the earth, and may teach their children so".' It is not just redemption (the exodus and Passover) the children need to hear, but the law from Sinai/Horeb.

---

8. Cf. the childhood of Jesus, Luke 2:40–52; the pastor's children, 1 Tim. 3:4, 12; Titus 1:6.

Again, most significantly, this theme of telling the next generation follows immediately, in Deuteronomy 6:4–9, on the *Shema*. To love the Lord the Redeemer is to obey the commands of God the Creator. This easy nexus of law and gospel is even clearer in Deuteronomy 6:20–25. The son asks (v. 20) the meaning of 'the decrees and the statutes and the ordinances that the LORD our God has commanded'. He is answered (vv. 21–23) in terms of redemption and the gift of the land, where (v. 24f.) law-keeping will lead to prosperity, because it is life in harmony with creation order.

When the next generation forget redemption they also forget creation order. The vicious cycles of the book of Judges epitomize this connection. In Judges 2:10, for example, we read, 'That whole generation was gathered to their ancestors, and another generation grew up after them, who did not know the LORD or the work that he had done for Israel.' They forgot, that is, the gospel of redemption ('the work he had done for Israel') and as a result they no longer knew the Lord himself, and their land became a disordered and lawless place (cf. Judg. 21:25). Indeed, in Joel 1:3 we find a paradoxical use of the 'tell the children' motif, in which they are to be told of the horrors of judgment lest they forget the seriousness of disobedience.

We may perhaps see in the later symbolic language of Zion the same intrinsic connection between law and gospel, creation and redemption. In Psalm 48:12–14 the believer is invited to 'Walk about Zion, go all around it, count its towers, consider well its ramparts; go through its citadels, that you may tell the next generation that this is God . . .' The ramparts, towers and citadels of Zion are here a symbol of divine security and promise, but may they not also stand as symbols of divine order, of law and gospel built together? Zion is at the same time a safe place and an ordered place. It is a suggestive image of law and gospel.

In Psalm 78:1–8 'the coming generation' are to be told both 'the glorious deeds' (v. 4) of the Lord, the wonderful deeds of redemption, and also (v. 5) his 'decree' and 'law'. In Psalm 34:11 the children are invited to be taught 'the fear of the LORD', which encompasses both gratitude for redemption and believing obedience to law.

In Psalm 22:30 the theme of task and service appears explicitly in the context of future generations. 'Posterity [lit. 'seed'] will *serve* him; future generations will be told about the Lord' (my italics). Nurture begins with telling the next generation about the Lord the Creator and Redeemer, about law and gospel; it issues in the next generation serving him in the task entrusted to humankind.

Godly motherhood
We have seen above the importance of godly fatherhood for nurture. Scripture also emphasizes the need for godly motherhood. In Psalm 22:9f. the

psalmist remembers that from his mother's womb and his mother's breast he was utterly dependent on the Lord, and that 'since my mother bore me you have been my God'. When from infancy a man or woman grows in subjective apprehension of this objective truth, and is led to know and trust this God, very often the role of the mother is pivotal. This seems to have been so for Timothy in the New Testament, who had a believing mother and grand-mother (Acts 16:1; 2 Tim. 1:5; 3:15) so that from infancy he was introduced to the Scriptures and pointed towards salvation.

It is possible that 1 Timothy 2:15 is relevant in this context. Paul says, rather enigmatically, that woman 'will be saved through childbearing' (*sōthēsetai . . . dia tēs teknogonias*); here 'through' (*dia*) cannot be understood in an instrumental sense (as though childbearing was the cause of the woman's salvation), for throughout Paul's letters (and the pastorals do not differ in this) salvation is only through God in Christ by faith. It is better to understand the 'childbear-ing' as a practical outworking of salvation in the life of a married woman.[9] Paul may be writing here against the cultural background of a protofeminist rejec-tion of the traditional women's roles of marriage and the bringing up of a family. It may be that he uses the verb *sōzō* in the sense that the practical out-working of salvation in the life of a woman may and usually will involve the valuable work of bearing and nurturing children.[10]

Opposition to mixed marriage

Opposition to religiously mixed marriage in the Old Testament is strong and persistent. We find it in Genesis 26:34f. (Esau); Genesis 28 (Jacob); Deuteronomy 7:3–5; Joshua 23:12; 1 Kings 3:1; 7:8; 9:24; 11:1–13; 16:31ff. (Jezebel); 2 Kings 8:18; Ezra 9 and 10 and Nehemiah 10:30; 13:23–27.

It is important to note that in the canon of Scripture the book of Ruth functions as a caution against interpreting the hostility to mixed marriage in simplistically racial terms; the underlying concern of the Old Testament

---

9. Markus Bockmuehl (personal correspondence) points out that there are close parallels to such a modal or circumstantial use of *dia* in v. 10, in 2 Tim. 2:2, in 1 Cor. 16:3, and (especially) in 1 Pet. 3:20.

10. There is a full treatment of the exegetical issues surrounding this verse in Mounce 2000, ad loc. We may note also the suggestion of Winter 2000:293 that the word usually translated 'childbearing'(*teknogonia*) in 1 Tim. 2:15 'refers not just to the birth of children but also to raising them'. In context this may be an affirmation of the moral significance of motherhood against the anti-motherhood trends of the 'New Roman Woman'. If correct, this text bears with considerable relevance on some trends in contemporary Western society.

writers is religious rather than racial. In this connection we note also the lack of censure in the accounts of the foreign marriages of Joseph (Gen. 41:50ff.) and Moses (Num. 12:1f.).

There are two moral dimensions to Scripture's opposition to a man marrying a non-Israelite woman. The first relates to the wife's influence on her husband, the second to her influence as the mother of their children. On the one hand, there is the likelihood that a wife whose allegiance is to other gods will turn the heart of her husband away from singleness of devotion to the Lord (supremely Solomon, 1 Kgs. 11:1f., but cf. the comment in 1 Kgs. 21:25 that Ahab was 'urged on by his wife Jezebel').

On the other hand (and this dimension is too often neglected), her influence on the children of the marriage will likewise be to turn them away from the Lord. This moral significance of motherhood is implicit in a number of places. In Genesis 26:34f. we are simply told of Esau's two Hittite wives that they were a cause of grief to Isaac and Rebekah. But in Genesis 28:1–5 Isaac's command to Jacob to find a non-Canaanite wife is explicitly linked to the repetition of the Abrahamic (and, as we have seen, Adamic) promise of fruitfulness and multiplication (v. 3), the purpose of which is that his people should take possession of the land. This makes the connection between godly nurture (and in particular godly motherhood) and the task of ruling God's land aright.

Again, in Nehemiah 13 there is a revealing insight into at least a part of the rationale behind the urgent concern and draconian measures taken by both Ezra (chapters 9 and 10) and Nehemiah (9:2; 10:30; 13:1–3, 23–27) against mixed marriage. Men of Judah had married women from Ashdod, Ammon and Moab. The result was that 'Half of their children spoke the language of Ashdod, and they could not speak the language of Judah, but spoke the language of various peoples' (Neh. 13:24). This is more than a merely linguistic observation. Language encapsulated and was the carrier of culture and religion; if they did not speak the language of Judah they would not acknowledge the God of Judah. A foreign mother meant a strange language; and a strange language meant other gods. That is why intermarriage matters so deeply, because of the moral and religious significance of motherhood.

The historian of the books of Kings appears to share this concern, with his repeated notes about the mothers (and either the mother's father's name, or the mother's place of origin, or both) of the kings of Judah, usually in close proximity to some evaluative comment about their kingship.[11] The identity and

---

11. 1 Kgs. 14:21, 31 (Rehoboam); 15:1f. (Abijah); 15:10 (Asa); 22:42 (Jehoshaphat); 2 Kgs.
    8:25–27 and chapter 11 (Ahaziah); 12:1 (Joash); 14:1ff. (Amaziah); 15:1ff. (Azariah);

roots of the mother often give a clue to the moral and religious character of the son. Some of these 'mother notes' are echoed by the chronicler.[12] And in 2 Chronicles 22:1–3 the chronicler makes the influence of the mother explicit: he adds to the account in 2 Kings 8:25–27 the comment that '[Ahaziah] also walked in the ways of the house of Ahab, for his mother was his counsellor in doing wickedly.'

The moral character of the mother

The moral significance of motherhood[13] is inseparable from the moral character of the mother. We must never allow the project of procreation to be disparaged as just 'making babies', for it ought not to be divided from the process of nurture. This points inescapably to the character of both parents, but since we are discussing motherhood we note how Scripture values the beauty of godly character above the transient beauty of outward form. Some 'lucky' husbands may get both, as David did when he married the beautiful and wise Abigail (1 Sam. 25), but a wise man will make sure he gives greater priority to 'discretion' above 'beauty', the latter without the former being 'like a gold ring in a pig's snout' (Prov. 11:22). However beautiful a woman may be, if she has a quarrelsome character she will make life at home miserable (Prov. 19:13; 21:9; 25:24; 27:15f.), as indeed will a quarrelsome man (Prov. 26:21). Outward beauty may be accompanied by a 'haughtiness' of heart, which leads to judgment (Is. 3:16 – 4:1). Lasting beauty that is deeply attractive to God is found in the heart and spirit (1 Pet. 3:3ff.).

If we ask what kind of woman this is, this godly wife and mother, the wisdom literature offers us a charming portrait of one. When the wise man concludes, 'Charm is deceitful, and beauty is vain, but a woman who fears the LORD is to be praised' (Prov. 31:30), he does so at the end of a wonderful acrostic poem (vv. 10–31) celebrating the virtues and benefits of 'a capable wife' ('a wife of noble character' NIV). This fine woman seems to be managing a wealthy family. There is not space here to extol all her virtues as the wise man does (and as many a wise husband will do today). In the context of our study we note her attitude to marriage (as a partnership), her competence and her generosity of spirit.

First, her attitude to marriage is cooperative partnership. 'The heart of her husband trusts in her . . . She does him good . . .' (vv. 11–12). She is her husband's 'helper' (Gen. 2:18). Their marriage is a partnership in which the

---

15:32ff. (Jotham); 18:1ff. (Hezekiah); 21:1ff. (Manasseh); 21:19 (Amon); 22:1f. (Josiah); 23:31 (Jehoahaz); 23:36 (Jehoiakim); 24:8, 15 (Jehoiakin); 24:18 (Zedekiah).

12.   2 Chr. 13:1f.; 20:31f.; 22:1–3; 25:1; 26:3; 27:1f.; 29:1f.

13.   Neuer 1990:149–151, 166–169 argues forcefully for the dignity, significance and demanding nature of motherhood.

two of them together are more effective in the service of God than two separate individuals ploughing their own furrows and carving out their own paths. Her attitude towards relationships, and specifically the marriage relationship, is that relationships are for the purpose of serving others, not pandering to her own needs. (It should go without saying that the husband ought to share this same attitude.)

This is not at all demeaning to the woman. This woman is far from being a 'doormat' kept in subjection to a tyrannical husband. Far from being cowed into silence or sullen assent, she opens her mouth in wise counsel (v. 26, 'She opens her mouth with wisdom, and the teaching of kindness is on her tongue'). So this attitude of partnership does not imply that her purpose in life is one-sidedly to serve and be useful to the man while he lords it over her; elsewhere Scripture speaks with penetrating cruciform challenge to any man who thinks like this (Eph. 5:25). Rather, her attitude is that together they serve God. Neither carves out a life for himself or herself; they claim no rights for themselves, but together as they serve one another their aim is to serve God.

Second, the poem celebrates her competence. She is 'capable' (v. 10) and her ability, her skill, her efficiency infuse almost every verse. She manages a household of some wealth. She is an able businesswoman; her life is far from a tightly circumscribed domesticity. She is practical, energetic and skilled. When we argue that marriage is to be understood in the context of the task of stewarding God's world, this may sound distantly grand and global, but it is earthed in the down-to-earth competence of this married woman who manages a home and business.

Third, however, it is instructive to note why she works so hard. 'She opens her hand to the poor, and reaches out her hands to the needy' (v. 20). Her love is indeed for her husband and children, who are very glad to have her as wife and mother (v. 28), but her love, being true love, extends also beyond the circle of the home and reaches out, as we might say, to Lazarus at the gate (in contrast to the wives of Amos 4:1). She understands that the purpose of hard work is not just to look after self, but also so that there is something to give to those in need. She is privileged, and her door is not closed to those who are not. She understands the message of Ephesians 4:28, 'Thieves must give up stealing; rather let them labour and work honestly with their own hands, so as to have something to share with the needy.'

Here is a fine sketch of godly motherhood, marriage as outward-looking partnership in the service of God in his world.

Outward-looking procreation and nurture

We are now in a position to see why procreation is rightly esteemed as a good and a blessing to be desired and valued. This is not for selfish reasons, either because parents want children because they find children sweet (they may or may not), or because in some way the parents need to be needed – as one famous actress said, 'I'm one of those people who needed to have children. I needed to have that centre to my life, that base';[14] nor is it because the parents desire sons or daughters to care for them in old age. It is because God has entrusted humankind with a noble task and that task cannot be carried out without a race of men and women conceived, born and nurtured to know, love and serve their Creator.

We conclude that the procreative 'good' of marriage is to be held in close conjunction with the costly project of parental nurture, and that both pro-creation and nurture are to be embarked upon with the goal of serving God in his world. This has wide implications for our teaching on parenting; it warns us against slipping into any ethical framework of parenthood that is self-serving for either parent.

In conclusion we must note an important corollary of allowing the ethic of task to control our understanding of procreation within marriage. The neces-sary conjunction between procreation and nurture safeguards us against allowing the ethic of task to be misunderstood as a purely functional (and thus sub-personal) ethic of sex. On the contrary, the enterprise of pro-creation and nurture is profoundly personal. It involves the couple's own relationship with God, their relationship with one another, their relation-ship with their children, and the developing relationship of the children with God.

Procreation before and after Christ: a critique of Karl Barth

We need at this point to address an objection that lurks in the back of the mind of many a Christian. We can understand the Old Testament emphasis on children, but has the coming of Christ not changed matters, so that from now on what really counts is not natural birth but spiritual birth? Augustine certainly thought so:

> Forsooth now (sc. after Christ) no one who is made perfect in piety seeks to have sons, save after a spiritual sense; but then (sc. before Christ) it was the work of piety itself to beget sons even after the carnal sense: in that the begetting of that people was *fraught with tidings of things to come* . . .
> (*On the Good of Marriage* §19, my italics)

---

14. Michelle Pfeiffer, *The Times* magazine, 15 April 2000.

The reason procreation mattered in Israel was that the Christ might come. So, argues Augustine, the 'time to embrace' (Eccles. 3:5) was BC, when sexual union was necessary, 'for the purpose of begetting and preserving a people for God, amongst whom the prophecy of Christ's coming must needs have had precedence over everything'. This is no longer so; now it is 'a time to refrain from embracing', because there are now 'among all nations . . . an abundant offspring to receive spiritual regeneration' (*On Marriage* §14; cf. S.15). What we need is not so much more people born by natural birth as more Christians born by spiritual regeneration.

Augustine therefore viewed the coming of Christ as an event that made sexual union itself a questionable activity. He has few followers today. None the less, a part of his inheritance has been developed and popularized in a most influential way by Karl Barth (*CD* III/1:312–324; III/2:296–301; III/4:141–143). Barth (as we have seen) placed great store on the marital relationship itself as an image of the divine covenant relationship of God with his people, Christ with his church; indeed, he taught that this relationship is the meaning of marriage. When it comes to procreation, however, Barth has the same attitude as Augustine: it is no longer really necessary since the Christ has come. He argues this from the history of salvation (*Heilsgeschichte*). Procreation in marriage was essentially a temporary priority, not needed before mortality entered the world and no longer needed now the Christ has come. He rightly points to the strong future orientation of the Old Testament, directed forwards in hope,[15] so that in prophetic anticipation the childless eunuch can be promised 'a memorial and a name *better than sons and daughters*' (Is. 56:5, my italics). And now these prophecies have been fulfilled, argues Barth, so that 'the necessity to procreate imposed by the history of salvation prior to the appearance of the Messiah has . . . fallen away' (Barth, *CD* III/4:143).

These arguments suffer from a number of weaknesses. First we may note that the forward-looking character of the Old Testament is at the same time both individual (pointing to Messiah) and corporate (Messiah's people and indeed the whole of humanity). Some of the genealogies do indeed have a pointed individual focus, with the lines of interest selected because they lead to the 'saviour'; this is so in Genesis 5 (selected to reach Noah) and in Genesis 11:10ff. (selected to reach Abraham). This kind of individual focus is, of course, shared by Matthew (1:1–17) and Luke (3:23–38), and by Paul's exegesis in Galatians 3:16 (the Abrahamic promise fulfilled in the 'seed' – singular –

---

15. This theme is also noted by Schillebeeckx 1965:81 in the recurrent use of the 'toledoth' motif, which (he says) points to the Christ to come.

that is, Christ). But the forward-looking focus is also on the growth of a people for Messiah to rule, and indeed the continuance of humanity for God to bless (e.g. the genealogies of Gen. 10 or 36). There is interest not only in Messiah but also in the general continuance of the human race, and even within Israel the interest is not exclusively on the line of promise (e.g. the many genealogies in 1 Chr. 1 – 9, ranging well beyond the Davidic line).

It is unconvincing to suggest that before Christ the piety of the Israelite seeking sons and daughters through marital intercourse was solely directed towards the faint hope that one might find oneself contributing to the genealogy of the Messiah. This cannot be the ethical underpinning of pre-Christian sexual intercourse. It would make the whole thing a kind of procreational lottery, so that if the 'messianic number' did not come up the whole enterprise would be rendered ethically vacuous. Besides, on this view there is a certain irony in the New Testament teaching that the Messiah's conception was achieved *without* parental sexual intercourse (cf. Luke 3:23, 'the son, *as was thought*, of Joseph', my italics).

We cannot collapse the promise of procreative blessing into the hope of the Messiah to the exclusion of Messiah's people. We see the tension, for example, in Exodus 1 and 2; in Exodus 1 the emphasis is on the wonderful multiplication of the people, and in Exodus 2 on the preservation of the 'saviour' Moses.[16] Both preserved people and preserved Preserver are part of the picture. The procreational good of pre-Christian marriage in Israel is directed both to the Messiah and to the continuance and multiplication of the people whom Messiah will rule. If it is argued that in Christ the teaching about the 'remnant' reaches its extreme, in that the remnant has collapsed into a single person, we must reply that such a theological systematization is hardly supported by the New Testament portrayal of real believers both at the time of Christ's birth (the godly group portrayed in Luke 2:21–40 including Simeon and Anna) and throughout his ministry. It is not persuasive to suggest that at the 'Christ-instant' in salvation history the people of God had collapsed to one man.

One argument sometimes adduced in support of a Barthian relativization of the procreational good of marriage is the silence of both Jesus and Paul in the context of marriage teaching about the blessing of having children. This is a tenuous argument. The most natural reading of Jesus' silence about children as a goal of marriage (as indeed on homosexual practice) is that here was

---

16. We see the 'special baby' motif elsewhere in both Testaments, for example in the births of Samson (Judg. 13); Obed (Ruth 4:13ff.); Samuel (1 Sam. 1); David's 'house' (2 Sam. 7); Is. 7:14; Mic. 5:2–5a; Luke 1:5–25, 26–38; Gal. 3:15–20 and Rev. 12:1–13:1.

an issue on which he had no controversy with the universal understanding of his day and culture. When asked about divorce (Mark 10) it would have been irrelevant to have included children in his answer, since this was not the point at issue.

Likewise, it is flimsy to argue from Paul's silence about procreation in 1 Corinthians 7 and 1 Thessalonians 4:1–8 that he regarded the intention to have children as having been superseded since Christ came. Whatever the immediacy of his eschatological expectations, the burden of proof lies firmly on those who would argue that Paul could possibly have commended the mutual duty of marital intercourse (1 Cor. 7:2) while not expecting or welcoming the conception of children that was bound to result.[17] It is much more likely that Paul took for granted the general intention to have children as part and parcel of what marriage is.

There are two significant lines of theological objection to the Barthian and Augustinian positions on marital procreation. The first and general one may be labelled as 'somatological'. Augustine especially is guilty of a body-spirit dualism which exalts regeneration while falsely marginalizing 'generation' (i.e. procreation). It is true (and a New Testament emphasis, for example in the Johannine epistles) that God builds his new covenant people by placing his (spiritual) seed within men and women so that they are born into his family. But the people in whom he does this regenerative work are men and women who have already been born naturally. This is so obvious that it is almost embarrassing to point it out; but it is important. The future for which Christians long is a new and restored 'heavens and earth', not some alien or gnostic concept of 'heaven'. We are not to be delivered out of this created order into some alien and unrelated order, but rather redeemed out of 'this evil age' into new heavens and new earth. The work of natural procreation and nurture is not evacuated of moral significance just because it is in itself insufficient to make a man or woman a child of God. To put it bluntly, there will be no child of God in the new age who has not first been a child of parents in this age.[18]

This tension between the ages leads into the second theological objection, which is eschatological. We live in the overlap of the ages, in which the new age has dawned, but on whom the shadow of the old still rests. So long as the

---

17. Even Meeks 1983:101 (commenting on 1 Cor. 7:1–16 and 1 Thess. 4:1–8), who thinks Paul's 'eschatological expectations made the question of procreation moot', admits that 'in that event the fact that he still allows normal sexual relations would be the more remarkable'.

18. Questions such as surrogacy or cloning and related issues of procreational technology lie outside the scope of this study.

old age continues alongside the new, this world will need succeeding generations of human beings to care for it, albeit imperfectly. The day when marriage (and therefore procreation) will be no more will be (according to Jesus in
Luke 20:36) when 'they cannot die anymore'. The need for the next generation will not cease until death ceases, and death did not cease at the first
coming of the Christ. We must say of Barth's argument in this regard that its
eschatology is over-realized.

Positively, the intention to have children is integral (for the believer) with the
great Christian theological theme of *hope*. We have children not simply because,
looking back to creation, we understand it as part of the creation mandate; we
have them as a sign that there is confidence and hope for the future. This has
been eloquently (if perhaps a little exaggeratedly) argued by Stanley Hauerwas.
The moral significance of our willingness to have children is 'our claim that we
have something worthwhile to pass on'. 'Fear and rejection of parenthood, the
tendency to view the family as nothing more than companionable marriage, and
the understanding of marriage as one of a series of nonbinding commitments,
are but indications that our society has a growing distrust of our ability to deal
with the future' (Hauerwas 1981:165f., and all of ch. 8).

In Scripture this theme of hope is eloquently expressed by the use of the
word 'generation'. Phrases such as 'from generation to generation' (e.g. Exod.
3:15) or 'a thousand generations' (e.g. 1 Chr. 16:15) are usually expressions of
hope and promise. But they are more than just synonyms for 'a long time';
they are only meaningful if that 'long time' is a time of ongoing procreation.
We may compare Jeremiah 16:1–4, where Jeremiah is prohibited from marrying or having children because of the imminence of terrible judgment, with
Jeremiah 29:6 (Jeremiah's letter to the exiles), where the injunction to marry
and have sons and daughters is not just a sign that the exile will be prolonged,
but also a sign (eloquently echoing the Abrahamic promise) that the Lord has
a purpose of good for those exiles. Procreation is allied to hope, nonprocrea-
tion to judgment. The absence of future generations of human beings is associated both in biblical thought and in plausible imaginative construction with
the retrogression of the world into chaos, so that the thorns and thistles of
Genesis 3 take over. Blessing is when 'the streets of the city shall be full of
boys and girls playing in its streets' (Zech. 8:5).

We do not need Scripture to teach us the need for the next generation. In
the Graeco-Roman world there are a number of examples of this need being
recognized and urged on people. Augustus issued 'decrees penalizing bache-
lorhood and rewarding marriage and child-bearing . . . In Athens, a childless
man was excluded from office. Plato remarks that there is an obligation to
women as well as men to procreate for the state' (Witherington 1980:595f.).

In contemporary fiction the novel *The Children of Men* by P. D. James (James

1992) conjures up a world in which fertility has fallen to zero and the youngest human beings are now young adults. It is a haunting picture – and it resembles what would have happened if previous generations had taken Augustine's teaching at its face value.

Consequences of procreation in the context of task

We are now in a position to draw some conclusions about the procreational good of marriage in the context of the responsible task of world stewardship. The ethical consequences that follow from this impact on the very practical issues of deliberate and involuntary childlessness and contraception. We consider each in turn.

The morality of chosen childlessness

We have argued the general truth that the birth and nurture of children is a blessing to be valued, and a task to be undertaken with joy in the presence of the Creator. If the Creator declares procreation a blessing, given to us to enable us to participate in the privilege of being his stewards in this world, we ought to value this as gift and blessing. It may be, and often is, an alarming blessing (because we are not sure if we can cope with it), an inconvenient blessing (impacting deeply on lifestyles) and a costly blessing, but it is to be esteemed as blessing not curse. This ought to be our fundamental attitude with regard to procreation.

In an illuminating analogy, William Temple spoke of early twentieth-century Britain as like a shop window in which the price tags had been switched around, so that we valued highly what we should have treated as cheap and we treated as cheap what we should have valued highly.[19] This analogy bears on attitudes to procreation today; sometimes, far from valuing a new life, we pay the doctors to take 'it' away.

What, then, may be said about the deliberate decision of a married couple not to 'try' to have children, the morality of chosen childlessness?[20] Any judgment in this area is fraught with pastoral danger. Too often the hidden agenda when a couple ask a pastor for guidance in this area is a desire to be told 'the rules'. Legalism lurks by every step. We need to be reminded of the wise pastoral words of the apostle Paul in another context (Rom. 14:4), 'Who are you to pass judgment on servants of another? It is before their own lord that they

---

19. Quoted by Michael Marshall in *Church of England Newspaper*, 13 July 2001, p. 7.
20. The discussion by Thielicke 1979:204–212, is deeply theological and illuminating.

stand or fall.' There is only one who sees the hidden motives and intentions of the heart, and it is not the pastor or ethicist.

We must not get this question out of proportion. Writing about the reluctance of some married women to have children, Jack Dominian comments, 'The answer to these problems is not to bully them to have children. If a small proportion of women do not procreate, the world will not come to an end' (Dominian 2001:84). There are, however, signs of a movement wider than just a small proportion of women. We have noted in Chapter 3 the falling birth rates in many developed countries. In a provocative article, Taylor and Taylor note that nowadays in Western culture, 'It appears at least as appropriate to ask why anyone would choose to have children as to enquire why they have chosen not to.' They suggest, 'Perhaps we need to face the awkward truth that having children in today's world is counterintuitive' (Taylor and Taylor 2001:23).

We must reject any attitude which treats blessing as curse. To deny a blessing and regard it as a curse is to place our wills at odds with God's will. Wilfully to place a low value on procreation within marriage and gratuitously to deny the possibility of this blessing must place a question mark over a couple's valuation of this as blessing. In his massive study of Roman Catholic attitudes to contraception, John Noonan observes that the value 'fecundity is good' lies at the heart of the Old Testament structure of thought about marriage (Noonan 1986:30). But this is not a matter of rules; it concerns aligning our values with the declared valuation of the Creator. We are to value what he values and to desire what he says is a blessing. (In the same way it is perverse to desire death when Scripture teaches us that death is God's judgment on human sin.)

Rodney Stark has shown that one of the salient distinguishing features of the early church was the refusal of Christians to countenance abortion or infanticide, in a world in which female infanticide was common (Stark 1996:97).[21]

The decision not to 'intend' children within a marriage may be taken for a number of reasons. Couples who choose childlessness are very sensitive to the charge of selfishness, and yet in contemporary Western society this charge must surely stick in some instances, if we are to believe the testimonies of some of these couples. Two examples from British newspapers will suffice to illustrate this. The *Independent*, on 17 November 1998, reports on a campaigning association, 'The British Association of Non-Parents'. The chairman says of himself, 'I have never wanted to be a father. I have never wanted that sort of responsibility. It is the fact that child-rearing goes on every bloody day for so long . . . I just do not want to devote myself in this way to children.' In *The*

---

21. Stark (1996:97f.) quotes the letter from one Hilarion to his pregnant wife Alis in 1 BC: '. . . if it is a boy keep it, if a girl discard it.'

Times on 21 June 1997 a Relate counsellor and spokeswoman is quoted as saying, 'It's usually a lifestyle thing. They have a life they enjoy and feel that children would change it too much.' The report goes on to explain that The British Association of Non-Parents wants 'to challenge the social tendency to glorify and romanticise parenthood', and the Christian ethicist will agree. They want to point out that bringing up children is 'exhausting, time-consuming, difficult and expensive'. Indeed so.

None the less, we need to question whether a marriage that is *in principle* closed to the hope of children is real love. We have seen that circumscribed love is an oxymoron. Paul Ramsey thoughtfully suggests that the fact that we procreate in the midst of our (sexual) love is 'a trace of the original mystery by which God created the world because of his love'. And therefore, 'To put radically asunder what God joined together in making love procreative [or] to procreate without love . . . means a refusal of the image of God's creation in our own' (Ramsey 1975:14f.).

In a similar vein, Stanley Hauerwas points out that real love is care and respect for others, irrespective of whether or not we have chosen them. Unlike conjugal ties, which are chosen, blood ties are not, for 'the most inescapable fact about families, regardless of their different forms and customs, is that we do not choose to be part of them' (Hauerwas 1981:165).

Rodney Clapp perceptively observes how learning to love our children (whom we have not chosen, even if we 'chose' to have them) is a practice of love that equips us to love the 'stranger'. As he puts it, by loving 'the strangers who are our children' we learn the 'transferable skills . . . we must use to welcome other strangers besides our children' (Clapp 1993:148). He entitles chapter 7 of *Families at the Crossroads* 'Welcoming Children and Other Strangers'. The next chapter is prefaced by a quotation from James T. Burtchaell's *For Better, For Worse*: 'The only home which is safe for anyone to be born into is the home that is ready to welcome someone who does not belong there by right of kinship, but belongs there in virtue of hospitality.' A society which grows to affirm deliberate and gratuitous married childlessness as a lifestyle will be a society moving in precisely the opposite direction. Clapp also observes that in the culture of the USA costly parenting does not fit easily with individualism and self-centredness.

> We have been coached so long and so thoroughly in the ways of autonomy and self-interest that we can no longer imagine why we should have children. After all, children cost a lot of money. And what could hinder my autonomy more than responsibility for children, who will surely impose their own expectations and limitations on my life?'
> (Clapp 1993:136).

It is sometimes argued that because children may put a strain on a relation-ship, couples who deliberately avoid children are more likely to stay together. So Penelope Leach writes,

> Having children – especially the first child – puts a bigger strain on a couple's relationship than anything else they ever do; some who stay together emerge stronger and richer, but a heck of a lot never recover. So a future of smaller families and more people choosing not to have children at all could well leave couples closer than they are today; for many, the purpose of being together would be *solely to pleasure and support each other* . . .
> (*CAM* magazine, No. 28, 1999, my italics)

Whether sociological analysis supports the assertion that deliberate childless-ness promotes marital stability is a moot point; that the philosophy advocated here is inherently selfish and introspective is not.

We would be guilty of ethical naïveté, however, if we failed to recognize that other motivations than selfishness are claimed in support of deliberate married childlessness. Fear is a significant one in a number of couples, who shrink from having children not because they deny this is in principle a bless-ing but because they think they are not 'ready for it', whether because of financial insecurity, psychological unfittedness or immaturity. The proper place for such fears to begin to be addressed is during marriage preparation, when the purposes of marriage are explained and embraced. To enter mar-riage involves a couple in accepting and aligning themselves with the Creator's purpose in instituting marriage; the general intention to have chil-dren is integral to this. It is not helpful, however, for the pastor to say to a couple, 'You should have thought of this before.' The theological theme that can inform pastoral engagement in these circumstances is adumbrated in Genesis 1:28f.; the *blessing* of fruitfulness and multiplication is immediately followed by the *provision* of all that is needful for humankind. The blessing of procreational responsibility is given along with the resources to enable humankind to sustain and carry out this responsibility. This, of course, sounds much too simple, and we need to be careful not to narrow its truth to any particular couple in isolation. If anything, it reinforces the need for society as a whole to value and support parenthood so that parents do not feel they have to carry this entire burden on their own.

There are Christian couples who say they have chosen childlessness in order to free themselves more fully for the service of God and the gospel of Christ. Just as in the nineteenth century many single women sacrificed the possibility of marriage for the sake of the gospel, so today (it is said) young couples may sac-rifice the possibility of children to the same end. I remain in general sceptical of this. The parallel with those who have renounced marriage is unconvincing; those who have 'made themselves eunuchs for the sake of the kingdom of heaven' (Matt. 19:12) may claim dominical support in a way that those who separate from marriage one of the created purposes of marriage may not. Too often behind such explanations lies a false spiritualization of the service of God, in which having children is essentially regarded as a selfish thing, whereas 'gospel ministry' is not. But, as we have seen, the costly project of the conception, birth and nurture of children is to be understood in the ethical context precisely of the service of God.

All the arguments so far have tended in one direction. We must now consider a final possibility, that there may be circumstances in which a couple long for children and would dearly love to have children, but feel that overriding obstacles have been placed in their way. Perhaps for reasons of age or hereditary health problems, they feel themselves frustrated in these yearnings. Their fundamental affective direction in this regard is wholeheartedly positive; they affirm God's valuation of procreation as a blessing. But in a fallen world they see the obstacles in their path to be so great that it would be irresponsible to embark on this project.

This possibility is eloquently described by O'Donovan, who suggests the moral possibility of a couple genuinely aligning their values with God's values and saying in their hearts, 'We would love to be entrusted with the blessing and task of children,' but perhaps for rare medical reasons they are convinced that these factors overwhelm the normal framework of ethical choice. His argument is worth quoting at length.

> A deliberate intention to prefer other goods (such as career or wealth) to the good of children would, in my opinion, constitute a lack of understanding consent and so, in traditional terms, a ground of nullity. A couple who do not see what children have to do with it are as far from understanding marriage as a couple who do not see what permanence has to do with it. But I would wish to distinguish very carefully between this couple and another who, while seeing quite clearly what children have to do with it, are persuaded for reasons that seem good to them (their age or health or genetic endowment, for example) that this good cannot be realized in their own marriage. There is a *reluctant* 'intention' not to have children which is perfectly compatible with a full understanding of marriage.
> (O'Donovan 1978:12)[22]

---

22. Cf. Atkinson 1979:89. Paul Ramsey likewise acknowledges this possibility when he speaks of a hypothetical couple who 'for grave, or for what in their case is to them sufficient, reason adopt a *lifelong* policy of *un*planned parenthood' (Ramsey 1975:9).

Involuntary childlessness

Many couples, however, would love to have children but are not able to; perhaps between one in seven and one in ten couples have difficulty in conceiving a baby (Cudmore 1996:55). The possibility does not fall within their sphere of choice at all. Some may have read this chapter so far with pain, wishing to affirm the blessing of children but aware this cannot be a blessing given to them. The pain of childlessness is a peculiar pain, described by one couple as 'that strange grief which has no focus for its tears and no object for its love' (Dickson 1997:93). It is the gradual loss of what might have been, a hope deferred that makes the heart sick (Prov. 13:12).

What does the gospel say to such a couple? We must affirm first that the purpose of marriage is to serve God. It is not (in any primary sense) to have children any more than it is (in any primary sense) to build relationship or promote social order. Further, we must affirm that, while the valuing of procreation as blessing is intrinsic to a proper understanding of marriage, the actual gift of children is not essential to making marriage true marriage (e.g. Augustine, *On the Good of Marriage* §17). It would be absurd (in a Christian framework) to claim that it was and I am not aware of any Christian writer who argues for this position (although see Thatcher 1999:120–124).

Further, children are a gift and a blessing, not a right. We must guard against the technological arrogance of all human talk that regards having a child as a human right. The argument against this is eloquently put in the Roman Catholic document *New Life: Church Teaching on Technology and Fertilization*. While infertility is 'a difficult trial', 'nevertheless, marriage does not confer upon the spouses the right to have a child, but only the right to perform those natural acts which are *per se* ordered to procreation'. 'A true and proper right to a child would be contrary to the child's dignity and value. The child is not an object to which one has a right, nor can be considered as an object of ownership: rather a child is a gift' (Connolly 1987:39f.). This proper understanding of child as gift prepares us for ethical limits on the lengths to which it may be proper to go in the search to 'achieve' parenthood; the study of these limits is outside the scope of this book.

Perhaps the most significant ethical implication in regard to involuntary childlessness impacts not on the couple concerned but on others around them. It is this: we ought to grieve with them and weep with them as they

---

In Ramsey's argument what renders their decision potentially moral is the determination to hold together the unitive and procreative dimensions of marriage, such that if either partner had a child it would be by the other and not outside of their exclusive sexual relationship. This is a different argument from O'Donovan's.

weep (Rom. 12:15). A friend struggling with childlessness wrote to me after hearing this in a talk. She was very struck by the teaching that others should grieve with her. She commented on how rare it is to hear such teaching in the churches she has known.

It is sometimes said that the strong affirmation of procreation that characterizes this chapter is insensitive to those who cannot have children. This is not so. To affirm the goodness of birth is not insensitive to those who cannot conceive or who suffer a miscarriage or a stillbirth, any more than affirming the goodness of marriage is insensitive to the widow. On the contrary, if we do not affirm this goodness, we cannot grieve with them. So we affirm that the longing of a couple to conceive is a good longing and their grief at not conceiving is a right grief; and we grieve with them, if we are taken into their confidence. They value what God values, and they are sad when that good gift is withheld from them or frustratingly postponed. They are right to be sad.

When the childless Hannah (1 Sam. 1) is described as weeping and losing her appetite (v. 7) and deeply troubled (v. 15) and in great anguish and grief (v. 16), we do not say to her, 'Snap out of it. Children are just a personal lifestyle choice, no more; whether or not you and Elkanah happen to have children is neither here nor there. It's not a good thing or a bad thing: it's just a thing. So what's the crying about?' No, we grieve with her and we pray with her (as has in the past been traditional at weddings) for the gift of children.

Contraception

We now consider briefly the moral question of the use of contraception within marriage. The debate tends to focus reactively around the arguments of Roman Catholic ethicists[23] based on 'natural law', that there is an inherent and unbreakable moral nexus between the unitive and the procreative aims in *each* act of sexual union. So Connolly expounds *Humanae Vitae* as affirming 'the inseparable connection between the two meanings of the conjugal act: the unitive meaning and the procreative meaning'. Contraception removes the procreative, artificial fertilization the unitive. Both separate the two goods and meanings of marriage (Connolly 1987:33).

Further, it is argued that deliberately to frustrate the procreative possibility in any act of sexual union is to damage the unitive significance of the act by circumscribing the self-giving of the one to the other. This latter argument is adduced by Brigid McEwen (McEwen 1997). Contraception separates pro-

---

23. Noonan 1986 gives a detailed account of Roman Catholic thinking and teaching about contraception. The review of the issues in Thatcher 1999: ch. 6 (with references given there) is also useful.

creative possibility from intercourse and makes the body lie, saying, 'I accept you, but not your fertility. I give myself to you, but not totally.'

A number of cogent criticisms from within a Roman Catholic framework are offered by Gareth Moore (Moore 1992: ch. 9).[24] But the most significant Protestant criticism is that it treats the marital relationship as if it were a sequence of isolated acts of sexual union, each of which must be considered and assessed separately in terms of morality. O'Donovan puts the critique admirably:

> What upset so many in the teaching of Paul VI's encyclical *Humanae Vitae* was that it seemed not to perceive the difference of structure between sexual relations in marriage and simple fornication. Chastity in marriage was analysed into a series of particular acts of sexual union, a proceeding which carried with it an unwitting but unmistakable hint of the pornographic. A married couple do not know each other in isolated moments or one-night stands. Their moments of sexual union are points of focus for a physical relationship which must properly be predicated of the whole extent of their life together. Thus the virtue of chastity as openness to procreation cannot be accounted for in terms of a repeated sequence of chaste acts each of which is open to procreation. The chastity of a couple is more than the chastity of their acts, though it is not irrespective of it either.
>
> (O'Donovan 1994:210; cf. Hauerwas 1981:186, n.12)

We may note in this context the observation of Thielicke that God has so ordered sex that it is only truly pleasurable in the context of ongoing relationship. He points out that sexual intercourse may be followed by disgust, even loathing, particularly of a prostitute (or, we might add, to the victim of coercive sex, cf. Amnon to Tamar in 2 Sam. 13:15).

> Actually the criterion of that which is more than merely instinctive, namely, the personal character of the sexual intercourse, is that gratitude and fulfilment survive the moment of ecstasy and that these moments are only the expression, culmination, and concentration of a continuing relationship which outlasts all changes of mood and feeling.
>
> (Thielicke 1979:38)

In the context of the life-relationship of a married couple, to value procreation as a blessing implies not necessarily openness to procreation in each act

---

24. Moore is particularly helpful in discussing what is and is not meant by 'an unwanted child'.

of sexual union, but rather that they ought (except perhaps in rare circumstances discussed above) to be open to the possibility (indeed the hope and desire) that God will bless their union with a child or children. There is a great moral difference between what used to be called 'planned parenthood' and 'planned *un*parenthood' (although even here the word 'plan' carries with it dangerous connotations of human autonomous control over the process).

Nevertheless, if (as has been argued) we are to understand the task of responsible stewardship of the earth as the primary ethical matrix within which marriage is considered, it follows that it may indeed be a matter of Christian freedom for a couple to make responsible decisions about the number of children they intend to have (always submitting themselves humbly to the possibility that God will give them a child unintended by them, and they will welcome that child too as a gift of God). Christian ethics has no statement to make about 'the right number of children a couple should have'; this is a matter of freedom and wisdom.

In fact, this governing ethic of responsible stewardship is precisely suited to proper consideration of issues of world population. It is not within the scope of this study to grapple with the ever-changing statistics of demographic profiles and totals, either of individual nations or of the world in totality.[25] But if the purpose of procreation is that there should be future generations to govern and rule the earth, it is perfectly proper to consider the possibilities either of some voluntary limitation of procreation or of encouragements to couples to have more children. Both possibilities are of contemporary relevance. In 1999 a newspaper article reported that in countries representing 44% of the world's population total fertility was below the replacement level; in the UK it has been so for more than two decades. Overall the world population continues to rise, but the rate of rise seems to be decreasing. The issues of responsible stewardship are not a simple matter of population totals as related to food resources (especially sustainable supplies of drinking water); they relate also to population profiles and in particular the ratio of the active workforce to the young and the elderly. It is sufficient *workers* that are needed.

In conclusion, we should note that there is a principled difference between the use of contraception within marriage in the service of 'planned parenthood' and the use of the same medical contraceptive techniques within or outside marriage with the explicit and long-term aim of preventing parenthood from happening at all.

---

25. See for example the reports by John Madeley, *Church Times*, 8 January 1999; Jeremy Laurance and Dominic Kennedy in *The Times*, 14 June 1996; Nicholas Schoon in *Independent*, 9 February 1999; Hugh Montefiore in *Church Times*, 28 June 1996.

Contraception and the ethics of premarital sex

It is sometimes claimed that Old Testament sexual ethics are primarily (even exclusively) concerned with procreation, pregnancy and paternity, rather than with sexual intercourse *per se*. So, with reference to the Old Testament adultery laws, Phillips claims, 'There is no thought of sexual ethics as such, but of paternity' (Phillips 1970:117). It is true that until the advent of reliable and readily available contraception any act of premarital sex ran a very considerable risk of leading to pregnancy. A man who married a woman and found she was not a virgin (Deut. 22:13ff.) and whose bride was found to be pregnant soon after marriage would not know if the child was his or not.

If paternity were the sole concern then we should have to admit that premarital sex with contraception was ethically of no concern to us. However, such an argument always assumes the marginalization of procreation as a purpose of sexual relationship. This chapter has argued strongly against such marginalization. We ought to desire the blessing of children as an integral part of any moral sexual relationship. Contraception with the aim of never having children from a particular relationship may break the link physiologically, but it cannot sever the intrinsic theological (and therefore moral) link in creation order.[26] A premarital sexual relationship is not rendered moral by the prevention of pregnancy.

Conclusion

We conclude that in general a couple determined to serve God (as all should) will wish for the blessing of children. They do not wish for children because they like children. They do not wish for children because they themselves need to be needed by children. They wish for children because they understand that humankind has been given a world to care for; and the next generation need to be conceived, born and brought up in godly nurture so that this may happen. One day, when death is no more and the new heavens and new earth are inaugurated, this need for successive generations will be transcended – but not yet. Until that day, nurturing children is not an alternative to godliness but rather a natural expression of godliness within marriage.

---

26. See Ramsey 1975: ch. 2 for an eloquent rebuttal of the separation of sexual 'love' from procreative intent.

10. INTIMACY AND ORDER IN THE SERVICE OF GOD

In order to redress a balance in contemporary thought I have tried (in Chapter 7) to show how the relational 'good' of marriage has been exaggerated out of biblical proportion with damaging effects. Instead I have argued that all three traditional 'goods' of marriage ought to be understood as subsidiary to the governing ethic of the service of God. In Chapter 9 I applied this thinking to procreation. In this chapter we consider the remaining two 'goods' of marriage.

Relationship in the context of task

The moment we suggest that the marriage *relationship* exists in order to facilitate the achievement of a *task*, doubts arise in our minds. Does this not inevitably reduce the relationship from one of love to one of function? Indeed, does it not trivialize sex and eviscerate it, removing the deeply interpersonal dynamic of desire and delight that most serious ethicists have wanted to affirm? We must grapple with this objection and consider how sexual desire and delight are to be related to the dignity of the human task under God.

The naturalness of sexual desire and delight
We begin by recognizing that sexual desire and delight is part of the natural backdrop to all the biblical texts. It is taken for granted and alluded to as a natural part of life. It is important to be clear that this is understood and affirmed throughout Scripture, as a brief survey of examples will show.

We may note the affirmation of beauty (possibly with connotations of sexual attractiveness) independent of any utilitarian context, for example, in the blessing of Naphtali as 'a doe . . . that bears lovely fawns' (Gen. 49:21); or the affirmation of the joyful garments of bride and bridegroom in Isaiah 61:10; or the 'delight' of the Lord the husband in his bride, like the joy of bridegroom over bride (Is. 62:4f.; cf. Ps. 19:5); or the king desiring his bride's beauty in Psalm 45:11 (interestingly in the context of the promise of pro-creation, v. 16f.); or the 'marriage song' in Psalm 78:63 (even though here, in the context of judgment, this song is absent); or the natural reference to 'beautiful young women' in Amos 8:13. Even when they cease because of judgment, weddings are remembered for 'the sound of mirth and gladness' when 'the voice of the bride and bridegroom' are heard (Jer. 7:34; cf. 16:9; 25:10; 33:11; Rev. 18:23). There is nothing surprising or strange about the Egyptians desiring the 'beautiful' Sarah (Gen. 12:10–20); or about Paltiel weeping behind Michal as she was taken from him to be given to David (2 Sam. 3:15f.).

Marital affection is referred to very naturally, for example in Ecclesiastes 9:9 ('Enjoy life with the wife whom you love'); in Genesis 26:8 (Isaac caressing or fondling his wife Rebekah; cf. 24:67, where his marriage to Rebekah is a source of 'comfort' to Isaac after the death of his mother); in Genesis 29:20 ('So Jacob served seven years for Rachel, and they seemed to him but a few days because of the love he had for her'); or Deuteronomy 13:6 ('the wife you embrace', cf. 28:54). Proverbs 5:18f. waxes eloquent about the joy the husband should have in the wife of his youth, satisfied by her breasts and captivated by her love. Elkanah and Hannah love one another (1 Sam. 1:5–8, specifically in the absence of children, Meilander 1995:74). It is taken for granted that the natural response to a spouse's death is grief (Gen. 23:1f., Abraham for Sarah, who has been loved long after she has fulfilled any procreative role; or Gen. 48:7, Jacob for Rachel; or Ezek. 24:15ff., where Ezekiel's wife is described as 'the delight of your eyes'). Song of Songs 2:5; 5:8 understand the dynamic of lovesickness.

We must never fall for the naïve parody that in the Old Testament the only motivation for sex was the desire for children (or, particularly, sons). Sexual attraction, desire and delight were as well known and accepted then as now. For one thing, the whole metaphorical structure of the Lord's marriage to his people would have been evacuated of meaning were this not so (Schillebeeckx 1965:86).

This natural 'taken-for-grantedness' of marital joy is carried over into the New Testament. The wedding at Cana (John 2:1–11) is naturally a time of cel-ebration when good wine will be used. In Matthew 24:37 judgment dividing married couples is a cause of shock and sorrow.

The goodness of sexual desire and delight

All of this is part of the natural backdrop to biblical thought. The Bible texts of all ages live in the same world as we do, so far as the underlying dynamics of sexual desire and marital delight are concerned. We must ask, however, why this is to be esteemed as good, beyond the obvious and ethically rather shallow observation that it can be pleasurable; for the association of sexual delight with the blessing of God suggests that it is good at a deeper level than the merely hedonistic. We may understand the relational *pleasure* of sex, but what is the relational *good*? In particular, what good does a sexual relationship do the couple and the world beyond the couple? In what way does the relational good of marriage serve the primary good of caring for God's world? The purpose of sexual union is not simply the good of the couple, but a wider outward-looking creation-serving good.

The answer *in nuce* is that faithful love cannot flow out from a marriage unless it is present as the heart of the marriage. As a good tree bears good fruit, so the usefulness of a marriage in bringing blessing to others is predicated on its nature as a marriage characterized by faithful love. Further, if a marriage is characterized by true love (which, as we have seen, can never be circumscribed by the boundary of the couple or even the family circle), then that love must overflow to bring blessing beyond itself.

This is true of God's marriage with his people, which exhibits precisely this overflow of love. The reason the divine bridegroom courts and loves his bride Israel is not that they should enjoy private bliss, but rather to bring blessing to the nations (a grand theme of Old Testament promise from Gen. 12:1–3 onwards). Israel is to be the bride of the Lord in order that she should be a light to the nations and in some sense become a mother figure to them as they come under her divine husband's wings. Just as Adam 'married' Eve that together they might till the garden, so the Lord 'marries' Israel that together they may properly rule and order his world.[1]

This gives us an ethical insight into the reason why a couple ought to build a relationship of love and trust. It is not that their relationship is an end in its own right. It is not even that the world may see in their love an image of the love of God for his people (though that may, wonderfully, be true). It is that as they engage in a joyful task they may work *together* rather than against one another; their care for God's world will be an overflow of the faithful love they have for one another.

It is important to be clear that we are not at all arguing against mutual delight in sexual union; quite the reverse. It might be thought that an

---

1. This phraseology was suggested to me by Dr Markus Bockmuehl in a letter.

unremitting outward and serving emphasis would place upon marriage a deadening burden of toil that is inimical to sexual delight. This would be to misunderstand the ethics I am commending. The restorative effect of sexual delight on husband and wife may perhaps be considered by analogy with the blessing of the Sabbath. Just as rhythms of Sabbath rest are instituted by the Creator for the sake of man (cf. Mark 2:27) to refresh him so that his work may be a joy, so sexual delight within marriage may refresh and restore husband and wife for the work to which the Creator has called them. As the Anglican churchman Jeremy Taylor rightly observed, married sex is not just for children or to prevent fornication, but also 'to lighten and ease the cares and sadnesses of household affairs, or to endear each other' (Bailey 1959:196, 207f.). Just as God gives rest in order that man may joyfully work (and not work for the sake of rest), so he gives husband and wife joy in sex that they may the more joyfully serve, and not the reverse. When reversed, sexual delight and relational intimacy become ends in themselves. The paradox and tragedy is that, having been made into idols, they inevitably disappoint, frustrate and fade. So often in a healthy marriage sexual delight creeps up on the couple at unexpected moments, in the midst of lives of active service and outward-looking work.

Just as the birth and costly nurture of children within marriage is a privileged part of serving God in his world, so also the sexual and relational intimacy of husband and wife serves this dignity and privilege, equipping man and wife to be in God's world what he intends them to be.

The mutual obligations of sex within marriage (1 Corinthians 7:1–6)

Treatment of most of 1 Corinthians 7 must be held over until divorce and singleness are covered by a forthcoming volume, but since verses 1–6 concern the sexual relationship of a couple, they will be considered here.

1 Corinthians 7:1

'Now concerning [peri de] the matters about which you wrote: "It is well [kalon] for a man not to touch a woman."' Paul begins what is usually regarded as a new section,[2] referring to matters they have raised with him. The reasonable assumption of many recent commentators[3] is that Paul quotes and immediately qualifies some slogan of his opponents. This is reflected in the NRSV

---

2. *peri de* (cf. 7:25; 8:1; 12:1; 16:1, 12).

3. E.g. Fee 1987; Collins 1992 (who says this view goes back to Origen, p. 252); Witherington 1995; Hays 1997; Barrett 1968.

speech marks: 'It is well for a man not to touch [i.e. touch sexually][4] a woman.'
This appears to be some kind of general claim that abstinence from sex is virtuous (*kalos* in the sense of 'morally good, noble, praiseworthy', BAGD) and
to be encouraged. The opponents may have been telling the unmarried they
ought to remain so, or they may have been telling the married they should
abstain from sex within marriage.[5] The latter is more likely (Fee 1987; Hays
1987), from the reference to depriving one another (v. 5). We do not know
why they urged such abstinence; it may possibly have been linked to philosophical ideas current in the Graeco-Roman world, that sexual intercourse
was draining of strength and otherwise unhealthy (Osiek and Balch
1997:104–106).

Paul immediately makes it clear that he disagrees. Later in the chapter,
when he uses the word *kalon* of the unmarried state (vv. 8, 26), it is not a moral
judgment, good as 'opposed to what is evil or vicious', but rather 'what is
expedient on account of there being so many troubles, vexations, and anxieties that are incident to married persons' (Calvin, *1–2 Cor.*:223), which is why
he can use the adverb *kalōs* in the reverse sense in verse 38 and also with the
comparative 'better'. This is not the voice of the ascetic Paul,[6] but of Paul the
wise pastor combating the ascetic Corinthians. They thought abstinence from
sex and marriage was good in a moral sense. Paul replies that they are wrong,
although it may be good in the sense of expedient.

This distinction is especially important in view of the later patristic tradition that identified Paul as an ascetic, one who held in principle a low opinion
of marriage 'and consequently encouraged his readers in the direction of
sexual asceticism, which is the rejection of one's erotic nature in order to
become more holy or closer to God'. In an important monograph, Deming
points out that 'not all forms of celibacy stem from a theology of sexual
asceticism', and that Paul should be seen 'as a cautious and measured proponent of the single lifestyle, a form of celibacy characterized by freedom from
the responsibilities of marriage and for which the absence of sexual fulfilment
was no more than an unintended consequence and an inconvenience, never an
end in itself' (Deming 1995:1, 2, 4; cf. Rosner 1994:149–153; Witherington
1995:174–176).

---

4. NIV 'It is good for a man not to marry' is misleading. Fee 1987:275 gives conclusive evidence from all nine occurrences of the phrase in Greek literature that, 'The idiom "to
touch a woman" . . . refers to having sexual intercourse.'

5. See Winter 2001:225f. for evidence that the absence of the personal pronoun does not
exclude the possibility that this refers to a man with *his* wife.

6. As Fee 1987:276 points out, 'Paul was simply not an ascetic'.

1 Corinthians 7:2–6

> But because of cases of sexual immorality, each man should have his own wife and each woman her own husband. The husband should give to his wife her conjugal rights, and likewise the wife to her husband. For the wife does not have authority over her own body, but the husband does; likewise the husband does not have authority over his own body, but the wife does. Do not deprive one another except perhaps by agreement for a set time, to devote yourselves to prayer,[7] and then come together again, so that Satan may not tempt you because of your lack of self-control [*akrasia*].[8] This I say by way of concession, not of command.

Human sexual urges will lead to 'cases of sexual immorality' (the likely translation of the plural *porneias*) unless the Christian community understands that the proper general response is to pair off so that, so far as is possible, each man has one woman and each woman one man (in other words, they form marriages).[9] In marriage there is a mutual[10] moral obligation on both husband and wife each to surrender their body to the other in willing sexual relations sustained so far as health permits over the lifetime of their marriage.[11] Abstinence may be allowed for prayer[12] (and will sometimes be inevitable for reasons of separation or health); but abstinence must not become a habit. In saying this we must also recognize that sexual desire changes with age, and eventually the time comes when 'desire fails' (Eccles. 12:5) even for the most vigorously libidinous (cf. David with Abishag, 1 Kgs. 1).

The mutuality 'runs counter to much first-century practice' (Winter

---

7. Winter 2001:232 suggests the prayer may have been specifically prompted by a crisis of famine in Corinth.

8. See Hill 1977. Hill argues that, whereas the Greek and Hellenistic concept of self-control was control of a man's other faculties by his faculty of reason, for Paul the element of 'power in oneself' has been removed, leaving open the theological possibility of this quality being God-given.

9. The danger of sexual immorality is also a motivation for getting married in Jewish tradition; cf. t.Levi 9:9f., 'Be on guard against the spirit of promiscuity . . . Therefore take for yourself a wife while you are still young.'

10. This mutuality incidentally prohibits polygamy, as noted by Barrett 1968.

11. Instone Brewer 2002:192–194 (and see n.7) suggests a background in Paul's thought in the rabbinic use of Exod. 21:10 here. This is possible, but see the perceptive cautions of Clark 1999:144 and nn.31, 32 there.

12. Cf. t.Naphtali 8:8, 'There is a time for having intercourse with one's wife, and a time to abstain for the purpose of prayer.'

2001:228) and cuts across any culture that regards sex as the privilege of the husband and the duty of the wife. It is just as much the duty of the husband and the privilege of the wife. Each owes the other the debt of full sexual love.

Far from it being 'good' for a man not to touch a woman, the right response is for each man to have one woman and to 'touch' and go on 'touching' her lovingly, and for each woman to have one man and do the same. Paul sets himself against the spiritual asceticism of his opponents and indeed the norms of the Roman world.[13] Husbands and wives are not to deprive one another of sexual relations. Today as a pastor, perhaps Paul would have expanded on this in terms of the ways in which husbands and wives may effectively deprive their spouses of a lasting sexual relationship by needless overwork, by preoccupation with work, by obsession with pornography, by the failure to make unhurried and uninterrupted time each for the other and in other ways.[14] The applications are numerous and important.

The only exception Paul allows is that a couple may (and we may sense the almost grudging way Paul allows this) abstain from sex by mutual agreement in order to have a special season of prayer. But even then they are not to do this for too long and they are to make sure they do not let abstinence become a habit, or it will lead to sexual temptations that could have been avoided. Even the option of temporary and spiritually focused abstention is only allowed as a concession (v. 6) (Fee 1987, ad loc.; Witherington 1995:175).

At the start of 1 Corinthians 7 Paul aligns himself with the fundamental Bible perspective that the sexual relation of marriage is good, to be sustained and encouraged. All that he goes on to say must be read in the light of this opening paragraph. Paul's teaching in verses 2–6 has been widely misinterpreted in exactly the opposite sense as a grudging admission that sex within marriage is a regrettable necessity for those poor souls who lack self-control, and even then purely for the negative reason of preventing their sexual frustration overflowing into immorality (Phipps 1982). Typical is Thatcher: 'St Paul taught the church at Corinth that marriage is better avoided. It is a concession,

---

13. Witherington 1987:178, n.33 observes that 'Roman matrons had been brought up to expect that once one had one's two to three children, one might expect to forego sexual relations thereafter. In the Roman view, sex in marriage was for procreation, not recreation.'

14. The verb for 'to devote yourselves' in v. 5 is *scholazō*, 'to have spare time, leisure'; the cognate noun *scholē* 'frequently appears in the Stoic-Cynic discussion on marriage' in the context of the need for free time (*scholē*) to study philosophy (see Collins 1999:257). That abstinence from sex makes more free time reminds us that free leisure time is necessary for sex. Married people must make space in busy lives for ongoing sexual relationship.

a second best, an escape for those who cannot control their sexual feelings (Thatcher 1999:32).[15] This is a misleading parody of what he actually teaches. It is revealing that the word 'concession' is applied by Thatcher in exactly the reverse sense to that in which Paul uses it in verse 6, where the somewhat reluctant concession is to allow abstinence from sex within marriage so long as it is strictly temporary and for a very strong reason.

What is not always appreciated is that the negative concern to prevent immorality and the positive valuation of sex within marriage are two sides of the same coin. There is no conflict between these reasons to commend marriage.[16] 'Paul's fundamental insight [is] that one of the good purposes of marriage is to provide sexual satisfaction for husband and wife together' (Hays 1997:131). The avoidance of temptation to immorality is achieved by the giving of sexual satisfaction each to the other in marriage.

It is important also that the sexual relationship and the wider marriage relationship be held closely together. Sexual desire and delight ought to be a natural overflow of married love. Indeed, those who counsel couples with sexual problems will testify that the large majority of sexual problems are symptoms of relational problems in the marriage.

Passion with fruitfulness (the Song of Songs)
The Song of Songs is the most positively erotic text in Scripture (although not the only one, cf. Is. 62:4f.). It would be unthinkable to consider Scripture's perspectives on the sexual relationship without considering its rich contribution. Although a full treatment falls outside the scope of this limited theological study, we must make some observations about how the Song relates to our themes.

'Human marriage' and 'divine marriage' readings
Even a brief glance at the Song raises problems of interpretation. How is it structured? Is it one coherent Song, a linear sequence of songs following a narrative plot, or an anthology of songs in no particular order but collected

---

15. Thatcher also quotes Brown 1989:55, where Brown claims that in 1 Corinthians 7:2, 'By this essentially negative, even alarmist strategy, Paul left a fatal legacy to future ages.' The negative patristic and later tradition has been well documented though not always in a balanced way by, e.g. Bailey 1959; Avis 1989:81ff., Brundage 1987. But note also the more positive aspects portrayed in Brooke 1989 and other parts of Brown 1989.

16. Cf. Barrett 1968, who notes that Paul 'does not say that marriage serves no purpose but that of acting as a prophylactic against fornication, but it does serve that purpose'.

because of a common theme? Where and how ought it to be subdivided? What is the nature of the association with Solomon? When, where and by whom was the song written? Are parallels or similarities in other literature illuminating or not (Brenner 1989: ch. 4)? These and other issues (including textual questions) are addressed elsewhere and lie mostly outside the scope of this study.[17]

It would be easy to become preoccupied with these puzzles. Instead we begin with the two most salient features to be taken into account in interpreting the Song. These are (a) that it is about sex, and (b) that it is in the Bible. The book centres on the tensions, desires and delights of the mutual erotic love of a man and a woman.[18] Were it not in the canon of Jewish and Christian Scripture we might leave it at that; here are secular love songs to be set alongside myriads of other secular love songs down the ages. But it is in the canon, and we must interpret it as a canonical text. For what reason is it there and in what way is it intended to profit us and equip us for godliness? Those who ask this question give two kinds of answers, often described (rather unhelpfully) as literal and allegorical/typological;[19] I refer to them as 'human marriage' readings and 'divine marriage' readings.

On the one hand, some (e.g. Gledhill 1994) say we have here a simple and beautiful affirmation of the rightness, wonder and goodness of heterosexual erotic love; we may explore in this Song the dynamics of such love and so enrich our thankful enjoyment of the gift of a good Creator who richly gives us all things for our enjoyment (1 Tim. 6:17). The wisdom writer who encourages the husband to rejoice in the wife of his youth so that her breasts satisfy him at all times (Prov. 5:18f.) might point this man to the Song for pure and

---

17. For an introduction to the history of exegesis see Rowley 1965:197–245. Brenner 1989 gives a concise overview of issues of interpretation from a feminist perspective. Gledhill 1994:19–39 gives a clear introduction. The most comprehensive recent technical commentary is Pope 1977. This includes a review of the histories of Jewish and Christian interpretation (pp. 89–132). See also the excursus in Bray 1996:159–164.

18. With most interpreters I take it that there is only one male lover and one female beloved. The hypothesis of a love triangle between one girl, her shepherd lover and King Solomon trying to win her love is unpersuasive (see the critique in Gledhill 1994:24–26). It is hard to see Solomon cast so unambiguously as villain in a canonical text. Above all, it requires a forced reordering of the text.

19. This is unhelpful both because the word 'literal' begs too many questions (especially with regard to such an enigmatic poetic text) and because 'allegorical' covers such a wide range of interpretations, too many of them uncontrolled and fanciful. And there are important conceptual differences between allegory and typology.

beautiful erotic stimulus to such marital love. Here is nakedness without shame, passion with purity. This is the 'human marriage' reading.

Others point out that we have elsewhere in Scripture the clue we need to understand why the Song is included. This clue is the motif of the Lord as the husband of his people his bride, or in the New Testament texts the fulfilment of this in the Christ as the husband of his bride the church. The Bible is a long story of salvation; this is its major theme and all its parts serve the telling of this grand story. When, for instance, the Bible speaks of the good gifts of food and wine ('a feast of rich food, a feast of well-aged wines, of rich food filled with marrow, of well-aged wines strained clear', Is. 25:6) it does so using good gifts of the created order to speak of the final order of redemption in the so-called messianic banquet. It is the same with sex and marriage. These are good gifts of the created order, but they feature in the Bible primarily as an image of salvation. The Song is in the Bible not simply to give us a beautiful portrayal of erotic love; it is there because that love is one of the controlling images of the love of the Lord for his people and her answering love towards him. This is the 'divine marriage' reading.

Historically it is almost certain that God's marriage is the prime, if not the only, reason why the book came to be in the canon (Bockmuehl 1997:18f., 22; Beckwith 1988; against Bloch and Bloch 1998:27–29). The rabbis were very insistent (perhaps because others questioned the apparently secular nature of the book) that

> No Israelite man ever disputed concerning Song of Songs that it imparts uncleanness to hands [i.e. is sacred scripture, Beckwith 1988:62]. For the entire age is not so worthy as the day on which the Song of Songs was given to Israel. For all the scriptures are holy, but the Song of Songs is holiest of all.
> (R. Aquiba in m.Yadayim 3.5)

The reason they could so vigorously assert its holiness was because it spoke to them of the love story of the Lord for Israel. The rabbis were scandalized that some were using verses from the Song in a bawdy way.

> He who warbles the Song of Songs in a banquet-hall and makes it into a kind of love-song has no portion in the world to come.
> (R. Aquiba in t.Sanhedrin 12.10)

> One who recites a verse of the Song of Songs and renders it a kind of song by singing it with a common melody [i.e. other than the traditional cantillation] and one who recites a verse in a banquet hall at an inappropriate time brings misfortune to the world.
> (b.Sanhedrin 101a)

And although some of the exegesis in the Targums appears to us uncontrolled (e.g. Alexander 1988:235 on the Aramaic Targum on Song 5:12), we must admit that to relate the Song to the grand narrative of Scripture is more persuasive than to confine it only to a secular affirmation of erotic love.

So, while there is no *a priori* doctrinal reason why Scripture should not contain a simple affirmation of the goodness of created sexual love, it is more consonant with its major theme of salvation for it to be in the Bible as a pointer to God's redemptive marriage with his people.

If the whole of the Old Testament foreshadows and is fulfilled in Jesus Christ, then the Song speaks with passionate anticipation of 'the marriage supper of the Lamb' and encapsulates the mutual eager desire of bridegroom and bride in these days of anticipation as we wait for the Son of God from heaven (1 Thess. 1:10). The Solomonic associations of the Song (whether the preposition *l*ᵉ in the superscription *lišlōmōh* is supposed to indicate authorship or subject matter or simply to categorize the Song with the 'wisdom' literature, Brenner 1989:23f. and ch. 7; Gledhill 1994:22–24) are consistent with such a Christological interpretation. The male lover is at the least a Solomon-like kingly figure (3:6–11), and the love described has royalty written all over it. This is not simply the love of a woman and a man, but of a woman and a king.

The 'divine marriage' reading can lay claim to a long and varied history in both Jewish and Christian readings (Pope 1977:89–132; Bray 1996:159–164; Evans 1987). Above all, it accounts for the happy inclusion of what would otherwise be a surprisingly explicit erotic text in the canon and ties in the theme of this text with a strong and enduring motif that runs through both Old and New Testaments.

None the less, for the purposes of our study we must remember that the 'divine marriage' reading carries with it the implication that human physical passionate exclusive sexual love between a man and a woman may be a beautiful and morally good experience. The passionate goodness of God's marriage infuses human marriage with possibilities of similar joyful passionate delight.

The morality of the Song

I have assumed the Song to be about marriage (or betrothal culminating in marriage), although it never explicitly says it is. There is no description of a wedding celebration and no formal statement that the lovers are husband and wife, even though the Song speaks of full sexual intercourse (most clearly in 5:1). Commentators have therefore sometimes taken the Song to signify cryptic approval of sex before marriage (e.g. Harvey 1994:63). Such commentators regard with scarcely veiled scorn the language of bride/bridegroom or husband/wife which are in their view imposed on the text by nervous

Christian writers worried that the Song might subvert Christian morality. So when Gledhill describes the song as the 'joyous, tentative explorations of love of the betrothed couple, culminating in their marriage and full sexual union in 5:1', Thatcher comments, 'This judgement probably reflects the desire to impose on the text an anxiety about the marital status of the lovers, about which the text itself is shockingly indifferent' (Thatcher 1999:85).

The text is certainly silent on the marital status of the lovers, but we can only interpret this silence as indifference if we utterly ignore the context of the Song in the canon of Scripture. Whenever a work became incorporated and recognized as a part of the Scriptures, it was inherent in its incorporation that it be interpreted in its canonical context. The canonical context of a work about the erotic love of a man and a woman is quite clear, namely that such love is to be expressed only within the public commitment we call marriage. This is part of the uncontroversial substructure of canonical ethics; it is historically irresponsible and tendentious to read the Song in such a way as to subvert the universal ethic of sex and marriage that surrounds it in the other Scriptures. If the lovers' marital status is unclear, the burden of proof is on those who wish to show they are not married, for this would be the unquestioned assumption of readers of a scriptural text. Here is vigorous joyful passionate poetry, and by and large the poet is content to leave the wider context to make the moral framework explicit.

Furthermore, within the Song itself we ought to note that marriage is really the only context that makes sense. It is a work in which *one* man and *one* woman are passionately and publicly devoted to one another. There is no third party to intrude.[20] The Song sets before us the loyal devotion of one man to one woman and one woman to one man, epitomized in the saying, 'My beloved is mine and I am his' (2:16).

There is also a public dimension to the poetic imagery. Commentators find it hard to agree exactly which verses are spoken by whom, but all agree that in addition to the man and the woman there is at least one 'chorus' of outsiders who listen or speak. (Brenner 1989:29 mentions a female chorus, the Daughters of Jerusalem, who both listen and speak [2:7; 3:5; 5:8f., 16; 6:1], and two male choruses [7:1–10; 8:8f.]). The details need not trouble us. This is poetry, and choruses may function as poetic devices in a variety of ways. But the mere fact that the Song does not consist *entirely* of the woman and the man singing or speaking the one to the other reminds the reader of the public dimension of their love. The Song majors on the desire for private sexual

---

20. We have already dismissed the love-triangle 'Shepherd hypothesis' as forced and unpersuasive.

intimacy, whether in the 'chamber' or out of doors (2:10, 'Arise, my love, my fair one, and come away . . .'), but it does so recognizing the desire of each that the world should know how beautiful is the other and how wonderful it is that they love one another. The crushing and stultifying effect of secretive or covert love is a long way from the joyful freedom of the Song which is only possible in the security of public recognition and, indeed, affirmation. Even the most explicit point of sexual consummation (5:1a) is followed by the public encouragement, 'Eat, friends, drink, and be drunk with love' (5:1b). We have in the Song a celebration of the public sexual and social union of one man with one woman, characterized by faithfulness. The morality is therefore most naturally taken to be that of marriage, pointing from human marriage to the divine marriage.

Is there an outward-looking ethic in the Song?
The critical issue for our thesis, however, is neither the nature of the marriage (human and/or divine) nor the morality of the relationship (marital or not), but rather the apparently introspective character of this love. It would appear that the Song of Songs is the part of canonical Scripture that accords least well with my thesis that marriage ought to be outward-looking. I have argued that marriage is instituted so that sex may be used in the service of God, that the relationship between man and woman is not and can never be an end in itself, and that marriage must be protected from the self-destructiveness of the introspective 'religion' of coupledom in which the supposed primacy of the relational good eclipses wider contexts of the service of God and others, and in particular of procreation and nurture of children.

The Song appears to stand in the path of this argument. It is no wonder that Barth placed it alongside his reading of Genesis 2:18ff. as the 'Magna Carta' of marriage in the Bible. He and others have noted that here we have the relational character of marriage extolled with no reference at all to pro-creation. Here, surely, the man and the woman are indeed gazing soft-focus into one another's eyes in precisely the way I have derided; they appear to be utterly consumed with devotion and desire for one another. 'The intense delight which the lovers take in each other is clearly an end in itself which is not justified by further reference to having children, pleasing God, or any-thing else' (Thatcher 1999:86). What are we to say to this?

It is too simple to avoid the problem by saying that the Song 'balances' (with its inward-looking relational delight) other Scriptures that emphasize the service of God. 'Balance' can easily be a mask for accepting dissonance in Scripture. If marriage is really about serving God in his world, we must ask *why* the man and the woman need to be absorbed in one another as they are in the Song. (We cannot claim it is *only* about the Lord's marriage to his people, in which such absorption is – exceptionally – justified, for the metaphor fails if it sets before us an *immoral* human marriage as the image of the divine marriage.) So let us assume that the man and woman are virtuous in being taken up in delight with one another as portrayed in the Song. In what way may such absorption in one another serve God? In what way does it differ from the self-seeking that characterizes so much relational idolatry outside the people of God? How does it escape Jesus' condemnation of us if we love only those who love us (Luke 6:32; Matt. 5:46)?

Spring flowers and autumn fruit
The answer may lie in a biblically sympathetic listening to the language of garden, vine, figs and other figures of fruitfulness which pervade the Song in a variety of contexts. Sometimes it is the woman's person or body that is a garden (4:12–5:1); at other times the signification is less clear (e.g. 6:2). But the age-old association of erotic love with springtime (notably in 2:10–13; 7:12) reminds us that springtime is welcome not only because it brings with it delightful fragrances and beauty to be enjoyed, but also because it promises the fruitfulness of autumn. 'The Lover goes to watch the spring, and to anticipate the harvest' (Landy 1983:193, commenting on Song 6:11). We love blossom on a tree not only because it is beautiful but also because it encourages us to hope for fruit. Beauty is not simply the opposite of ugliness, or delight of disgust. Beauty in the spring is the opposite of famine in the autumn. A garden in the imagery of the Song or the language of Eden is a vineyard or orchard rather than a collection of decorative flower beds.

In all the study there has been in recent times of the garden of the Song and the garden in Eden (notably Landy 1983:183–265; Frye 1982:107–114) too much of the conceptualization of the garden has been in romantic terms and too little recognition has been paid to the fact that a garden is where things are cultivated to *grow* and bear fruit that will both delight and feed people. Perhaps this is a result of scholarship emanating from the all-too-prosperous West in which it matters little whether a garden bears fruit or vegetables so long as it is aesthetically pleasing. Yet the aesthetic and the functional, blossom and fruit, do not appear from hermetically sealed and distinct containers; the latter is integral with the former.

Just so with erotic love. The idea that a man and a woman can enjoy the relational intimacy these lovers evidently enjoy without thought, expectation or even hope for fruitfulness is a very recent one. It would not have occurred to the writer or readers of the Song that such joy in sexual union should, or even could, be separated from the hope for fruit, most obviously in the birth of children. While it is true, therefore, that the Song focuses our attention with concentrated passion on the delight of the lovers in one another, the onus of proof must be on those who would deny the wider context of hope for the blessing of children and family. More generally, the language of fruitfulness that pervades the Song accords strongly with the emphasis of our study on marriage as instituted to serve God in his world, whether or not the gift of children is given to a particular couple.

Intimate lover and public king

Further, we ought to draw attention to a little-noted implication of the Solomon/king language. Part of the reason the beloved speaks of her lover as a king is surely that he is so fine, rich, grand and admirable in her eyes (this is true whatever the historical background). Also part of the reason, however, is that she understands that he is not an idle playboy but a man with a public persona, public respect and public function. Thus in 3:6–11 the poetic portrayal of Solomon's litter surrounded by mighty men equipped with swords and experts in war reminds us that, just as Solomon had a people to lead and protect (cf. the garden in Eden to tend and watch), so the lover cannot without interruption be intoxicated with the passionate embraces of his beloved, nor she with his: they will have work to do. Perhaps this is too obvious to be worth mentioning, but it is often ignored when it is assumed that the Song validates our contemporary ideals of endless romantic love.

If we press the question, 'What is the function of the lovers' passion?', we need to allow human marriage and divine marriage to interweave their meanings if we are to find an answer. The world's security and prosperity rely entirely on the passionate faithfulness of the Creator for his people, through whom he pledges his purposes for ultimate redemption for the created order he has made and which he loves. The fruitfulness of the world is inseparable from the passion of the divine marriage and, indeed, will only reach its consummation when the passion of the divine Lover is fully answered by the passionate answering love of the chosen beloved. There is a partial parallel of meaning in human marriage. The fruitfulness of a marriage depends on the faithful and passionate love of the marriage partners. This is true for the procreation *and nurture* of children, for whose nurture the faithful love of parents (so long as they live) is so important. It is also true in wider terms of the fruitfulness of marriage in serving God in his world. This at heart is why the lovers need to be so absorbed in one another, so that they may bear fruit in their relations with those outside and beyond their mutual adoration. It is for this reason the Song does not balance (in some uncertain sense) but positively complements the biblical perspectives that explicitly point to the public and procreational dimensions of marriage.

How are the relational and procreational goods of marriage to be compared?

Holding relationship and procreational intent together within marriage

We may ask at this point how the procreational and relational 'goods' of marriage (both understood now as subsidiary to serving God) relate to one another. It has been said only half in jest that 'literature is mainly about sex and not much about children, whereas in family life it is the other way round'. But how are we to assess sexual *relationship* and sexual 'fruit' (children) against one another? Is one more important than the other and, if so, which and why? These debates, which have at times characterized Protestant-Roman Catholic dialogue about contraception in not very fruitful ways, are not directly addressed in Scripture, which holds the love of lovers for one another in easy juxtaposition with their love for their children (cf. Titus 2:4, *philandrous . . . philoteknous*).

Since the pioneering work of Bailey it has been almost a truism of Protestant scholarship to affirm relational primacy and, at least to some extent, to distance ourselves from the traditional primacy accorded to procreation. I have already ventured some criticisms of the theological arguments in Barth used to support this change of emphasis see (see pages 170–175).

The question is important. On the face of it, the difference between the marriage relationship and other intimate relationships (such as parent to child, or between other close relatives or intimate friends) is precisely that in the sexual relationship there exists in principle and in nature a nexus between relational intimacy and procreational possibility. This nexus is written into the structure of sexual intercourse both in human anatomy and in Scripture. If it is finally broken there is perhaps no convincing ethical obstacle to the pursuit of sexual intimacy in all manner of other contexts, homosexual as well as heterosexual, transient as well as permanent (e.g. the suggestion of 'sexual friendships' by Thatcher 1993:172).[21] This has been clearly perceived by Hauerwas in a critique of a Roman Catholic report, *Human Sexuality*. Hauerwas writes,

> Once the connection between sexual intercourse and procreation is broken, and it has been broken in theory and practice for many Catholics, then it is by no means clear what basis you have for maintaining other judgments about the rightness or wrongness of certain forms of sexual expression. No amount of rethinking of

---

21. 'There will be countless other (i.e. non-procreative) contexts where sexual activity is an appropriate expression of love. That love will not have as its intended outcome children or be a commitment until death. These contexts are sexual friendships.'

natural law will be able to show that every act of sexual intercourse must be procreative; rather, what must be recaptured is that the connection between the unitive and procreative ends of marriage is integral to the Christian understanding of the political significance of marriage.

(Hauerwas 1981:185)[22]

The noncommensurability of relational and procreational intent

We have seen in our consideration of contraception that Roman Catholic ethicists insist that this nexus should be expressed in two ways. On the one hand every act of sexual intercourse (relational intimacy) must be open to procreational possibility; on the other, every procreational possibility (the intent to conceive) must take place in the context of sexual relational intimacy (hence rendering unethical certain forms of artificial insemination). Instead we have argued above that the proper ethical context in marriage is not a series of isolated acts of sexual union, but rather a lifetime of faithful union.

None the less, we must still affirm the fundamental nexus of sexual intimacy and procreational possibility in the context of marriage. Even when one or both of these twin purposes are frustrated (for example, by infertility or impotence), they are there in the background as the context of what has not been expressed, the nonexpression of which is the cause of frustration.

Even when we hold these goals together (as we must), however, we have to admit that their relationship is problematical. At the most basic level this has been explained by Paul Ramsey in terms of the conscious motivations of the future parents during the act of intercourse that leads to conception. He points out that even with a 'wanted' conception the will and desire during the act of intercourse is not directed towards the child but towards the husband or wife. Whether it may be in the back of the man's and/or the woman's mind that they long for a child or that they dread the conception of a child, during the act that leads to conception their desire is directed not to the child but to the one with whom they are enjoying sexual intimacy. Indeed, from the man's point of view, were he to be wholly directed in his affections at that moment to the as yet unconceived child, it is hard to see how he could avoid psychologically induced impotence.[23] As Ramsey nicely observes, 'He who remarks upon

---

22. In Hauerwas's thought the word 'political' refers particularly to the social expression of all Christian ethics as it is lived out in the community of the church (see Hays 1996:253–266 for a concise summary and critique of Hauerwas's thought in this regard).

23. Indeed, couples who have ongoing difficulty in conceiving often find their sexual relationship is adversely affected; they so much *want* to conceive a child that they find it hard to *want* one another.

the fact that he was once only a gleam in his father's eye is remarking ironically upon the fact that his earthly father, because the gleam was not on the son's account, was not really present with him in the moment he was created.' It follows that, 'An act of sexual intercourse itself is not an act of love and also an act of procreation in such a way that both these goods are wanted at the same time . . . In this sense every child is an unwanted child' (Ramsey 1975:4). Ramsey's observations, at one level all too obvious, point us to the fact that the procreative purpose and the relational purpose of marriage are not commensurable. They are different kinds of good, and we may not with any coherent meaning line them up one behind the other so that one alone may be assigned ethical primacy. This is a problem if they are competitors for the position of the primary purpose of marriage. But, as we have seen, the primary good of marriage is the service of God, and it is entirely acceptable to have two non-commensurable subsidiary goods in this way.

Moving the debates forward

Scholarly debates on this issue often circle somewhat fruitlessly around questions of artificial contraception. When we consider both 'goods' under the governing ethic of the service of God we may move the debate forward. The perceived Achilles' heel of the procreational emphasis has been that it easily dissolves into a mere functionalism. Is it really adequate, we may ask, to suggest that the goal of the man and the woman in marriage is to 'make babies'? And in particular, in the highly charged gender debates of contemporary thought, is it not demeaning to woman to suggest that her main role and contribution in marriage is to be the one in whom the baby is conceived, and who gives birth? Is this not reducing both parties, and especially the woman,[24] to that of an essentially subpersonal functionary? And is this not a woefully inadequate account of the joy and deep intimacy possible in sexual union, to consider it primarily in terms of conception (which, after all, is now technologically possible *in vitro*)?

In an incisive section of *The Ethics of Sex*, Helmut Thielicke analyses the question in terms of the *being* and the *function* of humankind (Thielicke 1979:19–24). There are two dimensions to man in his totality, 'man in his *being* and . . . man in his *function*' (Thielicke 1979:21). The former is man in relation to God, man as bearer of responsibility and value. The latter is man 'as he actively steps out of himself, accomplishes and effects something', whether to do with things or persons. So, for example, Marx accused capitalism of treating the

---

24. See Bailey 1959:234f. for a critique of the phrase 'the use of the woman' either for bearing children or as an outlet for male sexual desire.

worker in purely functional terms and failing to respect him as a human being. Goethe's character Werther, however, is an abstract 'being' who, Thielicke observes, would be much the better for having some function in life! Being and function in man need to be coordinated, not isolated. Thielicke's analysis corresponds with the ethical framework being put forward in our study, the double orientation of humankind as responsible to God on the one hand and entrusted with a task on the other.

In the case of sex these two dimensions are immediately related, the personal and the biological-functional. If sex were all about function (whether sensory pleasure or reproduction), then partners should be exchangeable at will, just as breeding animals are. The fact that we do not make promiscuity a social institution shows that 'we recognise that the *being* of the person is involved' (Thielicke 1979:23). Mere functionaries are interchangeable, so that if the procreational function alone is the goal, man may be regarded as 'an impersonal bearer of a propagative apparatus' (Thielicke 1979:23), just as in economics mere functionalism makes the worker replaceable at will.

Yet the task of world stewardship, under which marriage is considered, is not a mere function. It is a task entrusted with great dignity to humankind by the personal Creator, who calls people to carry out this task in the context of responsible relationship with himself. It is when the Creator is left out of account and replaced by the man who claims to be the master of his fate and the captain of his soul that the task becomes an impersonal function and those who carry it out replaceable functionaries (and, as Thielicke observes, sexual chaos results).

Because the task is personal, both the relational 'good' and the procreational 'good' of marriage are deeply personal. The marriage relationship must be stamped with the character of the Creator, in faithfulness and sacrificial love, because husband and wife are bearers of the task of ruling that Creator's world on his behalf and therefore in his way, which is the way of faithfulness and self-giving love. We shall return to this in Part Three as we explore the logic underlying the definition of marriage. The project of procreation is likewise deeply personal. It involves the nurture of the children of the marriage, and nurture is much deeper than pouring facts or even philosophies into their heads. Nurture is inseparable from the personal character and nature of the nurturers, as we have seen in our consideration of the biblical material (see pages 162–170). To consider marriage under an ethic of task is deeply consistent with fully personal emphases in terms of both the marriage relationship (the relational good) and the procreative activity and challenge (the procreational good).

It will be important also to guard ourselves against a further, even deeper, objection when we speak of marriage within an ethic of task. Even when we have established that the task under which marriage is to be embarked upon is a personal task because it is entrusted to us by God, enterprised in relationship with God and its end is the service of God, we have a further problem. This concerns the nature of marital love. The objection is this: if we are told that both our marital love and our marital intercourse are to be embarked upon to the end of serving God, does this not make our attitude towards our husband or wife that of regarding them as a mere means to that end?

This question is a special case of the general debate about the double commandment to love God and neighbour.[25] Do I love my neighbour *as a means* towards the *end* of loving God, or may I love my neighbour as an end in himself or herself? In terms of the writings of Augustine, do I regard my neighbour in the category of *usus* (use, towards a consequent end) or of *fruitio* (to be loved and enjoyed for their own sake)?

The answer of O'Donovan is that the categories of ends and means are inappropriate to this whole debate, because terminology of means and ends is essentially *deliberative*, focusing on a project to be achieved, easily slipping into a technological mindset in which we are in control. Love, however, by its nature, is not a deliberative project but rather called forth from us by the reality of the beloved (whether the spouse or the Creator), this reality being neither the creation of the lover's will nor deriving his or her importance from the lover's ambitions. Love is to do neither with means nor ends, but rather is determined by glad appreciation of the givenness of the other who is its object. It is the mystery of marriage that in it we are called to this nondeliberative love and that as this love is called out from us in the marriage partnership the Creator entrusts us with the task of pouring out that love in his service and in ruling his world.

The double ethical context of loving responsibility towards God and glad acceptance of God's task is the proper matrix within which the purpose of marriage is to be considered. Before we move on to see how the logic of this purpose works itself out in elements of definition, we must consider the public or institutional good of marriage under the ethic of task.

Sexual order in the context of task

In 1 Corinthians 7:2 Paul teaches that it is good if each man has his woman and each woman her man, 'because of cases of sexual immorality'. The important teaching that follows in verses 2–6 has been considered above (see

---

25. In what follows I have largely followed the argument in O'Donovan 1994:232ff.

pages 188–192). We noted there that the negative concern to prevent immorality does not conflict with, but rather complements, the positive valuation of sex within marriage. We should also note the strongly situational context of the teaching, so that, 'The repeated theme of sexual passion or misconduct and, in response, Paul's stress on self-control . . . probably tells us more about the problems in Corinth than about Paul's view of the purposes of marriage' (Witherington 1988:42). It is clear, however, that to avoid sexual chaos Paul commends the faithful sexual relationship of one man with one woman. In a similar vein we may also note 1 Timothy 5:11–15 with its cautious but realistic reference to the natural desires of younger widows.

The moment we suggest that marriage is God's remedy for sexual disorder we will be criticized for being too negative – but we cannot avoid this reason for marriage. We consider now how it too can be incorporated (with the other two 'goods') under the governing ethic of the service of God.

Outside Scripture, in church history, there have indeed been many negative attitudes to sex (e.g. Augustine, *On the Good of Marriage* §§5, 6, 8, 23, 25; *On Original Sin* §40, 42, 43; *On Marriage and Concupiscence* §7–9). Commentators make much of mocking these.[26] Part of the reason for these negative attitudes is that the 'good' of preventing sexual disorder is something introduced into thought about marriage only after the fall. It is intrinsically something removed from the age of 'man's innocency', whereas the relational and procreational 'goods' are integral to Genesis 1 and 2.

After the fall, the need for sexual desire to be restrained and channelled into godly paths becomes of great importance. It is right to point out that Scripture is, and the church ought to be, joyfully positive about sex within marriage. But even the most positive and affirming attitude to sex as a good gift of God in creation must recognize the terrible power of sex to destroy lives by introducing into human relations unique pain in the intimate violence of rape or abuse, of destructive jealousy, of acute injustice. We do not have to be killjoys to say that in a fallen world sex must be restrained by law. It is a

---

26. E.g. Bailey 1959. Note especially ch. 1 on the ascetic reaction to pagan licence, contrasted with positive Jewish attitudes to sex; ch. 3 on the moves during the patristic period to exalt virginity, the trend towards clergy celibacy, and the reactions of Augustine, Jerome and others to their own preconversion experiences; ch. 4, pp. 148–152 on medieval clerical celibacy and its abuses; ch. 5, pp. 167–169 on the Reformers' attacks on clerical celibacy, including treatment (p. 169) of Luther and Calvin on virginity; also pp. 170–173, Luther's and Calvin's attitudes to sex compared. See also the critique in Moore 1992: ch. 4, explaining why Augustine was so terrified of being mastered by passion.

necessary corollary of affirming the joy of ordered sex that we are negative about disordered sex.

We may note briefly three areas which make it clear that public restraint is necessary. The first is the tendency in the interior life of fallen man for sexual desire to be disordered, pulling men and women this way and that in apparently random fashion (hence the mythology surrounding Cupid and his arrows). We find ourselves victims of passions that may rage with tremendous power and force within our bodies. It is not unduly negative to argue that without public restraint such passions are often destructive. The lustful look (Job 31:1), the adulterous look (Matt. 5:27–30) and the difficulty for a young man of guarding pure thoughts (Ps. 119:9) all attest the raging instability that characterizes the sexual dimension of men and women, at least at some stages of life.

Second, we must be realistic about sexual arousal. There is a significant motif in Old Testament thought surrounding the concept of 'nakedness' ('erwâ) and in particular of 'uncovering nakedness'. The word 'erwâ and the idioms of 'uncovering', 'covering' or 'seeing' nakedness carry a variety of related meanings. In Exodus 20:26 Moses is forbidden to go up to the altar on steps lest his nakedness (i.e. his genitals) be exposed. In Ezekiel 16:36 the uncovering of nakedness is portrayed as an act of sexual provocation, to provoke sexual arousal in men. The same idea is present in Ezekiel 23:18. This idiom is profoundly suggestive for further study in the areas of sexual privacy and pornography (recognizing, of course, that often it is partial uncovering which is more arousing than total nakedness). Sexual order needs public constraints of privacy if it is not to disintegrate into the arousal of disordered desires.

Third, we must note the Bible's condemnation of prostitution in this connection. To prostitute oneself is to offer oneself sexually to another for an end other than the proper ends of sexual intercourse. This improper end may simply be money, or animal pleasure, or some supposed religious (idolatrous) purpose, but in each case it is instructive to note that the sexual activity is divorced from the context of lifelong partnership in the service of a task.

Although the selling of one's body for sex is universally condemned in Scripture, the existence of prostitutes and brothels has occasioned some debate in the history of the church. The argument has been used (for example by Augustine and Aquinas) that it may be the lesser of evils to allow brothels and prostitution as a kind of safety valve for male libido, thus safeguarding the purity and stability of the family structure in the rest of society. Prostitution is like a sewer under a palace, suggests Aquinas; it is revolting, but remove it and the whole palace becomes full of pollution (Bailey 1959:161–163). This view of male libido leaves much to be desired, however, and we may side with

Davenant, the Caroline divine, who robustly disagreed. Far from reducing the evil, he argued, brothels create and reinforce habits of lust; the problem is not that men must, as an outlet of natural desire, go to prostitutes, but that 'men make necessities of their own, and then find ways to satisfy them. There is no necessity that men must either debauch matrons or be fornicators; let them marry, for that is the remedy which God hath appointed' (Bailey 1959:210).

For these three reasons – the instability of fallen man's sexual desires, the dynamic of sexual arousal through 'nakedness', and the need for sexual intercourse to be ordered to the right ends – marriage is needed to maintain a healthy sexual order. God's world, which humankind is to steward, is an ordered world; it can only be governed aright in the context of ordered sexual relationships. This order is a public order. The strictly private and exclusive sexual relationship between a couple must be publicly known in order that it may be guarded and not intruded upon by a third party. Some of these themes will be taken up and treated more fully in later chapters.

Conclusion

We conclude by summarizing how the three 'goods' of marriage – procreation, public order and personal relationship – may be understood in the context of the big story of God's purpose to rule and order his world. Procreation is a blessing because, given our mortality, we need the next generation to carry on the task. Public order is necessary because the disorder introduced into the world by the fall is the very contradiction of the task. Relationship is integral to the task because it is a personal shared task and not merely an instrumental contract. The governing ethic of task enables us to move on in the next chapters to consider elements of the Bible's definition of marriage and to relate these to the Creator's purposes.

PART THREE

THE DEFINITION OF MARRIAGE

In Part Three we consider the shape of marriage using elements from the following working definition. This was first introduced in Chapter 4, where I defended the possibility of there being an objective definition at all.

Marriage is
the voluntary sexual and public social union
of one man and one woman
from different families.
This union is patterned upon the union of God with his people his bride,
the Christ with his church.
Intrinsic to this union is God's calling to lifelong exclusive sexual faithfulness.

In this chapter we consider the words 'the voluntary sexual and public social union'.

Sex is for marriage alone

I must first argue that the unmarried life is to be life without sexual intimacy, that sex is for marriage alone. Because sex between a man and a woman carries with it, inescapably, God's calling to public lifelong faithfulness (as we shall see in Chapter 15), it can only be moral within marriage, for marriage includes the public pledge of lifelong faithfulness. To love enough for sex is to love enough to have pledged that love publicly in marriage. Sex without that pledged public union may be accompanied by claims of love, but the claims are called into question by the failure to back them with public pledge. The underrated virtue of chastity is the practical correlate of faithfulness in the realm of sex, for in marriage it means faithfulness to the marriage bond, and outside marriage it means abstinence from sex. There is a clear sexual distinction between the married and the unmarried life. The two do not merge in fluid 'relationships' that develop into or out of sexual unions over time.

It has, however, been argued that the Bible does not prohibit sexual relations between unmarried people, and specifically that the word *porneia* (usually translated 'fornication' or 'sexual immorality') in the New Testament has no reference to 'pre-betrothal, pre-marital, non-commercial sexual intercourse between man and woman' (Malina 1972:17). We need to examine such claims.

The Hebrew and Greek words usually translated 'fornication' or 'sexual immorality' are different from those translated 'adultery'. Traditionally the former have been understood to refer to all sexual intimacy outside marriage. Since this view has been challenged, we look at the semantic range of these word groups (while recognizing that a word-group study will never exhaust a topic).[1]

In the Old Testament there are two major word groups used for sexual misconduct which is not (necessarily) adulterous. There are words for ordinary prostitution: the verb *zānâ*, the abstract nouns *z^enûnîm* (mainly in Hos.), *z^enût* (mainly in Jer., Ezek. and Hos.) or *taznût* (only in Ezek. 16, 23), and the word for an ordinary female prostitute (a *zōnâ* or *'iššâ zōnâ*). And there are the technical terms for the male and female cult prostitutes (the male *qādēš* and female *q^edēšâ*) in the Canaanite nature religions (e.g. Deut. 23:17f.; 1 Kgs. 14:24; 15:12; 22:47; 2 Kgs. 23:7; Hos. 4:14; and possibly Job 36:14). I will refer to these word groups by √znh and √qdš. The nearest equivalent Greek word group has the root *porn-*. The words are *porneia* (usually translated 'fornication' or 'sexual immorality'), *porneuō* (to commit *porneia*) or its emphatic equivalent *ekporneuō* (once in Jude 7), *pornē* (an immoral woman or prostitute), and *pornos* (an immoral man or male prostitute).

The √znh *word group*

√znh is used in the sense of straightforward financial prostitution, of Tamar in Genesis 38 (who is also called a *q^edēšâ* in v. 21f., the 'normal' and cultic kinds of prostitution seeming to merge, as they do in Deut. 23:17), of Rahab in

---

1. For example, when 1 Samuel 2:22 tells us that Eli's sons used to sleep with the women who served at the entrance to the Tent of Meeting, the √znh word group is not used, although the meaning is clear.

Jericho (Josh. 2, 6), of the mother of Jephthah (Judg. 11:1), of Samson's
woman (Judg. 16:1),[2] of the quarrelling women in 1 Kings 3:16 and of the
prostitutes who washed themselves in the blood of Ahab in 1 Kings 22:38 (cf.
Joel 3:3; Amos 7:17). The Israelite is not to let his daughter become a zōnâ
(Lev. 19:29) or the land will be 'full of depravity'. A priest is not to marry a
zōnâ (Lev. 21:7,14), nor is his daughter to become one (Lev. 21:9). The young
man is warned in the wisdom literature resolutely to avoid her (e.g. Prov. 5 – 7;
cf. Eccles. 7:26 where the word is not used).

Although this financial sense is common, however, we would be mistaken
to conclude that the concept of √znh is primarily financial (which would
exclude extramarital sex engaged in purely because of mutual sexual desire,
for example), for √znh overlaps with √qdš, and the latter was not done for
money.

Virginity was very important in Old Testament law. If a bride had premarital
sex with someone other than her husband, her behaviour is described as 'pros-
tituting' herself (√znh), whether or not this premarital sex was engaged in for
money (Deut. 22:13–21). The mere fact of a sexual liaison before marriage is
described as √znh. We see this same high valuation of virginity in the description of Rebekah in Genesis 24:16, 'a virgin' (bᵉtûlâ), which means a young
woman of marriageable age (not necessarily a technical virgin, Wenham 1972),
but here specifically describes a woman 'whom no man had known'.

In insisting on premarital virginity for a bride, no doubt the concern to be
sure of paternity was important. If (as must often have happened) a woman
became known to be pregnant soon after marriage, how could the husband be
sure she had not in fact been made pregnant shortly before marriage by
another man? Her child (for whom he would have to make provision) would
be the child of another man. Only if she is proved to be a virgin on her
wedding night can he be sure her child is also his child.

If concern for paternity were the only motivation, then we should have to
admit that contraception can ease this problem. Premarital sex, so long as it
did not lead to pregnancy, would no longer be an ethical problem. So long as
premarital sex was 'safe' (as we say), it would have to be accounted moral.

Such a line of reasoning is shallow and flawed. The core of the word group
√znh is neither prostitution for money nor (covert) paternity by another man;
it is that √znh is a turning aside from the public and open framework of
known community relationships into a secretive and covert liaison which lies

2. Hauck and Schultz 1968:584 suggest that both Judg. 11:1 and 16:1 are to be understood
   in the sense of a 'foreign' woman outside the tribe, but this seems unlikely, and is
   apparently contradicted in the same article on p. 585.

outside the structures and order of family life. All forms of √znh break the
sexual order of the open community or society. In Proverbs 23:27 the zōnâ is
placed in parallel with the nokrîyyâ ('alien woman' NRSV margin); she is the outsider or foreigner, the woman who does not belong with the covenant people
in the land. Prostitution involves a liaison outside the fabric of family and
society (Wright 1990:92–97). All extramarital relationships partake of this
'outsideness', whether or not the motive is financial. We see this often in the
metaphorical uses of the term; in Ezekiel 20:31, for example, the NRSV translates √znh by 'going astray'.

This same motif of 'turning outside' or away from home may perhaps also
be illustrated from Judges 19:2, where the Levite's concubine (*pîlegeš*) literally
'prostitutes herself' (*wattizneh*) from him when she goes back to her father's
home. She is not a prostitute, but in her action of deserting him she takes on
the character of one. She takes it upon herself to move outside the family
structure to which she belongs. This seems to be the sense.

√znh is deeper than simple monetary prostitution. 'The verb zānâ designates
primarily a sexual relationship outside of a formal union' (*TDOT* IV:100).

The porneia *word group*

'In the LXX the group *porneuō* is normally used for the root znh, while with
equal consistency *moicheuō* is used for n'p' (Hauck and Schulz 1968:584). The
word group derives etymologically from *pernēmi* (to sell), the idea being of a
prostitute for hire (Hauck and Schulz 1968:579f.). But, as with √znh, the range
of meaning is much wider than this.

In the LXX the predominant uses of *porneia*, *porneuō* and *ekporneuō* correspond to the metaphorical uses of √znh. *Pornē* is used to translate both zōnah
and qᵉdēšâh (e.g. of Tamar in Gen. 38); the LXX has no special term for cultic
prostitution.

In the New Testament this word group is used of literal prostitution in 1
Corinthians 6:12–20,[3] in Hebrews 11:31, in James 2:25 of Rahab (from Josh. 2,
6 LXX), and in Luke 15:30. It is used in 1 Corinthians 5:1 of what seems to be
an incestuous cohabitation of a man with his stepmother (see Chapter 13). In
John 8:41 there is allusion to the illegitimacy of those born *ek porneias*. It is
used in Matthew 21:31f. of the company Jesus kept, which included *pornai* (a
salutary reminder that a study of sexual ethics is gospel as well as law).

Old Testament metaphorical language is carried over into Revelation 14:8
and 17:1–19:10 (often) of 'Babylon the whore'. The word group appears in a

---

3. See Rosner 1998 for discussion of whether some kind of temple prostitution was
    under consideration.

variety of sin lists and contexts in which a number of sins or types of sinner are named: Matthew 15:19 (par. Mark 7:21); 1 Corinthians 5:9–11; 6:9; 2 Corinthians 12:21; Galatians 5:19; Ephesians 5:3, 5; Colossians 3:5; 1 Timothy 1:10; Revelation 9:21; 21:8; 22:15; and cf. Hebrews 12:16 where Esau has the character of a *pornos*.

The word group also appears in texts relating to the so-called 'apostolic decree' of Acts 15 (see Chapter 5), in 1 Corinthians 10:8 (see Chapter 8) and in the Matthean divorce texts (Matt. 5:32; 19:9).

The most satisfactory understanding of the *porneia* word group is the traditional one that in general (unless restricted by the context to some specific case) it refers to all sexual intercourse outside marriage. Three important texts support this conclusion.

First, in 1 Corinthians 7:2 Paul advises that 'because of cases of sexual immorality' (*dia tēs porneias*) it is better for each man to have one woman and each woman one man – that is, for people to be married. 'If Paul's only worry was cultic, commercial, incestuous, and adulterous relations, *if*, therefore, fornication was not considered to be forbidden, it is difficult to see why Paul has to look to marriage as a *remedium concupiscentiae*' (Jensen 1978:182). He argues as he does precisely because the opposite of *porneia* is marriage.

Second, in 1 Thessalonians 4:1–8 Paul tells the Christian men to abstain from 'fornication' (*porneia*, v. 3), since this would 'wrong or exploit' a brother. We can easily understand how adultery would do this. Had Paul had only adultery in mind we might have expected him to use the word *moicheia*, but in fact all premarital and extramarital sex is a wronging of another. It takes a temporary sexual partner and (because the liaison is temporary) robs them (and any future partner of theirs) of the possibility of unspoiled lifelong faithfulness. Extramarital and premarital sex are kinds of theft.

Third, in Hebrews 13:4 the writer brackets the adulterer with the fornicator (*pornos*) as together describing those who dishonour marriage. This confirms our conclusion that the traditional translation of *porneia* as 'fornication' or 'sexual immorality' (understood as any sexual intercourse outside marriage) is correct, unless the context makes it clear that something more specific (such as incest, 1 Cor. 5:1, or prostitution, 1 Cor. 6:12–20) is in view.

We conclude that sex is for marriage alone. Both the *porneia* word group and the √*znh* word group refer generally to sexual intercourse outside marriage.

Consent to sex and consent to marriage

God calls some (maybe most) men and women into marriage; those he calls must choose to consent or not to consent to enter marriage, and to marry a particular woman or man. Coerced entry into marriage is a contradiction in terms. This principle of consent inheres in the dignity given to humankind in creation, with a unique moral responsibility to the Creator and a unique task of stewardship over the creation.

There are several dimensions to such consent. There is, first, a distinction between consensual sex and consensual marriage.

Consent to sex

Biblical law and narrative unite in revulsion at nonconsensual sex. Rape is a form of intimate violence to be abhorred and lamented (Lam. 5:11); it is a disgrace in Israel (the burden of Judg. 19 – 21) and a sign of judgment (Zech. 14:2). The rape of Tamar by her half-brother Amnon (2 Sam. 13:14) is recorded with horror and pity.

The laws of Deuteronomy 22:23–29 distinguish between consensual and coercive sex. In verse 23f. a man 'meets' and 'lies with' an engaged woman 'in the town'; she does not cry for help and is therefore taken to consent. This is illegal consensual sex; both are guilty. But in verses 25–27 a man 'meets' an engaged woman 'in the open country', 'seizes her' (hifil of *ḥāzaq*, a verb with strong associations of violence) and 'lies with' her. The charitable assumption is made that the woman did not consent. This is regarded as rape and the man is punished. The case that follows (v. 28f.) seems to be about seduction rather than rape (in spite of the impression given in some translations) and parallels the similar law in Exodus 22:16f. The verb 'seize' (v. 28 NRSV, Hebrew *tāpas*) is not the violent word used in verse 25; it can mean 'to hold or handle' (cf. in Amos 2:15 of handling a bow); the phrase 'they are found' may signal consent; and the verb 'violated' has the sense 'had his will with her' (Mayes 1979:312, 304; Weinfeld 1972:286f.).

The biblical condemnation of coercive sex does not get us very far, however. After all, this moral value is shared in most cultures. In the contemporary Western world nonconsensual sex is just about the only surviving taboo.

To marry includes in principle consent to sex, ongoing self-giving in willing sexual intercourse with the marriage partner (1 Cor. 7:2–4). (Even if it is ongoing, it retains the character of consent and not coercion; the concept of rape within marriage is problematical but not meaningless.)[4] But consent to marriage goes beyond consent to sex. A prostitute may consent to sex and an extramarital lover to an ongoing sexual relationship; neither is marriage. We turn therefore from consent to sex to consent to be married.

---

4. See Brundage 1993 for studies from Western Canon Law on 'Implied Consent to Intercourse', including the issue of marital rape.

Consent to marriage: in its nature

In every culture marriage is entered by the giving of mutual consent. Anthropologists will teach us the great variety of ways in which this is expressed, both explicitly in words and implicitly in symbolic deeds. In every case in every culture consent has both a subjective dimension (the affective and volitional commitment of a man and a woman) and an objective dimension; they consent *to* something, they do not merely express their feelings for one another. To what (objectively) must they consent for their relationship to be marriage?

We may distinguish two facets of the consent to be married. On the one hand, the man and woman consent to a relationship which accords with God's (very simple) definition of marriage; they consent to enter marriage as marriage *is*. On the other hand, they ought to consent to align their goals within marriage to the ends for which God has ordained marriage (the subject of Chapters 6 – 10); they agree to enter marriage with an understanding of what marriage is ordained *for*.

Each facet needs a degree of public understanding; consent is 'informed consent'. Informed consent presupposes a culture (or subculture) within which the meaning of marriage is understood. It is rare for a couple to be able themselves fully to verbalize the nature and purposes of marriage, but each couple has some understanding from their culture of what and why marriage is.

The heart of marriage, to which a couple must assent, is that it is a union for life. Consent to a time-limited relationship cannot be marriage. This is expanded in Chapter 15.

Consent to marriage: in its ends

The nature of marriage is of a piece with the purpose of marriage. The reason why marriage is defined by exclusive lifelong faithfulness is because only marriage so defined can serve the Creator's purposes for marriage in his service. The mark of the Creator's relationship with his creation is faithful love, so the hallmark of faithfulness in the couple's relationship is the foundation of the couple's usefulness in the service of God (including the nurture of children when they are given this blessing).

No couple live together without goals, or at the very least hopes and expectations, whether openly expressed or secretly cherished. To consent to be married is to recognize that our goals ought to be God's goals; we enter an institution whose purpose has already been set, not one whose goals are created by us. This is why we devoted Part Two to the elucidation of these purposes.

Perhaps nothing casts clearer light on consent to the purpose of marriage than prostitution. Prostitution, whether 'sacred' or 'secular', is not condemned in Scripture only because it involves promiscuity, sex with more than one partner (although it does, cf. the emphasis of Jer. 3:1 on '*many* lovers'). What is most clear about prostitution is that it is sex for purposes other than the proper purposes for which sex is ordained. Whether it be the common harlot offering her body in return for money or the temple prostitute (male or female) engaging in sex as part of their employment, with partners whose motives are the religious promotion of fecundity and profit through intercourse, the goal of the union is not the service of God but personal gain. (The same critique would apply to the use of paid surrogates in sexual therapy to help clients 'practise' their newly acquired skills, Mickey 1995.)

When the prophetic tongue lashes the trading city of Tyre as a weary old prostitute having to go out on the streets to drum up fresh custom (Is. 23:15–18), the same separation of sex from its proper purpose is evident in the metaphorical language. The problem with Tyre is not that she engaged in trade with 'all the kingdoms on the face of the earth' (v. 17), for it is hard to see what is wrong with this; it is that she engaged in these unions for personal aggrandisement. Her motive was self-enrichment. This was (metaphorical) sex for self-fulfilment, not sex in the service of others in God's world.

The paradoxical story of Judah and his daughter-in-law Tamar (Gen. 38) also sheds light on this question of purpose. When Tamar's husband Er dies, his brother Onan refuses to give to Tamar her marital right, endeavouring to father a child for her to carry on the name of his brother (under the law of the Levir, or brother-in-law, Deut. 25:5–10). God's judgment on Onan, who 'spilled his semen on the ground' (v. 9, coitus interruptus), implies that Tamar was right to hope for a child; this was a proper goal of sex. After Onan's death his younger brother Shelah is promised to her, when he has grown up. When he grows up and is not given to her, Tamar disguises herself as a prostitute so that Judah will make her pregnant.

Judah's goal in sex was self-gratification (presumably), but Tamar's (for all the wrongness of the deception) was the child denied her by Onan's refusal properly to consummate their relationship and then by Judah's refusal to give Shelah to her. With all the moral complexity and (for us) cultural alienness of the story, the conclusion (v. 26) of Judah, 'She is more in the right than I, since I did not give her to my son Shelah,' implicitly recognizes the distinction between proper and improper ends in sexual relations. In paradox the 'prostitute' is shown to be 'in the right'.

We must be careful, however, not to exalt the desire for a child so much that it becomes an end that justifies any means. Lot's daughters are implicitly condemned in Genesis 19:30–38 for making their father drunk so that he would make them pregnant.

Most cultures accept that there are inappropriate motives for marriage.

There is a light allusion to this in Jane Austen's novel *Pride and Prejudice*. Jane earnestly asks Lizzy how long she has loved D'Arcy. Lizzy skittishly replies, 'It has been coming on so gradually, that I hardly know when it began. But I believe I must date it from my first seeing his beautiful grounds at Pemberley' (Austen 1813:288). We know she cannot be serious, for although she will indeed gain materially from her marriage, it is unthinkable that this would be a worthy motive.

It is easy to condemn those who marry for money or status, but a more insidious wrong motive has insinuated its way into our culture: romance. Romance has attached to itself a raft of benefits focused on self-fulfilment and the realization of dreams (notably the dream of 'the right one for me'), but because this is not God's purpose for marriage, it is a self-defeating goal. Besides, as Hauerwas nicely observes, even if we seek to marry 'the right person', in practice 'we always marry the wrong person. We never know whom we marry; we just think we do. Or even if we first marry the right person, just give it a while and he or she will change' (Hauerwas 1981:172). Paradoxically, it is when we jointly embark on the endeavour of serving God in his world that romantic pleasure sometimes takes us by surprise. As a goal it evaporates, but as an unsought blessing it may be greeted with delight and thanksgiving.

Marriage was not ordained in order to promote the selfish pleasures (whether sexual or material) of either partner; it was ordained so that in the delight and security of faithfulness man and wife should enjoy serving God in caring for his world. A couple ought to agree together to serve God. This service often embraces the nurture of children; it always involves building a home that is not an isolated and self-centred dwelling but a secure outward-looking social unit engaged in serving people in God's world.

This is perhaps why the wisdom writers castigate the man who goes to prostitutes for squandering his wealth (Prov. 29:3) – he ought to have been using his strength, his energies, his wealth, his talents, in building up a home in which God was served. Instead he dissipates these in a disordered way which tends to move the world towards chaos rather than cosmos. To understand, at least in a measure, the proper ends of marriage gives to the whole project an outward-looking orderliness which promotes lasting love.

Traditional debates about consent in marriage law (both civil and ecclesiastical) have focused mainly on the capacity of the parties to the marriage to offer free and informed consent. Matters such as freedom from duress and the age, maturity and mental health of the parties are considered (e.g. defective consent may result from mental incapacity, duress, fear, mistaken identity or a fundamental misconception as to the nature of marriage (Church of England 1935:8ff.; Church of England 1955: chs. 3, 4; Atkinson 1979:91).

The reason why these debates have focused on the capacities of the moral agents (the man and the woman) to consent is that they took place for the most part in a public culture in which the fundamental nature and ends of marriage were uncontroversial. This is no longer so. Debate now (and this is perhaps the key to ethical discussion of unmarried cohabitation) needs to focus on the nature and ends of marriage and what it means for a couple to consent to this nature and these ends.

Immediately, however, we have a problem. This discussion could easily be sidetracked down a pathway of subjective psychologizing, in which we purport to analyse or morally assess the states of mind and emotion of the parties to a marriage. What were their thoughts and inward hopes, their cognitive and affective understandings, as they gave what they said was consent to be married? Did they in some subjective sense have their mental fingers crossed behind their backs as they said what they said? If the husband had a bad attack of 'cold feet' as his bride walked down the aisle, such that he really wondered if he was doing the right thing, but yet he managed to get the promises spoken, was his consent defective? Can he, at a later date, say, 'I don't think I really meant it'? What if they did consent as best they knew how, but had different ideas of the importance of the commitment to lifelong faithfulness, such that one interpreted this as more of an optional extra whereas the other understood it to be central? One young man whose wife had deserted him soon after their marriage said to me that he did not think his wife had really understood what marriage was and meant it when she married him; this, in his judgment, cast doubt on the reality of the marriage in the sight of God.

Such a path of subjective judgment is both pragmatically unworkable (both in law and pastoral practice) and theologically misguided. It is precisely in the matter of consent that the nature of marriage as *public* commitment (a 'sexual *and public social* union') comes to the fore. A publicly spoken consent *is* in general consent of the person who speaks it. Consent is not a private matter of the thought-life but a public affair of the spoken word and deed. It is those who 'stand by their oath even to their hurt' (Ps. 15:4) who are acceptable to God. Integrity is harmony between the affections of the heart and the actions of life; moral judgments of others in this life can only be based on the actions of life, and therefore on the charitable assumption of integrity, that people mean what they say. Indeed, the judgment of God will be based upon our deeds (remembering that a word is a spoken deed, an outward action of the person who speaks), since our deeds are the only sure evidence of our hearts (e.g. Rom. 2:6).

As an illustration of this truth we may take the comment of Vaisey in an appendix to *The Church and Marriage*. Discussing the concept of 'intention' (i.e. the intention to enter marriage understood as lifelong exclusive union), Vaisey notes,

> There may . . . be a *consensus ad idem* which is not a *consensus ad matrimonium*, and if, for
> instance, it could be established in a particular case that the parties were in point of
> fact contemplating a union for a limited period, e.g. for seven years, and that their
> minds were solely directed to such a limit of time, and that they had conspired and
> arranged between themselves to utter the words appropriate to a life-long union
> *without intention* – then in such a case there would be no marriage.
> (Church of England 1935:75)

Now this is a legal statement and in order to 'establish' that the words of the
marriage commitment had been spoken with a different *intention* it would
never be possible simply to refer to the thoughts of the parties to this deception. Evidence is in principle something that can be brought into the public
domain; it would be necessary to adduce spoken or written evidence, evidence
in words, to weigh against the evidence of the words spoken in the marriage
service.

This distinction between private thought and public commitment was
clearly recognized in *The Church and the Law of the Nullity of Marriage* in its discussion of 'defective intention'. To allow someone later to evade marriage
responsibility by saying 'I didn't really mean it' would be to 'allow people to
take advantage of perjury'. The intention of the parties 'must be collected
from the words of the rite which they employ and not from any private intentions which they may have' (Church of England 1935:27). However, the
context is wider than simply 'the words of the rite which they employ', since
even these words gather their meaning from a cultural context.

It follows that the public cultural framework within which marriage is
entered is critical to the assessment of consent. It may be that (for example in
a church marriage service) there is, before the vows are exchanged, a public
reminder of the nature and purposes of marriage. The couple then clearly and
explicitly assent to enter marriage as understood and explained in this pream-
ble. Or it may be (more ambiguously) that the couple exchange vows in a cultural context in which more of the nature and purposes of marriage are taken
for granted. So, in a civil ceremony in Britain, the vows follow a very concise
statement of what the state understands marriage to be. But this concise statement is (or used to be) a reminder of a much wider shared cultural understanding of what marriage is for.

We ought also to note that the cultural context is wider than just the spoken
words. To take a trivial example to make this point, an actor and an actress on
a film set may go through the whole of a marriage service, including the pre-
amble and vows, but it will be clearly understood by everybody that this is
acting and that their words express only pretended consent (Church of
England 1955:24).

It is very important for a couple to be able to know that they are married. In particular they need to have objective grounds for knowing that the consent of each is a valid consent. Much debate in church history has focused on nullity: in particular, under what circumstances may consent be allowed to be so defective as to render a marriage invalid? The Reformers spoke into a church culture in which the whole concept of nullity had come to be terribly abused, so that a strong theoretical doctrine of marital indissolubility existed side by side with easy practical divorce under the name of annulment for those with sufficient influence or wealth. Against this we ought to urge proper consent as part of marriage, while laying the burden of proof in a particular case firmly on those who would assert that consent was inadequate. We ought to assume adequate consent in the absence of strong and objective evidence to the contrary. Otherwise we unwittingly weaken the security which is part of the Creator's loving purpose in instituting marriage in the first place. A married person ought to be able to know with confidence that he or she really is married and not to be in constant fear that some arcane grounds for nullity might be unearthed by their spouse (Atkinson 1979:162–170).

Unmarried cohabitation and consent

When we come to consider the practice of nonmarital cohabitation perhaps the most critical ethical question is, 'To what have these couples consented in agreeing to live together?' Clearly they have consented to ongoing sexual relations. Usually there is some understanding that this precludes sexual relations with others while the cohabiting relationship lasts. Often also there is the expectation from at least one of the partners that the relationship has a future; newly cohabiting couples sometimes assure their families that they would not have agreed to live together if they did not expect their relationship to last. In terms of public commitment, however, the relationship is surrounded by a haze of ambiguity. And usually the degrees of commitment between the two people are unequal; the relationship has a tendency to asymmetry of commitment. Perhaps the woman thinks, hopes and expects it will be more lasting than does the man (cf. Morgan 2000:48). But neither has any public commitment to engender security.

In considering the ethics of nonmarital sex (i.e. nonadulterous but not within marriage), it is instructive to return to Deuteronomy 22:23–29. We saw above that only the second of the laws (vv. 25–27) is about rape. The first is the seduction of a betrothed ($\sqrt{rs}$) girl, the last (v. 28f.) the seduction of a girl who is not betrothed. We saw that this last law roughly parallels that in Exodus 22:16f., the main differences being that in Exodus the girl's father may decide not to give the girl in marriage and that in Deuteronomy the man not only marries her but loses the right to divorce her (Hugenberger

1994:256–260). Discussion of the precise interpretation of these differences is outside the scope of our study. What we need to note is the difference of seriousness between the seduction of the betrothed girl and the seduction of the unbetrothed girl. The former is more serious and has about it the character and seriousness of adultery (even though betrothal falls short of marriage in that it precedes consummation), which is why it is regarded as a capital offence; a pledge of sexual loyalty has been broken. In a later age the pregnancy of Mary the betrothed of Joseph would presumably have been assumed to reveal sexual sin of this kind (Matt. 1:18–25).

The latter is quite different in seriousness. The girl was not pledged to be married. When she consents to have sex with this man, she is not doing right, but the wrong she and the man are doing is of a different order. They are engaging in a union which in its created nature carries with it the calling and moral obligation of lifelong public exclusive loyalty, but they do so in an ambiguous context (to say the least) in which it is not clear that they accept this moral obligation. The law, however, does recognize this inherent obligation and imposes it upon them, as it were retrospectively, so that (unless, in Exodus, the father withholds his consent) they must marry.

In effect the community recognizes that inherent in sexual intercourse is a meaning *in some ways* equivalent to the spoken oath of marriage; we may perhaps term this an 'oath sign'. Either this intercourse is and remains immoral, or else the partners must accept (even retrospectively) the moral obligations inherent in the act. There is a wider dimension to this, expressed in the concept of the father's consent on behalf of the woman's family. But it is instructive to consider the arguments of Hugenberger, who seeks 'to demonstrate that sexual union (*copula carnalis*), when engaged in with consent (i.e., both parental, in the case of dependent daughters, and mutual), was understood as a marriage-constituting act and, correspondingly, was considered a requisite covenant-ratifying (and renewing) oath-sign for marriage, at least in the view of certain biblical authors' (Hugenberger 1994:248; cf. 248–265).

In his detailed history of 'informal marriage' in England from 1750 onwards Stephen Parker notes how, often in this period, when a man made a woman pregnant the local community regarded them as effectively married; that is to say, the man was obliged to take upon himself the responsibilities of husband and father, to care for the woman and her child. The man might or might not willingly accept this responsibility, but he had little choice. Parker comments, 'The approach to sex was therefore far from casual: it was located in a general belief in the ability of public opinion to command obedience to community values' (Parker 1990:19).

This concept of the wider community imposing upon the couple the obligations of the relationship into which they have entered, even if they have not chosen to accept these obligations, is suggestive of a way forward in the debates about unmarried cohabitation in contemporary society. It seems to me defensible to argue that the wider community (if it is to act in line with the created order) ought to understand that sexual relationship is either immoral or carries with it this moral obligation of permanence, and therefore ought in its laws to express this understanding by expecting of the cohabiting couple that these obligations will be honoured (or penalizing them as immoral). In other words, it ought to re-establish the concept of common law marriage. This is to recognize the unbreakable deontological nexus in the created order between sexual relationship and responsibility to God for enduring faithfulness.

This would mean that if either party wished to 'walk out' of the relationship, they could not (as at present) do so without accountability to wider society and therefore without doing some kind of justice to the abandoned partner. Such a development in society would afford protection to the weaker party, which is precisely one of the major functions of marriage. Traditionalists may be horrified at this suggestion, which will seem subversive of marriage, and undoubtedly there are significant advantages in verbalizing and consciously accepting the commitment to permanence before witnesses. For a Christian believer this public and explicit acceptance of what marriage is and means must be right. Nevertheless, it seems to me that for society as a whole it is better to understand cohabitation as containing within its 'symbolic' meaning the *obligations* of marriage than to allow couples without scandal to live together with no such commitments, which is close to the current situation. Either cohabitants accept the obligations of faithfulness or their relationship is immoral; they cannot be at the same time moral and uncommitted to faithfulness.

It is important for Christian people to insist that the public vows do not change the moral status of a relationship from one in which transience is acceptable to one in which permanence is expected. No sexual relationship is at the same time moral and intentionally transient. When a man and a woman wish to live morally together they owe each other exclusive lifelong faithfulness; this is the only moral context for sexual relations. God calls them to faithfulness, whether or not they recognize this. The one who walks out of a cohabiting relationship is not exempt from God's condemnation simply because they never promised to stay. The public pledges are not an extra degree of commendable commitment volunteered by particularly virtuous couples, thus moving their relationship up to a higher ethical level. The public pledges admit and recognize the moral obligation that God has already laid on them by virtue of their existing relationship.

Some have argued that we may redefine betrothal to mean prenuptial cohabitation, thus rendering such cohabition moral because it carries with it the *intention* or *hope* of subsequent marriage (Thatcher 2002). This, however, is confused thinking. If 'betrothed cohabitation' is to be moral, it must carry the public pledge of lifelong faithfulness; that is to say, it needs to be marriage. Thatcher appears implicitly to recognize this when he writes, 'Marriage begins not with a wedding but with betrothal' (Thatcher 2002:61); in which case what he is actually doing is redefining what we call 'a wedding' to mean a post-nuptial celebration not far removed from a wedding anniversary party.

The question arises as to whether a culture's understanding of the meaning of a nonverbal act (cohabitation) can change with time, so that society may come to recognize (in law) responsibilities in cohabitation beyond those that present-day cohabitants would choose to accept. Put another way, the question is whether a public *understanding* of the meaning of an action (living together) may become so strong as to amount to an implicit *undertaking* from the parties involved that in living together they take upon themselves the obligations of faithfulness. Such a link between public understanding and personal undertaking is, after all, implicit in other use of symbolic language; we all understand that to shake someone by the right hand while stabbing them in the back with the left is a form of violent treachery in which the symbolic meaning of the handshake is contradicted by the attack. A handshake *means* acceptance or friendship; to shake the hand is *understood* by society to mean this, and therefore to shake the hand is to *undertake* this kind of relationship. If society came to understand cohabitation as it used to understand common law marriage, as the union of one man with one woman for life, then the action of moving in together would implicitly carry with it the undertaking of faithfulness. It does not at present.

Stephen Parker claims that there is an unconscious continuity in Britain between the relatively informal marriage arrangements common before the Hardwicke Marriage Act (1753) and the contemporary practice of unmarried cohabitation. Although, 'The State most certainly does not *call* these relationships (sc. unmarried cohabitation) marriage . . . It does . . . increasingly regulate them *as if* they were marriage' (Parker 1990:1, 28). Parker suggests that the Hardwicke Act was 'the high point of formality' in which the law stamped a uniform and inflexible definition on marriage. It was less formal before, and the history since has been of 'a gradual, if ambiguous, retreat' from this position (Parker 1990:2, 47; cf. Gillis 1988; also Outhwaite 1995, which covers very fully the history, substance and effect of the Hardwicke Act).

The weakness with Parker's analysis is the question of permanence. In the informal arrangements (often lumped together as 'common law marriage') that preceded the Hardwicke Act it was always understood that for a relationship to be moral it must be intended and pledged for life. Today we see a category or spectrum of relationships (unmarried cohabitation) in which the intention of permanence is far from clear, if it is present at all. Indeed, unmarried cohabitation is precisely a relationship existing in parallel to marriage, but deliberately excluding the public pledge of lifelong faithfulness. In this central respect it is unlike common law marriage.

None the less, it might perhaps be possible for society to change its perception of unmarried cohabitation so that it carried with it the expectation and obligations of permanence. In his vigorous critique of unmarried cohabitation Pratt writes that 'mutual consent is at the heart of marriage' and this consent has not been given by cohabitees (at least not by both); they have opted for cohabitation as a way of avoiding this consent. 'They would not say thank you if Parliament passed a law regarding them as married: they have chosen not to be!' (Pratt 1994:16f.). This is true. But whether or not the individuals wish it, a society may (arguably ought to) recognize in law the moral obligation to permanence which is laid on such couples by God (unless their union is immoral, in which case society ought to discriminate *against* it). That a couple may wish not to accept these responsibilities is one thing, but if this is – as I argue – the actual moral obligation in the sight of God, it may be that society ought to impose these responsibilities on cohabiting couples. We would then be endowing a symbolic action (living together) with meaning and obligations in law. I make this suggestion rather tentatively.

Consent and consummation

Consent – to sex, to marriage in its nature, and to marriage in its ends – is essential to marriage. The question has therefore been asked in the past, 'Ought the inception of marriage to be defined by public consent *alone*?' That is, when a couple publicly promise in the present tense (*per verba de praesenti* rather than *per verba de futuro*, which is engagement, a declaration of intent to be married in the future) to take one another as man and wife, we are to account them married, whether or not the marriage is consummated in sexual union. (This is, of course, what we do in both civil and ecclesiastical wedding ceremonies.)

This question has a long history (Brooke 1989: chs. 6, 11). Both consent and consummation are intrinsic to marriage. Scripture recognizes that an unconsummated union is seriously distinct from a consummated one. This distinction is implied in the episode in Genesis 20 where Abraham effectively turns his marriage to Sarah into a clandestine marriage. Abimelech 'took' Sarah (v. 2). The use of this verb (*lāqaḥ*) might suggest he had intercourse with her, but in verse 4 it becomes clear that he had not 'approached' (*qārab*) her, indicating sexual intercourse. And the absence of sexual intercourse meant that his action in 'taking' her (into his harem, perhaps) did not have about it the character of the 'great sin' of adultery. Sex is very significant. Marriage is distinctively about sex; what distinguishes marriage from other relationships such as kinship or friendship is precisely that it involves sexual intercourse. Scripture never envisages marriage without sex.

It would seem to follow that known and permanent incapacity for sex renders true marriage impossible. The question of incapacity for sexual relations has naturally concerned both pastors and lawyers. Usually the point at issue is male impotence, although the principle under discussion is any physical (and presumably psychological) incapacity of either partner for sexual intercourse. *The Church and Marriage* listed four main principles on which marriage is based. The fourth of these is 'competence' to be married, which includes being above the age of consent,[5] not being already married, not being too closely related, and also physical capacity. But it insists that, 'With regard to physical impotence, only the parties themselves can impeach a marriage on this ground, and the impotence must be proved as having existed at the time of the marriage, and not to have been a subsequent development.' Likewise, *The Church and the Law of Nullity of Marriage* lists both the wilful refusal to consummate and also sexual impotence as 'defects which make a marriage voidable'. It is important to note that both these reports focus here on the physical capacity for sexual intercourse rather than the capacity to have children. Thus the 1935 report in a footnote denies that 'the actual possibility of procreation' can be allowed to define marriage – a woman who has had a hysterectomy, for example, can contract a valid marriage (Church of England 1935:8f.; cf. Church of England 1955: ch. III, which excludes 'incurable sterility).

These discussions too easily sink into absurdity, however. *The Church and the Law of Nullity of Marriage* discusses differing Anglican and Roman Catholic perspectives on the distinction between the man achieving penetration and the man being capable of actually deposing semen in the vagina (Church of England 1955: ch. 5). It is precisely this kind of Pharisaical nicety that points up the fruitlessness of this line of argument. In a matter so intimate, how may impotence subsisting at the time of marriage be proven? How may anyone hope to prove, for example, that a man knew he was permanently impotent at the time of contracting a marriage and deliberately deceived his wife about this until the time came when she expected sexual relations and was disappointed? This will only be possible in the most exceptional circumstances in which the man's permanent impotence is a matter of medical record.

There is a much stronger case for marking the beginning of a marriage by

---

5. The distinction between childhood and adulthood as regards sexual intercourse is of great importance today.

consent than by consummation, even if we admit that deliberate nonconsummation would be grounds for nullity (this including one partner knowing before the exchange of consent that they could never have sex and concealing this from their partner).

We may note the seriousness with which the Old Testament law regards the pledge of betrothal ($\sqrt{'rs'}$) in Deuteronomy 22:23–27. The woman is engaged to be married, which in their culture seems to have meant present-tense exchange of consent (with an agreement that consummation will follow at a later date), rather than our engagement (which is a future-tense declaration of *intent*). Since marriage is characterized (even defined) by faithfulness, faithfulness to such vows of consent defines entry into the married state; in this law the woman who breaks such vows is guilty of adultery.

There is a nice example of the application of this principle by Pope Alexander III in the twelfth century. Brooke records the case of Agnes, Countess of Oxford, married by *verba de praesenti* to Aubrey de Vere, First Earl of Oxford, when Agnes was about twelve years old. Between the giving of this (present-tense) consent and the consummation, however, Agnes's father, Henry of Essex, was disgraced and de Vere decided the marriage was not as auspicious as he had thought. He sought to annul it. Agnes appealed and Pope Alexander III eventually ordered the earl to share his bed and board with her as man and wife. He was to do this within twenty days of the arrival of the Pope's mandate, or else the bishop was to lay an interdict on his lands and excommunicate the earl. The earl complied with this unusual order, the marriage was consummated, and they had at least five children. Brooke wryly comments, 'One can hardly imagine a more inauspicious beginning to a marriage ...' (Brooke 1989:153–157, 128). Alexander III's scriptural logic was presumably clear and straightforward. De Vere had pledged himself to Agnes in marriage and must therefore give her full marital rights (1 Cor. 7:3–4). Consummation must follow consent to be married; to withhold it would be unjust.

An interesting variation on this argument is found in Luther's polemical work *On the Babylonian Captivity of the Church*. Luther discusses the case of a man who, while engaged to one woman (B), has intercourse with another (C). The Catholics said that his intercourse with C was an impediment to his going on to marry B. Luther argues the reverse: that his solemn promise to B stands. He is bound to marry her. His intercourse with C was in the nature of adultery, since he was promising her what he had not in his power to give (Luther, *Babylonian*:382–389). For Luther, as for Alexander III, consent to marry takes precedence over sexual union.

Having argued that present-tense consent must define entry to marriage, we must immediately enter a caveat. This caveat leads into a crucial discussion of the public nature of marriage. We may introduce this by considering the argument of the Reformer Martin Bucer. In his work 'Marriage, Divorce and Celibacy', Bucer disagrees passionately with the concept of marriage being defined *per verba de praesenti* alone. His reasoning is pastoral: what if two rash and infatuated youngsters make promises to be married and happen to make them in the present tense? Are they to be held to be married, such that they must now live together as man and wife even though there has been no consummation and they may very soon regret what they have said? So Bucer argues that the distinction between promises in the present tense and promises in the future tense is one of Pharisaical nicety which should not be sustained. Only when the promises are accompanied by consummation may they be said to be married (Bucer, *Marriage*:408f.).

This debate about consent and consummation may seem arcane, but it comes back again to the nexus of public and private which is in many ways the key to ethical discussion of marriage. Brooke sensitively comments,

> As facts of ordinary experience consent and consummation seem equally important. But the great difficulty of defining and applying acceptable rules to the entry to marriage is that it is both a very private, intimate, personal bond between a man and a woman, and a public act from which all sorts of consequences which concern many folk besides the partners may flow. Its definition is too intimate a matter to be left to the crudities of the law; yet it is also too public a matter to be left to the private convictions of the partners. The outward and the inward views of marriage have always been, and must be, in some degree of tension, even conflict.
> (Brooke 1989:129f.)

While the ruling of Pope Alexander III expresses the biblical concept of marital obligation (that when a man and woman have publicly consented to be married *now* each *ought* to give their body to the other in sexual love), the concern of Bucer arises when the consent is not properly public. These rash promises were made in secret (Bucer, *Marriage*:409f.). Had they declared their intent solemnly to make these vows in public, then their families would have protected them from their own stupidity. Bucer's pastoral concern leads him to insist on the consent not just of the couple (who may be influenced by 'blind love and the desire of the flesh', Bucer, *Marriage*:320) but also of parents or guardians. This familial widening of consent is considered in the next section.

Consent of individuals and consent of family

Bucer's concern prompts an important discussion. Again and again our discussion of the definition of marriage brings us back to its public dimension. This is true for consent, which is more than a private agreement.

The distinction between choice and consent

It is important first to distinguish consent from free choice; they are not coterminous. The idea that a man or woman may freely (i.e. in an unconstrained or unfettered way) choose a marriage partner is a curiously recent one, and one that may be thought to owe more to half-digested ideas of Cartesian personalism than to a biblical view of the human moral agent. No man or woman has ever enjoyed free choice. Every marriage decision is limited by a myriad of constraints, whether of geography, class, culture or family. It is not only Romeo and Juliet who encounter obstacles to choosing the spouse of their dreams, not least because most never get the chance even to meet him or her. So when in his otherwise valuable study *Marriage and its Modern Crisis* Alan Storkey asserts, 'Declared choice is . . . the fulcrum of the wedding service,' and goes on to claim that some arranged marriages (and principles of endogamy or exogamy) compromise this principle of free consent because they compromise the scope of marital choice, we ought to demur (Storkey 1996:47).

It is a paradoxical principle of the gospel that voluntary submission does not compromise freedom (this is expounded with peculiar power in 1 Pet. 2:13 – 3:6). To consent to submit to the will of another is not the same as being coerced into subjection to the will of another. Consent is a decision of my will, whereas coercion is the exercise of theirs. To consent, therefore, to the proposal of another does not threaten moral agency or responsibility (indeed, in the light of Phil. 2:5 – 11 it may be seen to enhance it). It is possible, indeed often virtuous, freely to consent to do something which might not have been what we ourselves would have chosen had we been unconstrained.

In the matter of consent in marriage, this distinction is important. It is too easy to pour scorn on arranged marriages as sub-Christian. On the contrary, arranged marriages in some cultures may sometimes be wise and loving arrangements – so long as the couple themselves freely consent to the arrangement. They must be free to consent or to refuse any marriage that is proposed. This is in principle not very different from the freedom of a woman to accept or refuse a proposal of marriage from a man. She is not (in most cultures) free to say, 'No, I won't marry you, but I will marry John Smith whom I prefer.' This choice may not be open to her unless John Smith has also proposed or is willing to accept her proposal. An individual's freedom extends only to the making of proposals or the acceptance or otherwise of proposals or arrangements that are offered.

Consent and families

Contemporary commentators tend to discuss cultures in which a father 'gives away' his daughter in marriage (e.g. Caleb in Josh. 15:16 or Saul in 2 Sam. 3) in terms of patriarchy and its damaging effects, but there is another side to the debate. It is true that a society in which families have a large say in marriage decisions will have instances of injustice and harsh judgments. None the less, the alternative of free floating freely choosing individuals is not a panacea for true humanness. In a study of the family in premonarchical Israel (i.e. in the period between the settlement of the land and the monarchy) Carol Meyers writes eloquently of how the sense of identity in that agrarian context is bound up with family, and how this differs from our contemporary Western concept. On the family farm the family's work was inextricably linked with its survival, so one did not think in individualistic terms. On the contrary, 'The profound interdependence of family members in self-sufficient agrarian families . . . created an atmosphere of corporate family identity, in which one could conceive not of personal goals and ventures but only of familial ones.' In this context, 'Work and family were not independent spheres, just as property and families were not independent entities.' By contrast, in the Industrial Revolution there grew up the modern family which is separated from its economic basis, which lies in an external domain, the workplace. This 'fosters the notion of individual choice, interests, freedoms, gratification, and fulfilment'. In an agrarian setting, 'People *belong* to a family rather than, if they so choose, *have* a family' (Meyers 1997:21f.).

In Meyers' view the most radical discontinuity between biblical origins and the modern Judaeo-Christian world is 'the corporate identity and family solidarity of the early Israelite farm family as opposed to the achievement-oriented individualism of the industrialized West'.

Philip Slater has written, 'The notion that people begin as separate individuals, who then march out and connect themselves with others, is one of the most dazzling bits of self-mystification in the history of the species' (quoted in Stone 1979:425). It seems to me that we ought to be more open to ideas of parental or wider family consent as part of the public matrix of marriage. I have quoted Martin Bucer on this above, but it is fitting to close this discussion of consent with his pastoral judgment in this regard. In *De Regno Christi* he reiterates his insistence that the consent of parents or guardians is essential to a valid marriage. His motivation is to safeguard the interest of both the parents (whose family will be deeply affected by the marriage choices of their children) and the spouses, who need (especially if they are young) to be protected against the consequences of rash judgments. Marriage needs 'the counsel and consent of parents, or, in their absence . . . the counsel of those whom everyone justly ought to have in the place of parents, such as tutors, guardians, relatives, patrons and special friends' (Bucer, *De Regno Christi*:321). He is strongly against clandestine marriages. As a pastor, however, he is aware that no system of wider consent is perfect. Parents can withhold consent for reasons of cruelty; if they do, he recommends that the magistrate should have the power to overrule them.

Having said all this about the pastoral wisdom of wider consent, we must be very careful to guard the principle of consent by the parties to the marriage themselves. There are too many terrible examples of duress to allow us to become complacent (Church of England 1955: ch. 4). Probably the most vigorous biblical insistence on the principle of free consent is to be found in 1 Corinthians 7:36–38. This short section has a number of exegetical cruxes and my exegesis follows the excellent treatment by Fee, in which he argues that what is in view is an engaged man being pressured by some in Corinth (in line with their dictum in verse 1 that 'It is good for a man not to touch [sexually] a woman') not to go ahead and marry his fiancée. Fee points out the repeated insistence on what we might call free consent (here by the man, although the same would apply to the woman). The man must settle the matter in his own heart; he must be under no compulsion (*anagkē*); he must 'have authority' concerning his own will; and he must make up his own mind. 'This verbal tour de force strongly suggests that outside influences might lead him to take such an action' [i.e. not marry his fiancée] but against his own will' (Fee 1987:353).

Marriage as public institution

In his massive study of British marriages from 1600 to the present, John Gillis notes, 'Marriage has been and always will be a public as well as a private matter, whose history is not just that of the lovers but of all those who are in any way touched by their relationship' (Gillis 1988:321). In an essay entitled 'Sex in a wider context' Linda Woodhead notes how sex insists on breaking the bounds first of the individual (by attachment to another) and then of the couple (both by children and by the whole social reality of relating to others *as a couple*): 'Contrary to what is commonly held today, there is no private realm hermetically sealed from the wider and impersonal public realm' (Woodhead 1997:107–110).

We noted in Chapter 3 that privatization, the retreat of marriage from the public sphere, is at the heart of a damaging paradigm shift. This privatization is not new. In 1935 the introduction to *The Church and Marriage* lamented, 'There is in many quarters a revolt against any view of marriage which emphasises its social aspects and obligations, and an increasing tendency to regard it as a purely individual affair' (Church of England 1935:3). It goes on to insist that 'forms must be observed which are recognised by the community and are free from any imputation of clandestinity' (Church of England 1935:10).

(Indeed, the Hardwicke Marriage Act of 1753 was entitled 'An Act for the Better Preventing of Clandestine Marriages', Outhwaite 1995:169.)

In his influential treatment of marriage, Barth does include the public dimension. Marriage cannot be 'a purely private undertaking. Even the smallest cottage of the happiest of lovers cannot be habitable inside unless it has at least a door and a few windows opening outwards. *At some point* it finds itself implicated in affinities and friendships as part of the Christian and civil community' (Barth, *CD* III/4:224, my italics). And yet for Barth 'the genesis of marriage' is still the interpersonal covenant love of the couple, and this *leads on* to the creation of a new social unit in relation to those outside. 'A wedding is only the regulative confirmation and legitimation of a marriage before and by society.' For Barth any view that equates marriage with the wedding ceremony is 'a dreadful and deep-rooted error', falls into Roman Catholic externalism and formalism and loses the inner dynamic of the relationship (Barth, *CD* III/4:225).

Against Barth, I suggest that the public creation of a new social unit is not an extra ('at some point') but intrinsic to the genesis of marriage, which is not created purely by the covenant love of a couple. Indeed, the covenant love of the couple is not so much the genesis of the marriage as the vocation to which husband and wife are called by God by virtue of being married. It does not matter what the dynamics of interpersonal covenant love were or were not before the marriage was entered; what matters before God is the response of the man and wife to the calling of God to live out covenant faithfulness in the marriage once they have entered it. The public dimension is not merely a corollary of marriage; it is at the heart of marriage.

In Western culture we have followed the logic of Barth's thought far beyond his intention. We have got used to thinking that sex is a private matter between consenting adults and that, for example, 'law has no place in the bedroom'. Such private romanticism is deeply misleading. Again and again in our study we have observed the distinction between sexual relationship considered as a private arrangement and the same relationship recognized in the public domain. This ought not to surprise us. If, as we have argued, the primary moral matrix of marriage is the responsible task entrusted to humankind to steward God's world, then marriage cannot be a matter of so-called private morality (indeed, the phrase 'private morality' is itself an oxymoron). It is necessary therefore to explore further the public dimension of marriage as a relationship initiated, hedged and bounded by public recognition and support.[6]

---

6. As Longenecker 1984:xii recognizes, there is no strict divide between social and personal ethics, and sexual ethics span this boundary with peculiar force. See also Atkinson 1979:87–89 on the institutional framework of marriage.

The public nature of marriage is the social expression of the theological truth that marriage is a joining together by God.

The wedding and the honeymoon: public feast and private intimacy

Public feast

It may seem surprising that in our study so far we have not considered the word 'marriage' itself in the Scriptures. Indeed, it may seem even more surprising that in the Hebrew Scriptures there is no common word or word group that simply designates marriage as an institution or 'to marry' as a verb,[7] or 'husband' and 'wife' as distinct from 'man' and 'woman'. All this is true, but of little significance since the concepts are not dependent on simple denotative words.

It is instructive at this point, however, to consider the Greek word *gamos* (marriage), along with *gameō* (I marry), *gamizō* or *gamiskō* (both meaning 'I give in marriage'). These words occur in a number of contexts, but one of the most common is the use of the word *gamos* to designate a wedding banquet or feast.[8] Indeed, in the LXX the only member of the word group to appear is *gamos*, where this is its usual meaning.[9] The only New Testament use of the word to designate what we might call the institution of marriage is in Hebrews 13:4.

Thus in the New Testament and the LXX our attention is directed not usually towards the interpersonal dynamics of the ongoing marriage but to the public celebration of the inauguration of the marriage, the marriage feast. The guests at Jacob's marriage to Leah (a *gamos*, Gen. 29:22 LXX) would have been disappointed to hear that marriage is 'just a piece of paper', since the LXX *gamos* translates the Hebrew *mišteh*, which means literally 'a drinking'. Three times in the LXX of Esther there is a *gamos* (Est. 1:5; 2:18; 9:22) and always it means a public feasting.[10]

A *gamos* is precisely not the intimate candlelit dinner for two, but the joyful and exuberant public celebration of the marriage. A man and a woman know when they are married, and everyone else knows, and rejoices – this is the sense of the word. The couple do not drift gradually into a relationship such that the *gamos* feels like a graduation ceremony (as so often today after premar-

---

7. The √*b'l* is used in this sense on a few occasions (see BDB: 1166), but most marriages are spoken of without a technical term.

8. Matt. 22:2ff.; 25:10; Luke 12:36; 14:8; John 2:1ff.; Rev. 19:7, 9.

9. Gen. 29:22; Est. 1:5; 2:18; 9:22; the other occurrences are in Tobit, 1 Maccabees and Ben Sirach.

10. Indeed, in the Hebrew text neither in 1:5 nor 9:22 is there any clear connection even with a wedding.

ital cohabitation). They marry and subsequently work at living out the implications of the relationship into which they have entered. It is part of the essential paradox of marriage as understood in the Bible that the privacy and
intimacy of the couple are known about, supported and affirmed by as wide a
spectrum of community and family as is possible.

Private intimacy

It is precisely this bipolarity of publicity (the wedding) and intimacy (the honeymoon) that gives to marriage its stability and security. Both poles are necessary. And both are under threat. Paradoxically, as we live in a culture where the
publicity of sexual commitment is being diluted by drift into ambiguous relationships, at the same time sexual intimacy is made public. While on the one
hand public commitment publicly recognized is being weakened by nonmarital cohabitation, at the same time we live in a society in which the intimacy of
sexual union is paraded for all to see in the growing acceptance of pornography in the mainstream media. Yet the public dimension of marriage is
intended to protect, not to expose, the private dimension of sexual intimacy.

It is instructive to consider the uses and connotations of the Hebrew word
'erwâ, whose general meaning is 'nakedness' or specifically 'the genital area',
the 'private parts' (male or female) that Paul refers to as being treated with
greater honour (1 Cor. 12:23). The idiom 'to uncover nakedness' (*'erwâ* with
the verb *gālâ*) is often used (particularly in Lev. 18 – 20) as a euphemism for
sexual intercourse. It may also be used in the sense of allowing one's genital
area to be uncovered, or perhaps to dress or almost undress in a deliberately
provocative way, to arouse a stranger to desire, for 'nakedness' may be uncovered literally, photographically or suggestively (to the imagination). This seems
to be the sense, for example, in Ezekiel 23:18 ('When she carried on her whor-
ings so openly and flaunted her nakedness', the openness conveyed by the
repeated use of *gālâ*). The concern to prevent any danger of this appears to lie
behind the law of Exodus 20:26 that forbade Moses going up to the altar on
steps lest his nakedness be exposed,[11] and the law of Exodus 28:42 that the
priest is to wear linen undergarments to cover (*kāsâ*) his nakedness, the
purpose being to cover his private parts. Both to uncover one's 'nakedness'
voluntarily and to have it exposed by force (e.g. Is. 47:3 of the 'virgin daughter
of Babylon', Ezek. 23:10, 29) or seen by others (Lam. 1:8; Hos. 2:9f.) is a cause
of shame. Almost always the association is not so much literal nakedness

---

11. Cassuto 1967:257 suggests a deliberate contrast to the practices of certain peoples in
    the Ancient Near East 'whose priests ... used to perform every ritual ceremony in a
    state of nakedness'.

(which may simply be for medical reasons) but rather sexual desire, sexual union, sexual abuse or sexual provocation. Indeed, there is sometimes an element of ambiguity or overlap between the 'seeing' of nakedness and actual sexual activity. For example, it is not clear what Genesis 9:22f. means by saying that Ham 'saw' (*rā'â*) his father's nakedness. The severity of Noah's response in verse 24f. suggests to some commentators that some sordid details have been suppressed and that perhaps Ham even committed sodomy with his father (Sarna 1989, ad loc.; Phillips 1980).

'Nakedness' conveys an image of vulnerability that ought to be exposed only in the context of a private and legitimate sexual union.[12] When a man 'covers' a woman's nakedness in marriage (as Ezek. 16:8 or, in intention, Hos. 2:11) the implication is that 'it is understood that henceforth the woman shall be covered to all except her husband'.[13] The marriage union is the only safe place for sexual uncovering.

The benefits of public recognition

Alongside the privacy of sexual intimacy (which is to be guarded) there ought to go the security of public recognition. We explore now some of the benefits of this.

Protection against inadvertent intrusion

At the simplest level publicity is a protection against unwitting intrusion into the pledged relationship. Outsiders need to know who is married to whom lest any unwittingly intrude or threaten to intrude. This is why Abimelech is so scandalized by Abraham's behaviour in Genesis 20.

It is not just necessary to know who 'belongs' (sexually) to whom at present. For the security of marriage it is necessary also to have a clear public understanding of the enduring and exclusive nature of that mutual belonging. The whole dynamic of sexual relationship involves perhaps the deepest vulnerability of which human beings are capable. It is for this reason that protection is necessary. Sex without security is riven with anxiety and the fear of hurt. We need the security of a public hedge around private intimacy to protect us from the possibility that in opening ourselves to that intimacy our vulnerability will be exploited to harm us.

A concern to protect the weak was the driving force behind the moves in

---

12. Even when used by Joseph metaphorically when accusing his brothers of spying, in Gen. 42:9, 12 ('the nakedness of the land'), it is used to convey an image of vulnerability that ought not to be seen by strangers.

13. Greenberg 1983:227; cf. Levine 1989:120.

the late medieval church towards bringing marriage into the ecclesiastical domain. How were the weak to be protected from exploitation by a bigamist, or children under the age of consent from being unfairly pressed into a marriage? Answer: by encouraging marriage *in facie ecclesiae*, which 'means publicly, in the presence of the local community of the church or parish; not privately or secretly or clandestinely' (Brooke 1989:250). In the late eleventh and early twelfth centuries marriage was increasingly marked by ecclesiastical ceremony. Long before a ceremony in the church building became common, the public nature of marriage was guarded by marriage 'at the church door' (first mentioned in documents of the twelfth century and in common parlance by the fourteenth century).[14]

This movement culminated in Lord Hardwicke's Marriage Act of 1753, which enforced church marriage as the only valid marriage in England (as had been done in Roman Catholic countries since the Council of Trent) until civil marriage became part of English law in 1836. This was not primarily because it was thought that ecclesiastical involvement improved the union in some religious way, but rather as a protection against the perceived dangers of clandestinity (Bailey 1959:204f.; Haw 1952:142–150; Brooke 1989:139ff.). This safeguard is now equally maintained by properly publicized civil marriage. However it may be achieved, it is essential for any ordered society to know who 'belongs' (mutually and sexually) to whom.

Protection for the weak in the matter of consent: the strange case of Shechem and Dinah (Genesis 34)
It is attractive in our culture to suppose that 'I', as a free-floating moral agent, may consent to enter or decline a proffered sexual relationship. In reality such unattached 'freedom' means slavery of the weak to the manipulative. There is a tragic Bible episode that points up for us the need for consent to be made publicly in the context of family and community support. This is the strange case of Shechem, the Hivite prince, and Dinah, the daughter of Jacob and Leah (Gen. 34). This episode is often called 'the rape of Dinah', since it begins with Shechem's coercive sex with Dinah (v. 2). But what follows makes it clear that this is very different from, say, the rape of Tamar by her half-brother Amnon (2 Sam. 13), in which we see the familiar tragic sequence of obsession, rape (v. 14) and aversion (v. 15). By contrast Shechem goes on being deeply attached to Dinah (Gen. 34:3, lit. 'his soul stuck to her'; cf. Gen. 2:24). It becomes apparent to the reader only near the end (v. 26) that throughout the drama Dinah has

---

14. Brooke 1989:212 cites Chaucer's 'Wife of Bath' of whom Chaucer said, 'Housbondes at chirche dore she hadde fyve.'

been in Shechem's house. In other words, they have been cohabiting. We are not told what Dinah felt and thought about this. It is possible she was kept entirely against her will, but in view of Shechem's ongoing love for her and his sustained pressure to be allowed to marry her it seems more plausible that his affection was not entirely unreciprocated (Sternberg 1985:445–475; cf. Kass 1992). What is clear, however, is that Dinah in this drama is an individual isolated from the network of her family relationships. She is in a way the epitome of the typical young unmarried cohabitant.

This sorry drama points us to a profound theological connection between the question of consent and coercion and the distinction between publicly supported marriage and a 'private' arrangement of cohabitation. It does not take much sensitivity or knowledge of human nature to understand the mixed feelings and conflicting emotions of Dinah, who was a young woman (cf. v. 4 'this girl' *yaldâ*) making decisions about her affections and loyalties *on her own*. Going back to the pastoral arguments of Bucer about consent, we may observe here that had Dinah had the public counsel and support of her family (and particularly her father, who sadly seemed to have cared as little for Leah's daughter as he had cared for Leah), she would have been freed from the physical and emotional coercion to which she was undoubtedly subjected. The value of marriage as a public covenant recognized and supported by the wider family and community is highlighted here; the absence of this public and societal dimension leaves the parties in a cohabitation all too vulnerable to exploitation and coercion. There is a theme here worth exploring.

The buttressing of integrity with public vows

Public commitment buttresses a private pledge. In one sense, whenever a man and a women pledge themselves to be married they enter into a covenant to which there is at least one witness: according to Malachi 2:14, 'the LORD was a witness between you and the wife of your youth'. In this sense there is no such thing as a clandestine marriage. Whenever a man and a woman consent to marry one another, the Creator is witness and holds them to account to maintain and uphold lifelong exclusive faithfulness.

It would be wrong, however, to deduce from this that human witnesses are unnecessary. On the contrary, human witnesses encourage both marriage partners to understand the seriousness of the promises they make and at least to approximate in human society the impact of the divine witness.

Hauerwas perceptively notes that 'the church's traditional condemnation of "secret marriages" involves substantive assumptions' that are relevant in every age. This condemnation rightly implies that 'we should not trust our declarations of love unless we are willing to commit ourselves publicly. For there is surely no area where we are more liable to self-deception than in those contexts where love is mixed with sexual desire.' When we embark on sexual liaisons without public pledges, this constitutes '*prima facie* evidence that the love is not true'; the test of true love is the willingness to pledge that love in front of witnesses (Hauerwas 1981:186f. and endnote 14).

While in a world before the fall it might presumably be said of any man or woman that a spoken word is a bond – for they would live each moment *coram Deo* – in the world after the fall there is a tragic difference between the fragility of a word spoken in private and the strength of a word spoken in public. When a word is spoken in public, on a solemn occasion in front of witnesses, the entire public persona and integrity of the speaker are placed on the line behind that word. It is much harder to break, even if the speaker later wishes he or she could break it. As Ramsey has suggestively put it, marriage is not just a re-enactment of the marriage of Adam and Eve, before the fall. There is something about marriage after the fall which is like the 'skins' God lovingly made to protect and care for Adam and Eve after their disobedience. 'God has ordained marriage to restrain and remedy the defects in us, to protect us against threats which imperil our true good' (Ramsey 1975:19).

In an echo of Reinhold Niebuhr's saying ('Man's capacity for justice makes democracy possible. Man's inclination to injustice makes democracy necessary'), Ramsey writes,

> Man's capacity for responsible fidelity to the being and well-being of another of opposite sex makes marriage possible (and this is what we mean by saying that in every marriage there is something of the marriage of Adam and Eve in the garden of Paradise); yet man's inclination toward unfaithfulness and irresponsibility makes marriage necessary (and this is what we mean by saying that in every marriage there is something of the first marriage after the Fall).
> (Ramsey 1975:20)

Public recognition of the marriage commitment is a bulwark against the instabilities of the individual will. Left to ourselves, our human individual wills are not steady, faithful and resolute. We vacillate and are tossed around by winds of emotion, by storms of suffering and by shakings of personal insecurity. This is peculiarly true of marital love. In marriage the union is not merely between two free-floating individuals, but between wider families in the context of a place in the structure of the community. In this way, 'The unstable emotions of *eros* are provided with a suprapersonal counterbalance that gives permanence to the relationship' (Thielicke 1979:107, of ancient Israel).

This counterbalance works in two complementary ways. On the one hand, in a society which respects marriage individual married people know that in their attempts to build their marriage those around are on their side. They understand and sympathize with the request to make time to build the marriage, with the need to devote energy to refreshing the marriage. These desires and obligations are respected, so that the married couple, while they have their own struggles, need not feel they are taking on the world around them as well. This is how it ought to be in a culture that respects marriage. This is why it is appropriate for those who debate public policy to argue for policies in law and taxation that encourage and support the marriage commitment.

On the other hand, we must not neglect the important aspect of fear and even taboo. When a person is finding marriage hard and beginning to wonder if he or she would be better giving up and taking steps to break the marriage, a vital part of the moral matrix of decision-making is how other significant people around will view such a decision. If those around will shrug their shoulders and say, in a fatalistic way, that sadly these kinds of incompatibility do sometimes surface and really there is nothing to be done about it but recognize the fact and split up, then the struggler is more likely to do just that. But if the deliberate abandonment of a marriage partner (whether by adultery or desertion) would be greeted with dismay and horror by those around, the struggler will be afraid of these consequences, will recognize the wider social cost of breaking this marriage and will thus be strengthened in the resolve to do all that is possible to mend the marriage. The fear of such disapprobation is a good and healthy fear; it is an echo (albeit an imperfect one) of the fear of God who is the divine witness to the marriage.

It is one of the marks of a society that begins to despise marriage that the guilty party in a break-up is viewed with benevolent neutrality by neighbours and friends. If we are to align our judgments with the order of creation we ought to admire and support those who persevere with difficult marriages and we ought to be appalled and dismayed by those who do not.

Such a blunt statement is easy to misunderstand. What I mean is that we ought unequivocally to regard the action of breaking a marriage as sinful – not as inevitable or merely sad, but as a morally sinful act. And therefore we ought to treat the one who does this as we treat any other fellow sinner, not as morally inferior to us (for we are sinners too), but as needing to repent.

Again, it is important (and we shall return to this in our discussion of divorce) to recognize that to speak in simple terms of 'the action of breaking a marriage' hides a great deal of moral and interpersonal complexity. The 'breaker' is not necessarily the one who does the legal formality of filing for divorce. The breaking of the marriage may well have been initiated and even effectively completed in other ways before this, by adultery or desertion or persistent abuse or cruelty; and the filing for divorce may in some circumstances merely be the insistence that this brokenness be properly recognized in law. It is the morally irresponsible actions that initiate and lead to the breakdown of the marriage which we must abhor and from which we must ourselves flee.

Public vows, like the skins on Adam and Eve, recognize human weakness, that present passion is not enough, that we are not by ourselves trustworthy people. A vow is a commitment and not a prediction, but it is a public commitment, buttressed by the support of the wider community. 'The Christian knows and men generally should know, that "I love you" may simply mean, in all sorts of subtle and deviating ways, "I love me and want you"' (Ramsey 1975:20). The vow faces us with the possibility of having to give and not receive. It is foolish to trust myself to be faithful, let alone to ask someone else to rely on me, without the public commitment of the marriage covenant. 'The promise is realistically designed to remedy the element of sin in all human love and to preserve the finest, most intimate of human relationships in a fallen world' (Ramsey 1975:21).

Thus, for example, there is a great difference between a cohabiting couple privately assuring one another that they want to stay together for life (and perhaps promising this, even in the words of the wedding service, by the fire-side one evening), and the same couple making the same commitment to permanent faithfulness publicly – not just in front of family and friends, but in principle in front of all society (for that is what a wedding achieves). As Stafford sceptically comments, 'Private promises are as durable as the morning dew' (Stafford 1993:118).

When I make such a public commitment (unboundedly public, since the wedding certificate is a public document available to all to inspect), I place my whole integrity as a person in the wider community on the line. This 'quality of commitment' can never be matched in the private assurances of lovers, be they never so sincerely meant. It is not the 'formal registration' which is at issue, but the investment of my whole persona (in its full range of relation-ships) in the commitment to permanence.

In Forster's thoughtful assessment of cohabitation (Forster 1994:19), he notes that it is not easy – for a cohabiting couple – to assess the extent to which their relationship is marked by 'lifelong intent'. This is true. But when he goes on to observe that 'the same is now sadly true of marriage' he seems to miss the crucial point that for a married couple, whatever their private thoughts and perhaps conflicting emotions and expectations, there lies behind them a public, explicit and unconditional commitment of each to the other for life.

The phrase 'preceremonial sex' is sometimes used in the debates over pre-marital cohabitation[15] (by which I mean cohabitation where the partners say

---

15. E.g. Joy 1986, who argues that preceremonial sex lies outside the category of *porneia*. Quoted in Stafford 1993:117f.

they intend to marry). The connotation of the word 'preceremonial' tends to be minimalist, as if to imply that this sex happens to take place before the ceremony, but really this is no more than an issue of dates in the diary. The intention is there by the man and woman to be faithful and to be married; who cares if they begin to live together before they get around to telling the wider society that this is their intention? 'Any sex they have will be pre-ceremonial but not pre-marital' (Thatcher 1993:84). Such language tends to imply that 'ceremony' is more or less equivalent to 'formality'. This is ethically naïve; public vows are substance not mere formality.

The painful ambiguities of nonmarital relationships

The value of public marriage surfaces with peculiar force at times of sickness and bereavement. One of the less recognized tragedies of unmarried cohabitation is the pain of relational ambiguity introduced into times of sickness, grieving and funerals. For a married couple there is no doubt that the wider community ought to support the bereaved spouse in his or her grief, to focus their grief on the widow's grief, and to give that person priority of support and honour. This is clear and unambiguous: the spouse is next of kin and the loss is above all his or her loss. By contrast, when one partner in a cohabiting couple dies, perhaps young, perhaps after just a couple of years of living together, the grieving process is fraught with the added pain of relational ambiguity. In particular this focuses on the tension between the grief and claims of the dead person's parents and the pain and attachment of the cohabiting partner. The clear transfer from parents to spouse at a marriage is replaced by a muddy uncertainty as to quite where these various parties stand in relation to one another. It is true that this ambiguity is gradually diluted with time, so that for a couple who have cohabited for many years and perhaps have children of their own we are all pretty clear about relationships and priorities. None the less, the uncertainties over the preceding period are to be regretted, and this regret is usually recognized when the muddy waters of cohabitation are interrupted by premature death. We may almost say that the terrible irruption of premature death is a kind of hard litmus test of morality; it brings into sharp focus the promptings of conscience.

Protection for the weak when marriage breaks

One of the major benefits of clarity in marriage is the protection it affords to the weaker or innocent party when a marriage breaks. We have said that public marriage endeavours to give social expression to the divine calling to faithfulness; correspondingly, it endeavours at its best to give social expression to the divine displeasure at unfaithfulness and the divine concern for justice for the oppressed. Where marriage is considered as at heart an interpersonal relationship of two individuals, one feature that tends to be lost or diluted is justice when it goes wrong. It is all too easy (at present) to walk out on a nonmarital relationship without social disapproval and without being called to account under law for obligations to the abandoned partner. This ought not to be. A society that has regard for creation order ought to expect of the one who walks out that social justice obligations will be respected. This is the moral basis for all attempts to safeguard in law the interests of the spouse left behind and of children of the marriage.

Because the public commitment of marriage is such an important protection for the weak, it may be that we should consider unmarried cohabitation not so much in the category of sin (as in the catchphrase 'living in sin') but more in terms of foolishness. To enter into a union in which God expects of us lifelong exclusive faithfulness without the protection and clarity of the public acceptance of that calling, which we call marriage, is very foolish. Those who slip, by conformity to the culture around, into unmarried cohabitation are not to be shunned as 'unclean' – but they are to be pitied and therefore encouraged to see why God has patterned marriage not merely around the moral obligation of faithfulness but around the clear and public acceptance of that obligation by both parties, a public acceptance buttressed by both the support and the sanctions of wider society.

The blessing of being well connected

But there is a wider aspect of the public nature of marriage. It has deep theological echoes and ties public marriage yet more deeply into the great themes of the story of redemption. The whole business of public records, certificates and genealogies is marginalized whenever there is a nonmarital cohabitation. Yet this despised 'piece of paper', the marriage certificate, may speak to us theologically of the blessing of connectedness. To be married is to be tied into a web of publicly attested and recorded loyalties; to cohabit unmarried is to be a blip under the microscope of the observant social scientist.

As the Babel story of Genesis 11 so graphically portrays, the curse of sin leads to *scattering* and division between peoples; it lies behind the fragmentation of the human race, the difficulties in communicating, the hostilities and barriers between peoples. Again and again in the story of salvation the remedy is spoken of in terms of gathering and barrier-breaking. Israel and Judah are split by sin; they will be gathered into one in the time of salvation (e.g. Ezek. 37:15–28). 'Whoever does not gather with me scatters' (Matt. 12:30). 'There will be one flock, one shepherd' (John 10:16). And in Old Testament Israel there is a sense that this is, or ought to be, one people connected to one another, who will image to the world what a united humanity under the rule of God ought to be. We see this in the seemingly endless genealogies in 1 Chronicles 1 – 9, or in

Genesis 5, 10, 11. Contrary to the claim of Barth, these are not only genealogies leading to the Messiah; they do not focus only on David and through him to the Christ. They include all kinds of people in different tribes. The unifying motif is surely that here are people who matter very much and who are *connected* to other people who matter. The people of God are not isolated individuals but integrated and (in the proper sense) well connected. This is what it is to be part of humanity as humanity was meant to be.

There are no doubt all manner of social reasons behind the dilution and weakening of marriage at different times and in various cultures, but surely among them are the social forces that tend to move people around so that they begin to think of themselves primarily as individuals rather than as members of wider families. This trend has been noted in Chapter 3. A perceptive article appeared in a journal about 'The Decline and Fall of the Surname'. The writer observes that when people introduce themselves they tend (in contemporary Western culture) just to use their first name.

> Simon introduces himself to me as 'Simon' because he is welcoming me to first-name acquaintance at the outset. When he goes to a conference he writes 'Simon' on his name badge. The world is his friend. No need to stand on ceremony. Simon lives in a world with no strangers, just friends he hasn't met yet . . . But who is Simon (or Sally or Fred)? He stands in front of me with a smile, but there is something unconnected about him. Mark Eliot is Andy Eliot's brother, Tina Wallace is Mike Wallace's wife, Paula Perkins is a cousin of the Perkins family I knew when I lived in Puddletown. Llewellyn Jones may speak with a Yorkshire accent, but is evidently of Welsh stock. But Simon? By introducing himself in this way, he has, as it were, sealed himself in a vacuum. Does he not think of himself as a member of a family – his parents' son or his sister's brother?[16]

Such free-floating personhood is a sign of curse not of freedom. We are not persons at an isolated point in time, but persons with histories and futures, and in these histories and futures we had and will have all manner of relations with other persons. To relate to another person is to engage in building not merely isolated points of contact (the connotation of 'acquaintance') but rather a shared story. We cannot do this without implicating our pasts and futures with one another (Moore 1992:60f.). Nor do our histories begin with our births. We look through the photographs or written records of our ancestors with a sense of continuity. The sense of distance is obvious; it is the continuity ('this was *my* great-grandfather') that gives it its interest and sometimes its pathos.

We cannot finally escape our wider ties, however hard we try. The tragedy

---

16. Julia Cameron, in *Evangelicals Now*, April 1995, p. 11.

and sometimes irony of these ties come back like a boomerang to haunt us. When Juliet realizes that Romeo bears the hated name of Montague, she cries,

> What's in a name? That which we call a Rose,
> By any other word would smell as sweete,
> So Romeo would, were he not Romeo call'd,
> Retaine that dear perfection which he owes
> Without that title. Romeo, doffe thy name,
> And for thy name which is no part of thee,
> Take all my selfe.
> (*Romeo and Juliet*, act 2, sc. 1)

As Scruton points out, however, 'As the tragedy shows, it is precisely this that Romeo cannot do. To doff his name is to doff his identity, as the child of these particular parents, heir to this particular debt of vengeance' (Scruton 1986:77). Jennifer Lash's novel *Blood Ties* plays on similar themes of disconnectedness and interconnectedness (Lash 1998). We live with connectedness and the only question is whether that connectedness will be characterized by curse or blessing, by scattering or gathering.

This is why it is not possible finally to separate the affine relationships of marriage from the kinship relationships of blood. We have endeavoured strongly to connect marriage with the birth *and nurture* of children; this reminds us that the purpose of marriage is integral with the goal of intergenerational harmony, a world in which it is true that 'Grandchildren are the crown of the aged, and the glory of children is their parents' (Prov. 17:6). It is perhaps no accident that in Malachi we find both God's strong hatred of the action of 'putting away' in divorce (Mal. 2:16) and also at the end the ministry of 'Elijah' described in terms of the restoration of intergenerational harmony as the only way to avoid curse: '[Elijah] will turn the hearts of parents to their children and the hearts of children to their parents, so that I will not come and strike the land with a curse' (Mal. 4:6).

Conclusion

We conclude that marriage must be entered by consent. At the heart of this is consent to ongoing sexual relationship, committed to exclusive faithfulness for life and aligned to the Creator's purposes for marriage. We have seen that consent cannot consistently be considered as a private or purely individual concept; it carries with it a necessary public and wider familial dimension. The public dimension of marriage is not an ethical extra to make marriage better, but is of the essence of marriage as instituted by God.

12. ONE MAN AND ONE WOMAN

Marriage is
the voluntary sexual and public social union
of one man and one woman
from different families.
This union is patterned upon the union of God with his people his bride,
the Christ with his church.
Intrinsic to this union is God's calling to lifelong exclusive sexual faithfulness.

In this chapter we consider the phrase 'one man and one woman'. There are two parts to this: heterosexuality and monogamy.

1. Heterosexuality ('one *man* and one *woman*') – a brief footnote to the debates

I will comment on heterosexuality only very briefly. It will be clear from this study that I follow the traditional biblical teaching in this area, but so much ink has been spilled and so many voices raised in anger over the homosexuality issue that it is hard to know what constructive contribution this study can make. It would be superfluous simply to go over the arguments in summary form; the bibliography will suffice for those who wish to do this. The centrality that Scripture gives to marriage in all its treatment of sexuality will be evident throughout this study. The overwhelming exegetical arguments in favour of the traditional understandings of the texts that prohibit homosexual practice have been well treated elsewhere.

My goal in this brief section, therefore, is to correlate the traditional understanding of marriage as a heterosexual institution with the framework of the ethic of the service of God expounded in Part Two, and in particular with the procreational good and blessing associated with marriage. I argued in Part Two that the creation institution of marriage is set within the context of the dignity and task given to human beings made in the image of God to rule over God's world in responsible and responsive love to their Creator. The man and the woman are together to serve God in their union, and indeed God's purpose for the marriage union is to promote this task of caring for his world. We saw there that the faithfulness of the relationship is essential to the purpose of marriage because it must reflect the faithfulness of the Creator. We saw that marriage must be a publicly ordered institution since the task is to govern an ordered world, to promote order and fruitfulness and to contain and control pressures towards disorder.

Those who advocate the possibility of faithful publicly pledged homosexual unions argue that such unions can indeed serve this ethic. Two men in union or two women in union may, it is argued, live faithfully together in a social unit that serves God in his world and that conforms to public social order – so long as homosexual unions gain the public recognition for which such advocates strive. Both the relational good and the public order good may in principle be served in a homosexual union, it is argued.

The critical issue in this debate is procreation. As the late Robert Runcie observed in a radio interview in 1996, 'Once the church accepted artificial contraception they signalled that sexual activity was for human delight and a blessing even if it was divorced from any idea of procreation. Once you've said that sexual activity was a matter of delight and pleasing to God in itself [*sic*] then what about people who engaged in same sex expression and who are incapable of heterosexual expression . . .?'[1] The key phrase in this statement is 'even if it was divorced from *any idea of* procreation' (my italics). Sexual union ought never to be divorced from *any idea* of procreation: if it is, the goals of the couple are disordered from the values of the Creator. A sexual relationship ought to accept that the procreation and nurture of children are intrinsic to the structure of sexual relationship.

Such a claim needs to be carefully expounded, or it will be open to the very obvious objection that it excludes the infertile or the aged from 'proper' marriage. No such exclusion is in view. What is meant is that every married couple

---

1. Quoted in *The Briefing*, No. 176, p. 8f.

ought to align their valuation of procreation with God's very positive valuation. They ought to value the gift of children as a good gift and a blessing, and understand why this gift serves God's purpose in the raising of the next generation to steward his world, until such time as the age to come is consummated and death shall be no more.

Thus, if this gift may be bestowed, a couple will long for it and be saddened if it is not granted. And if, by reason of age or medical condition, they know that this gift cannot be given to them, they will still have a fundamental attitude of heart that would have loved this gift had it been possible. And if this gift has been given and the couple have decided responsibly not to have more children, they will forever be grateful to God for the children they have, and every act of sexual union will be as it were a loving reminder of that gift. It is always possible to have this attitude of heart with heterosexual intercourse, for the intrinsic structure of the act between the man and the woman is intended and designed towards this end. The relational delight and the procreational blessing are different kinds of end, but they are coordinate rather than competitive or contradictory.

In a fundamental way, however, it is never responsibly possible to adopt this attitude in homosexual genital activity. The whole structure of the male and female person is ordered such that only in heterosexual intercourse is conception, gestation and procreation part of the proper and natural ordering of sexual union. With the current fast pace of technological development it will no doubt be objected that the time may come when, with the assistance of medical technology, conception may be possible for lesbian couples, but it is hard to see how lesbian or male homosexual sexual union *in itself* can ever be a procreative act. It is in the light of this that we are to understand the natural law arguments for heterosexual marriage (in terms of the physical structure of the human body, male and female), the scriptural advocacy of marriage, and the scriptural texts which prohibit homosexual intercourse.

2. Monogamy ('*one* man and *one* woman')

Monogamy is predicated on monotheism. The deepest reason why marriage is between *one* man and *one* woman is that there is *one* God and *one* created order. Before we see why this is the fundamental reason, we need to consider the phenomenon of polygamy in the Old Testament. When we have done so we move to the theological-biblical arguments adduced in support of monogamy.

Polygyny in the Old Testament

The major problem with any biblical-theological argument for monogamy is that the Old Testament records, and is largely untroubled by, polygyny practised by some of its most significant men (see careful analysis in Hugenberger 1994:106–122; for a different perspective see Kaiser 1983:182–190). How are we to reconcile this with a theological defence of monogamy?

First, we must be sceptical about the shallow assertion that the Old Testament entirely accepts polygamy as a normal and commonplace practice. This is an oversimplification. There are indications that some Old Testament writers regarded polygamy with disapproval. Perhaps the clearest is also the first, the case of Lamech in Genesis 4:19–24, in which a clear impression is given of an unsavoury character for whom bigamy is of a piece with his other sinful characteristics. So Murray writes, 'The context suggests, to say the least, that the taking of two wives is co-ordinate with the other vices,' and that this passage is 'an indirect indictment of [polygamy's] wrong' (Murray 1957:46). It is possible that the puzzling passage Genesis 6:1–4 is in part a critique of polygamy and/or the use of harems by powerful kings ('sons of the gods') (Kline 1961).[2]

Further, where multiple marriages are described, the picture of family life that results is far from harmonious.[3] Jacob's family is a prime example of this, but we could say the same of Abraham with Hagar and Sarah (Gen. 16), of Elkanah with Hannah and Peninnah (1 Sam. 1), or indeed of David, whose family misery arose significantly from the sons and daughters he had by different women. (Disapproval of Solomon's wives focuses not so much on their multiplicity as on their religious pluralism.)

It is common to read assertions such as, 'In Old Testament Judaism, as everybody knows, polygamy was common' (Stafford 1993:31). This is not so. It is, of course, part of the cultural background for pagan kings, such as in the Babylonian and Persian empires (e.g. Dan. 5:2, 23; Est.), but in his careful study Hugenberger claims that apart from tribal leaders (including the patriarchs) and kings, 'the only clear instance of a non-monogamous marriage for any "commoner" is Elkanah in 1 Samuel 1' (Hugenberger 1994:108).[4] Emmerson agrees

---

2. However, exegesis that understands the 'sons of the gods' as human figures has not commanded wide support (see Westermann 1987, ad loc.).

3. It is impossible to be clear about the exact distinctions between the 'wife', the 'concubine', the 'slave-wife' and the 'captive-wife' (Hugenberger 1994:106–108).

4. Old Testament examples include Abraham (Gen. 16, 25), Esau (Gen. 26:34f.), Jacob (Gen. 29ff.), Gideon (Judg. 8:30f.), Elkanah (1 Sam. 1:2), David (e.g. 2 Sam. 3:2ff.; 5:13; 1 Chr. 3:1–9; 14:3–7), Solomon (1 Kgs. 11:1–3), Rehoboam (2 Chr. 11:18–21), Abijah (2 Chr. 13:21), and Joash (2 Chr. 24:1–3).

that, 'Apart from the patriarchal narratives and the stories of Gideon and Samson, there is little reference to anything other than monogamy. With the exception of royal harems, Samuel's father Elkanah alone in the books of Samuel and Kings is the husband of more than one wife' (Emmerson 1989:383). To have more than one wife was a significant sign of power and wealth that few could achieve. Indeed, a reference to more than one wife may simply be another way of saying that a man was rich and successful: this is almost explicit in 2 Chronicles 13:21 ('But Abijah grew strong. He took fourteen wives, and became the father of twenty-two sons and sixteen daughters').

But what of Old Testament texts that seem to signify neither disapprobation nor even neutrality, but actual approval of polygamy? Hugenberger treats a number of claimed examples of this. It is worth briefly reviewing some of these before endeavouring a conclusion about the overall Old Testament witness.

Jeremiah 3:6–13 and Ezekiel 23 portray Yahweh as a bigamist, married simultaneously to the southern kingdom Judah and the northern kingdom Israel. It would be precarious, however, to press this feature of these metaphorical texts so as to argue that the prophets thought bigamy was godly, not least because in these texts the 'wives' are also sisters, which is explicitly prohibited in Leviticus 18:18. The point of the parables is the culpable unfaithfulness of both Israel and Judah.

In 2 Samuel 12:8 the Lord says to David, 'I gave you . . . your master's [i.e. Saul's] wives into your bosom.' Does this imply that David's polygamy with these women was good? Such a conclusion would misunderstand the attitude to divine agency in the books of Samuel and Kings. In these books there is a very strong doctrine of the sovereignty of the Lord, such that if an event happens we are to understand that ultimately the Lord causes it. (We see this in the famous alternative descriptions of the census, where in 2 Samuel 24:1 the Lord incites David to take it, whereas in 1 Chronicles 21:1 it is Satan. Both perspectives are true, but in the perspective of Samuel-Kings divine agency behind an action does not signify simple moral approval of that action.) So, just a few verses after the verses we are considering, in 2 Samuel 12:11, as part of David's punishment the Lord (again the Agent) will 'take your wives before your eyes, and give them to your neighbour, and he shall lie with your wives . . .' We cannot conclude that Absalom's actions (the fulfilment of this judgment) are morally approved simply because the narrative attributes their happening to God's agency. It would be precarious therefore to take 2 Samuel 12:8 to signify acceptance of polygamy.

Exodus 21:10f. regulates the conditions of a slave-wife, such that if her master takes another wife (simultaneously) he is not to reduce her maintenance. Deuteronomy 21:15–17 rule somewhat similarly for a bigamist whose firstborn is the son of his less-favoured wife, that he must give this firstborn the rights of the firstborn none the less. Both these laws assume that bigamy will take place, but it would be a misunderstanding of Old Testament law to assume that they signify tacit approval, any more than the regulations governing divorce and remarriages in Deuteronomy 24:1–4 signify approbation of divorce. A practice may be regulated to ameliorate its worst effects, without that practice being fundamentally approved. In an important article, Gordon Wenham notes that the world of law is not the same as the ethical world of the writer. While law regulates actions, and law presupposes an ethical framework, we must not confuse the legally enforced minimum of behaviour with the ethical ideals of the writers. If 'the law . . . represents the floor below which human behaviour must not sink', there is also an 'ethical ceiling . . . as high as heaven itself . . .' (Wenham 1997:25f.). These laws certainly show that bigamy was allowed; they do not indicate that it was approved.

It is sometimes assumed that the law of the Levir (Deut. 25:5–10) actually necessitates bigamy, since even if a surviving brother is already married he is required to act as husband to his dead brother's widow. Hugenberger argues persuasively that this law may well have taken as read that it applied only to the oldest *unmarried* brother. Since the law is clearly incomplete, making no provision for a case where there is no brother at all or where the brother is too young, it is reasonable to suppose that it may have other unwritten assumptions. Hugenberger notes that in Genesis 38 (see page 218) the obligation to give a son to Tamar devolves first to Er's younger brother Onan and then to Shelah when he is of age. This would be consistent with a practice whereby the levirate duty devolved on the oldest unmarried brother. Hugenberger also notes that the Targum for Ruth 4:6 has the next of kin excusing himself on the grounds that 'I am already married; I have no right to take an additional wife, lest it lead to strife in my home.' Although he admits this is a later commentary, he suggests it may point to 'what must have been a common understanding in its day, namely that an existing marriage would exempt one from performing the duty of the levirate' (Hugenberger 1994:115).

Lastly, the prohibition of marrying two sisters simultaneously in Leviticus 18:18 is taken to imply that marriage to two women who were not sisters would be acceptable. We may approach this text in two ways. It seems likely (as with Exod. 21:10f. and Deut. 21:15–17) that here again bigyny is allowed but not necessarily approved. The prohibition of Leviticus 18:18 is directed at preventing the more grievously divisive case of marriage to two sisters and so limiting the evils of bigyny.[5]

---

5. Tosato 1984 has argued that this text actually prohibits polygyny. He does this by reading 'sister' to mean 'fellow member of the covenant community' in this verse alone.

While the Christian theologian might like to argue that the Old Testament is clearly hostile to polygamy, it is hard to sustain this with responsible exegesis. For example, when the chronicler records the beginning of the reign of King Joash of Judah (2 Chr. 24:1–3) he comments (v. 2f.), 'Joash did what was right in the eyes of the LORD all the days of the priest Jehoiada. Jehoiada got two wives for him, and he became the father of sons and daughters.' If the chronicler disapproves of the action of Jehoiada in getting two wives for Joash, we can only say he has kept very quiet about his disapproval.

The Old Testament did not forbid polygamy, nor very clearly disapprove (for the most part). It is concerned with the telling of a much bigger story, of which the polygamy of kings is mostly but a minor prop on a grand stage. The Old Testament writers were not primarily concerned to teach us moral lessons about the sex lives of its kings and patriarchs. These men lived in cultures where it was acceptable for the rich and powerful to have more than one wife. Had the narrators turned aside to indicate approval or disapproval of every action described, the story would never have been told.

If the Christian theologian wishes to argue for monogamy, this must be done from wider theological perspectives, to which we now turn.

Possible rationales for monogamy

The argument from Genesis 2:24

The first argument is from the creation Scriptures, which have a theological significance above the historical narratives. Genesis 2:24 is the programmatic text for marriage; it records that a man (one man) leaves his father and mother and cleaves to his wife (one wife). Adam did not have two or more women (bigyny or polygyny), nor did Eve have two or more men (biandry or polyandry). The LXX (as quoted in Matt. 19:5; Mark 10:8; Eph. 5:31) draws attention to monogamy by its insertion of 'these two' (*esontai* hoi duo *eis sarka mian*). Even without this translator's clarification it is very difficult to inject the thought of polygamy into this text. Murray comments that, as for divorce so for polygamy, 'from the beginning it was not so . . . the principle of monogamy is inherent in this verse' (Murray 1957:29f.).

It is likely also that the references to the overseer (*episkopos*) being 'a man of one woman' (*mias gunaikos andra*) in 1 Timothy 3:2 and Titus 1:6, and to the widow as being 'a woman of one man' (*henos andros gunē*) in 1 Timothy 5:9 have this same sense, that moral uprightness in the sexual realm involves the union of *one* man with *one* woman (Mounce 2000, ad loc.).

Arguments from the nature of sexual love

The second kind of argument is not from Scripture or theology, but from 'how things are'. It is suggested that it is in the nature of true sexual love that it both gives and longs to receive totally and with total reciprocation. So Barth, in spite of his suspicion of natural law, argues that because love means choice, the choice of one marriage partner, it excludes by its definition truly loving more than one. 'The man who thinks it is possible and permissible to love many women simultaneously or alternately has not yet begun to love.' Indeed, 'Don Juan is not a hero but a weakling in the sphere of love' (Barth, *CD* III/4:195).

Thielicke develops a comparable, if more pragmatic, approach. He observes that males appear able to separate their sexual (and in particular physiological) nature from their whole self, and therefore to practise polygyny with little difficulty (although with fundamental moral compromise). Women, however, are not in general able to make this separation of sexuality from selfhood. 'Since this separation [*of personhood from physical sex*] is seemingly possible in the man, but obviously [*sic*] impossible in the woman, monogamy is based primarily upon the wholeness of feminine selfhood' (Thielicke 1979:89; cf. 86–98). Only by treating women badly and forcing on them an unnatural separation can men practise polygyny. (Like most scholars Thielicke does not trouble himself with the possibility of polyandry and uses polygamy synonymously with polygyny; polyandry has never been a serious contender in the market of family values, for rather obvious reasons.)

These arguments are not without persuasive value, but they are inadequate, for they rely on pitting one observer's theory of human sexual nature against another's. More seriously, they tend to lean on some intrinsic equation of sexual union with 'full personal union', and it is not clear what 'full personal union' means, let alone whether or why sexual union must necessarily be of this kind (see pages 349–355). Indeed, such an equation runs the risk of loading sexual union with a burden of interpersonal relational expectations it was never meant to bear. Certainly in Barth there is a gargantuan sense of theological weight freighting marriage, and it is no surprise that Barth must allow that only over time can a couple make a judgment as to whether in fact God has joined them together and they really were 'meant for each other and no one else' (Barth, *CD* III/4:196).

The argument from God's covenant with his people

Barth himself, of course, is not so theologically naïve as to base his argument ultimately on observed behaviour. He moves fairly quickly to assert, 'It is God's election and covenant which gives unconditional and compelling character to the requirement of monogamy' (Barth, *CD* III/4:198). This leads us to the third and strongest of the usual arguments for monogamy: that the structure of marriage is to image the exclusive love of the one God for his one chosen people, and therefore must be intrinsically monogamous. We can no more envisage bigyny than that the Lord should choose two separate peoples as exclusively his own; and we can no more countenance polyandry than we can the chosen people giving their loyal love to several gods. Like a golden thread running through the covenants from Abraham onwards is the one God who wants, offers and will himself achieve an exclusive relationship of mutual love and loyalty with his one people. 'You alone of all the peoples of the earth will be my people and I alone, brooking no rivals, will be your God.' This healthy jealousy runs like a castle wall around the structure of monogamy. This argument is undoubtedly the strongest and most deeply theological of the three.

However, since (as we shall see) the Bible sees a strong continuity between redemption and creation, we may press this redemption structure back to see its origin in creation itself.

The argument from the one Creator and his one creation

In order to see how monogamy is predicated on monotheism we must go back to the beginnings of the big story, the metanarrative, of the human race. Genesis 1 and 2 set before us one true Creator God who freely creates one universe (we must allow this expression 'one universe' because the oxymoron 'many universes' is now part of public discourse in connection with discussion of the so-called strong and weak anthropic principles). It is essential in the beginning that there should be one God and one cosmos, for the integrity and order of the cosmos depends upon this unity. Were we to allow more than one god we would introduce a principle (or antiprinciple) of conflicting order into the cosmos, which is exactly what polytheism does. And were we to allow more than one 'cosmos', the different cosmoses being separated by some deep ontological gulf, we would also introduce disorder; for if the supposed cosmoses are ordered to one another (as, for example, the sea and the dry land in Genesis 1) then they are just parts of one ordered cosmos, and if they are not ordered to one another then there is an antiprinciple of disorder introduced.

From the beginning, therefore, there must be one God and one cosmos, the former creating the latter out of free love and choice, the latter obligated towards the former to respond with wholehearted thanks and praise (which is why not giving thanks to him goes to the heart of sin, Rom. 1:21). Just as the fundamental character of the Creator is faithful love, so that he keeps all his promises to his creation, so also the fundamental moral obligation of every human being is to respond to the Creator in undiverted love and loyalty as part of one ordered and fruitful whole.

When sin enters the world and judgment comes, it is characterized by scattering. This is the theme of the judgment on the builders of the tower of Babel (Gen. 11). Repeatedly in Scripture scattering is a mark of judgment, notably in Israel's history with the divided kingdom, picked up again and again in the prophets with the promise of future reunification. Gathering into one people is a mark of salvation. The reason why there must be *one* chosen people worshipping *one* God is ultimately not because of some later structure of redemption but because of the original structure of creation. Redemption, if it is to restore the integrity of creation, must fashion *one* people from whom blessing will spread out into the world (cf. the collective 'seed' of Abraham, which is Christ, Gal. 3:15–22). This one people must be singular, indicating harmony, cosmos and integrity, rather than plural, connoting division, chaos and disintegration.

Conclusion

Barth and others are right to see monogamy imaged in the covenant love of the one God for his one people, but this redemptive structure is itself rooted in the covenant love of the one Creator God for his one undivided cosmos. In its small and often humdrum way the marriage of one man and one woman images this redemptive restoration of creation order. Monogamy is predicated on monotheism.

13. GUARDING THE FAMILY CIRCLE

Marriage is
the voluntary sexual and public social union
of one man and one woman
from different families.
This union is patterned upon the union of God with his people his bride,
the Christ with his church.
Intrinsic to this union is God's calling to lifelong exclusive sexual faithfulness.

We consider now the restriction, 'from different families', the prohibition of incest.

Introduction

'A woman may not marry her daughter's daughter's husband . . .' Many an older Anglican has puzzled during a dull church service over the seemingly arcane prohibitions in Archbishop Parker's 'Table of Kindred and Affinity wherein whosoever are related are forbidden by the Church of England to marry together', but incest features more prominently in the Bible than we might expect. Alongside the 'obvious' sexual sins, repeatedly we find mention of incest. The more a society disintegrates into sexual chaos the more important the incest prohibitions become. This was true in Bible cultures, and it is true today. In this chapter we enquire not so much into the precise extent of the prohibitions, but into the rationale behind them. If we know why incest is prohibited, we will be able to judge whether the biblical limits are absolute or cultural in their extent, and what principles ought to guide us in applying them today.

The Bible teaches that only those in different families may marry. Nearly every society has held to this principle in some way and recoiled in horror from (at least some) incestuous unions. Marriage must be exogamous. Sexual relations must be forbidden within the family circle, except between husband and wife. Baldly to state this begs two questions. How extensive is 'the family circle'? And why is this prohibition necessary? Both the extent and the rationale of the prohibition have been the subject of debate in Christian history (Church of England 1940, 1984; Murray 1957:53, n.8).

The biblical material is of various kinds. Most of the laws are in Leviticus 18, sometimes with sanctions in Leviticus 20 and/or curses in Deuteronomy 27, and echoes in the Prophets. There are accounts in the History books of unions forbidden in Leviticus 18 but sometimes passed over in the narratives. The reason for this would seem to be the same as the reason for polygamy not being condemned, that the narrators have a much bigger story to tell and do not trouble to comment on the morality of each and every action described in its telling. In the New Testament Paul refers to an incestuous relationship in 1 Corinthians 5:1; John the Baptist condemns Herod for having his brother Philip's wife (Matt. 14:3f.). There is also the law of levirate marriage (Deut. 25:5ff.; cf. Matt. 22:24ff. and parallels), which appears to contradict an incest prohibition. Of all these texts the fundamental one is Leviticus 18.

Leviticus 18

Although not all the chapter relates specifically to incest, to understand the incest prohibitions it is important to consider the chapter as a whole. Verses 1–5 set the laws in the ethical framework of law and grace. These laws are to be kept not in order to gain grace but in response to redemption already given (v. 2 reminding of, for example, 11:45). Verse 3 stresses the importance of God's people being distinctive.

Verses 6–23 are sexual laws. The last few are not about incest, although, as we shall see, they give clues as to the context within which the incest laws should be understood. The principle behind the first and major section is given in verse 6: 'None of you shall approach anyone near of kin to uncover nakedness: I am the LORD.' 'Anyone near of kin' translates *šᵉ'ēr bᵉśārô*, literally 'flesh of your flesh', where two virtually synonymous words for relatives are used for emphasis. To 'uncover nakedness' refers literally to the exposure of the sexual organs; here it refers to sexual intercourse.

The verb translated 'to approach' (*qāraḇ*) is used in this context about the intention to have sexual intercourse. It includes the actual uncovering of nakedness (i.e. the intercourse, cf. Deut. 22:14 'when I lay with her'), but it also suggests what modern colloquial English means by 'to make advances' (included perhaps in the sense of Gen. 20:4) and draws our attention to the fact that sexual intimacy is not usually a sudden and spontaneous event; it tends to have a history in the imagination and the desires, at least of one party. This is important in the context of family intimacy which follows.

It is important in this connection to note that these prohibitions apply for all of life. So, for example, if verse 8 were simply prohibiting a man from having his stepmother while his father and stepmother were married this would appear superfluous in view of the prohibition of adultery in verse 20. What is prohibited is the man even considering the faintest possibility or hope that at any stage of his life such and such a relative could ever be a sexual partner. Even the beginning of an imagined 'approach' in the mind is to be ruled out absolutely.

The passions in the human heart can be very strong, and it is not unknown for a man to hope that a certain marriage will break down (or even that a certain man should die) so that he may have that woman for himself. Within the family circle he is to be brought up to understand that there is a lifetime absolute prohibition on this, even should the husband in question die. Unlike the 'neighbour's wife' (who would be available in principle if the 'neighbour' dies), a man's stepmother will never ever be available sexually to him, and therefore he is not even to think about the remotest possibility of this ever happening. In some way it is a stronger prohibition than adultery, because it is a prohibition for all time. It is never right to wish a husband dead (or divorced) in the hopes of getting his wife, but there is a sense in which the close family circle must be absolutely and especially guarded against even the possibility of sexual relationships intruding. Such is the gravity of the protection needed to safeguard nonsexual family security and intimacy.

The laws which follow expand on this principle. Each is given in terms of the restriction of a man's choice, but the principle must surely apply reciprocally. Some of the prohibitions concern relationships of consanguinity (vv. 7, 9, 10, 12, 13); others involve affinity, relationship via a marriage bond – either the man's own marriage, or the marriage of one of his relatives (vv. 8, 11, 14, 15, 16, 17).[1]

The following relationships are forbidden.

---

1. Relatives by affinity are the spouse or former spouse of any of one's relatives and any relative of one's spouse or former spouse' (Church of England 1984: §6).

(i) Mother (v. 7)

The reason why a man may never have sexual intercourse with his mother is both because her 'nakedness' (i.e. her sexuality) is the 'nakedness' of his father (v. 7a) and also because she is his mother (v. 7b). Both because she is his mother and because she is married to his father, she will always be too closely related to him for sex between them to be allowed. Even were his father to die or divorce his mother, she could never be his.

(ii) Stepmother (v. 8)

Incest with a mother is rare. Incest with a stepmother is more common, not least because a stepmother may be close to the age of the father's son. Any society afflicted by sexual chaos will have a proliferation of step-parent relationships; in many homes a son may be attracted to his father's new 'woman'. Perhaps for this reason, most of the biblical material about incest relates to this prohibition. It was a capital offence (Lev. 20:11); it attracts a curse (Deut. 27:20); it was the sin of Reuben (Gen. 35:22; cf. 49:4 and 1 Chr. 5:1), of Absalom (2 Sam. 16:21f.; cf. 15:16; 20:3) and potentially of Adonijah (1 Kgs. 2:22; cf. 1:1–4). It is condemned in Ezekiel 22:10a and (it or something very similar) in Amos 2:7.

In verse 7 a mother was forbidden to a man both because she was his mother and because she was his father's wife. The second of these is sufficient on its own and is the basis of verse 8: by virtue of her sexual relation with the man's father she is and will always be out of bounds for the man. Were sons to make advances to their fathers' wives, the damaging effects on family order would be severe. We do not need to subscribe to some simplistic theory that women were considered as chattels (Countryman 1989: ch. 2) to see how family order would be threatened by such practices. (Besides, an exclusive focus on male authority issues fails to explain the prohibition of v. 13, the mother's sister.)

Paul condemns a relationship of this kind in 1 Corinthians 5:1, where he speaks of a man *having* (present participle) his father's wife/woman. The present tense and the need for such strong rebuke suggests an ongoing public relationship, perhaps a cohabitation.[2] Paul does not explicitly refer to Leviticus 18 in his

---

2. Church of England 1984 tries to argue that since the verb *echein* (to have) need not imply that the man and his stepmother were *married*, the problem was simply that they were living in an illicit (i.e. unmarried) relationship. We cannot therefore argue from this text, the report suggests (§§77–81), that Paul saw any problems with affine *marriage*. But, as the minority report points out (§269), the exegetical key to the text is not the precise connotation of *echein* but the condemnation of the practice as something even pagans will not tolerate, 'a description which can only refer to the affinal relationship of the couple'.

rebuke, but argues that the church ought to have been horrified because this does not occur even among the pagans.

(iii) Half-sister (v. 9; cf. Lev. 20:17; Deut. 27:22; Ezek. 22:11)

This prohibition covers a half-sister on either side and so, *a fortiori*, a full sister. The reference to the place of birth covers both a half-sister born to the man's father in the same (paternal) home and also the half-sister born to his mother in another home while she was (presumably) in a previous marriage. Because either half-sister may now be living in the same home as the man, marriage is not ever to be in view.

Abraham's marriage to Sarah would come under this prohibition (Gen. 20:12), but the morality of it is not commented upon in Genesis. Tamar's desperate suggestion that Amnon might (exceptionally) be allowed to marry her (2 Sam. 13:13) would also have contravened this law.

(iv) Granddaughter (v. 10)

Since the granddaughter through both son and daughter is forbidden, it is very likely that this prohibition covers *a fortiori* that of a father with his own daughter (Levine 1989:120), which is also implicitly forbidden in verse 17. Genesis 19:30–38 (Lot's daughters) strongly suggests disapproval of the practice.

(v) Stepsister (v. 11)

We are not certain what 'begotten by' (*môledet*) means. There are, however, four possibilities.

1. If *môledet* means 'descendant' in the literal sense of natural daughter, then it duplicates half of verse 9 (the half-sister with a common father). This is possible, albeit untidy. But, if so, the phrase 'your father's wife's daughter' would be an unusual way of describing the woman who was also 'your father's daughter'.
2. It is sometimes argued that when verse 9a refers to 'your father's daughter' this means your full sister, whereas verse 9b means the half-sister with a common mother. Verse 11 can then be read of the paternal half-sister without duplicating verse 9. But the symmetry of verse 9 suggests it is about the two kinds of half-sister (as assumed above).
3. It has been suggested that verse 9 speaks of the illegitimate daughter of the man's father, his daughter by a mistress rather than by his wife. Verse 11 then adds to this the case of the legitimate paternal half-sister. This reading is alien to the context of Leviticus 18, which nowhere addresses the distinction between legitimate and illegitimate births. It also leaves the curious lacuna of the illegitimate maternal half-sister.

4. The most likely solution appears to be to take *môledet* here to refer not to natural but to legal parentage. This woman was born to the man's father's wife in a previous marriage, but is now adopted into his father's home and line. She is therefore a stepsister, who 'is both legally and socially one's sister and must be treated as a full or a half sister' (Hartley 1992:295f.). The reason why she is forbidden to the man is that she is now a part of the same family circle as him, as sister, and confusion will be caused if he begins to make sexual advances to her.

(vi) Aunts (vv. 12–14)

The following three laws may be taken together. They begin (v. 12f.) with natural aunts on each side (father's sister or mother's sister), forbidden also in Leviticus 20:19 (but note the marriage of Moses' parents, Exod. 6:20). This is followed (v. 14) by the aunt by marriage on the father's side (cf. Lev. 20:20).

There is, however, no prohibition for the aunt by marriage on the mother's side. This asymmetry is one of the 'ragged edges' which caution us about being too dogmatic concerning the precise delineation of the prohibitions. While we may (as Calvin did, and as we see in Archbishop Parker's table) tidy it up and make it symmetrical by including the maternal aunt by marriage, there may well be some cultural reason for the asymmetry. It may be that, whereas the aunt by marriage on the father's side (v. 14) would have been part of the family circle in 'the father's house', the aunt by marriage on the mother's side would not. We cannot be sure.

(vii) Daughter-in-law (v. 15)

This prohibition is also mentioned in Leviticus 20:12 and Ezekiel 22:11. The paradoxical episode of Judah with Tamar (Gen. 38: 11–30) relates to this law.

(viii) Sister-in-law (v. 16)

The assumption here is that the man's brother has died or that the marriage has ended in divorce; otherwise it would already be covered by the prohibition of adultery, a capital offence, whereas the penalty here (Lev. 20:21) is childlessness. Since it is hard to see how literal childlessness can be a penalty *in law*, Murray suggests that this may be a legal penalty by which any children of the union are rendered illegitimate, 'so that in a civil sense they would be childless' (Murray 1957:250f.).

The law of the brother-in-law or *levir* (Deut. 25:5ff.) appears to contradict this prohibition. The custom whereby a deceased man's brother marries his widow in order to raise up a family for her is known in a variety of forms in different cultures. It is found, for example, in the Hittite Laws and the Middle Assyrian Laws, as well as in some Hindu cultures (Driver 1902:281; Tigay

1996:482f.; de Vaux 1973:37f.). In the Bible the law appears only in
Deuteronomy 25:5–10. It is presupposed as the cultural background in
Genesis 38 (Judah's sons and Tamar), which suggests that Deuteronomy
'does not create a new institution, but merely codifies an old one' (Driver
1902:281). An extension of this custom appears to be in the background of
Ruth 4, since Naomi has no surviving son and Boaz acts not as *levir* but as *gō'ēl*
(kinsman-redeemer).

This law is concerned with the integrity and continuity of the family and
their ancestral land. It is not some quasi-mystical or superstitious concern for
the dead man to 'live on' (Tigay 1996:482), but rather a practical concern with
property and family continuity. The brothers 'reside together' (v. 5) on the
family land. The law prevents this land (or part of it) passing outside the
family to 'a stranger' (v. 5 *'îš zār*). The concern is not so much the family
'name' (mentioned only in v. 6) as the division of the ancestral property.[3] The
significance of the sandal (v. 9) is that ownership of land is symbolically
effected by the owner walking over it (cf. Gen. 13:17). When the brother's
sandal is torn off he loses any rights he would otherwise have had to the land
(cf. Ruth 4:7 for a sandal signifying a transfer of ownership) (Driver 1902:283;
Mayes 1979:329).

This concern with family continuity in the context of working the land ties
this law to God's purpose for marriage in the context of caring for his world.
It also enables a theological link between the levitical prohibition and the deuteronomic law of the brother-in-law. The usual explanation of critical scholarship is simply that the levitical law (part of the so-called Holiness Code) dates
from late in Israel's history and therefore we need not be surprised that its
laws contradict earlier practices or customs.[4]

Traditionally, however, 'The two laws are usually harmonised by the supposition that Leviticus prescribes the general rule, which is superseded in the law
of Deuteronomy by the exceptional circumstances there contemplated'
(Driver 1902:285).[5] This is the understanding of the Talmud (Tigay 1996:232).
If Murray is correct to understand 'childlessness' in Leviticus 20:21 as a legal
penalty (which makes much more sense than literal childlessness, which is not
within the scope of legal punishment), then the correlation between the two

---

3. Mayes 1979:328; Josephus, *Antiquities* 4.254; Driver 1902:282 ('to prevent a family
   inheritance from being broken up, and . . . passing into strange hands').

4. E.g. Mayes 1979:329: 'In the later Holiness Code (Leviticus 18:16; 20:21) such
   marriages are forbidden.'

5. Driver continues, 'As the conditions under which the marriage is permitted are very
   precisely described in Deuteronomy, this explanation may be the correct one.'

laws (or the general law and its exception) may be this: if a man dies leaving a son and heir, his brother is not to 'muscle in' on the family property by marrying his widow. If he does, the children of this new marriage will be legally disinherited so that the dead man's family will not be disadvantaged. However, if a man dies leaving no son,[6] then his brother is to marry his widow and keep the property in the family.

We have noted in our discussion of polygamy (see page 251) the possibility (perhaps suggested in Gen. 38) that it is implicit that the levirate duty devolves on the oldest *unmarried* brother.

(ix) Both a woman and her daughter or granddaughter (v. 17)

This is similar to Leviticus 20:14 and Deuteronomy 27:23, which prohibit a man from having a woman and her mother. Here Leviticus 18 applies this principle to the next two generations. This also (implicitly) forbids a sexual liaison between a man and his daughter, since (by definition) he has had such relations with his daughter's mother.

(x) Two sisters both living (v. 18; cf. Gen. 29:21–30)

The condition that both women are alive at the time of the bigamy means this is not the same as the preceding laws, which apply for all time. We have moved beyond incest for the last few laws.

Tosato argues that 'sisters' should here be taken to mean any Israelite women, in which case this law would be a general prohibition of polygyny (Tosato 1984; cf. Murray 1957:252–255). Since the usual usage in Leviticus 18 is of actual sisters, however, this is unlikely.

(xi) Menstruating woman (v. 19; cf. Lev. 12:7; 15:20; 20:18; Ezek. 18:6; 22:10)

Conservative commentators tend to gloss over this awkward law. It is 'distinctive in that it governs a man's sexual relations with his own wife' (Levine 1989, ad loc.). In Leviticus 12:7 and 15:20 the context is of ritual uncleanness, which would not seem to have enduring moral significance. However (as we shall see when we consider vv. 24–30 below), there are good grounds for taking Leviticus 18 to have enduring relevance. In church history different views have been taken as to the ongoing applicability of this law (Bailey 1959:208f.).

My very tentative suggestion (recognizing that the rationale of this law is

---

6. Or possibly child of either sex. The LXX translated son by *sperma* and Jewish scholars have so interpreted it, in the light of Num. 27:8 which allows daughters to inherit if necessary. The Sadducees appear to have shared this understanding in Matt. 22, where *sperma* is also used.

not now accessible to us) is that it may be included in Leviticus 18 because it adds an important element to the scenario of male sexual greed in Canaan. In Canaanite society, it seems, the men wanted sex a great deal; they wanted it on their terms, with whom they wanted and when they wanted. The incest laws come in the context of other laws, all of which restrict male sexual greed. If the others govern with whom a man may have sex, this addresses the male impatience that says, 'I want it now and I am not prepared to wait.' The casting aside of this law goes naturally with a male attitude to sexual intercourse which pays little regard for the natural desires or rhythms of the woman.

(xii) Adultery (v. 20; cf. Exod. 20:14; Deut. 5:18; Lev. 20:10; Ezek. 18:6, 11, 15; 22:11)
The inclusion of this prohibition in Leviticus 18 reminds us that the fundamental biblical attitude towards sex is positive within marriage, which should be honoured (Heb. 13:4), and negative in all other contexts.

(xiii) Offering children to Molech (v. 21)
Sacrificing children to Molech is forbidden at greater length in Leviticus 20:1–5 and alluded to in Deuteronomy 18:10; 2 Kings 16:3; 23:10; Isaiah 30:33; Ezekiel 23:37–39 and Micah 6:6f.[7]

It is not, on the face of it, a sexual sin. It is possible that the children who were sacrificed were those born of the unions between men and cultic prostitutes at the pagan shrines. If this were so, it would provide a natural reason why the law should be included in this context.

(xiv) Male homosexuality (v. 22; cf. Lev. 20:13)
This is a simple prohibition of male homosexual practice. (There is no evidence from the text that its meaning is restricted to homosexual cult prostitutes.)

(xv) Bestiality (v. 23; cf. Lev. 20:15f.; Deut. 27:21)
This is the only one of these laws which includes a woman in its address.

The word 'perversion' comes from the root 'to mix' – this is 'a forbidden "mixture" of the species' (Levine 1989:123). Mary Douglas emphasizes the relationship between holiness and conformity to 'the categories of creation'. 'Holiness requires that individuals shall conform to the class to which they belong' (Douglas 1966:53). These categories must be kept distinct.

---

7. Levine 1989:258–260 has a useful excursus on 'The Cult of Molech in Biblical Israel';
   cf. Hartley 1992 on Lev. 20:2.

Concluding section: ethics for all humankind (vv. 24–30)

Verses 24–28 are very important. The pre-Israelite inhabitants were 'vomited out' of the land because their sexual behaviour flouted these laws. Their society was full of sexual greed. Although they had no law from Sinai, no special revelation of God, they ought to have known that such unrestrained sexual greed was abhorrent to God and to 'the land' (an eloquent way of referring to the order of creation). And because these behaviours are naturally disgusting, it is not only the Israelite (v. 26) who must avoid them, but also 'the alien who resides among you'. The order of creation teaches us to avoid these practices.

In this regard the sexual ethics of Leviticus 18 are quite different from, say, the food laws of Leviticus 11. The Canaanites were not 'vomited out' of the land because they ate unclean food; they knew no better, and besides, the food laws were given to Israel as a sign of their distinctiveness. The sexual ethics, however, are taken by the New Testament as read, as a natural part of the created order.

The problem of the narrative accounts of incestuous relationships (Abraham, Moses' parents, etc.) is usually resolved in one of two ways. Either commentators use this as evidence for the lateness of the levitical 'holiness code', which is often dated roughly at the time of Ezekiel – those who wrote it had different (priestly) concerns, it is argued, from the historians; or a contrast is drawn between patriarchal religion and Yahwism after Sinai, so that we are to understand that some fundamentally new moral standards were introduced at Sinai. This is problematical in view of the logic of 'vomiting out' in the final section of Leviticus 18, which strongly suggests that the Canaanites, even without any scriptures or special divine revelation, *ought to have known* that these kinds of behaviour were abhorrent.

I would like to suggest another way of understanding Leviticus 18 which does justice to the narrative accounts of 'illicit' relationships, to the place of Leviticus in the Mosaic law, and to the whole of Leviticus 18 (including the non-incest laws). It is this. The uncondemned relationships of Abraham, Moses' parents, etc., suggest that Leviticus 18 is not simply setting before Israel a clear system of law. The miscellany of non-incest laws at the end of the list reinforce for us a horrible portrayal of a *society* in which (mainly male) sexual greed had become endemic. All the behaviours described are symptoms of this. The Canaanites are spewed out of the land because sexual greed became generally accepted; their culture even approved of it. When the historians recorded some marriages which contravened the letter of Leviticus 18, they did not need to register divine disapproval; the individual morality of these patriarchs and others was not material to the narrative in hand. Such an understanding recognizes the pastoral reality that an *individual*, especially in a desperately corrupt society, may take a close relative to wife (because it is an accepted practice) without himself burning with sexual lust in any exceptional way. But when a society as a whole fails to recognize these taboos, it is corrupt and comes under judgment (cf. the logic of Ezek. 33:25).

What is the rationale for the incest prohibitions?

We consider several theories.

View 1. A genetic rationale: the dangers of inbreeding

Were the rationale for these prohibitions genetic, the affinity prohibitions would not be accounted for. Whatever the dangers of inbreeding,[8] this cannot be the rationale for the incest laws.

View 2. Marriage creates a union as lasting as blood ties

We consider next the suggestion that marriage creates a union as strong and deep as ties of blood, that affinity is on a par with kinship. An early example of this view is a letter of Basil to Diodorus in the fourth century, in which Basil seeks to persuade Diodorus that a man should not marry the sister of his deceased wife, because she is a sister to him also, through his marriage to his late wife (Church of England 1940:31f.). Because the man and his wife are one flesh for ever, her sister is his sister. That is to say, the affine bond made by marriage renders her a close relative in perpetuity to her brother-in-law just as strongly as if she were his brother by blood. Marriage bonds are as strong and lasting as blood ties.

This view has been supported by Gordon Wenham: 'Marriage, or more precisely marital intercourse, makes a man and wife as closely and permanently related as parents and children' (Wenham 1979a:31f.; cf. Wenham 1979b:36–40; Heth and Wenham 1984:105f.). Wenham argues that the lifetime prohibition of marriage with affine relatives alongside the similar prohibition for kinship relatives implies that 'marriage thus creates both vertical blood-relationships in the form of children and horizontal "blood"-relationships between the spouses' (Wenham 1979a:39). This alone, he suggests, explains why even after the death of a spouse a man may not marry his deceased wife's

---

8. Church of England 1940:15–17 has a brief discussion of this. The biological evidence needs updating, but would not affect the argument that no purely genetic rationale can explain the prohibitions of Leviticus 18, since it is in general irrelevant to considerations of affinity.

former close relatives, because by virtue of his marriage they become his own close relatives.

Two features of Leviticus 18 cast doubt on this. The first is the lack of symmetry (v. 14, aunt by marriage on father's side only). The second is the difference in the *extent* of forbidden unions through kinship and affinity (extending through two or even three kinship links, vv. 9f., 12f.,[9] but never through more than one married link of affinity); a consistent equation of kinship with affinity would require, for example, the prohibition of a man marrying his (late) wife's stepmother. The Church of England report *Kindred and Affinity* is right to conclude that 'the selection of affinity prohibitions which appears in the Levitical list could not have been made by anyone who supposed that all the relatives of a wife were related to her husband *in the same manner as if* they had been his own relatives by blood, and that whatever is true of his relatives by blood is also true of his relatives by marriage' (Church of England 1940:28, my italics).

We may note also the theological difficulty with the equation of kinship with affinity: that blood unions are a *necessary* part of a person's identity, whereas marital unions are the result of human freedom and choice. For example, a man cannot, being himself, have a different mother or son from those he has; but he can, while remaining himself, choose to have a different wife (O'Donovan 1978:11).

View 3. We must obey Leviticus 18 as it stands

This view says that Leviticus 18 is the law of God for all cultures in all ages and must simply be obeyed as such, without extension, reduction or rationalization. Whether or not there is a rationale is not for us to ask. This view was one significant reaction to the trend in the medieval church to extend the incest prohibitions sometimes absurdly. On the basis of View 2 (above), at one time in the medieval period a man was prohibited from marrying his sixth cousin or his wife's sixth cousin (Brooke 1989:134f.; Church of England 1940: ch. VI; Bailey 1959:142–148). 'The effect was that in many small towns and village almost any marriage that a man could make was liable to be declared null' (Church of England 1940:36).

In the early years of the continental Reformation the Reformers reacted strongly against this, because it enabled easy divorce in practice by couples who were granted annulment as a result of 'tendentious genealogical enquiry' (Brooke 1989:269). The Reformers argued that we must go back to Leviticus 18 as it stands.

---

9. E.g. in v. 12 the kinship links are (1) from the man to his father; (2) from the father to his parents; (3) from his parents to their daughter (the father's sister).

View 4. We must rationalize and systematize Leviticus 18

The problem with View 3 (above) is that there are ragged edges in the list. It will not quite do, argued Calvin, to take Leviticus 18 as extensive and comprehensive. Rather, it is illustrative of the degrees of relationship which involve incest. Calvin was not the first, but was one of the most influential, to argue that there are implicit in Leviticus 18 principles which need to be applied in a more systematic way, using 'argument by analogy' (e.g. for aunts with nephews and uncles with nieces) (Calvin, *Harmony*:102). Calvin's approach has been very influential in the Anglican Communion, being adopted by Archbishop Parker in his Table of Kinship and Affinity which was incorporated in the *Book of Common Prayer* (Church of England 1940:41–45; cf. Murray 1957:49–54 and Appendix B).

View 5. The argument from charity (Augustine)

Augustine made the theological suggestion that the rationale for the incest prohibitions is that exogamous marriage multiplies the number of people to whom a person is closely related; it thus increases the sum and extent of human charity. Exogamy is a socially desirable antidote to introspective clannishness. He argued this in *The City of God* in a passage 'quoted throughout the Middle Ages' (Church of England 1940:46). 'The underlying purpose (sc. of the ban on incest) was that one man should not comprise many relationships in his one self but that these connexions should be severally distributed among individuals and in this way serve *to weld social life more securely* by covering in their multiplicity a multiplicity of people' (Augustine, *City of God*, §15.6). If a man has to marry outside his family circle, then 'the number of people united by close ties' will be increased and the extent of charity and hence concord in the world will also be increased (cf. Bucer, *De Regno Christi*: ch. 17). This theory is attractive but speculative.

View 6 and conclusion. The protection of the family circle

The simplest and most persuasive principle for the prohibition of incest is that the family circle (close kin, Lev. 18:6) must be protected from the destructive effects of sexual possibility. Apart from husband and wife, the family circle needs to be protected against even the suggestion or faint future hope of sex. Once this possibility is admitted to be within the bounds of normality, the most destructive jealousies and hatreds begin to destroy the security of nonsexual family intimacy. The most helpful, exegetically reasonable and pastorally realistic solution is to understand that the purpose of the incest prohibitions is to protect the family circle from the terrible disorders introduced by these sexual possibilities.

This is recognized in the original Israelite context by Carol Meyers, who suggests,

> The relatively large number of prohibited liaisons among consanguinal and affinal kin arises from the necessity to create taboos among the residents of an extended family household . . . Incest taboos, in such a context, serve as coping mechanisms for dealing with the tensions and temptations present when closely related persons live in close quarters. At the same time, they maintain the possibility for endogamy within the larger hamlet or village population, the *mišpāḥâh*.
> (Meyers 1997:18)

The approach that sees family order and properly ordered relationships as the underlying rationale is consistent with the work done by Mary Douglas on the Holiness Code which stresses the love of order and the horror at confusion underlying this (Douglas 1966).

We find an illustration of this in 1 Timothy 5:2. In a context in which church is considered as 'household' (1 Tim. 3:15) or family, Timothy is to treat the younger women 'as sisters – with absolute purity', with the implication that if they are sisters they cannot be potential mistresses or lovers. The harmony of the church family, as with the natural family, must be guarded by the strict exclusion of sexual confusions and ambiguities.

In church history, 'Originally the intention underlying the impediment of affinity seems to have been the avoidance of domestic discord by precluding the possibility of wedlock between persons likely to be members of the same household' (Bailey 1959:144).

The incest prohibitions are a necessary protection of nonsexual intimacy within the family circle from the depradations of sexual greed and the associated jealousies aroused by a multiplicity of sexual possibilities. We must exclude 'disturbing sexual emotions from the home circle' by a strong taboo and cultural revulsion (Church of England 1940: ch. 7). This rationale is sometimes argued along the lines of the need to avoid 'confusion of roles', as Basil also did in his letter to Diodorus (cf. Church of England 1940:37f.).

The report *Kindred and Affinity*, in a still valuable section on what they call the anthropological reasons against incest, puts this rationale clearly. Relationships between parents and children

> are incompatible with the possibility of courtship and mating. They require of the parents guardianship, instruction, and self-forgetful affection, and these things must be given equally to all their children. They require of the children respect and obedience. The brothers and sisters living in the same family must also stand by each other with help and affection in daily and hourly association. It is essential to all these

relationships that they should be maintained with a steadiness on which each member can rely . . . To this unity of the family jealousies and hatreds would be disastrous, and these must arise if any thought of sexual relations within the inner circle of the family could be entertained.

The report continues,

> The same considerations apply in their measure to the prohibitions of sexual relations between less closely related members of the joint family, so long as the joint family is a social unit in which all the members live and work together.
> (Church of England 1940:20f.).

If, as I suggest, this is the rationale underlying Leviticus 18, then the question of counting the precise degree of relationship (whether by Roman or canonical computation)[10] may be to some extent a matter of culture. What matters is whether or not two people share membership of the same family circle (Church of England 1940:33).

The lifetime nature of these prohibitions is very important. The majority authors of the report *No Just Cause* argued against a lifetime ban on sexual union between a stepchild and step-parent. While a stepchild is in the same household as the step-parent, and certainly while the stepchild is a minor, the impediment should remain, but it need not be lifelong, they argued. It is worth quoting the cogent criticism of this in the minority report:

> The case which was most commonly made (in debates in the House of Lords) for retaining the impediment on the marriage of step-parents and step-children was that in this type of family the parent-child role needs to be established and protected. By ruling out the possibility that step-parent and step-child could ever marry, the existing impediment reduces the temptation for them to see each other as likely sexual partners (which implies, of course, the child's seeing his or her natural parent as a sexual rival for the affection of the step-parent).
> (Church of England 1984, §242)

---

10. There have historically been two ways of calculating how closely related two people are. Roman civil law measured relationships by the *sum* of the steps (= *gradus* = degree) from the common ancestor to the two persons concerned (e.g. five to a first cousin once removed). This is still retained by the Orthodox Church. The Western Church later (eighth century) adopted Germanic reckoning, now known as canonical computation, which takes the larger of the two numbers of steps to the common ancestor (e.g. three to a first cousin once removed). See Church of England 1940:33 for explanation.

Churches have differed in their assessment of the implications of nonmarital sexual liaisons on impediments to marriage (discussed briefly in Church of England 1940:72f.). Two principles are involved. On the one hand, to allow a secret or little known, perhaps even casual, liaison to be deemed to create a marriage impediment introduces into marriage the potential for terrible uncertainty. It is surely unacceptable for a man or woman to be faced with the possibility that it will later come to light that, through a secret union of their spouse with one of their relatives perhaps many years before, their marriage may be annulled.[11]

On the other hand, a well known public cohabitation between one party and a close relative of the other would seem to create an impediment. 'It would be repulsive if a man who had been known to have lived with a woman for years could claim to marry her mother or her daughter' (Church of England 1940:73). The Roman Catholic Church calls this 'the impediment of common decency'. The key issue is therefore not the legality of the previous union, and certainly not its ecclesiastical validity; rather, it is whether it was public or secret. So the report *Kindred and Affinity* suggests that an impediment of affinity should not only be created by marriage (church or civil), but also 'by habitual or notorious cohabitation' (Church of England 1940:73). This issue is all the more relevant in our contemporary cultural climate.

We conclude that the condition of marriage being between people from different families is intended to protect the harmony of the family circle from confusions of role and destructive jealousies. There are characteristics (e.g. of responsibility, of discipline or dependence) which rightly pertain, for example, to the relationship of father to daughter, and these characteristics are not the same as those between man and wife. One man ought not to stand towards a woman (or vice versa) in a multiplicity of relationships, because of the confusion this brings. This principle transfers poignantly in contemporary society to the more general taboo of sex between adults and children.

---

11. So, Church of England 1940:73 rightly comments, 'It would, strictly speaking, be necessary before the solemnisation of a Marriage to demand evidence that there is no impediment arising from previous misconduct between one of the parties and a relative of the other – and to make this demand is almost impossible.'

14. GOD'S PATTERN FOR MARRIAGE

Marriage is
the voluntary sexual and public social union
of one man and one woman
from different families.
This union is patterned upon the union of God with his people his
bride, the Christ with his church.
Intrinsic to this union is God's calling to lifelong exclusive sexual faithfulness.

We turn now to the statement, 'This union is patterned upon the union of
God with his people his bride, the Christ with his church.'

> Wilt thou have this man to thy wedded husband, to live together after God's
> ordinance in the holy estate of matrimony? *Wilt thou obey him, and serve him*, love,
> honour and keep him, in sickness and in health; and forsaking all other, keep thee
> only unto him, so long as ye both shall live?
> (*Book of Common Prayer*, Marriage Service, my italics)

For many years almost every bride in England was asked this question and
said, 'I will.' Not any more. There has been a sea change in the relations of
men and women. This chapter is about a husband's headship and a wife's submission. It is long, out of proportion to its importance in our study, only
because its subject matter and the exegesis of the texts are so controversial.

In 1975 Paul Jewett could assume a general familiarity with Ephesians

5:22–33, 'because of its traditional use in the marriage ceremony of the church' (Jewett 1975:58). We could not assume this today. The Joint Liturgical Commission of Great Britain has produced a marriage service 'For Christians from Different Churches' (i.e. denominations). The list of Scripture readings from which couples are to choose omits the only three Bible passages which directly address husbands and wives: Ephesians 5:22–33; Colossians 3:18f. (vv. 12–17 are listed, but the passage stops just short of the verses in which husbands and wives are actually addressed); 1 Peter 3:1–7 (Joint Liturgical Group 1999:20). While we can understand the inappropriateness of the last of these, it is hard to avoid the impression that we are embarrassed by the teaching of these passages about the wife's submission and the husband's headship. If these passages are read in church, there are sniggers (if it is generally assumed that we do not believe they are relevant any more) or a perceptible increase in tension (if it appears that some still do). Commenting on 1 Corinthians 11:2–16, Richard Hays observes, 'The preacher who works from the Revised Common Lectionary will never have to deal with this text' (Hays 1997:191).

When reading these and similar scriptures, there are three (broad-brush) responses. Some conclude that the Christian Bible is irremediably patriarchal and all or much of it must be rejected in our enlightened age; they differ as to whether, having done this, there is anything worth salvaging that may bear the name of Christian theology.[1] Such writers usually have a hidden axiom that 'equality' between men and women must govern all scriptural hermeneutics.[2] Others suggest that male-female asymmetry of these kinds (headship, submission, etc.) is one of the sad dislocations introduced by the fall (alongside, for example, slavery). It was not present before the fall, it will not be present at the end, and in Christ (in whom 'there is no longer male and female', Gal. 3:28) it is being remedied. Where the Bible is patriarchal, this reflects not its enduring theology but a temporary phenomenon that the

---

1. Daphne Hampson (1990) is a prominent example of a feminist writer who concludes that there is not. Others, depending on their wider doctrinal framework, differ in the openness with which they reject the teaching of Scripture. For example, the commentator Andrew Lincoln (1990:392–394) makes it clear both that Ephesians 5 is patriarchal in its teaching and that he rejects it as valid today. He writes of a 'contemporary appropriation of Ephesians', but by 'appropriation' it is hard to avoid the impression that he really means 'evacuation' (cf. the treatment of Best 1998).

2. See the perceptive critique of Thatcher in Barton 2001:23. Barton vividly describes a similar negative approach to the Old Testament (that of Sue Walrond-Skinner) as being 'a kind of contamination theory, according to which the Old Testament . . . is polluted by patriarchalism' (p. 32).

gospel comes to heal. A third group argue that, while much sinful dislocation is evident in male-female relations, none the less these texts witness to
an enduring complementarity in creation order, and this calls for our attentive and thoughtful obedience.

The literature is vast on all the texts and prejudices run deep on all sides,
but some important marriage texts address the issues and no biblical theology
of marriage would be complete without an attempt to grapple with them. (I
have restricted myself to consideration of marriage and by and large omitted
wider considerations of the attitudes of Jesus and Paul to women and Paul's
teachings on leadership in churches.)

If there is any fresh contribution here, it concerns our theme of marriage in
the service of God. The question is not simply how husbands and wives ought
to relate, but how they ought to relate so that in their marriages they serve
God. This outward-looking focus may shed some fresh light on the issues.

Creation and fall

In his detailed study of Paul's teaching about women, Perriman notes that,
while the material is largely practical ('addressing such mundane issues as the
wearing of head-coverings while praying and prophesying'), it is 'drawn
around two important theological focal points: the creation of man and
woman as narrated in the first chapters of the book of Genesis, and the recreation of men and women in Christ' (Perriman 1998:174). This is true of
the non-Pauline texts as well. We begin with creation, in which we note two
anthropological features, the created distinctiveness of male and female, and
their created complementarity. Men and women are different, and they are
asymmetrically different.

a. Created sexual distinction

There is no such thing as an androgyne human being. The idea is literally mon-
strous, neither taught nor hinted at in Scripture (Jewett 1975:24–28; Perriman
1998:176f.). There is only the human male and the human female (Gen. 1:27).
The first question we ask about a baby is, 'Is "it" a boy or a girl?' with some
reluctance to use the neuter pronoun even in that question, for we know he or
she cannot be 'it'. Woman was made from man in the drama of Genesis 2; she
and the man were not together made from an androgyne original.[3] The idea

---

3. Cf. Plato, *Symposium*: 58–65, with its famous idea of men and women being the halves
   (through Zeus's punishment) of original spherical wholes, whether male (leading to

that, before Eve was made, Adam was a sexually undifferentiated human androgyne has no support in the text. Such an idea makes little sense of his unrequited longings *before* his deep sleep (alluded to in Gen. 2:23: 'this *at last* is bone of my bones . . .'). The Adam we meet after the creation of Eve is the same Adam as before. Our embodied nature as male or female is fundamental to our humanity.

In his forthright treatment of this theme Barth insists we must not desire to rise above our gender 'to a third and supposedly higher mode of being, possible to both sexes and indifferent to both' (Barth, *CD* III/4:156). The idea of an asexual being, abstractly human, transcending sexual distinctiveness, may seem attractive, but it has no biblical basis; it puts a wrong division between our embodied existence and some supposed 'spiritual' level of being. Our sexuality is not 'external, incidental and transient . . . but rather an inward, essential and lasting order of being as He and She, valid for all time and also for eternity' (Barth, *CD* III/4:158). Barth is incisively critical of the 'myth of the androgyne' found in Berdyaev's work *The Destiny of Man* and equally critical of Simone de Beauvoir's *The Second Sex*, in which, although there is no androgyne myth, sexuality is imposed on men and women by their culture (as in the famous quotation, 'One is not born a woman, one becomes one') and must be resisted or reshaped as part of the struggle for true humanness (Barth, *CD* III/4:159–162).

At the heart of the debates is the distinction between sex and gender (or sexuality). It is said that, whereas sex is anatomical and physiological, gender is a cultural construct. Gender or sexuality is 'our self-understanding and way of being in the world as male and female' (Nelson 1979:17f.). We cannot do much about sex, but we can recreate gender by changing the way we understand it. At the simplest level this is uncontroversial: male and female dress codes vary from culture to culture and through history; there is wide variety in how masculinity and femininity are perceived and expressed. The crucial question is whether the order of creation extends to gender distinctions at all, or whether these distinctions are entirely under our authority as autonomous and creative human cultural agents. Elaine Storkey expresses the centrality of this question in her book title *Men and Women: Created or Constructed?* (Storkey 2000).

We must insist that, because we are embodied persons (not spirits imprisoned in bodies), our gender perceptions ought to be grounded in our bodily

---

homosexual halves), female (leading to lesbian halves) or hermaphrodite (leading to heterosexual halves). Philo of Alexandria was strongly influenced by this Greek mythical androgyne concept; he regarded 'Man' as originally created to be the 'Idea' of Man, incorporeal, immortal, neither male nor female (Jewett 1975:24).

existence. We cannot allow some dualistic caesura between our anatomy and our whole personhood (Meilander 1995:71f.). 'A person . . . cannot be split into a sexual corpse and a sexless psyche' (Neuer 1990:26). Such a view has been called a 'Kantian feminism', in which the genus 'person' is as independent of sex as it is of race or class. Such ideas of ungendered personhood are a moral blind alley (Scruton 1986: ch. 9). 'Man and woman are not an A and a second A whose being and relationship can be described like the two halves of an hour glass, which are obviously two, but absolutely equal and therefore interchangeable' (Barth, *CD* III/4:169).

It is an irony that when holistic approaches to the human person are widely advocated (e.g. in medicine), they are denied by the reductionist approach to gender which regards men and women as identical apart from the accident of a few anatomical differences. Rather, our anatomical differences point to whole-person differences which we neglect to our cost.

We need to beware, however, of overconfident attempts to delineate exactly what these differences are. The popularity of John Gray's *Men are from Mars, Women are from Venus* (a best-seller in more than 38 languages, we are told) suggests the stereotypes are widely recognizable (Gray 1993), but the Bible does not encourage dogmatism in this area. The delineation of the differences is as hard as saying where a cloud begins and ends. When Emil Brunner and others attempted such a 'phenomenology or typology of the sexes', Barth pointed out scathingly that 'probably every third man and certainly every second woman' objects that he or she does not fit into the typology. And, devastatingly, he asks, 'On what authority are we told that these traits are masculine and these feminine?' (Barth, *CD* III/4:151–153). The 'authority' is the shifting one of anthropological study; Christians beware!

For all that the differences puzzle us greatly, we ought to expect the whole of our embodied existence to be touched and shaped by our sex. We must be sceptical of philosophies that minimize sexual distinction and seek to merge humankind into one androgyne mass.

b. Created complementarity

Genesis 2:24 suggests that we ought primarily to read Genesis 2 as about marriage and only secondarily about the wider relations of men and women. In it we find that the woman was given to the man to be 'a helper as his partner' ('*ēzer kᵉnegdô*, Gen. 2:18). She was not God's provision for his loneliness, but rather the only suitable partner to work with him in the task of tilling and keeping the garden (v. 15). But what kind of helper? And what kind of partnership? These are the questions of this chapter.

Several features in Genesis 1 and 2 suggest male prominence or precedence (Perriman 1998:177f.). The first, in 1:26f., is masked by the NRSV translation:

> Then God said, 'Let us make humankind ['*āḏām*, 'man'] in our image, according to our likeness; and let them have dominion over the fish of the sea . . . So God created humankind [*hā'āḏām*, 'the man'] in his image, in the image of God he created them; male and female he created them.

The text moves between 'man' (singular, masculine, generic) and 'them' (plural, male and female). We cannot avoid the fact that the Hebrew text, when referring generically to humankind, uses the word '*āḏām*, which is also used of the man (as distinct from the woman) later in the narrative (e.g. 2:8). The human race takes its title from the man and not from the woman. The man is created first in Genesis 2 (which Paul understands as significant in his allusions to it in 1 Cor. 11:7f. and 1 Tim. 2:13). He is given his task in the garden before the woman is created (Gen. 2:15). God speaks to the man the words of permission and command before the woman has been made (2:16f.). The woman is created out of the man. In the poetic exclamation of delight in 2:23 the man gives to the woman her name, 'Woman' (a 'naming' paralleled in some way after the fall in 3:20).[4]

Both male and female are made in the image of God (Gen. 1:26f.). In this image the woman is given a great dignity. She alone is qualified to be the man's helper in the great task entrusted to them. The word 'helper' ('*ēzer*, LXX *boēthos*) has no necessary connotations of inferiority.[5] It focuses not on the status of the helper (who may be greater, lesser or equal), but on the need of the one to be helped. There is no suggestion that the man is to exercise dominion over the woman; rather, together they are to exercise dominion over the created order (Gen. 1:26–28). Indeed, the drama of Genesis 2:18–23 emphasizes the woman's unique superiority to the animals. Yet the texts also draw attention to the precedence of the man. A faithful treatment of the texts must wrestle with both the dignity of the woman and the priority accorded to the man.

The emphasis on the man continues in Genesis 3. After the disobedience God calls 'to the man' (*āḏām*), 'Where are you?' and the man answers (v. 9f.).

The disobedience narrated in Genesis 3 affects the whole human condition. Genesis 3:16 speaks specifically to the fallen condition of the woman.

---

4. Perriman 1998:180 is correct to note that the namings here, both of the animals and of the woman, are acts of recognition rather than necessarily acts of rule. Nevertheless (as he agrees), they do reinforce the impression of male precedence.

5. E.g. The word '*ēzer* is used of the Lord as the helper of his people (e.g. Ps. 70:5; Exod. 18:4, the name Eliezer); cf. Perriman 1998:179, n.9.

To the woman he said,
'I will greatly increase your pangs in childbearing;
in pain you shall bring forth children,
yet your desire shall be for your husband,
and he shall rule [*māšal*] over you.'

There are three ways of understanding the words 'he shall rule over you'.

1. It is the origin of patriarchy. Patriarchy stems from the dislocation in male-
    female relations which is God's punishment; before the fall there was no
    male precedence of any kind. We must reject this reading, for it rides
    roughshod over all the indicators of male prominence in Genesis 1 and 2
    (noted above).
2. It records a sad transformation of male primacy from a blessing to an
    abuse. The good order of male leadership before the fall changes into male
    oppression and female subjugation. The woman 'had, indeed, previously
    been subject to her husband, but that was a liberal and gentle subjection;
    now she is cast into servitude' (Calvin, quoted in Neuer 1990:79). 'The sub-
    ordination of the woman to the man was intended from the beginning; but
    now that the harmony of their mutual wills in God is destroyed, this subor-
    dination becomes subjection'. 'From being his wife's leader (Genesis ii.18),
    the man had become her tyrant (Genesis iii.16)' (Schillebeeckx 1965:25).
    This interpretation is consistent with biblical theology. While partnership
    as the man's helper in doing *the task given by the Lord* is a joyful calling, sub-
    jection as the man's slave in doing *tasks given by the man* will be (and has often
    been) a sorry plight.
3. It is a simple reaffirmation of the good created order, the neglect of which
    had contributed to the fall (Neuer 1990:79–81, citing Aquinas and Luther in
    support). There is nothing necessarily negative about the verb 'to rule'
    (*māšal*), which is used elsewhere of God's good rule (e.g. Is. 40:10). To be
    ruled may be a good or a bad thing depending on the ruler. The fact that the
    verse begins with the pain of childbirth does not mean the whole verse is
    necessarily negative; her desire for her husband is not obviously a punish-
    ment.[6] And if male oppression were a punishment for Eve's sin, it might
    appear that Adam is being rewarded when he too deserves punishment
    (Perriman 1998:183f.).

---

6. It has even been suggested (from the similarity with 4:7) that the woman's 'desire' for
    her husband is in fact a craving for independence and a desire to dominate her
    husband. See Wenham 1987:81 and the reference to article by Foh there.

Thus 'he shall rule over you', far from being a regrettable consequence of the fall, may be a reaffirmation of the good created order which, had it been followed, might have prevented the fall. The woman has come out from under the protective and spiritually beneficial 'rule' of her husband, with disastrous consequences. Now she must return to her proper place in God's order.

The narrative of Genesis 2:4b–3:24 sets before us the following order. 'Yahweh God is supreme; the man is the highest of the creatures, with the woman closely associated but subordinate to him; least of all are the animals' (Walsh 1977:161–177). The serpent subverts this order, placing himself at the top, and the woman above the man (by speaking with the woman and then arranging for her to 'lead' the man), with God forgotten. We may understand 'he shall rule over you' (3:16) in the sense not of punishment but as the reconstituting of the original good order. This may be supported by the reference to the man having obeyed his wife's leading in verse 17 (where the idiom 'listen to the voice of' means to 'obey', Wenham 1987:82). He allowed her to lead him into sin, when he should have been leading her in righteousness. It is because of male precedence that the responsibility for the fall is laid at his feet rather than hers.

Perhaps it does not much matter whether we understand 'he shall rule over you' in sense 2 or 3. Either way, we must understand from Genesis 1 – 3 that some kind of order of male primacy is a part of the good created order, however distorted it has subsequently become. What is probably of greater significance for our study is that in Genesis 3:9–19 all the dimensions of the purpose of marriage have come under judgment. The relation of Adam and Eve is spoilt by mutual recrimination and blame, childbearing becomes painful, and the care of the earth becomes a matter of toil and frustration. When the man and woman break out from serving God in his garden together, the deleterious effect on their marriage is total in its scope.

Other Old Testament issues

The relationship between men and women in the remainder of the Old Testament is a vast topic and a proper treatment would take us well beyond the scope of this study. It would need to encompass customs and laws, prophetic perspectives and wisdom insights. Any responsible treatment will, however, take into account the complexity of the issues and will not be content to repeat parrot fashion the simplistic claims that wives were regarded as their husbands' 'property', or that there was a simple and inequitable double standard in laws regarding adultery (Wright 1990:90–92 and ch. 6; Hugenberger 1994:243–247, 313–337; Emmerson 1989:382–385). The Old Testament is set against a background of cultures that were firmly patriarchal, but for much of the time it simply records the marriage customs in passing comment on their morality. The writers are concerned with a much larger story of salvation which will in time sit in judgment on all these cultures, as it does on ours.

New Testament texts

The question for the New Testament texts is how they read creation in the light of redemption. The age to come has broken into this age. Churches are to form countercultural communities in which the life of the age to come is lived out. They are to live in this world, but with the values of the age to come. This produces tension and leads to suffering. The New Testament teachings on the complementary relations of men and women must be read in this context.

For reasons of space, we focus as much as possible on texts that address marriage rather than wider issues of male-female relations (e.g. in church leadership). For this reason, 1 Timothy 2:8–15 and Titus 2:3–5 are not given separate treatment.

Galatians 3:28 – male and female in Christ: a programmatic text for social reform?

'There is no longer male and female; for all of you are one in Christ Jesus.' What is new about the new creation in Christ for relations between men and women? In every debate the presence of Galatians 3:28 is felt. Whether or not it was seminal in Paul's thought, it has been seminal in feminist writing of all hues. It has been asked to bear much weight, and we are faced with 'a bewildering array of possibilities for interpretation . . . both in technical and in non-technical studies'. It 'has become a hermeneutical skeleton key by which we may go through any door we choose' (Snodgrass 1986:161). The history of its exegesis 'illustrates the fact that all too often meaning is in the eye of the beholder and that without proper care and attention to its context, text becomes pretext' (Witherington 1980:593).

Richard Longenecker argues that there is a qualitative distinction between creation, in which 'hierarchical order, subordination and submission are generally stressed', and redemption, 'wherein freedom, mutuality and equality take prominence' (Longenecker 1986:82; cf. Longenecker 1984 in which programmatic importance is given to Galatians 3:28). If Longenecker is right, then we need to be very cautious about extrapolating created complementarity into the contemporary world.

With Longenecker, many regard this text as programmatic, perhaps echoing a formula used in baptism (Fiorenza 1983:208f.; Witherington 1980:596f.; Fung

1988:175; against Perriman 1998:189f.) and relating to a wider programme of social egalitarianism within the churches. It is 'the Magna Carta of Humanity' (Jewett 1975:143), the 'Emancipation Proclamation for Women' (Stendahl 1966, in Witherington 1980:593–604). Here is Paul the liberator showing his most penetrating insight into the social and ecclesial implications of the gospel of Christ.

If this is so, the texts where the New Testament (and especially Paul) teach women's subordination have either been misunderstood (so that they do not really teach this) or are not truly apostolic (being deutero-pauline, as is usually claimed for the pastorals, often for Ephesians and sometimes for Colossians, or a later interpolation, as some suggest for 1 Cor. 14:34f.), or perhaps represent a temporary phase in Paul's developing thought (Snodgrass 1986:165f.).[7]

Alternatively, these hierarchical texts are the temporary accommodation of the apostles to make their churches respectable in the culture of the day: 'That Paul did not spell out the implications for slaves and women more than he did is not too surprising if one allows for his concern for missions. Other factors, no doubt, were the fear of social upheaval and the fear that the Christian movement would be seen as a political force and, as a result, would be stamped out' (Snodgrass 1986:179). To preach 'wholesale emancipation from societal constraints' would have been 'illusionary enthusiasm that hinders the advancement of the gospel and threatens the unity of the church' (Fiorenza 1983:207).

Always in this line of interpretation, however, the fundamental gospel principle is represented by Galatians 3:28. It is like an arrow whose trajectory we must now follow to its logical (invariably egalitarian) conclusion.

For all the popularity of this interpretation, it suffers from a massive exegetical difficulty.[8] It is far from obvious that any of this was in Paul's mind. Far from being the *locus classicus* in which we find the heart of the apostolic teaching about men and women, 'Galatians 3:28 contains an incidental reference to men and women as part of a treatment of a subject other than men's and women's roles, and the single phrase (sc. "not male and female") is not explained at all' (Clark 1980:138).

What Paul says about men and women is an illustration of his main thesis in Galatians, which is that *all* people who have faith in Christ are fully incorporated into Christ and saved by him. Just as Jew and Greek are saved this way,

---

7. The problems with theories of development in Paul's thought are legion, as evidenced by the lack of consensus accompanying any theory.

8. Perriman 1998:184–195 offers a convincing and thorough rebuttal of exaggerated egalitarian arguments for the significance of Galatians 3:28 (from an author who himself argues wherever he responsibly can for the egalitarian case).

so are slave and free, male and female. This is a deep and marvellous truth, but it is not the radically egalitarian truth many commentators wish it to be (cf. the detailed study of Hove 1999).

There are four occasions in Paul's letters where he sets alongside one another two or more of the contrasts between men and women, Jew and Gentile/Greek, slave and free (cf. Rom. 10:12f., which mentions just Jew and Greek). These are Galatians 3:28; 1 Corinthians 7:17–24; 1 Corinthians 12:13 and Colossians 3:11 (in the last two the male-female contrast is not mentioned).[9] In these texts Paul teaches first that none of these human distinctions have any religious significance; they do not affect full membership of the family of God in Christ. Second, as a consequence of this, they ought not to cause divisions within the body of Christ. Paul's thought has a religious basis (our common membership in Christ) and a social and ecclesial consequence (the obligation to live in harmony with one another).

Thus in 1 Corinthians 7 contentment in our 'called' state (whether married or unmarried, slave or free, circumcised or uncircumcised) is possible because these distinctions have no significance so far as our status or relationship to God are concerned. Where there are legitimate possibilities of change (slave to free, unmarried to married), this is a matter of Christian freedom.

In Colossians 3:11 the social sins (such as slander, abusive language and lying, v. 8f.) so often exacerbated by social distinctions (v. 11) are not to be allowed to divide those who are in Christ, because we are together forgiven (v. 13), with Christ ruling in love in our hearts by his word (vv. 14–16). (Incidentally, since Paul goes straight on in v. 18f. to tell wives to be subject to their husbands, presumably he does not regard this ordering within marriage as being inconsistent with the unity in Christ he has just extolled.)

The statement in 1 Corinthians 12:13 is similar to Colossians 3:11; it too is written to promote unity within the body of Christ. The basis of that unity, explicit in 1 Corinthians 12, is our common baptism in the one Spirit. This is an important link with Galatians 3:28. In Galatians the major thrust of Paul's argument is that taking upon oneself the law of Moses is unnecessary for justification before God, because justification is fully entered by faith in Christ. This includes the gift of the Spirit in all his fullness (3:1–5). Those who by faith in Christ are Abraham's seed (corporately in Christ) inherit the promise to Abraham and become children of God.

Galatians 3:26–29 is an emphatic statement of Paul's conclusion. The translation below is as literal as possible.

---

9. Perriman 1998:193 plausibly suggests that in Corinth and Colossae gender was not proving a divisive force and so Paul has no need to mention it in these contexts.

For *all* [10] (of) you are sons[11] of God through faith in Christ Jesus.
For *as many as* were baptized into Christ have put on Christ.

There is neither	Jew nor Greek,
There is neither	slave nor free,
There is not	'male and female' [*arsen kai thēlu*].

But if you are of Christ, then you are Abraham's seed, heirs according to promise.

The main emphasis is on Jew and Greek. This previously significant distinction matters no longer for salvation. The most natural understanding of the second and third pairs is that they emphasize the same point; neither social status nor gender affect salvation in Christ. Salvation is the focus throughout. Paul returns to this theme of seed, inheritance and promise in verse 29. There is room for debate as to quite how his Jewish-Christian or Judaizing opponents would have described the underprivileged status either of slaves or of women in terms of salvation. The negative view of women is usually illustrated from the daily benediction recited by a Jewish man, thanking God that he has not made him 'a heathen, a woman, or a brutish man'. In a Gentile context similar views are attributed to Thales, who remarked that he had three reasons for gratitude, 'that I was born a human being, not a beast; a man and not a woman; thirdly, a Greek and not a barbarian'.[12]

The institution of male circumcision implicitly gave men a more complete entry into the people of God (an entry not dependent on relationship to a woman in the way that a woman's entry was usually perceived as dependent on relationship to a circumcised man, whether her father, husband or son). Baptism (of men and women equally) represents an important change in this respect (Clark 1980:141).[13] Also, if the Judaizers in Galatia were arguing for full Jewish cultic observance, the laws concerning women's ritual impurity at

---

10. Both 'all' (*pantes*) and 'as many as' (*hosoi*) are given emphasis by being placed first in their respective sentences.

11. Although the NRSV 'children' is not a literal translation of *huioi* here, in view of Paul's argument in v. 28 such an inclusive sense is clearly in Paul's mind. However, such an inclusive translation loses the surprise of the original, that 'sons' should so *emphatically* include believers of both sexes.

12. b.Mehahoth 43b; Diogenes Laertius I.33, both quoted in Witherington 1980:594. On p. 593 Witherington also gives (minority) rabbinic evidence for the view that women were equal with men in the sight of God. See also Fiorenza 1983:217; Clark 1980:145–147; Longenecker 1990:157.

13. Although, as Witherington 1988:77 points out, we should not make too much of this given the evidence of proselyte baptism into Judaism in New Testament times.

times of menstruation and after childbirth might have made it harder for
them to feel they had equal access to God (Witherington 1980:595). Whatever
the precise background of thought, it seems clear that at least in contemporary Judaism, 'Only the free male Israelite was a "first-class citizen", a fully
responsible member of the worshipping community' (Clark 1980:147–149).
Before the destruction of the temple the second-class religious status of the
women was vividly experienced every time their access in the temple stopped
at the Court of Women.

Although it is not possible to argue that women or slaves would have been
excluded from the people of God, none the less they had a lower status. Paul's
emphasis here seems to be on the *full* acceptance of all these people into the
people of God and their *full* endowment with the Spirit of God as the down
payment guaranteeing their inheritance. This was in contrast to both Jewish
and Graeco-Roman backgrounds (Perriman 1998:187f.; cf. Snodgrass
1986:168–170). It has been suggested that Paul may have had Joel 2:28f. in his
mind at this point, with its vision of the democratization of the Spirit within
the people of God so that both sons and daughters, and indeed male and
female *slaves*, are the recipients of his ministry and gifts (Snodgrass 1986:175;
Allen 1976:99, n.18; cf. Perriman 1998:192f.).[14] This is likely; Paul returns to
the gift of the Spirit in Galatians 4:6.

But what does Paul mean by his enigmatic change of structure so as to use
the phrase 'male *and* female' rather than continuing with the 'neither . . . nor
. . .' pattern he has used of Jew or Greek, slave or free? It seems likely that this
is an allusion to the LXX of Genesis 1:27, which suggests that the *created* nature
of human beings as male and female is in his mind (Witherington 1980:597;
Fung 1988:175; Longenecker 1984:75, n.6).

It is unconvincing to argue that Paul envisages that in Christ there is the
'eschatological restoration of man's original divine, androgynous image', as
later Gnostics understood this verse (Meeks 1974:197). The whole idea of
androgyny is alien to Paul's (and all biblical) thought; for he never sets
redemption against creation (Snodgrass 1986:177).

Nor is it persuasive to say that Paul regarded the distinction between men
and women as being 'abolished' in some way in Christ, any more than the distinctions between Jew and Gentile and between slave and free were abolished.
Many Jewish Christians may well have continued to circumcise their sons and

---

14. Perriman 1998:192f. also points to Paul's adaptation in 2 Cor. 6:16–18 of the promise
    to David, 'I will be to him a father, and he will be to me a son' (2 Sam. 7:14). This
    becomes, 'I will be to you a father, and you will be to me sons *and daughters*.' As
    Perriman points out, this adaptation is in line with Is. 43:6.

to keep the food laws and Sabbaths. It is unlikely Paul would have been troubled by this; indeed, he himself seems to have observed the law at least some of the time (e.g. Acts 24:18). He continued to regard himself as a Jew, albeit a fulfilled one, rather than a Gentile (Jewett 1975:143). Slaves continued to be slaves, for the most part (cf. 1 Cor. 7:21–24). Clearly, males continued to be males and females to be females. Paul knew that.

In a well argued article, Witherington (1980) notes that the terms 'male' and 'female' (as opposed to 'man' and 'woman'), together with the likely allusion to Genesis 1:27, direct our attention specifically to marriage and procreation ('be fruitful and multiply'). He then suggests that the reason Paul uses 'male *and* female' is because some Judaizers were urging that the best way for women to become full members of the covenant community was to marry a circumcised believer and have children by him. Paul insists that in Christ there is no necessity for the believer to marry and have children (rather as in parts of 1 Cor. 7). A male on his own or a female on her own (not necessarily 'male *and* female' together in marriage) can be full members of the covenant community. This is an intriguing possibility, but must remain speculative.

Paul saw no incongruity in passionately asserting that in Christ there is no male and female while at the same time insisting on the proper order of headship and submission in marriage (see Eph. 5:21–22ff. and Col. 3:18f.). When arguing about these and other sexual distinctiveness issues, he repeatedly looks back to Genesis 1 and 2 (Witherington 1980:598). Those who see radical egalitarianism in Galatians 3:28 are forced to argue that these and other inegalitarian texts in Paul are either non-Pauline or reflect some kind of retreat of Paul from his egalitarian vision. It is better to hold the two together and to recognize that the wonderful salvation truth of the full possession of the Spirit by all believers is entirely consistent with the assertion of some kinds of created orderings, including between husband and wife in marriage.

It may even be that, in using the phrase 'male *and* female', Paul is consciously alluding to the fact that *this* division (unlike Jew-Greek and slave-free) goes right back to creation. It owes its existence neither to human sin (as does slavery) nor to the covenant of God with Abraham (as do Jew and Gentile), but to creation itself. Paul's use of it here may be climactic and emphatic: 'If *even* these good created distinctions are no longer of religious significance in Christ, *how much more* ought you not to give religious significance to that between Jew and Gentile.'

Having established that Galatians 3:28 is about salvation (rather than an egalitarian social programme), it would be a mistake to conclude that it had no social implications for the ways in which men and women actually relate to one another (Snodgrass 1986:163f.; Clark 1980:151–155). Every salvation truth has social implications. The Jew-Gentile issue certainly did, for table fellowship (Jewett 1975:144). But the social implications are not those of simplistic egalitarianism. Perhaps the most illuminating commentary is in 1 Peter 3:7, where (in the context of male headship, Hurley 1981:127) Paul reminds the men that their wives are fellow heirs (*sunklēronomoi*) with them of the grace of life. To be in Christ is to inherit together the promise to Abraham and his seed (the theme of Galatians). The husband is not the mediator of the promise or the Spirit to his wife, nor the wife to her husband. Just as in creation they are to be partners in the service of God, so in salvation that partnership involves each of them and both of them together in full membership of the family of God. If he can pray, so can she; indeed, they are to pray together (perhaps the most natural implication of 1 Pet. 3:7). These truths challenge both the male chauvinist who despises his wife and the independent feminist who considers she can get along very well without her husband.

Paradoxically, we may need to apply this in reverse today. Peter needed to stress that the wives were fellow heirs, but in church culture today too often it is the women who press ahead with Christian growth while their husbands lag behind. Perhaps we need now to stress that husbands too are to enjoy full membership of the people of God. A provocative thought.

The equality in salvation taught in Galatians 3:28 is to be held in harmony with the texts that speak of headship and submission, to which we now turn.

1 Corinthians 11:2–16: headship and culture
Because 1 Corinthians 11:3 connects headship with the relationship of God to Christ it is important for our study, but it comes in a bewilderingly difficult passage.[15] It has spawned a vast scholarly and popular literature.[16] And the radically egalitarian assumptions with which our culture approaches this text render it more difficult than it need otherwise be.[17] If we are prepared to allow

---

15. The case for this passage being a non-Pauline interpolation is weak and supported by no textual evidence. See the concise rebuttal in Witherington 1988:78f. and the more detailed arguments of Murphy-O'Connor 1976; cf. Fee 1987:492, n.3.

16. Probably the clearest recent introduction is Fee 1987:491–530, with invaluable footnotes and references to other literature (especially 492, n.7). For a readable and concise complementarian view, see Schreiner 1991. See also the recent egalitarian arguments of Perriman 1998: ch. 4.

17. Fee 1987:493, n.8 notes how harmful it is 'when the prior conclusions both for and against women's equality determine how one is going to understand the text'. He goes on realistically to admit that 'on this issue' he himself 'is also a person of his times, for good or ill'.

ourselves to be taken with the flow of the text even when it challenges our prior assumptions, we may learn important truths from it, even though the detailed background is hidden from us.[18]

It is difficult to discuss the exegetical issues from any readable English version, so I use a very literal translation (similar to Fee 1987 but with fewer interpretative features), laid out to indicate the structure of the argument, with comments interspersed with the text.

Introduction

> [2] I praise you because you remember me in all things;
> even as I passed on [*paradidōmi*] to you,
> (so) you are holding on to the things passed on [*tas paradoseis*].

In verse 1 Paul exhorts the Corinthians to be imitators of him as he is of Christ. Now he praises them for holding to the traditions he has passed on. His praise contrasts with his rebuke in verse 17 at the start of his correction of their behaviour at the Lord's Supper. Since in verses 3–16 he also corrects at least some of them (albeit more gently, Fee 1987:491, 530), it seems that verse 2 is a general positive comment against which all his subsequent criticisms in chapters 11 – 14 are to be set. He encourages them to 'hold on' more consistently.[19]

A theological principle stated

> [3] I want you to know that
> of every man [*pantos andros*] the head is   Christ
> (the) head of woman (is)   the man
> (the) head of Christ (is)   God.

The practical issue becomes clear in verse 4f., but Paul begins with theology. Although Fee plays down the significance of this theological statement, its position at the beginning of the argument suggests it is important.

---

18. Fee 1987:492, n.5 is realistic about our ignorance of early Christian meetings.

19. Hays 1997:182f. suggests that when the women dispensed with their head coverings they thought they *were* following Paul's teachings about male-female equality in Christ. Likewise, Fiorenza 1983:226 suggests Paul is not rebuking them for doing what they knew was wrong, but rather 'introducing regulations and customs which were observed in other Christian communities' (cf. v. 16 and 14:33).

There is an order of headship: God, Christ, man/husband, woman/wife.[20] It is not clear why he does not follow the logical order of 'Christ-God', 'man-Christ', 'woman-man'; it may be that he includes 'the head of Christ is God' at the end because he wishes this intra-trinitarian relationship of headship to act as a theological control over the other two. Headship cannot mean a superiority of being, since Christ is not in his being inferior to the Father (Schreiner 1991:130). The relationship of Christ to the Father must be the final control of all ethics of male headship, for in this relationship there is equality of being combined with voluntary subordination. This would seem to be the unfallen paradigm for the husband-wife relation, which rules out male tyranny, passive female subservience, female rebellion and male abdication.

The meaning of kephalē (head) in 1 Corinthians 11

The crucial hermeneutical issue is usually taken to be the meaning of the word 'head' (*kephalē*). The arguments range to and fro between 'authority' and 'source' (Schreiner 1991:127–130; Grudem 1985; Fee 1987:502f. and n.42; Kroeger 1987; Fitzmyer 1993; Dawes 1998:122–149; Bedale 1954:211–215; Best 1998:189–196). On the former (and traditional)[21] interpretation, 'A is the head of B' indicates that 'A is in some kind of authority over B'; on the latter, it means that 'A is the source or origin of being of B (as in the head of a river)'.

In a recent contribution Perriman argues against both these meanings. On the one hand, he gives cogent evidence that the metaphorical meaning 'source' is rare and unlikely to be Paul's meaning. On the other, he argues that the metaphorical use does not *necessarily* include the exercise of authority; rather, the core idea is that of 'prominence'. More precisely, the primary metaphorical range of meanings of the word may be 'mapped' as follows.

---

20. Hays 1997:185 comments that the context here 'does not give us much help' in ascertaining whether married couples were specifically in Paul's mind. Winter 2001:127 says, 'The very mention of the word "veil" by Paul would automatically indicate to the Corinthians that the females under discussion in this passage were married,' since taking 'the veil of the bride' was an essential part of getting married and 'the social indicator by which the marital status of a woman was made clear to everyone' (our nearest equivalent being a wedding ring). cf. Perriman 1998:89f. Other commentators think that the very general nature of Paul's argument tells against narrowing it to married couples (e.g. Fee 1987:501, n.38).

21. Although Fee 1987 disagrees with it, he notes (502, n.41) that 'all commentaries up to Barrett and Conzelmann' (i.e. 1968/9) take this traditional view, with only the occasional published study reading it otherwise.

(1) the physical top or extremity of an object, such as a mountain or river or pillar (e.g. Judges 9:25, 36; 3 Kingdoms 7:4, 27; 8:8, LXX = 1 Kings 7:16, 41; 8:8); (2) more abstractly, that which is first, extreme, either in temporal or spatial terms; (3) that which is prominent or outstanding; and (4) that which is determinative or representative by virtue of its prominence.

(Perriman 1998:13–33, quoting from p. 32)

Three kinds of argument may be used to assess the theories. First, we may consider the use of the word *kephalē* in extrabiblical Greek literature. This is of more limited use than is sometimes acknowledged, since metaphors change their usage over time and in different cultures and contexts; we would need to be persuaded that a particular usage was influential on Paul. Second, we may study the use of the word in the LXX; this is more significant, since the influence of these Greek translations of the Old Testament on Paul are admitted by all (e.g. he usually quotes the Old Testament from the LXX). There is a *prima facie* case for arguing that the LXX should be the primary lexical matrix within which Paul's usage should be understood. And third, we must give the highest value of all to the indicators from Paul's own usage of the word in his letters.

The extrabiblical uses seem to be inconclusive (and I am not competent to assess them). Perriman has mounted a strong case that the meaning 'source' 'has virtually no support in the Septuagint' (Perriman 1998:25f.; cf. O'Brien 1999:414, n.215; Cotterell and Turner 1989:141–145. O'Brien concludes that 'head' carries the sense of 'master' or 'lord'). Perriman also argues that the metaphorical figure of 'head' 'was not used in the Septuagint to denote a position of authority. The basic sense . . . appears rather to be that which is first, foremost, prominent, pre-eminent' (Perriman 1998:20). His arguments from the LXX for dismissing 'source' and 'head' are different. He dismisses 'source' firmly: 'The "source" interpretation has been seized upon rather uncritically by interpreters anxious to excise from Pauline thought what has been regarded as the cancer of sexual prejudice' (Perriman 1998:32). Indeed, as Hays argues,

Some interpreters have attempted to explain away the hierarchical implications of v. 3 by arguing that *kephalē* means 'source' rather than 'ruler'. This is a possible meaning of the word, and it fits nicely with v. 8 . . . however, in view of the whole shape of the argument, the patriarchal implications of v. 3 are undeniable.

The patriarchal implications of the text 'are imbedded in the structure of Paul's argument' and 'cannot be explained away by some technical move, such as translating *kephalē* as "source", rather than "head"' (Hays 1997:184, 192).

When it comes to 'authority', Perriman's argument is more nuanced. The word *kephalē* in the LXX is sometimes used of those who did exercise authority, but the metaphorical use of the word focuses, he says, primarily on their prominence rather than on their authority. Perriman's point is that 'head' does not *necessarily* carry connotations of authority, but always of prominence. So, for example, Naboth is seated by King Ahab at the 'head' of the assembly (1 Kgs. 21:12; in the Alexandrian codex of 3 Kingdoms 20:12 it reads *en kephalē tou laou*, Perriman 1998:18, n.8) because he will be prominent and visible, not because he has authority. On the other hand, when David (2 Sam. 22:44; cf. Ps. 18:43; 17:43 LXX) speaks of himself as 'head of the nations' (*eis kephalēn ethnōn*), he does mean authority. If Perriman is right, the contexts in Paul's own usage will determine whether or not 'authority' is in view when he uses *kephalē* in 1 Corinthians 11 and Ephesians 5.[22]

Thus, although the meaning 'source' is compatible with what Paul says in 1 Corinthians 11:8f. about the woman being 'out of' the man, and meanings may be constructed for God being the source of Christ (at his human birth or in his eternal origin) and (perhaps) for Christ as the source of man, we will be on surer lexical ground when we assume the word speaks at least of primacy or pre-eminence.

In 1 Corinthians 15:27f. Paul speaks of the voluntary submission of the Son to the Father when he hands over the kingdom. Since in Ephesians 5:22–24 headship is closely linked to submission, it seems likely that when Paul speaks of God as the head of Christ in 1 Corinthians 11:3 he has also in mind this submission of Christ to God. The concept of authority is never far from Paul's mind, but needs careful treatment since 'authority' is itself a word with a considerable semantic range.

Application of the principle

> [4] Every man praying or prophesying having down/against the head shames his head;
> [5] But every woman praying[23] or prophesying uncovered as to the head shames her head.

Paul moves with two closely balanced statements to the issue he wants the Corinthians to address. The context is prayer (speaking to God in public. and prophecy (speaking for God in public, Fee 1987:505), in the context of the

---

22. See the criticism of Perriman's treatment of Eph. 5:23f. in O'Brien 1999:413, n.211.

23. It is clear from v. 13 that this is not a hypothetical example; the women were actually praying, and the natural supposition is that they were also prophesying (whatever that meant).

public meetings of the church (Witherington 1988:80f.).[24] Paul says nothing of her dress at other times.

The balance of the subsequent text suggests his major concern was how the women should behave, with his statements about the men acting as foils to this.[25] Paul's practical goal in this section is to persuade the Corinthian women to wear a head covering[26] while praying and prophesying in the public gatherings of the church.

We are not sure what 'having down/against the head' (*kata kephalēs echōn*) means for the man, but the contrast with the uncovering of the woman's head and the similar usage of the phrase elsewhere[27] suggests the head being covered.[28]

The inappropriate behaviour of verses 4 and 5 (whatever it is) brings shame to his or her 'head'. This may mean it brings shame to the person concerned (as suggested by the parallel in v. 14b – 'dishonour *to him*'; 15a – 'glory *to her*'; cf. Acts 18:6), or that for the man it brings shame on his metaphorical 'head',

---

24. Perriman 1998:85f. suggests Paul speaks only of the times when a woman leads in prayer or prophesies, and that during the remainder of the meeting he is not concerned about her covering. This is possible and supported by v. 13 with its emphasis on her uncovered head *while she prays to God*.

25. Note the extra material relating to women in vv. 5c, 6, 10, 13, 15b. See Fee 1987:495f. It seems unlikely that the men were actually covering their heads or wearing their hair long.

26. We do not know what kind of covering; see discussion on v. 15 (also Fee 1987:496f.; Perriman 1998:86–88). The suggestion that Paul wanted the women to put their hair up in a 'bun' rather than let it hang long and loose is perhaps less likely (*pace* Hays 1997:185f., Fiorenza 1983:227ff.). The verb *katakalyptō* (cover) in v. 6f. refers to an external covering up or hiding (e.g. LXX Is. 6:2; Gen. 38:15) (besides, the men of v. 7 could hardly put their hair up in a bun!); Est. 6:12 (LXX) refers to Haman covering his head in shame, and uses the same phrase *kata kephalē* as in v. 4 here. See also extra-biblical uses quoted in Schreiner 1991:126. It seems unlikely it covered the face.

27. Est. 6:12 (LXX); Plutarch (see Fee 1987:506f. and n.60).

28. Fee 1987:506–508 discusses the options and background. Witherington 1988:81f. gives evidence that it was customary in Jewish and in Graeco-Roman culture for adult women in public, and especially in religious meetings, to wear a head covering. 'This may be contrasted with the evidence that girls, maidens, harlots and immoral wives were expected to be bareheaded in various contexts.' It has also been suggested that the *pneumatikoi* of 12:1ff. had dispensed with this under the influence of the wild ecstatic behaviour in some of the mystery cults (though it is not clear that the women were uncovered in these cults).

i.e. Christ, and for the woman it brings shame on her metaphorical 'head', i.e. the man/her husband (Fee 1987:506), linking with the principle enunciated in verse 3, and with the teaching about the woman being the glory of the man in verse 7. Or it may cover both (Hooker 1963:411; Perriman 1998:86), since presumably bringing shame on Christ/the husband at the same time brings shame on the man/the woman.

Paul does not tell us why such inappropriate head covering or uncovering brings shame,[29] but it is reasonable to assume from verse 3 that in some way it contravenes the divine order of headship.

Analogy to reinforce theme of disgrace

> For it is one and the same thing for her to be a shaved person.
>
> [6] For if a woman is not covered, let her also be shorn (i.e. she might as well be shorn (Witherington 1988:85);
>
> But if it is disgraceful for a woman to be shorn or shaved,[30] let her be covered.

Paul assumes that (for whatever cultural reason)[31] his readers will agree with him that a woman with shaved or shorn head is in disgrace. We need not know the background to this. Here he says that if a woman 'is not covered' she might as well have a shaved head. That is to say, an uncovered head has for him all the negative and shameful connotations of a shaved head. Presumably his readers agree with him about the shame of a woman's shaved head, but have yet to be persuaded of the comparable shame of a woman's head uncovered in prayer or prophecy. So he moves to a substantial theological argument, from creation.

---

29. Perriman 1998:93f. has a number of suggestions but thinks the primary issue was the dangers of the *sexuality* of the women being publicly displayed. Some of Perriman's argument is persuasive, but it is curious (if sexuality is the key) that there is no clear indication that the woman's *face* was covered; indeed, it seems unlikely, since she is praying or prophesying. But surely a woman's face is a primary focus of sexual attractiveness and so 'glory' (in Perriman's sense). See also Winter 2001:121–123 for evidence that to pull the toga over the head was associated with some pagan sacrificial rites. See also pp. 127–130 for cultural background on the shameful nature of a woman having the head uncovered or shaved.

30. The distinction between hair cut short (shorn) and the head being shaved is of no consequence in the argument. See Fee 1987:511, n.82.

31. Witherington 1988:255, n.43 has suggestions for cultural background. Fee 1987:510f. suggests it is simply that a woman with shaved head or shorn hair looks like a man and breaks down gender distinctions. See also Perriman 1998:91.

Supporting arguments from creation: (i) Glory

> [7] For on the one hand [*men*] a man ought not to cover the head
>   being [*huparchōn*] the image and glory of God;
>   but on the other hand [*de*] the woman
>   is the glory of (the) man.

Paul 'raises the theological stakes by introducing a new line of argument based on his reading of the Genesis creation story' (Hays 1997:186). The concept of 'glory' is the key to this verse. The main sense is brightness or splendour (cf. 2 Cor. 4:4, which speaks of 'the glory of Christ who is the image of God'). Probably it is used here in the sense of reflecting honour back on the one who is glorified (hence NRSV 'reflection'). When 'the glory of God' appears it is the outward shining of his being and causes those who see it to bow down. Likewise, the man ought to bring honour to God so that when others see him they give praise to God. In the same way, the woman ought to bring honour to the man (which may suggest that Paul has husbands and wives particularly in mind here). Just as the woman's inappropriate behaviour (v. 5) brings shame on her 'head' (husband), so her right behaviour ought to reflect well on him.

Paul would have agreed that woman as much as man bears the image and likeness of God (Gen. 1:27). His omission of 'image' in the second part of the verse may reflect this (Hooker 1963:411), as also the fact that he does not use 'likeness' but rather 'glory' (a word not present in Gen. 1:27). He is not denying that woman is made in the image of God as much as man. The point he is probably making is that the wife is to reflect honour on her husband by the way she behaves. Some of the Corinthian women were not doing this. His point is similar to the motif in the wisdom literature in which a good or bad wife reflects back on her husband's reputation (e.g. Prov. 12:4; 31:12, 23; cf. Perriman 1998:93 and n.24).

He goes on to explain why her life ought to reflect honour on her husband.

Supporting arguments from creation: (ii) Priority and purpose

> [8] For man is not from woman [*ek gunaikos*], but woman from man [*ex andros*].

As in 1 Timothy 2:13,[32] Paul sees the prior creation of the man and the subsequent creation of the woman in Genesis 2 as having enduring significance for the relations of men and women.[33]

---

32. On 1 Tim. 2:8–15 see the recent and comprehensive treatment by Mounce 2000.

33. This is nothing to do with much later gnostic ideas of emanations from God (*pace* the odd comments of Thielicke 1979:10).

[9] For also man was not made for woman's sake [*dia tēn gunaika*], but woman for man's sake [*dia ton andra*].

Paul follows the narrative flow of Genesis 2. The woman was made from the man because it was not good for the man to be alone. He needed, and God provided, a helper suitable for him, to be a partner in the task of caring for God's world.[34] By being such a glad and willing helper in serving God (not serving her husband), she reflects honour on him. We find this truth hard to accommodate, because we forget that the woman was made not to serve her husband but to help her husband in the service of God.[35] The distinction is vital and Paul returns to it by allusion in verse 11f.

The cooperative nature of shared service is evident in Titus 2:3–5. Here the younger women are to be encouraged (among other things) to be lovers of their husbands (*philandrous*), lovers of their children (*philoteknous*), good managers of their households (*oikourgous agathas*),[36] and at the same time submissive to their husbands (*hupotassomenas tois idiois andrasin*) in order that the word of God may not be discredited (*blasphēmētai*). At one level this may be understood as a concern that the behaviour of these women should be consistent with the highest ethical standards of their culture. But Paul can only commend this because he understands that in these respects his culture is consistent with created order. The culture is right to value relational faithfulness in marriage (lovers of husbands) and the caring nurture of children (lovers of children), and to see the woman running the household as fulfilling an important, responsible and valuable role.

Paul values these women being good managers of their households. Debate about patterns of marriage often includes discussion of the distinction between the so-called 'public' and 'private' spheres. In the traditional pattern, it is said, the husband goes 'out' of the home into the public sphere (the 'city

---

34. Perriman 1998:181 suggests that 'when Paul speaks of the woman as having been created "for the sake of the man", it is likely that he is thinking fundamentally of the creation of the woman as the sexual counterpart to the man.' However, as Perriman himself notes, this presumably would work equally in reverse (in line with the sexual mutuality of 1 Cor. 7:1–6. But it is essential to Paul's argument here in 1 Cor. 11 that it should *not* work in reverse, and therefore the context of task seems more central to Paul's thought than the context of sexuality *per se*.

35. Schreiner 1991:133, 'to help (the man) in the tasks God gave him'.

36. To manage a household was a much bigger thing than 'running the home' in a contemporary Western family. It often involved the oversight of slaves and the management of overlapping family and business finances.

gate' in Old Testament language), while his wife remains 'in' running the household. This seems to be the pattern assumed in Titus 2:5. It has been the dominant pattern in many cultures, including most, if not all, of the cultures in which the Bible literature was written.

Unlike the pattern of headship and submission treated above, however, there does not seem to be any theological reason why this cultural pattern *ought* always to be followed. We need to be careful to distinguish creation principle from cultural patterns in any particular period. We must beware cultural traditionalism as much as the dogmatic radicalism that rides roughshod over biblical exegesis.

Paul's arguments from creation in verses 7–9 are firmly asymmetric. When Fee (1987:517f.) insists on seeing here *only* sexual distinctiveness (the woman must not appear to be the same as the man) and interdependence (the man and the woman need each other), he misses the one-way logic which infuses Paul's argument throughout. Distinctiveness and interdependence would equally be implied if Paul's argument had been reversed, exchanging men and women at every stage. Fee claims that subordinationist readings 'do Paul an injustice' (Fee 1987:524), but readings that fail to give due weight to the asymmetry of his argument are less than fair to the text Paul wrote.

Interim conclusion

[10] For this reason the woman ought to have authority[37] over the head, because of the angels.

There are three uncertainties in this verse. The second and third would presumably have been clear to the Corinthians and perhaps had featured in their previous correspondence with Paul.

First, 'For this reason' (*dia touto*) may refer backwards (Barrett 1968; Witherington 1995; Hooker 1963; Fitzmyer 1957/8; Schreiner 1991), forwards (the usual use in Paul's letters), or both (Fee 1987:518). It is therefore unclear where verse 10 fits in to the flow of the argument.

Secondly, 'To have authority over the head' (*exousian echein epi tēs kephalēs*) most naturally in Greek usage means that the woman herself exercises authority over her own head.[38] This reading has seemed to cut so strangely across the

---

37. RSV 'veil' relies on a minority manuscript reading, *kalumma* for *exousia*.

38. '*Exousia* is found nine times in 1 Corinthians alone and always refers to a power or authority held in one's own hand' (Witherington 1988:79). Ramsay 1907:202ff. described the idea that it referred to someone else having authority over the woman as 'a preposterous idea which a Greek scholar could laugh at anywhere except in the N.T.' cf. Fee 1987:518–521

flow of the argument that most commentators and translations suggest that here *exousia* (authority) is some kind of shorthand for a head *covering* as a cultural symbol of being *under* authority (i.e. of her husband).[39] Such interpretations are last resorts when faced with overwhelming arguments that this is not what the Greek means, attributing to 'authority' 'a passive sense, which is otherwise unknown' (Fitzmyer 1957/8:48–58).

Hooker (1963) focuses on 'glory' and the covering of the face. The context is prayer; the man, being the glory of God, should have his face uncovered, but the woman, being the glory of man, ought to cover her face *in this context*, lest the glory of man obscure the glory of God in prayer. 'Her head must be covered, not because she is in the presence of man, but because she is in the presence of God and his angels – and in their presence the glory of man must be hidden' (Hooker 1963:415). (Hooker suggests that in practice it would be the men who would be distracted in worship by the women's attractive uncovered faces.) One major problem with this proposal is that it is far from clear that the covering Paul speaks of would have covered the *face* at all.

An alternative is that Paul was telling the women they ought to keep their own heads under control, to exercise authority over their heads, perhaps by keeping their hair properly done up or their heads properly covered. Although Hays (1997:187f.) supports this, it seems better to agree with Hooker that it is a 'quaint' and curious idea.

Winter suggests that 'authority' means 'sign of marriage', but it is less clear why the word *exousia* is used here (Winter 2001:131).

Hooker also suggests that the covering functioned as a sign of the new authority *given to women* in the church to play an active part in the public worship of God (Hooker 1963:415f.). This is a variation of the suggestion (Robertson and Plummer 1911:232) that the covering is to preserve the *dignity* of the woman. This suggestion has been presented in a greatly intensified form by Fiorenza, who argues that the whole purpose of the passage is that Paul wants the women to wear bound-up hair 'as the symbol of women's prophetic-charismatic power' (Hays 1997:230).

Schreiner (1991:134–136) argues against Hooker's suggestion on several grounds, perhaps the most significant being that, since *exousia* is so rarely used symbolically (here of a head covering), it is possible that it may take this unusual passive meaning in this case. He also points out that, if verse 10 had been a vigorous affirmation of the woman's new-found freedom in Christ, the qualification Paul enters in verse 11f. would hardly be necessary. This is a

---

39. Hooker 1963:414 objects that on this reading, since the context is prayer and prophecy, the man likewise ought to wear a symbol of being under the authority of Christ.

substantial exegetical point, but nevertheless the linguistic argument from the otherwise universally active sense of *exousia* (as indicating the subject's, i.e. the woman's, exercise of her own authority) cannot be so easily overridden (Perriman 1998:95–97). Hooker's suggestion is possible, but needs to be carefully interpreted (see below) in such a way as to be consistent with the rest of Paul's argument.

Perriman (1998:97–99) suggests that the problem in Corinth was not protofeminist women, but rather feminist men in tension with modest conservative women. The men were encouraging the women to pray and prophesy with head uncovered (as they, the men, did), but the women were reluctant to do so, on grounds of feminine modesty, not wishing to draw attention to their feminine charms in public like this. In verse 10 Paul tells the men that the women have the right (authority) to cover their heads if they so choose, as in fact they were doing. Perriman admits that the picture of the women's behaviour suggested by 1 Corinthians 14:34f. seems to conflict with this. It remains to be seen whether this reconstruction will prove convincing.

Thirdly, 'Because of the angels' (*dia tous angellous*) leaves all commentators puzzled (Fee 1987:521f.). It ought to support 'for this reason' (*dia touto*), connecting with the rest of Paul's argument.

Some have suggested that the angels (like the 'watchers' of Gen. 6:1–4) are evil and lustful and the women have to wear a head covering either so as not to display their charms and risk attracting their unwelcome advances or as a quasi-magical charm to frighten them away (Fitzmyer 1957:54; Perriman 1998:99 and nn.41f. there). This is highly unlikely; nowhere else in the New Testament are angels spoken of as evil and the concept of the women as weak, vulnerable or endangered is utterly foreign to the context of the passage (Hooker 1963:412; Fitzmyer 1957:54).

Winter (2001:133–138) argues that the word *angellos* ought here to be translated 'messenger'. This is the interested or suspicious outsider who comes into the Christian meeting and reports back to others about what went on (cf. Gal. 2:4). Paul's concern is the public reputation of the Christian meetings; they must not be considered disorderly or socially subversive. The women must not look as though they have lax sexual morals. This interpretation is attractive (but see the comments of Fee 1987:521, n.34 and Perriman 1998:99, n.40).

Others have pointed out texts (e.g. 1 Cor. 4:9; cf. 1 Tim. 5:21; Ps. 138:1) that may suggest angels are spectators of this world; in particular perhaps they are guardians of the natural order of creation. 'To some extent authority for the created order has devolved upon them, and we would therefore expect angels to be concerned with seeing that the ordering of things established at the creation is maintained' (Hooker 1963:412; cf. Fitzmyer 1957:55; Perriman 1998:100). Perhaps they are considered to be present in a special way at gatherings for public prayer (Fitzmyer 1957:55–57). This would link with the reasons put forward in verses 7–9, which do relate to creation order.

We do not know the background. Whatever Paul meant, presumably the Corinthians would have understood, since Paul makes no attempt to defend or elaborate.[40]

Very tentatively I suggest that the most plausible reading of verse 10 is that Paul concludes from his preceding argument ('for this reason' looking backwards) and because of the created order (the concern of the angels) that a woman ought (in their culture) to wear a head covering in public worship. She has authority (the right) to pray and prophesy in public, and the head covering is the cultural symbol that in so doing she understands that the created order of headship (v. 3) still stands.[41] By making use of her new right to participate in public worship she is not arrogating to herself an existence independent of man or a wrong headship over man.

Balancing creation principles: interdependence and dependence

[11] Nevertheless, neither (is) woman apart from[42] man, nor (is) man apart from woman in the Lord.

[12] For just as the woman is from the man, so also the man is through the woman [dia + genitive]; and all things are from God.

'Nevertheless' (plēn) signals that Paul wishes to enter a qualification at this point. He is concerned that his arguments so far are open to misinterpretation. He has offered bold asymmetric arguments to persuade the women to dress appropriately, but he understands that these issues are sensitive, all too easily misunderstood by the women and misappropriated by the men. So he teaches two balancing truths, neither of which contradicts or undermines his argument thus far.[43] First, men and women are deeply dependent each on the other

---

40. The phrase 'probably alluded to previous discussions and would have been understandable to the Corinthians' (Witherington 1988:79).

41. In this I am close to Witherington 1988, who writes (p. 89), 'New creation for Paul does not obliterate the original creation order distinctions ... Paul endorses the new freedom of women but still maintains the old creation order distinctions in a transferred and transformed sense.'

42. The suggestion popularized by Fiorenza 1983:229 that chōris here means 'unlike, different from' is unlikely. If Paul is arguing for the insignificance of gender differences he might as well not have embarked on vv. 3–10.

43. He does not contradict what he has just said; else why bother saying it? (pace Fiorenza 1983:230: 'Differences which might exist on the basis of nature and creation are no

(v. 11), not least since even if Eve came from Adam, every subsequent man has been born of woman (v. 12a). Second, both men and women are utterly dependent on God, living 'in the Lord' (v. 11) and owing their existence to God ('from God', v. 12). Paul does not contradict his previous argument and teach that men and women are now radically equal when previously they were not (*pace* Fee); he teaches their mutual interdependence on one another and their common dependence on God.

In this Paul is not teaching that the creation order in relation to men and women has been abrogated in Christ, or that the order of headship was a consequence of the fall (which would contradict v. 3). Rather, he is taking us back to the order of creation before the fall, in which the help of the woman is given to the man in the presence of God in order that together they may serve God.

Argument from cultural appropriateness

> [13] Decide among yourselves these things: is it appropriate [*prepon*] for a woman to be uncovered praying to God?
>> [14] Does not nature [*physis*] itself teach you that
>> on the one hand [*men*] if a man grow his hair long it is dishonour to him,
>>> [15] but on the other hand [*de*] if a woman grow her hair long it is glory to her
>>> because the hair has been given her in the place of [*anti*] a covering.

Before concluding, Paul appeals to them not now on the grounds of creation (vv. 7–12) but on grounds of cultural appropriateness (this is the significance of the words *prepon* and *physis*). By 'nature' Paul cannot here mean anything intrinsic to how men or women are made, since long or short hair results not from birth but from cultural decision (whether or not to have it cut). He uses the concept in a slightly different sense from Romans 1:26f., probably more in line with accepted philosophical discourse in the Stoic tradition; he refers 'to the "natural" feeling that they shared together as part of their contemporary culture' (Fee 1987:526f.; cf. Winter 2001:132 for the association of effeminate

---

longer present in the worship assembly of the Christians'). Fee 1987 seems to regard v. 11f. as having theological priority over vv. 3–10 when he downplays v. 8 and says that v. 12 teaches us that '*in a much more significant way*, "all things," both man and woman, "come from God"' (504, my italics). However, it is clear that in terms of the *action* Paul urges, the most significant teaching is vv. 3–10; the women ought to wear head coverings; v. 11f. is a qualification to prevent misunderstanding of this teaching, but it is not his main point.

looks with homosexuality). 'All first-century cultures possessed means by which the polarity of the sexes was defined with various conventions; hair length was one such feature in Roman Corinth' (Winter 2001:133).

But how does hair length here connect with Paul's concern for head coverings earlier? In verse 15b he says the woman's hair has been 'given her' (presumably as a 'natural', culturally accepted custom) 'in the place of a covering'. The word 'covering' (*peribolaion*) probably signifies some kind of shawl or 'wraparound', rather than a veil (*kalumma*).[44] Although *anti* ('in the place of') often means 'instead of, as a substitute for', here Paul cannot mean that a woman's long hair will serve as an acceptable substitute for a covering, since this would undermine his argument so far.[45] The word may have its alternative sense of equivalence (BAGD:73); that long hair was accepted as appropriate for a woman is a helpful analogical pointer to the fact that (artificial) head covering had the same cultural significance, showing a woman taking her proper place in the social order. In these two respects (long hair and head covering) their culture could be viewed as consistent with the order of creation.

Parting shot

[16] And if anyone thinks to be contentious, we do not have any custom such as this [*toiautēn*, i.e. women covering the head in public meetings] nor (do) the churches of God.

Paul points out to the Corinthian women who wanted to introduce this cultural novelty of uncovered hair in corporate worship that it is indeed a novelty and not one accepted as appropriate either by Paul or by the other churches (whether just Pauline or all, Witherington 1988:84). The behaviour of the women (and perhaps also the men) in Corinth was leading to quarrels which did not build up the church. They should not be rebelling against these appropriate cultural expressions of masculinity and femininity, but rather cooperating with them.

Conclusions

Much in this passage would presumably have been well understood by the Corinthians in the context of their dealings with Paul, but is hidden from us.

---

44. Witherington 1988:83, who points out that the garment Paul is talking about comes down from the head (v. 4 *kata kephalēs exōn*), which would not be appropriate for a facial veil; also that to pray or prophecy while deliberately covering the mouth (i.e. with a facial veil) would appear perverse!

45. Fee 1987:528f. As Witherington 1988:83 points out, 'A woman's hair might be her *doxa*, but it is very unlikely Paul would call it her *exousia*!'

Scholars make suggestions, some enlightening but all provisional. None the less, there are conclusions we may draw even without knowledge of the cultural background.

Fee is perhaps right that Paul's tone is quite mild in this passage, milder than the passage that follows. He appeals to their judgment (v. 13, while clearly hoping their judgment will agree with his). He reasons and seeks to show the rightness of his case and the disgrace of the opposite, but he does not directly rebuke. It may be that Paul recognizes that applying theological principles to culture is not always straightforward. He considers the Corinthian women (for they seem to be the problem) to be wrong, but he majors on reasoning with them. He expects his readers to share with him a common cultural understanding[46] that certain things are shameful and others honourable. They all know (vv. 5c, 6) that a shaved woman is a disgrace; they know from how things are in their culture (v. 14f.) that long hair on a man signifies dishonour and long hair on a woman glory. That we do not 'know' these things simply reflects the fact that in our culture these things do not have the same significance.

What matters is that Paul is prepared to apply the theology of creation to the cultural expression of relations between husbands and wives. The two theological principles we found in creation are reiterated here; they ought to find expression in any culture.

(i) The distinctiveness of the sexes

Men and women are different and their differences go much deeper than physical anatomy. This is clear from Paul's argument (Fee 1987). There are patterns of behaviour and demeanour that are appropriate for men, and other patterns for women. Men ought not to look like women, nor women like men, and each ought gladly to accept the distinctives of masculinity or femininity (Schreiner 1991:130f.). This is an imperative of great relevance in our culture.

(ii) The asymmetrical interdependence of the sexes in the service of God

To say Paul is teaching that men and women are distinct is not enough, however.[47] There is an obstinate asymmetry about Paul's teaching that mirrors

---

46. 'Paul was concerned about head coverings only because of the message they sent to people in that culture' (Schreiner 1991:138).

47. Fee 1987 is right to stress the importance of sexual distinctiveness, but misses the asymmetry of the argument when he refuses to go further. Hays 1997 recognizes that Paul teaches both distinctiveness and an order of hierarchy, even though he refuses to accept the latter as valid.

the male precedence we noted in Genesis 1 – 3. The man is the head of the woman, not the woman of the man; the woman is the glory of man, not the man of the woman; man was not made from woman, but woman from man; neither was man made for woman, but woman for man. Neither is to think of themselves as independent of the other, let alone as independent of God (v. 11f.), yet they are not simply equal but different partners. Since male precedence is argued here from creation, Christian theology ought to take it seriously. We must seek both to understand what it means and to correct misunderstandings (as Paul does in v. 11f.).

The service of God is critical to the understanding both of headship and of mutuality. In verse 3 the headship of the man to the woman is set within the context both of the headship of Father to Son in the Godhead and of the headship of Christ to the man. When headship is removed from these theological controls, it becomes oppressive. Those who understand headship to be about authority must never claim that this means the woman ought simply to do the will of the man; for only as the man serves the will of God is the woman's help as it was meant to be. It is 'in the Lord' (v. 11) and in recognition of our common dependence on God (v. 12) that we are to work together in his service.

Paul's teaching here seems to be conditioned by women (perhaps reacting against the abuses of patriarchy) behaving as if they can 'go it alone' in their behaviour, whether by ceasing to be gladly feminine or by reluctance to co-operate in the marriage partnership. By their contentious and disorderly behaviour they bring disrepute upon the gospel. In the absence of proper order (which includes Christian subordination of the wife to the husband, and headship as sacrificial serving authority) there will be rivalry rather than partnership between the sexes. Perhaps in Corinth the women needed reminding both of their interdependence with the men and that they were made 'for the sake of' man, as partners in a shared God-given task. Disorder (and in particular a wrong attitude to subordination) leads to rivalry in which the weakest go to the wall; the task will be neglected. Proper order will promote sexual relations in the service of God.

1 Corinthians 14:33b–35/36

This passage touches only tangentially on marriage and must be treated here very briefly.[48] The context is proper order in the gatherings of the church

---

48. Accessible recent treatments are to be found in Perriman 1998: ch. 5; Fee 1987, ad loc.; Carson 1991; Witherington 1988:90–104. In my view Perriman's treatment of this passage is excellent.

(14:26–40). The suggestion that verse 34f. is a non-Pauline interpolation is unconvincing, in spite of the few (late and Western) manuscripts that have verse 34f. transposed to after verse 40 (Perriman 1998:103–107; Witherington 1988:90–92; Carson 1991:41–45. *Against* Fee 1987:699–705). Probably verse 33b ought to be taken as the introduction to this passage, rather than with what precedes, but we cannot be sure (Perriman 1998:107f.; Carson 1991:140f.).

An important question is how the prohibition on women speaking in church gatherings may be reconciled with the fact that in 1 Corinthians 11:5, 13 Paul expects them to pray and prophesy in public, provided that their heads are properly covered. A number of suggestions have been made (Perriman 1998:108–113). One is that what Paul is treating here in chapter 14 is the kinds of teaching debates that were involved in the weighing of prophecy (v. 29). It is these debates, with all the associations with teaching authority, in which the women are not to participate, lest they 'lord it' over their husbands, who were likely to be there (Carson 1991:151–153; 1997:121ff.; Hurley 1981:185–194; cf. Witherington 1988:101f., criticized in Carson 1991:146). This is possible but speculative; we cannot be sure that in Christian meetings there was such a clear distinction between prophesying and the weighing of prophecy, nor that the weighing of prophecy was so clearly an exercise of authority (Fee 1987:703f.; Perriman 1998:111f.).

A thoughtful reconstruction has been offered by Perriman (1998:121f.), who observes from verse 30 that it seems people *stood* to contribute to the public gathering of the church. He suggests that what Paul forbids is disorderly chattering by the women while still seated; they would not take their turn to stand and contribute. But when a woman, in proper orderly fashion, takes her turn to stand, covers her head, offers prayer or gives prophecy, this is acceptable (1 Cor. 11:5, 13).

We still need to ask, however, why Paul singles out the women. It may be that in their context it happened to be mainly, or even only, the women who chattered in a disorderly way; we cannot know. But Paul's prohibition is addressed not to the disorderly in general (though no doubt he would have disapproved of disorderly men too, cf. vv. 26–33), but to the disorderly women in particular. Nor is his prohibition addressed to the uneducated in general (whether or not all the women were uneducated, which is unlikely),[49] but to the women in general, whether or not they were uneducated. In view of the word 'submit' (*hupotassomai*), with its associations elsewhere in Pauline thought, and

---

49. Baugh 1995:45–47 rebuts the suggestion that all the women in Ephesus were uneducated.

the somewhat puzzling clause 'as the law says' (usually in Paul a reference to Scripture in some form), it seems most likely that (as in chapter 11) Paul refers to the appropriate submission of wives to husbands, a creation principle found in Genesis 2 (cf. 1 Cor. 11:8; 1 Tim. 2:13f.). The disorderly chattering of the women (almost all of whom would presumably have been married and mostly with their husbands present) was not only improper because it disrupted the meeting, it also showed a scandalous lack of respect for their husbands. Because such respect is a creation principle, Paul is especially sensitive to contravening its contemporary cultural expression. His ruling was not local (for it extended to 'all the churches'), but it was contemporary, for it concerned the cultural expression of a creation principle.

The wider cultural background was generally negative about women participating in public meetings at all, the exception being the disreputable mystery religions (Perriman 1998:113–119). Against this background it was risky to have the women participating at all in public prayer and prophecy. We may imagine that Paul was especially concerned to avoid any appearance to the outside observer that the Christian assembly was disorderly or disreputable, and in particular that it scandalously dismissed the conventions governing relations between the sexes.

The household codes: principled or pragmatic?

Every culture has conventions governing relations within society and the household. In Graeco-Roman culture these conventions focused on relations between governing authorities and citizens, slaves and masters, parents and children, and between husbands and wives. The New Testament addresses these relations, most significantly in Colossians 3:18–4:1 (often considered to be the earliest); Ephesians 5:21–6:9 and 1 Peter 2:13–3:7 (other relevant texts include Rom. 13:1–7; 1 Tim. 6:1f. and Titus 2:1–10). Following Luther's word *Haustafel* (a table for the household), these are often called 'household codes' or *Haustafeln*. We do not know whether Paul and Peter adapted these teachings from models found in Stoic philosophy, Hellenistic Judaism, the wider world of Graeco-Roman moral philosophy, or a mixture of these; whatever their models, they radically Christianized them (Balch 1981; Achtemeier 1996:206f.; Best 1998:519–527; Witherington 1988:42–47; O'Brien 1982:214–219; Lincoln 1990:355–359).

Women had a low status in the culture. Summarizing the views of the intellectual elite of the Graeco-Roman world, Achtemeier writes,

> Dominant among the elite was the notion that the woman was by nature inferior to the man. Because she lacked the capacity for reason that the male had, she was ruled rather by her emotions, and was as a result given to poor judgment, immorality,

intemperance, wickedness, avarice; she was untrustworthy, contentious, and as a result, it was her place to obey. Such a view of women was also sedimented in legal tradition: women could not vote or hold office, could not take an oath or plead a case in court, could not be the legal guardian of their own minor children, and were legally dependent on either their father or a guardian.

(Achtemeier 1996:206f.; cf. Balch 1981:139–142)

Achtemeier notes that in the reign of Augustus there was a measure of relaxation in these legal restrictions, but the general picture is unchanged.

The New Testament teachings on the relations of men and women radically undermine these views while appearing to confirm the underlying asymmetry. It is important to understand how they do this.

For Christian moral theology the question of how these New Testament codes apply in the contemporary world, if at all, arises from the theological question of *why* the apostles included this material in the way they did. The following major rationales have been suggested. They are not mutually exclusive and they may not apply identically for all the relations treated (for example, the rationale for slaves may not be the same as the rationale for wives).

(i) A concern for order within the churches which were threatened by disintegration through a false intoxication with liberation in Christ

When the women and slaves heard that in the gospel they were admitted equally into full membership of the people of God (Gal. 3:28), it would not be surprising if they began to question and indeed flout (where they could) the cultural conventions of patriarchy and slavery. Indeed, it seems (e.g. Rom. 11:13–32) that tensions also arose because of rivalries between Jewish believer and Gentile believer in some contexts. The apostles may have included the household codes and related material to keep proper order in churches threated by rivalry and disorder (Balch 1981:106f.).

(ii) An apologetic and missionary concern that the public reputation of the churches should be respectable so that the message of the gospel should gain a hearing

We have seen this element above in our consideration of 1 Corinthians 14:33b–36.

(iii) A desire to minimize tensions with surrounding society so as to reduce persecution

This links closely to (ii). Any minority religion needs to consider (iii) and any proselytizing one (ii). If the young churches were seen as hotbeds of sedition, undermining the proper order of the household, dissolving social morality and threatening the stability of the wider *polis*, it would be hard to gain a hearing for the gospel. They would be met with suspicion, rather as cults visiting door to door are viewed today. Before long informal persecution or formal pressure from the authorities would follow. For both reasons (ii) and (iii) it was important that the churches should be, and be seen to be, places where proper social order was maintained.

Good behaviour in the sight of outsiders is important in the light Matthew 5:16 (Selwyn 1947:373, 428). This concern is evident in 1 Thessalonians 4:12 and Colossians 4:5 (in both of which we find the phrase *pros tous exō*) and in 1 Peter 2:12 with its interest in 'your way of life [*anastrophē*] among the pagans [*en tois ethnesin*]'. It may also be the logic underlying 1 Timothy 2:2–4.

We should not, however, be over sanguine about the hope that the good lives of Christians would lead either to the conversion of others or to a reduction in persecution (cf. 1 Pet. 4:4). The apostles were more deeply concerned that the righteousness of God be vindicated. In 1 Peter 2:12 the good lives of believers will force the hostile outsider to glorify God 'when he comes to judge' (*en hēmera episkopēs*, in the day of visitation); this is more likely to mean that on the Day of Judgment they will have to admit (albeit reluctantly) that the Christians were in the right rather than that they would be converted beforehand (Balch 1981:87). The missionary motivation for respectable conduct may not have as strong a scriptural base as is sometimes supposed. The apostles were more concerned that Christian lives should *be* good, than that they should be seen or thought to be good. This leads to our final, and most significant, motive.

(iv) A belief that a particular ordering is intrinsically right, being rooted in creation order and not merely according with cultural custom

Only if this last motivation can be established do the household codes have enduring validity. If Christians simply had to be thought to be good (i.e. respectable), then the principle would press us to conform to each succeeding culture's respectability. But if they commended behaviours as actually *being* good (in the sight of God), then what was good then is presumably good now.

The great dividing line in commentators on these passages is between those who affirm some or all of motivations (i)–(iii) and those who see *also* in some places motivation (iv). Any or all of the first three motivations can coexist with the fourth. The first three may be pragmatic or they may be principled; if they are principled, then they may stand in judgment over contemporary culture. It would be hard to exaggerate the importance of this hermeneutical distinction.

With these preliminary considerations in mind, we turn first to the overlapping addresses to wives and husbands in Colossians 3 and Ephesians 5.

Colossians 3:18f. and Ephesians 5:21/22–33

In the household code of Colossians, Paul[50] speaks to wives (3:18) and husbands (3:19), to children (3:20) and fathers (3:21), to slaves (3:22–25) and masters (4:1). Likewise in Ephesians, he speaks to wives (5:22–24, 33b) and husbands (5:25–33a), to children (6:1–3) and fathers (6:4), to slaves (6:5–8) and masters (6:9). There are close parallels; it is often thought that Ephesians develops the household code found first in Colossians. Ephesians says more about marriage, although it is still not a comprehensive treatment, saying nothing about the wife's love for the husband and nothing about children (who are, however, not far away in 6:1–3). Our study will follow the order of Ephesians 5.

Ephesians 5:21: transitional verse

²¹ Be subject to [*hupotassomenoi*] one another out of reverence for Christ [*en phobē Christou*].

The relation of verse 21 to verses 22–33 is a matter of debate. On the one hand, although most translations make verse 21 begin a new sentence, the participle *hupotassomenoi* is the last of a series of participles dependent on the verb 'be filled' (v. 18): speaking (*lalountes*, v. 19), singing and making melody (*adontes kai psallontes*, v. 19), giving thanks (*eucharistountes*, v. 20), and submitting (v. 21). All these are to be done as believers are filled with the Spirit; they are not strictly imperatives, but rather 'dependent participles of result which describe the overflow or outworking of the Spirit's filling believers' (O'Brien 1999:387f.). This is how Spirit-filled believers behave towards one another. And yet, on the other hand, verse 21 also introduces the motif of submission which leads in to the passage that follows. It is 'a hinge verse' (O'Brien 1999:399).

There is a minor textual uncertainty in verse 22. Some early manuscripts omit the verb *hupotassomai* in verse 22, so that the meaning has to be carried forward from the participle *hupotassomenoi* in verse 21, thus linking verse 21 to the section that follows. If this is so, then we must (grammatically) understand verse 21 as introducing the section that follows, so that it reads, '. . . being in submission to one another out of reverence for Christ, wives to your husbands . . .' Other manuscripts include the verb separately in verse 22 (albeit in four alternative ways), enabling us to place a major punctuation mark at the end of verse 21 and to read verse 22 as the start of a fresh section. It seems

---

50. I accept Pauline authorship of Colossians, Ephesians and the pastorals. My reasons for doing so lie outside the scope of this study.

likely that the shorter reading (with no verb in v. 22) is original, the verb being variously supplied later in verse 22 in the interests of clarity when a Scripture reading was to begin with verse 22 (as is done in most English translations).[51] (The imperative form appears in Colossians 3:18.)

In favour of seeing verses 21–33 as an integral section is also perhaps the hint of an *inclusio* formed by the use of 'fear' in verse 21 ('in the fear of Christ') and verse 33b ('wives should "fear" their husbands') (Lincoln 1990:352; O'Brien 1999:388, n.110; against Best 1998:516).

It is important to clarify how verse 21 links exegetically to verse 22, because the former appears to refer to mutual submission (each to the other) while the latter is clearly one-sided submission (wives to husbands). The other three uses of 'one another' (*allēlōn*) in Ephesians all refer to reciprocal relations (4:2, 25, 32).

There are three main options (O'Brien 1999:398–405; Lincoln 1990, ad loc.; Best 1998:515–517).

First, verse 21 undermines verses 22–24, 33b (Sampley 1971:114ff.). On this reading verse 21 expresses Paul's true intent, egalitarian mutual submission of each believer to each other believer independent of gender. Paul places verse 21 here so that when we read the section that follows we realize that although, for reasons of respectability, he feels he must say the patriarchal things, he does not really mean them. But, as Lincoln observes, 'if he disagreed with it (sc. the patriarchal ideas of submission and headship), why would the writer have made such extended use of it' as he immediately does (Lincoln 1990:366; cf. Best 1998:516)? Verses 22–33 are a significant extension of Colossians 3:18f. View (1) is not persuasive.

Secondly, verse 21 teaches mutual submission and thereby exercises a control over the one-way subordinate relations that follow, in line with Paul's teaching elsewhere about the nature of Christian brotherly and sisterly relations and in particular the nature of Christian leadership (Barth, *CD* III4:172; Bilezikian 1985:154ff.; Keener 1992:168–172). 'The household code which follows (Ephesians 5:22–6:9) is a special application of the Christian grace of submission . . . Christians should not be self-assertive, each insisting on getting his or her own way.' They should count others better than themselves (Phil. 2:3–8). The leaders ought not to 'lord it' over the flock (1 Pet. 5:3). Paul himself, with all his self-conscious apostolic authority, could call himself the

---

51. See Metzger 1971, ad loc. and the critical apparatus in UBS Greek New Testament. Also Lincoln 1990:351, n.a; Best 1998:531 ('a lectionary reading could hardly begin with a verbless sentence'). The alternative readings probably testify to a very early tradition of beginning this section of the letter at v. 22 rather than v. 21.

Corinthians' 'slave' for Jesus' sake (2 Cor. 4:5) (Bruce 1968:382). Those who advocate this view usually understand Paul as teaching that husbands should submit to their wives (at least in some way) as well as wives to their husbands, despite what follows.

Thirdly, the difficulty with the second option is that 'submission' is not a reciprocal quality. If A ought to submit to B, then it is virtuous for A to submit to B, but not for B to submit to A. Indeed, if A submits to B, it is not logically possible for B to submit to A. Kings ought to serve their subjects, but not submit to them. Paul immediately applies submission in stubbornly nonreciprocal ways (O'Brien 1999:401–404; Clark 1980:74–76; Knight 1991:166–168). The Christian virtue is to submit *to those to whom I ought to submit*. In verse 21 Paul therefore means, 'Let each of you subordinate himself or herself to the one he or she should be subordinate to' (Clark 1980:76). 'The apostle is not speaking of *mutual* submission in the sense of a reciprocal subordination, but submission to those who are in authority over them' (O'Brien 1999:404).

These appropriate (and one-way) subordinations are spelled out in the sections that follow, wives to husbands (but not husbands to wives), children obeying parents (but not parents obeying children), and slaves obeying masters (but not masters obeying slaves). When Bruce speaks of 'submissiveness' being a Christian grace, it is not clear that this is *in general* correct. Humility (including mutual humility, Phil. 2:3; 1 Pet. 5:5) and service towards one another (John 13:14f.) are general Christian virtues, just as arrogance and self-serving are general vices. Submissiveness is a virtue only in the sense that I ought to submit to those to whom I ought to submit, in God's proper ordering. Masters and husbands are given challenging injunctions, but masters are not told to *submit* to their slaves, nor husbands to their wives. The noun *hypotagē* (subordination, subjection, submission) is not a general virtue.[52]

Even the mutuality in the word 'one another' (*allēlōn*) in verse 21 is dependent on the context. For example, in James 5:16 ('Therefore confess your sins to one another, and pray for one another, so that you may be healed') *allēlōn* is used twice, once of confession, once of prayer. In each case it is not completely mutual. Not every believer confesses, but only those who are sick because of sin; not every believer prays, but rather those who are seeking to

---

52. The four New Testament occurrences are 2 Cor. 9:13 (submission to the confession of the gospel); Gal. 2:5 (Paul's *non*-submission to the false-believers in Jerusalem); 1 Tim. 2:11 (women) and 3:4 (the overseer's children). In each it is not the quality of submissiveness that is in view, but the object of submission, and whether or not it is a *proper* object of such.

help the sick. So *allēlōn* may be restricted by its context to a nonmutual meaning (Clark 1980:76, n.4).

The third view seems to be correct. The idea of mutual subordination arose only as 'an exegetical tactic commonly employed by those wishing to mitigate the hierarchalism of the subsequent passage' (Perriman 1998:52). It does not derive from exegesis.

Verse 21, however, is a transitional verse with connections of thought to what comes before and after.[53] As Best comments, 'Authors do not necessarily think in paragraphs . . . There is at times perhaps a greater flow in the argument than editors care to admit' (Best 1998:515; cf. O'Brien 1999:378; Hurley 1981:140). The fact that 'submitting to one another' comes at the end of a series of participles about entirely mutual behaviour (presumably any or all the believers could speak, sing, make melody or give thanks), and the strong general association of *allēlōn* with mutuality may well suggest that Paul is reminding the Christian husbands that the submission of their wives does not give them licence to become arrogant or self-serving. The challenge to husbands is a major emphasis in the passage that follows. To evacuate verse 21 completely of mutuality might seem to reduce its force in Paul's argument. He might almost as well have left it out and made it quite clear he was starting an entirely new section in verse 22.[54] The tension between mutuality and order may be precisely the nuance Paul needs to make his point when he moves to the 'household code'.

The phrase 'in the fear of Christ' expresses a very strong awe and reverence. This sets the whole subject of submission firmly within the matrix of serving Christ. Most of the problems in contemporary debate result from extracting the issue from the lordship of Christ, so that we begin to think in terms of secular attitudes and self-serving power plays. But both sides of the submission Paul enjoins in the verses that follow are to be acted out in the conscious presence, and under the lordship, of Christ.

---

53. The suggestion of Martin 1991:67f. that by linking v. 21 with the context of the Christian meetings in the preceding passage, Paul is 'remarking in v22 that it is in services of public worship that a woman ought to be submissive to her husband', is unlikely (especially in view of *en panti* in v. 24). (cf. the criticism in Witherington 1988:48).

54. *Contra* Perriman 1998:52, who suggests the emphasis and point of v. 21 is that submission is to be 'in the fear of Christ' rather than reluctant or grudging. But why does Paul say 'one another', rather than just, 'Wives, be submissive to your husbands in the fear of Christ'? And why make 'submitting yourselves' a participle linking back to v. 18?

Ephesians 5:22–24: wives – headship and submission

> [22] Wives, (be subject) to your husbands as (you are)[55] to the Lord [*hōs tō kyriō*].[56]
>
> [Colossians 3:18: Wives, be subject to your husbands, as is fitting in the Lord (*hōs anēken en kyriō*).]
>
> [23] For [*hoti*] the husband is the head [*kephalē*] of the wife
> just as Christ is the head [*kephalē*] of the church,
> the body of which he is the Saviour.
> [24] Just as[57] the church is subject [*hypotassetai*] to Christ,
> so also wives ought to be, in everything, to their husbands.

Wives are to submit to their husbands (*tois idiois androis*) rather than women to men in general. This passage is explicitly about marriage.

We ask two questions: What did Paul mean here by headship and submission? And why did Paul mean this (i.e. what is the underlying rationale, theological and/or pragmatic)?

What did Paul mean by headship and submission?
It is clear from the strong parallel structure of verses 23–24 that what he means by submission is the counterpart to what he means by headship. The church is subject to Christ because (*hoti*) Christ is the head of the church; the wife is subject to the husband because the husband is the head of the wife. The obligation to submit is grounded in headship and the meaning of headship in this context is therefore strongly conditioned by the meaning of submission.[58]

---

55. NRSV 'you are' is an interpretative insertion by the translators.

56. Had Paul meant that wives should submit to husbands 'as to a lord' (i.e. treating their husbands as lords or masters), we would have expected *hōs tois kyriois* here. The singular reference is clearly to Christ.

57. NRSV does not translate *alla* (but) at the start of v. 24.

58. Against Perriman 1998:55–57 whose attempt to dissociate headship from submission is not at all convincing. His endeavour to present Ephesians 5:22–24 as originally nonhierarchical is a weak section in his otherwise careful study. To argue as he does that only '*as long as* the man has the sort of prominence that a patriarchal society attributes to him, the woman should be submitted to him' is to evacuate vv. 22–24 of any substantial theological meaning. When he admits (p. 57), 'We cannot say for certain that Paul consciously thought of the headship of the man as provisional in this way,' we may say this is an understatement; he would have been very surprised.

Submission

We begin with submission, since this is much more common in the New Testament than the metaphorical concept of headship. The verb *hypotassō* (to subject, subordinate) and the noun *hypotagē* (subjection, subordination, obedience) occur between them forty-two times in the New Testament, mostly in Paul.[59]

The root idea is that of *taxis*, which means order, appointment or arrangement, and presupposes some superior authority which (or who) has arranged things or people in some way. So, for example, what we would call the rota for service in the temple of which Zechariah's section was a part is called a *taxis* (Luke 1:8). The writer to the Hebrews speaks of 'the *taxis* of Melchizedek' (or of Aaron), by which he seems to mean an orderly succession (Heb. 5:6, 10; 6:20; 7:11, 17). For a community to be *kata taxin* is to be orderly as opposed to chaotic (1 Cor. 14:40; cf. v. 32, 'the spirits of the prophets are subject to the prophets'; also Col. 2:5). The opposite of good order is chaos.

The noun *hypotagē* denotes a state of subjection, whether voluntary or involuntary, welcome or unwelcome. In Galatians 2:5 Paul insists that he, Barnabas and Titus absolutely refused to submit (lit. to be *en hypotagē*) to the Judaizing false-believers in Jerusalem. In 2 Corinthians 9:13 he is pleased to see evidence of 'obedience [*hypotagē*] to the confession of the gospel of Christ' by generous participation in the collection for the saints. In 1 Timothy 2:11 the women are to learn quietly 'in all submission' (*en pasē hypotagē*);[60] and in 1 Timothy 3:4 the overseer is to keep his children in submission (lit. having his children *en hypotagē*). The central idea seems to be that the one in submission does the will of the one to whom he or she submits, whether this will be good or bad, whether doing it be welcome or unwelcome.[61]

The majority of New Testament uses (38 out of 42) are of the verb *hypotassō* rather than the noun *hypotagē* (Delling 1972:39–46). For ethics these are more significant, since they focus on the action of some moral agent rather than simply on an experienced state. The verb *hypotassō* in the active (literally 'to arrange under', O'Brien 1999:399) refers to the action of bringing

---

59. See Delling 1972:27–48 for these and cognate words in Greek literature, the LXX and the New Testament. Also O'Brien 1999:399 for a concise summary.

60. The question to whom or what the women here are to be in submission lies outside the scope of this study. See Mounce 2000.

61. Delling 1972:40 claims that the middle voice *hypotassomai* 'does not mean ... to do the will of someone but rather "to lose or surrender one's own rights or will"'. It may be right that the emphasis is on self-negation, but it is hard to see how this differs in practice from doing the will of the one to whom one submits.

someone or something into submission, whether they wish to submit or not: 'the subordination expressed may be either compulsory or voluntary' (Delling 1972:41).

The submission of all things to God and Christ

In the New Testament the subject of the active verb is always God or Christ (Delling 1972:41). God subjects creation to frustration (Rom. 8:20) and he subjects all things to the man Jesus Christ (Heb. 2:5, 8; 1 Cor. 15:27f.; Eph. 1:22; these texts are all strongly linked to Ps. 8:6). In Philippians 3:21 Christ makes all things subject to himself. In Romans 8:20 ('the creation was subjected to futility'); 1 Peter 3:22 ('angels . . . made subject to him') and 1 Corinthians 15:27 ('All things are put in subjection') we also find a 'divine passive' with the same sense of involuntary subjection by God or Christ. And when in Luke 10:17, 20 we read of the demons being made subject (*hypotassetai*) to the disciples in Jesus' name, we must take this middle in the passive sense, since it is clear they submitted because they had to, not because they chose to.

The submission of Christ to God

The only active sense in the New Testament is of God or Christ enforcing the submission of the created order. All the other uses are of voluntary submission, using the middle voice (*hypotassomai*). The supreme example is Jesus himself, as 1 Corinthians 15:24–28 explains.

> Then comes the end, when he (Christ) hands over the kingdom [*paradidō tēn basileian*] to God the Father, after he has destroyed every ruler and every authority and power. For he must reign until he has put all his enemies under his feet. The last enemy to be destroyed is death. For 'God has put all things in subjection under his feet' [Psalm 8:6]. But when it says, 'All things are put in subjection,' it is plain that this does not include the one who put all things in subjection under him. When all things are subjected to him, then the Son himself will also be subjected [*hypotagēsetai*] to the one who put all things in subjection under him, so that God may be all in all.

There is a vast moral difference between the involuntary subjection of all things under Christ's feet by the Father and the voluntary handing over of the kingdom to the Father by the Son. The rebellious created order is forcibly subjugated; the Son places himself gladly in submission to the Father. The same word *hypotassō* is used of both, but the context must decide the moral nature of the submission described. In the former, the moral agent is the Father, who acts to bring all things into submission to Christ. In the latter, the moral agent is the Son, who chooses to hand over the kingdom and to place himself (*hypotassomai*, middle voice) in submission to the Father.

The submission of the believer to God

We may perhaps speak of the fundamental 'vertical' ordering of 'God – Christ – all things' as a 'metataxis', an order that controls all other orderings. But we would be mistaken if we simply included all human beings as part of 'all things', for in Christ the believer is given the moral privilege of being enjoined *voluntarily* to submit to God. Four texts speak of this dignified submission.

1. James 4:7, 'Submit yourselves [*hypotagēte*] to God.' The moral address is to human beings who are enjoined voluntarily to place themselves under God.
2. Hebrews 12:9, 'Moreover, we had human parents to discipline us, and we respected them. Should we not be even more willing to be subject [*hypotagēsometha*] to the Father of spirits and live?' NRSV 'willing to be subject' picks up from the future tense the same moral sense of the voluntary submission of the human will to the will of the Father.
3. In Romans 10:3, speaking with sadness of his own people the Jews, Paul writes, 'Being ignorant of the righteousness that comes from God, and seeking to establish their own, they have not submitted to God's righteousness [*tē dikaiosunē tou theou ouk hypetagēsan*].' They ought to have submitted their wills to the righteousness God has ordained and given up the attempt to establish their own.

   These texts are not the simple counterparts of those that speak of God bringing all things into submission under Christ. That was a compulsory subjection enforced (in the end) upon the whole created order. This, by contrast, is a voluntary submission. Voluntary submission as a calling of God is the key to the various submissions between human beings to which we turn below. It is emphasized in our fourth text.
4. 'For this reason the mind that is set on the flesh [*to phronēma tēs sarkos*] is hostile to God; it does not submit [*ouk hypotassetai*] to God's law – indeed it cannot' (Rom. 8:7). Paul speaks of the work of the Spirit in the believer. By the Spirit of God alone the believer is enabled voluntarily to submit to God, because the Spirit works in the believer at the deepest level of human personhood, the level of the human spirit. So when the believer chooses to submit, this is not a submission enforced from outside but a joyful submission embraced from the heart.

The distinction between the relation of Christ to 'all things' (which he subjugates) and his relation to the church (which by the Spirit voluntarily submits to him) is noted in Ephesians 1:22, where Christ is said to be 'the head over all things for the church' (*kephalēn hyper panta tē ekklēsia*). Christ's headship over all things is of a different order from his headship over the church. We return to this below.

We consider now the five contexts in Scripture where human beings are enjoined to be subject to other human beings.

(i) Submission to civil authorities
In Romans 13:1–7 Paul tells all people to be subject (vv. 1, 5) to the governing authorities. He reiterates this in Titus 3:1. Peter says the same in 1 Peter 2:13.

(ii) Submission of slaves to masters
In Titus 2:9 Paul tells slaves to be subject to their masters (cf. 1 Tim. 6:1). Peter says the same in 1 Peter 2:18. In Ephesians 6:5 and Colossians 3:22 he tells them to obey (*hypakouō*), which suggests that in this relationship submission is equal to obedience. The two concepts are not identical and usually the context decides whether simple obedience is included with subordination.[62]

(iii) Submission to church leaders
In 1 Peter 5:5, Peter tells the young to be in submission to the elders (probably here the church leaders). In Hebrews 13:17 this is spoken of in terms of obedience (using *peithō* in the passive) and compliance or yielding (*hypeikō*).

In 1 Corinthians 16:15f. we find a revealing passage for the possible association of submission and shared service in a task.

> Now, brothers and sisters, you know that members of the household of Stephanas were the first converts in Achaia, and they devoted themselves to the service of the saints; I urge you to put yourselves at the service of such people [*hypotassēsthe tois toioutois*], and of everyone who works and toils with them.

As in marriage, so in church: submission means the willingness to do the will of another *so as to help them in the shared task of doing the will of God*. The household of Stephanas were toiling for the gospel; in this context Paul enjoins the other believers to submit to them, to allow them to give the lead in doing the work and not to make it harder for them by being uncooperative.

(iv) Submission of children to parents
Luke 2:51 speaks of the boy Jesus being in submission to his parents. The overseer is to make sure his children are 'in submission' (1 Tim. 3:4). Elsewhere children are told to obey their parents (Eph. 6:1; Col. 3:20), so Paul seems to have understood submission for them (as for slaves) to include obedience.

---

62. Delling 1972:41. But note the observation of Lincoln 1990:367f. that submission and obedience are 'frequently synonymous'.

(v) Submission of wives to husbands

Wives are told to submit to their husbands in Ephesians 5:24; Colossians 3:18; Titus 2:5 and 1 Peter 3:1 (cf. v. 5; also, with less clarity as to the context and whether it is all women or just wives, in 1 Tim. 2:11 and 1 Cor. 14:34). They are not explicitly told to obey (*hypakouō*), although Sarah obeyed Abraham and is held up by Peter as a good example (1 Pet. 3:6).

Submission and obedience

From this survey of submission we may learn that the fundamental concept shared by all the uses is that the one who submits does the *will* of the one to whom they submit. The word itself says nothing about whether this is a good thing or a bad thing, a voluntarily embraced submission or an enforced subjection, but it always involves the *will* of one being given up in some sense or to some degree to the *will* of the other.

Having said this, there is a great dividing line through the concept, separating submissions that are enforced and submissions that are gladly accepted. We have seen this in the distinction between the enforced subjection of all things to Christ and the voluntary submission of the believer by the Spirit to Christ and to God, following the example of the voluntary submission of Christ himself to the Father.

The submissions enjoined by Scripture between human beings are to be the voluntary acts of spiritual men and women. God's word comes in each case to the one who is to submit; the other is not told to keep them in subjugation. 'Those who are to be subordinate, wives, children, and slaves, are addressed as moral agents' (Lincoln 1990:367).[63] Citizens are to make themselves subject to the authorities, slaves to masters, children to parents, believers to church leaders and wives to husbands. The only time when submission is to be enforced is in the context of parents disciplining their children (1 Tim. 3:4; cf. Heb. 12:9). Even then, as soon as the believing children are of age and can hear the word of God, it is addressed to them, telling them to obey their parents (Eph. 6:1; Col. 3:20). In particular, husbands are never told to make sure their wives submit to them, or to keep them in submission. Submission 'is something they must do themselves. Paul does not tell husbands to insist that their wives perform this duty' (Witherington 1988:50).

---

63. O'Brien 1999:406 comments that although the concept of reciprocal obligations in these relations is not unknown in discussion of households in the Graeco-Roman world, 'there are no extant examples which are as thoroughgoing as Colossians 3:18–4:1 and Ephesians 5:22–6:9 in this emphasis on reciprocal obligations'.

Headship

Paul uses the word *kephalē* (head) seventeen times in his letters.[64] Nine of these are in 1 Corinthians 11:3–16 (a mixture of literal and metaphorical, discussed above). Seven of the remaining eight are in Ephesians and Colossians, and the eighth is not relevant to our discussion.[65] We have agreed with Perriman that 'source' is very unlikely to be the primary metaphorical meaning, both because it lacks any clear support in the LXX and because it is not a common feature of all the New Testament uses. We may agree further that the fundamental idea of pre-eminence or prominence seems to unite all the LXX uses, and take as our starting point that it means this at the least. We list below Paul's remaining uses of *kephalē*.

1.   Colossians 1:18: 'He is the head of the body, the church; he is the beginning, the firstborn from the dead, so that he might come to have first place in everything.'

2.   Ephesians 1:22f.: 'And he [God, v. 20] has put all things under his [Christ's] feet and has made him the head over all things for the church, which is his body, the fullness of him who fills all in all.'

3.   Colossians 2:9f.: 'For in him the whole fullness of deity dwells bodily, and you have come to fullness in him, who is the head of every ruler and authority.'

4.   Colossians 2:18f.: 'Do not let anyone disqualify you, insisting on self-abasement and worship of angels, dwelling on visions, puffed up without cause by a human way of thinking, and not holding fast to the head, from whom the whole body [*kai ou kratōn tēn kephalēn, ex hou pan to sōma*], nourished and held together by its ligaments and sinews, grows with a growth that is from God.'

5.   Ephesians 4:15f.: 'But speaking the truth in love, we must grow up in every way into him who is the head, into Christ, from whom the whole body, joined and knit together by every ligament with which it is equipped, as each part is working properly, promotes the body's growth in building itself up in love.'

---

64.   Excluding Rom. 12:20, which is in a quotation from LXX Prov. 25:22.

65.   In 1 Cor. 12:21, in the context of the extended metaphor of the church as the body of Christ, Paul mentions by way of illustration that, 'The eye cannot say to the hand, "I have no need of you," nor again the head to the feet, "I have no need of you."' Here 'head' is just one of the many members of the body and is not used with any specific metaphorical sense of 'headship'. We may leave this reference to one side.

In these five texts Christ's headship is used in two different ways: he is head over all things and he is head of the church.

First, Christ is the head over all things, who are brought into submission to him by God (Eph. 1:22f.; Col. 2:9f.; cf. 1 Cor. 15:27f. and Heb. 2:5, 8, which make use of Ps. 8 and thereby link Christ's headship to the dominion given to humankind in Gen. 1:26–31). This is a rightful and an enforced authority.

Secondly, Christ is the head of the church, to which he relates as head to body. This is different from his headship over the created order. This is stated in Colossians 1:18 (in a context which stresses his pre-eminence, v. 18b). The nature of this relationship is expanded in Ephesians 1:22f., which speaks of his headship over all things as being 'for the church, which is his body, the fullness of him who fills all in all'. The idea seems to be that in union with Christ, the church which is his body may enter into that beneficent dominion over the created order that was given in creation to Adam; Christ's headship over the created order is 'for the church' because it enables the church to enter into this rule with him.

A similar thought may be found in Colossians 2:9f. In union with Christ the believer comes to 'fullness in him, who is the head of every ruler and authority'. A related truth is taught in Colossians 2:18f. and Ephesians 4:15f. Here the emphasis is not on the rule of the church's head over creation, but on the blessing he gives to the body as its head. As the church holds fast to the head, the whole church is nourished and held together and grows up into maturity in relation to him.

When Paul writes that God is the head of Christ and Christ of man in 1 Corinthians 11:3, it seems clear that in both relations he has in view this voluntary and beneficial submission. The enforced subjugation experienced by the rebellious created order is not in view. Likewise, since the headship of husband over wife is paralleled with that of Christ over the church (in the context, v. 23, of his being the Saviour of the body), it is clear that this too is to be a beneficial relationship voluntarily entered into by the wife because she understands it will be for her blessing.

Indeed, in Ephesians 5:22–24, this context of blessing is so much in the front of Paul's mind that even before he moves to address the husband he mentions that Christ is the Saviour of his body the church. It is sometimes suggested that the concept of Christ as Saviour also has an analog in the role of the husband as protector or nourisher of the wife; while it is possible to understand some such analogy in a way that is consistent with verses 25–33, it is not clear that this was directly in Paul's thought at this point, since by the word *autos* (he) he emphasizes that this is true of *Christ*; also, the word Saviour (*sōtēr*) is not used in the sense of protector or nourisher elsewhere in the New Testament

(O'Brien 1999:414f.). Most commentators (e.g. Lincoln 1990:370–372; O'Brien 1999:415) also suggest that the adversative 'but' (*alla*) at the start of verse 24 reinforces the view that the 'Saviour of the body' statement applies only to Christ; Paul resumes with 'notwithstanding this difference'. Nevertheless, the fact that when Paul speaks of Christ's headship he immediately thinks of the blessing of salvation for the church accords with the major thrust of verses 25–33 challenging husbands to make their headship similarly beneficial. This is 'a theological "trailer" for what follows' (Best 1998:535).

We conclude that when Paul tells wives to submit to their husbands he has in mind a voluntary, morally honourable and Spirit-given willingness to do the will of the husband rather than insisting on their own will, so that together they may serve the will of God (cf. Lincoln 1990:368–370).

Earlier in Ephesians Paul has described the church's relation to Christ. Lincoln writes of this,

> If one asks what the writer thinks is involved in the Church's subordination to Christ, one can look for an answer to the way in which he depicts the Church's relation to Christ in the rest of the letter. The Church receives God's gift of Christ as head over all on its behalf (1:22). In the building imagery of 2:20, 21 the Church looks to Christ as the crowning stone of its structure and the one who holds it all together. It opens itself to his constant presence (3:17) and comes to know his all-encompassing love (3:19). The Church receives his gift of grace (4:7) and his gifts of ministry for its own upbuilding (4:11, 12). It grows towards its head and receives from him all that is necessary for such growth (4:15, 16), including teaching from him (4:20, 21). The Church imitates Christ's love (5:2) and tries to learn what is pleasing to him (5:10) and to understand his will (5:17). It sings praises to him (5:19) and lives in fear of him (5:21). The Church's subordination, then, means looking to its head for his beneficial rule, living by his norms, experiencing his presence and love, receiving from him gifts that will enable growth to maturity, and responding to him in gratitude and awe. It is such attitudes that the wife is being encouraged to develop in relation to her husband. (Lincoln 1990:372; cf. O'Brien 1999:416f.)

The phrase 'in everything' (v. 24) prohibits us from understanding Paul to mean some carefully circumscribed submission, restricted to one sphere of life alone. He is not speaking about uncontrolled or unguarded submission, as if he meant the husband's authority to override the authority of God.[66] This

---

66. Fiorenza 1983:269 interprets this phrase to mean that 'the submission of the wife to her husband is on a par with her religious submission to Christ'. This is not what Paul says.

would be a caricature of the apostle's teaching. Rather, he envisages the wife's submission as being a general submissiveness extending to every area of life. This will help the couple function effectively as a coherent unity in their marriage (O'Brien 1999:417f.). They are not a pair of barrack-room lawyers arguing the precise categories or subdivisions of life in which headship does or does not apply; they are 'one flesh' partners working together under one head to serve God.

What is Paul's rationale in speaking of headship and submission?
In Ephesians 5:22 Paul says the submission of the wives to their husbands is 'as to the Lord' (*hōs tō kyriō*). In Colossians 3:18 it is 'as is fitting in the Lord' (*hōs anēken en kyriō*). What do these mean? In particular, does he command wifely submissiveness *only* because this was respectable behaviour for married women in their culture (which it was)?

The apostles did have a strong concern for the good repute of the Christian churches in contemporary society.[67] The behaviour of believers was to bring honour not shame on the gospel. In 1 Peter 2:12, just before the section on submissions (treated below), Peter writes, 'Conduct yourselves honourably among the Gentiles, *so that* [*hina*], though they malign you as evil-doers, they may see your honourable deeds and glorify God when he comes to judge' (my italics). When it comes to the judgment, even their most malicious critics will have to admit that their lives were free from shame and scandal (cf. 1 Pet. 3:15f.). And in Titus 2:4f. the behaviour of the wives, including their submissiveness to their husbands, is '*so that* [*hina*] the word of God may not be discredited' (my italics).

There are, however, two ways to interpret this motivation. They might privately have deplored the cultural norm of patriarchy and enjoined submissiveness reluctantly for the purposes of mission, hoping that in due course patriarchy would be abolished; or they might have wished to affirm (albeit in a modified form) something of this cultural pattern as being in harmony with the created order.

Following the former approach, Perriman suggests that 'the subordinate condition of the woman is more an accepted social reality than an express apostolic regulation' (Perriman 1998:55). What Paul means is that, since wives have to submit anyway (this is expected from them in their culture), they ought to do so 'as to the Lord' so that their submission is transformed from a demeaning and debasing experience forced upon them by a patriarchal

---

67. Cf. Jewish diaspora apologetic by Josephus, who likewise argued that Judaism was not subversive of the ethics of proper subordination in society (Lincoln 1990:358).

society to one in which their freedom in Christ is expressed by the dignity of voluntary and uncoerced submission. But, he assumes, Paul would rather society had not expected this submission in the first place: 'He is not teaching them to be subordinate but how to deal with the subordination that society generally expected of them.' The ideal is equality, and the apparently patriarchal teachings in the New Testament are the apostles modifying and ameliorating patriarchy by bringing it into the sphere of being 'in Christ'; they are introducing Christian teaching to make the best of a disorder (Perriman 1998:52f.).

This approach is appealing in an egalitarian culture, but it faces an enormous exegetical problem. Paul develops the patriarchal theme in Ephesians with considerable warmth and passion along lines suggested to him by the long Old Testament theme of the marriage of the Lord to his people his bride (this development in marked contrast to slavery, where the New Testament writers offer no such theological rationale). Best ignores this wider scriptural theme when he says, 'No logical reason dictates the drawing of a parallel between the relationship of Christ and the church and that of husband and wife' (Best 1998:559). He claims that Christ could equally have been portrayed as wife with the church as husband, and that the only reason the writer puts it this way is that he lived in a patriarchal culture (and the grammatical convenience that *ekklēsia* is feminine). On the contrary, there is a deeply scriptural and theological reason. This motif of the divine marriage is central to the grand story of the Bible; it is not an occasional or *ad hoc* argument produced to make a particular point in a specific situation. This theological motif strongly suggests that when Paul speaks of the submission of wives to husbands he does so, not with hesitation or regret, but because he understands that this theme ties the marriage relationship on earth to the great drama of salvation. The reason submission is 'fitting in the Lord' (Col. 3:18) is not simply that this will prevent the gospel being brought into disrepute in a patriarchal society, but that it is rooted in the good created order. Paul says that patriarchy in any culture is a distorted expression of a good and beneficial patriarchy; he does not reject all patriarchy.

If we jettison this teaching as merely culturally determined, we lose the most powerful and passionate argument in all of Scripture that speaks to counter the endemic sin of men's cruelty and injustice in the treatment of their wives. If we lose verses 22–24, we lose also verses 25–33: 'Theologically, we are not free to retain a supposedly exalted view of Christian marriage with its loving service, commitment, trust, and growth, on the one hand, and to jettison hierarchical patterns of submission or subordination, on the other' (O'Brien 1999:408). Verses 22–24 are a vital but easily misunderstood teaching which ought never to be heard apart from verses 25–33.

Ephesians 5:25: husbands — what they are to do

[25] Husbands, love your wives . . .
(Colossians 3:19, Husbands, love your wives and never treat them harshly.)

Forty words have been addressed to wives, but now 115 to husbands (O'Brien 1999:409). In Graeco-Roman culture it was not new to teach that wives ought to submit to their husbands. Paul's hearers would probably expect him to go on to tell husbands to keep their wives in submission. He pointedly does not do so (O'Brien 1999:419; Best 1998:540).

The connection with the divine marriage has implications for both wife and husband. For the husband, it immediately invites the question of how the Lord relates to his people. The answer from beginning to end of Scripture is that he relates to them in sacrificial love and gentleness.

In Colossians 3:19 Paul does not develop the theme; he is content with his pointed command that husbands not be harsh to their wives (*mē pikrainesthe pros autas*). Pastorally there is much need for this command, for male harshness and unkindness is endemic in marriage and its detrimental effect on the self-esteem of wives is a source of great pain.

In Ephesians 5 Paul dwells on Christ's marriage to show how husbands are to love, the end to which they are to love, and the underlying rationale, why they are to love.

Ephesians 5:25–28: husbands — how and to what end they are to do this (1) as Christ loved the church

[25] Husbands, love your wives,
just as [*kathōs kai*] Christ loved the church and gave himself up for her,
   [26] *in order to* [*hina*] make her holy by cleansing her with the washing of water by the word,
   [27] *so as to* [*hina*] present the church to himself in splendour, without a spot or wrinkle or anything of the kind –
   yes, *so that* [*hina*] she may be holy and without blemish.
[28] In the same way [*houtōs*], husbands should love their wives . . .

The first explanation of the manner in which husbands should love their wives is in verse 25: they should love them 'just as Christ loved the church and gave himself up for her'. The love of husband for wife is to be modelled on the cross. It is to be self-sacrificial love and not the self-serving enjoyment of some misguided concept of privilege. Christian headship in marriage is marriage in the shape of the cross; most contemporary debate misses this central point. For Christ to be head of the church was not a cheap or comfortable calling; it involved crucifixion.

C. S. Lewis writes of the husband's headship,

> This headship, then, is most fully embodied not in the husband we should all wish to be but in him whose marriage is most like a crucifixion; whose wife receives most and gives least, is most unworthy of him, is – in her own mere nature – least lovable . . . The chrism of this terrible coronation is to be seen not in the joys of any man's marriage but in its sorrows, in the sickness and sufferings of a good wife or the faults of a bad one, in his unwearying (never paraded) care or his inexhaustible forgiveness.

Lewis speaks poetically of the 'crowns' given to the man in pagan marriage (which is vacuous and empty) and in Christian marriage.

> The sternest feminist need not grudge my sex the crown offered to it either in the Pagan or the Christian mystery. For the one is of paper and the other of thorns. The real danger is not that husbands may grasp the latter too eagerly; but that they will allow or compel their wives to usurp it.
> (Lewis 1960:97f.)

The major thrust in Ephesians 5:22–33 is the challenge to husbands. Paul's hearers would have been surprised by this. The women would not have been surprised by verses 22–24 (there would have been no sharp intakes of breath when it was read in church, although they might have wondered what was coming next when they heard 'the body of which he is the Saviour'), but the men (or at least the newly converted) would have reacted in amazement at verses 25–33.

> After the exhortation to wives to submit . . . what might well have been expected by contemporary readers would be an exhortation to husbands to rule their wives. It was not unknown outside the New Testament for a husband to be enjoined to love his wife; but it was rare.
> (Lincoln 1990:373f.)

Paul goes on to the goal of Christ's headship over the church. Three times in verse 26f. he uses *hina* (in order that) to express the purpose of the cross. The Lord Jesus Christ died in order that he might make his church holy, washed, cleansed, perfected in sinless beauty so that on her wedding day (probably a reference to the parousia, O'Brien 1999:424f.) he might be able to enjoy her with no trace of aversion but only joy and delight (cf. 2 Cor. 11:2).[68]

---

68. Lincoln 1990:375 (cf. O'Brien 1999:422–424) points to the background of 'washing' both in baptism and in the traditions of a bride having a ceremonial prenuptial bath (cf. the ideas both of washing and of fine clothing in Ezek. 16:1–14).

While verse 26f. may be an aside by Paul unrelated to human marriage (Witherington 1988:54f.), the fact that in verse 28 he goes straight on to, 'In the same way [*houtōs*]' suggests that the command to husbands relates not only to the manner of their headship (sacrificial) but to its purpose. The most natural way in which this theme of purpose may be taken over into a Christian marriage is that the husband takes upon himself the goal of being such a husband whose love will lead his wife into growth in personal and spiritual maturity (for there is no dichotomy between these two), so that his great aim in marriage is not his self-fulfilment but the blossoming of his wife. 'Husbands should be utterly committed to the total well-being, especially the spiritual welfare, of their wives' (O'Brien 1999:422–424). This might sound a little self-righteous, as if he from his Olympian spiritual height can raise up his wife to his level; it is in fact deeply humbling. No husband can take this responsibility seriously without himself being deeply conscious of his own need for cleansing, holiness and growth in grace.

At this point Paul moves from looking ahead (sacrificial love with a view to growth in spiritual maturity) to looking back. If the path ahead for the thinking husband appears too hard a road, he needs some encouragement to persevere.

Ephesians 5:28–33a: husbands – how and for what reason they are to do this (2) as their own bodies because they are one flesh

[28] In the same way, husbands should [*opheilousin*] love their wives as they do their own bodies. He who loves his wife loves himself.

[29] For no one ever hates his own body [*sarx*], but he nourishes [*ektrephei*] and tenderly cares [*thalpei*] for it, just as Christ does for the church, [30]because we are members of his body.

[31] 'For this reason a man will leave his father and mother and be joined to his wife, and the two will become one flesh' [quoting Gen. 2:24 LXX].[69]

[32] This is a great mystery, and I am applying it to Christ and the church [*egō de legō eis Christon kai eis tēn ekklēsian*].

[33] Each of you, however, should love his wife as himself.

(cf. Lev. 19:18; Lincoln 1990:361)

If the first answer to the question, 'How should husbands love their wives?' was 'as Christ loved the church', the second is 'as they do their own bodies'.

---

69. There are two insignificant deviations from LXX: *anti toutou* replaces *heneken toutou* to translate 'for this reason'; and Paul omits *autou* ('his') after 'father' and 'mother'.

This carries with it a motivation. A husband should love his wife as he loves his own body; just as no-one (normally)[70] hates his own flesh but rather nourishes and cares for it, so should a husband love his wife. To 'nourish' (*ektrephein*) is also used (in 6:4) of the care of children, and to care tenderly (*thalpein*, 'to cherish') in 1 Thessalonians 2:7 of a nurse's loving care of children.

The theological truth is that the believers are members of Christ's body (v. 30); the ethical truth is that husband and wife are one flesh (v. 31; Gen. 2:24). Christ nourishes and tenderly cares for his church, because (*hoti*) we are members of his body. For the same reason the husband ought to love his wife as himself, for she is one flesh with him (flesh, *sarx*, being used interchangeably here with body, *sōma*, as indicated by the use of *sarx* in v. 29a, translated 'body' in NRSV).[71]

The well-being of the one is intimately connected with the well-being of the other. When the church hurts, Christ her head hurts; when the church grows in grace, Christ rejoices. In the same way, when the wife hurts, her husband hurts; when the wife is blessed, the husband is blessed. And although it is true that wives need to be taught to love their husbands (Titus 2:4), it is perhaps even more true pastorally that husbands need to be taught to love their wives.

What does Paul mean when he describes 'this mystery' as 'great' (v. 32)? The usual meaning for *mystērion* (mystery) in Ephesians (in its other five occurrences, 1:9; 3:3, 4, 9; 6:19) is the great purpose of God which was once hidden but has now been revealed, the union of Jew and Gentile believer in Christ. The emphasis is on the profundity of the mystery (as wonderful) rather than on its impenetrability. Probably this same meaning is in view here, focusing especially on the depth and intimacy of the union between Christ and the church (Lincoln 1990:380f.). Genesis 2:24 is quoted to lay emphasis on the wonder of the 'one flesh' union (and not because there is some mystical analog in the Godhead to the man leaving his mother and father, O'Brien 1999:430, n.283).

The Vulgate translated *mystērion* as *sacramentum*, from which developed the idea that human marriage is a sacrament of the church conveying grace to husband and wife. However, the meaning of *sacramentum* changed significantly in the process (Atkinson 1979:42f.). In Ephesians 5 it is the union of Christ and the church rather than human marriage that is described as a *mystērion*, as Paul

---

70. O'Brien 1999:427, 'Although some eccentrics have engaged in self-mutilation, and ascetics have sometimes regarded it as meritorious to make their bodies uncomfortable, people generally do not act in this way.'

71. Lincoln 1990:354, 378, who notes the same interchangeability of use in 1 Cor. 6:16.

makes clear when he goes on to say that he is speaking (literally, not 'applying') at this point of Christ and the church (O'Brien 1999:430f.).

O'Brien (1999:432–435) argues that, given the use of Genesis 2:24 and the major thrust of the passage towards human marriage, the 'mystery' is not just the divine marriage but the fact that the relation of Christ to the church may be spoken of as a marriage and *therefore used typologically of human marriage*. It is neither the divine marriage on its own nor human marriage on its own, but the startling use of the former to illuminate the latter that constitutes the 'mystery' (cf. Best 1998:557).

It is sometimes claimed that verse 32 means that Paul's main aim is to teach us about the relation of Christ to the church. But when Paul says, literally, 'I am speaking concerning Christ and concerning the church,'[72] this does not mean Paul's whole purpose is to teach us about Christ and the church. The main thrust of the passage is to persuade husbands and wives in marriages to behave rightly towards one another. Paul uses Christ's marriage as a means of teaching us about human marriage rather than vice versa.

In verse 33a *plēn* (however) rounds off the discussion ('in any case', 'now', O'Brien 1999:435, n.307) and brings his readers back to the main point in hand, which is that the husband should love his wife as himself. The appeal is emphatically individual (Best 1998:558), to stress the moral obligation of *each* husband (and presumably each wife) before God to respond to this teaching.

The similarity of this command to Leviticus 19:18 was first noticed by Jerome. As Best wisely comments, however, it needs to be treated with great care. The way in which a husband loves his wife (who is one flesh with him) is quite different from the way he loves his neighbour in general (and in particular his neighbour's wife!) (Best 1998:558).

Ephesians 5:33b: wives – final reminder

and a wife should[73] respect [*phobētai*] her husband.

Both sides of the headship-submission relation must be heard together; so Paul ends with a final reminder to wives, using the strong word *phobeomai*. Literally this means 'to fear'; in this context it has the sense of submissive respect. It links back to the general reference in verse 21 to submission being 'in the fear of Christ', suggesting that whatever the fear of the husband means, it is conditioned, qualified and governed by the fear of Christ.

---

72. *legō eis Christon kai eis tēn ekklēsian.* For the idiom '*eis* + acc.' to mean 'concerning' see Acts 2:25. NRSV 'applying . . . to' is misleading here.

73. A rare New Testament use of *hina* in an imperative sense (see O'Brien 1999:436, n.313).

We have in Ephesians 5 an incomparably beautiful pattern of married relationship. Neither male chauvinist patriarchy nor secular feminist egalitarianism can approach this pattern for beauty or blessing. It is a pattern which challenges all our presuppositions of how marriage ought to be.

1 Peter 3:1–7

The beautiful picture of the husband's love in Ephesians 5 invites the objection of countless women down the ages that the men in their lives have not behaved like this; it is for them an unrecognizable portrait of a man, a cruel delusion to set against the harsh reality of their shattered experience. What is a woman to do if her man does not behave towards her remotely as Christ does to his beloved church? Ought she still to be submissive?

Here in 1 Peter we have a powerful address to Christian believers under pressure. In 1 Peter 2:13–3:7 Peter addresses some of the same ordered relationships that Paul treats in his household codes, with the addition of the civil authorities (treated separately by Paul in Rom. 13), omitting children and parents, and with no separate address to masters.

Peter considers these relations specifically in the context of injustice. He knows that for his readers submission may be to a harsh master or an unbelieving husband (not addressed in Eph. 5 or Col. 3, but cf. 1 Cor. 7:12–16). Just as Christian headship is modelled on the cross, so Christian submission is to walk in the way of the cross. Both headship (expressed in sacrifice) and submissiveness (to unjust authority) are expressions of the way of the cross. This is particularly so for the slaves with harsh masters, who suffer for doing right and whose demeanour is to be modelled on the innocent suffering of Jesus on the cross (2:21–23). It is still in the background when Peter addresses the wives.

1 Peter 3:1–2: submission and its motive

[1] Wives, in the same way [homoiōs], accept the authority of your husbands [hypotassomenoi tois idiois andrasin],

so that [hina], even if some of them [ei tines] do not obey the word, they may be won over without a word [aneu logou] by their wives' conduct, [2] when they see the purity and reverence of your lives.

'In the same way' links this passage to what precedes, possibly tying in the address to wives with that to slaves (beginning at 2:18), although he uses the same word to introduce his word to husbands in verse 7. The verb *hypotassomai* is used in 2:18 and 3:1 in the form of a participle that functions as an imperative (and is translated this way in NRSV, Selwyn 1947:175; Balch 1981:97; cf.

Achtemeier 1996:209). The parallel is only partial, but just as some slavery will be to harsh masters, so some marriages will be to unbelieving husbands.

As with Ephesians 5:22 and Titus 2:5, the word *idiois* ('your' or 'your own') emphasizes that 'the subject is the marriage relationship, not women and men viewed generically' (Michaels 1988:157). 'This word delivers the passage from any charge of inculcating the "inferiority" of women to men, and shows that the subordination is one of function, within the intimate circle of the home. St Peter's teaching implies that every institution must have a head for practical purposes, and that in the home this should be the husband' (Selwyn 1947:182f.).

Peter does not tell wives to submit only to unbelieving husbands. The phrase 'even if some' (*ei tines*) shows that there are some believing husbands in the churches to which Peter writes (for Peter expects some to heed v. 7). And the 'holy women' of verse 5f. were not married to unbelieving husbands; at least Sarah was not (Selwyn 1947:183, 435; Michaels 1988:164f.; against Achtemeier 1996).[74] None the less, Peter has unbelieving husbands particularly in mind at the beginning of the passage. The husband who does not obey the word may be one who actively opposes belief (including the belief of his wife). The verb *apeithō* (to disobey) has this hostile sense in Acts 14:2; 19:9 and Romans 15:31, and against a social background in which 'a wife was expected to accept the customs and religious rites of her husband', this seems likely (Balch 1981:99; Achtemeier 1996:210, n.60).

The purpose of wifely submission when the husband is not a believer is that those who do not obey the word (i.e. the gospel) may be won over (i.e. converted)[75] without a word. This is not a reference to the silent wife, but rather to the wife whose main instrument in winning her husband to the faith is her conduct rather than nagging preaching of the word at home (Achtemeier 1996:210).

Her life is to be characterized by 'purity and reverence' (*tēn en phobō hagnēn anastrophēn hymōn*, 'your pure reverential way of life' – the phrase *en phobō* is virtually an adjective since *phobos* has no cognate adjective with the meaning reverent, Michaels 1988:158). Since purity is a virtue (broader than 'chastity') with reference to God, and reverence is so closely associated with it here, it seems

---

74. Achtemeier 1996 (though he recognizes that there are Christian husbands in these churches) claims the passage 'intends to say nothing about the subordination of women to men in general, nor even within Christian Marriage' (p. 208). The former statement may be true (it is about marriage not more general relations); the latter is not. Achtemeier's reference to 1 Cor. 7:4 does not prove the total equality he claims.

75. The verb *kerdainō* is used of winning (or winning back) in a spiritual sense in Matt. 18:15 and 1 Cor. 9:19–22 (Selwyn 1947:183; Achtemeier 1996:210, n.66).

certain that the reverence is not towards the husband (since fear of the husband is spoken against in v. 6) but towards God (the sense it has also in 1:17; 2:18; Selwyn 1947:183; Achtemeier 1996:210; Michaels 1988:158). She does not revere her husband; she submits to her husband and reveres God. The wife may submit to her husband even if he is an unbeliever, but her primary obligation is to be pure and fear the Lord. This provides a control to the concept of submission in marriage.

Reverence to God was important if the husband insisted that the wife follow the same gods as him, and forbade her from following Jesus Christ. Plutarch certainly thought the wife should worship only the gods in which her husband believed (Achtemeier 1996:207, n.35; 211, n.75). For her life to be marked by purity and reverence towards God would inevitably place a limit on her submission to her husband.

Peter then gives an illustration and contemporary application of one dimension of submission.

1 Peter 3:3–4: submission and its manner

> [3] Do not adorn yourselves outwardly by braiding your hair, and by wearing gold ornaments or fine clothing;
> [4] rather, let your adornment be the inner self with the lasting beauty of a gentle and quiet spirit, which is very precious in God's sight.

They are not to have the outward adornment (*tēn exōthen . . . kosmos*) but rather the hidden or inner self (*ho kruptos . . . anthrōpos*). There is no doubt a cultural background to this (Achtemeier 1996:211f.; Balch 1981:101f.). The outwardly 'showy' hairdo and dress alluded to in verse 3 (cf. 1 Tim. 2:9;[76] also often among Jewish and Graeco-Roman writers, Selwyn 1947:183f.; Michaels 1988:159f.) was an expression not only of godless luxury but here specifically of wives expressing their independence of their husbands and their rights to self-expression, perhaps even sexual freedom as well (Michaels 1988:164).

Instead they are to have 'the lasting [*aphtharton*, imperishable, by contrast with physical beauty] beauty of a gentle and quiet spirit, which is very precious in God's sight'. Because they fear God they are to value what God values, to account precious what is precious in his sight, which is a gentle and quiet spirit. The contrast seems to be with the noisily assertive independence epitomized by the dress and hairdo of verse 3.

---

76. There are several points of contact between 1 Tim. 2:8–15 and this passage (Selwyn 1947:434); cf. the satire of Is. 3:18–24.

1 Peter 3:5–6: submission exemplified

> [5] It was in this way long ago that the holy women who hoped in God used to adorn themselves by accepting the authority of their husbands [*hypotassomenai tois idiois andrasin*, echoing v. 1].
>
>   [6] Thus Sarah obeyed Abraham and called him lord. You have become her daughters as long as you do what is good and never let fears alarm you.

This argument is more than just an illustration, as is commonly supposed. It begins with 'for' (*gar*, not translated in NRSV) and supports verses 1–4 as an argument from spiritual pedigree, analogous in some ways to the pedigree of the suffering righteous used by Jesus in Matthew 23. The phrase 'holy women' is unique in the New Testament; its meaning appears to be those women who, by their evident hope in God (as the characteristic orientation of their lives) were most clearly in the spiritual line of Sarah (perhaps particularly Sarah, Rebecca, Rachel and Leah, Michaels 1988:164). To be a daughter[77] of Sarah is the female equivalent of being a 'son' of Abraham; it is to be a child 'by spiritual likeness and descent' (Selwyn 1947:185), to show the family likeness of an authentic woman member of the people of God (cf. Luke 13:16). This is a line of women characterized by setting their hope on God ('hoped in God' translates the imperfect participle *elpizousai*, suggesting this was their habitual or characteristic attitude). Because they set their hope in God and feared God, they submitted to their husbands.

Going back to the beginning of the people of God (Sarah is not a randomly chosen example, cf. Is. 51:2), Sarah obeyed (*hypēkousen*) Abraham. Although submission (*hypotassomai*) and obedience (*hypakouō*) are not identical, their meanings overlap and it seems that Peter considers them virtually synonymous in this context. When Peter says that Sarah called Abraham 'lord' (*kyrios*), he is probably alluding to Genesis 18:12 LXX (where she refers to Abraham as *ho . . . kurios mou*) (Achtemeier 1996:215 and n.141). Peter takes this use of the title as illustrative of Sarah's general attitude of obedience; he is not here interested in the particular context, in which Sarah is sceptical about the angelic promise of a son, having a 'lord' who is so old (Michaels 1988:165)!

Although Achetmeier claims that 'The "holy women" function . . . not so much as models of moral behaviour to be imitated as examples of women who have followed the path here described' (Achtemeier 1996:214), the

---

77. The word is *tekna* (children) but in this context clearly means female children. In another context (Gal. 4:21 – 5:1) Paul can speak of the whole church having Sarah for its mother.

distinction is unduly nice; Peter presumably hopes the wives among his readers will model themselves on the example of these 'holy women'.

At the end of the verse Peter writes (literally), 'of whom [i.e. Sarah] you became children doing good [*present participle*] and not fearing [*present participle*] any terror'.[78] The past tense, 'became' (*egenēthēte*), with the present participles (doing good, not fearing) tell against these participles being conditional ('if you do good . . .') (Achtemeier 1996:216; Michaels 1988:166); rather, they enlarge on the characteristic behaviour of Sarah's spiritual daughters.

But why does Peter mention the absence of fear at this point? It may be that the unbelieving husbands were making life very difficult, even frightening, for their Christian wives. Perhaps they were trying to prevent them practising their new-found faith. Achtemeier writes of 'a husband who may use fear and intimidation in the attempt to compel activity inappropriate for her as a Christian' (Achtemeier 1996:217). If this is so, Peter may be stressing that the only proper object of fear is God. They are to give proper Christian submission to their husbands, but they are to fear God alone (cf. Matt. 10:28). It is important that Christian submission (in whatever context) is motivated not by fear of the one to whom we submit, but rather by the fear of God. This is profoundly subversive of tyrannical oppression in any context (indeed, it contains within itself the seeds of the destruction of slavery). It subverts the tyrannical abuse of male authority in a marriage. The tyrant always wants to *force* submission upon his subjects, and when a subject submits, not out of fear of the tyrant, but voluntarily out of the fear of God, this draws the sting of tyranny and uncomfortably reminds the tyrant that he would have no power unless it had been given him from above.

1 Peter 3:7: to the husband

> [7] Husbands, in the same way [*homoiōs*], show consideration for your wives in your life together, paying honour to the woman as the weaker sex, since they too are also heirs of the gracious gift of life – so that nothing may hinder your prayers.

---

78. *mē phoboumenai mēdemian ptoēsin.* The noun *ptoēsis* may mean (actively) intimidation or (passively) fear or terror (BAGD). The phrase may echo Prov. 3:25 LXX (so Selwyn 1947:185, 435; Achtemeier 1996:216; Michaels 1988:167); this reads, *kai ou phobēthēsē ptoēsin epelthousan oude hormas asebōn eperchomenas* ('And do not fear terror coming nor the storm coming to the wicked'), although the verbal parallel is not strong. If this is the background the idea may be that in their purity and righteousness these Christian wives may be confident in their ultimate security, no matter how badly they may be treated by their husbands.

Because Peter's major emphasis has been on the oppressed (the slave of the harsh master, the wife of the non-Christian husband), he has devoted more space to the wife (in contrast to Paul in Eph. 5). But he adds a vital verse addressed to any husband who will listen.[79] Presumably this excludes most of those who currently will not obey the word (v. 2). Achtemeier (1996:208f.) sees here the egalitarianism of Christian marriage contrasted with the regrettable subordinationism of a mixed marriage. The only reason, according to him, for the wife in a mixed marriage to be submissive is to minimize conflict. This reading ignores the 'if some . . .' (*ei tines*) of verse 1, with its clear implication that what follows is not only for mixed marriages; and it shows no consideration for the harmony of Scripture, and in particular Ephesians 5. This verse is Peter's equivalent to Paul's commands to the Christian husbands in Colossians 3 and Ephesians 5.

The phrase translated 'for your wives' is *tō gynaikeiō*; *gynaikeia* in normal use is an adjective meaning 'feminine, pertaining to women'. Here it is used substantivally in place of the noun *gynē*. Achtemeier (1996:217) suggests that this 'points to a wider meaning and probably refers to the way males in a household deal with its female members, including of course the man's wife but not limited to her'. The usual meaning of *synoikeō* (live together), however, is both social and sexual cohabitation (Michaels 1988:168), which suggests that the reference continues to be to husbands with their wives, although the word may point to the way a man needs to relate to his wife specifically *as a woman*, taking account of the difference of sex.

'Show consideration for . . .' (*synoikountes kata gnōsin*) is literally 'living together with, according to knowledge'. The knowledge may be an understanding of the nature (and in particular the vulnerabilities and weaknesses) of the wife, hence 'show consideration for . . .'; this is probably the sense in which 'knowledge' is used in 2 Corinthians 6:6 and 2 Peter 1:5, what Selwyn calls 'practical understanding and tact' which 'calls for . . . such instruction for Christian marriage as is contained in much modern literature on the subject' (Selwyn 1947:186). '"Living with a woman" is not a mere physical function but something a man must *know how to do*' (Michaels 1988:168). Alternatively, the phrase 'according to knowledge' may refer to the knowledge of God, so that the husband is to live together with his wife as one who knows, and lives by the knowledge of, God (Achtemeier 1996:218).

He is to pay honour to his wife, to treat her with dignity as a person of

---

79. It has been suggested (Michaels 1988:169) that, balancing vv. 1–6, this addresses primarily Christian husbands of non-Christian wives. But there is no indication in v. 7 of such a limited focus and the reference to 'fellow heirs' tells against it.

value and weight in the sight of God, 'as the weaker sex' (*hōs asthenesterō skeuei*, as to the weaker vessel). The word *skeuos* (vessel) is used of both men and women elsewhere (1 Thess. 4:4; 2 Cor. 4:7; Acts 9:15); with the imagery of pottery it can emphasize vulnerability and this seems to be the sense here. The husband is to remember the relative weakness of his wife at the most simple and uncontroversial level of her physical constitution (Achtemeier 1996:217). Peter cannot be speaking of her lesser wisdom, since the Christian wife of a non-Christian husband (who is foolish enough not to obey the word) is wiser than her husband. That women in general are physically less strong than men in general is widely understood. Even in an egalitarian age they compete separately in most sporting events. As Selwyn commented in 1947, this description of women 'cannot be held to apply to character or to ability, nor is it true of health or physical endurance without many reservations. And yet the Apostle's phrase answers to some deep-seated truth which both sexes alike still agree to recognize' (Selwyn 1947:187).

The husband is to remember that his Christian wife is a fellow heir (*synklēronomos*) with him of the gracious gift of life. He is to treat her as such. The implication of the end of the verse is that the husband who does not treat his wife with honour, as a fellow heir of the gift of life, will place an insuperable obstacle in the way of his or their prayers. 'For the Christian man to ignore [this verse] is to have God ignore him' (Achtemeier 1996:209). The prayers may be those of the husband (since Peter is addressing them in this verse), or those of husband and wife together (as joint heirs of life; cf. 1 Cor. 7:5). On the former reading, it is the disobedience of the husband which inhibits his prayers; on the latter, it is the loss of unity in the marriage that weakens their joint prayers. Either would be true.

To warn of hindered prayer is to make the command of verse 7 as forceful as possible. For God not to listen to prayer is supremely serious. But Achtemeier is inaccurate when he writes, 'The point is clear: men who transfer cultural notions about the superiority of men over women into the Christian community lose their ability to communicate with God' (Achtemeier 1996:218). This is not what Peter says. He says that a husband ought to live together with his wife 'according to knowledge' (considerately and/or conscious of God), treating her with honour as the weaker sex and as a fellow heir of the gracious gift of life. The point is not whether the husband has some particular understanding of 'superiority' or 'inferiority' or 'equality' (all of which are bandied about much too loosely), but rather how he *behaves* towards his wife. The question is not the abstract one, 'How does he *think* of her?' but the concrete one, 'Does he *honour* her?' The words 'honour' and 'fellow heir' are strong indicators that in the thinking of Peter submission is entirely consistent with equality of value and worth in the sight of God.

In conclusion, some more general points about submission are worth making. Some of these could have been made in connection with Ephesians 5 and Colossians 3, but they are particularly appropriate in the context of unjust authority in 1 Peter.

Christian submission is not conditional on the character of those occupying an office or entrusted with a status

God's ordering of human relationships relates to the status of the one exercising authority and not to his or her character. So, for example, we should honour our parents. This is the fifth commandment. 'Honour your father and mother, so that your days may be long in the land' (Exod. 20:12). The son or daughter is to honour his or her parents, with obedience while a child, with respect at all times, and with loving care in their old age. The commandment is not conditional on the character of the parents. They may be kind parents or cruel parents; they may be fair or have favourites; they may be honourable or shameful. Fathers and mothers are to be honoured because they are fathers and mothers, even if they are bad fathers and mothers. They are to be honoured because of their position in God's order. This is not reversible: we may never say, 'Actually this is all very well, but our temperaments are such that it will be better if my parents honour me.'

The supreme example is the boy Jesus. At precisely the time when Mary and Joseph had signally failed to understand him or his calling, we read (Luke 2:51) that 'he went down with them and was obedient to them (*ēn hypotassomenos autois*)'.

It is the same with the submission of the citizen to the civil authorities (1 Pet. 2:13–17; Rom. 13:1–7), the submission of the slave to the master (1 Pet. 2:18–25) and the submission of the wife to the husband. These orderings are not conditional on character and they are not reversible.

This concept of order related to status or position is alien to contemporary thought. We usually consider that our response to an individual is to be conditioned by their character and behaviour, but we ought also to respond because of the office they hold. God has not made humankind to be disordered. The opposite of order is anarchy; societies disintegrate under the pressure of their own disorder, which is the law of the jungle, the survival of the fittest, a continual fighting for a better place in the pecking order.

Christian submission is God-centred

Submission in Scripture is at root the willingness of the penitent believer to submit to God (e.g. Jas. 4:7; Rom. 8:7; 10:3). Rebellion is the essence of sin; submission is at the heart of repentance and faith.

It follows that appropriate submission in human relationships is an expression of submission to God. In each of 1 Peter's three applications this is apparent.

1. 1 Peter 2:13, *'For the Lord's sake* accept the authority of every human institution . . .'; the believer does not submit to authority because of human compulsion but because he or she submits to the Lord, and recognizes that human authority is part of God's order.
2. 1 Peter 2:19, the slave who is ill-treated is to 'endure pain while suffering unjustly', 'being aware of God'. He submits even to an order which is far removed from God's original order, but he submits 'being aware of God'. He submits to his master not because he is forced to, but because he is conscious of God.
3. The God-centredness of submission is not so explicit in 1 Peter 3:1–6 as in Ephesians 5:22 ('as . . . to the Lord'), but there is a hint in verse 4. The 'lasting beauty of a gentle and quiet spirit . . . is *very precious in God's sight'*. The submission of this ill-treated wife is not born of necessity but because she lives her life conscious that it is lived 'in God's sight'.

Christian submission is free not forced
We have already noted that the word of God about submission in Ephesians 5 and Colossians 3 comes not to the husbands (that they should make their wives submit) but to the wives as responsible moral agents (in contrast to Aristotle, who addresses only the males, the master, the husband, the father; Balch 1981:96). The same Christian freedom is apparent in all Peter's examples of Christian submission. This is crucial; misunderstanding this is at the root of most secular feminist objections to these teachings.

Christian submission to God, and Christian submission to God's order, is free not forced. It happens when God by his Spirit writes his law in the heart of the believer so that in his or her inner being there is delight in God's law (Rom. 7:22), a desire of the heart to submit to God, and thus to place oneself in line with God's order, in society, in human relations and specifically in marriage.

Peter is very emphatic about this free response to God. 'As servants of God, live as free people, yet do not use your freedom as a pretext for evil' (1 Pet. 2:16). Submission to the civil authority is not a demeaning thing; it is the free response of the servant of God. Being set free from sin frees us to obey God. This is the context of Christian submission.

Christian freedom is a precious gift, not to be surrendered, that we become slaves of anyone (1 Cor. 7:23). Christian submission is an expression of Christian freedom and a demeanour of wonderful dignity. We are called to it whether or not those to whom we submit are worthy of our submission: we submit if they are placed in headship over us in God's order. And when sub-mission is properly fulfilled it carries with it dignity, honour, beauty and human worth. When Jesus stood before the unjust power of Pontius Pilate he had about him an awesome dignity as he said, 'You would have no power over me unless it had been given you from above' (John 19:11).

If this freedom characterizes Christian submission in general, it charac-terizes the submission of the Christian wife in particular, who even in submis-sion to a hard husband will not let fears alarm her (1 Pet. 3:6). Christian submission is the free decision of the believer who is unafraid because she knows her status and security before God.

A Christian may be called to submit in one relationship and exercise authority in another
If we say submission is demeaning we neglect this truth, which ought to be obvious on any reading of the New Testament. To take a simple example, if a woman is a wife and a mother, in the marriage relationship she is to live out appropriate submission; but also, alongside the father, she is to exercise authority and discipline over her child (e.g. in Prov., or Deut. 21:18–21). To take another example, a citizen who is also a husband and father is to live out appropriate submission to the civil authorities, and at the same time to exer-cise authority as a father and loving headship in his marriage. None of these offices, whether of submission or leadership or authority or headship, says anything about the worth of the one who occupies it.

What do headship and submission in marriage mean in practice?

Those who accept that Scripture teaches an enduring order (enduring because rooted in creation) of the husband's headship and the wife's submission must ask how this order is to be worked out in the concrete realities of married life. In so doing we must be very careful to guard against the natural desire for precise rules in areas that are governed by Christian freedom. So often when discussing these things we hear the request, 'Tell me what you think the rules ought to be,' in this regard or that in a marriage. We want to know whether in our marriages it is a simple case of 'I tell you what to do and you do it', or 'You tell me what to do and I do it', or 'We discuss and in the end the strong-est personality wins'.

Christlike headship and Christlike submission (both modelled on the cross) form a delicate and beautiful dynamic that cannot be pinned down with rules. It is the free response of the Spirit-filled believer, man and wife, to the revealed reality of marriage rooted in creation order. Man and wife both indi-vidually and together are to live under the gentle authority of God, learning to love his will and to serve him together in his world. They are partners entrusted with the task of caring for the garden. Everything about the order of marriage comes back to this 'vertical' relatedness to God and this outward-looking purpose of together joining in the task entrusted to us.

It may be helpful to identify four ways in which the proper order of marital headship can be subverted. In this way, by focusing on what it is *not*, we approach a clearer understanding of what it *is*.[80] Two of these subversions are the work of the husband, two of the wife.

a. The tyrannical husband

The pages of secular and church history and of Christian theology are filled with terrible examples of men behaving badly. Males throughout history (including the history of the church) have arrogated to themselves the prerogatives of God. In marriage this makes us domineering, insistent on our autonomous rights to make our decisions and to impose them on others (and in particular on our wives). We have patterned our leadership not on the cross but on the pagan crown of despotism, in so far as we have been able to get away with it.

Here is Barth's lively portrayal of the male tyrant.

> [The tyrant] need not be cruel or bad-tempered. There are quiet, gentle, amiable, easy-going tyrants who suit women only too well, and it is an open question in which form the male tyrant is worse and more dangerous. The distinctive character of the tyrannical ... man is that he does not serve the order (sc. God's order) but makes the order serve himself. It interests him only in so far as he falsely supposes that it confers distinction upon him and gives him an advantage over woman. He changes it into an instrument for the seizing and exerting of power in favour of his supposed masculine dignity and honour, wishes and interests. It is not for him a duty, but a need and a pleasure, to take precedence of woman. It is for him an end in itself to take advantage of her ... He preens himself, as the peacock its feathers. In his own refined or crude, convincing or ridiculous manner, he plays as best he can the part of the male.
> (Barth, *CD* III/4:178)

It cannot be emphasized too strongly that the husband's headship is never to be insisted upon or enforced, whether by physical force (for this is physical abuse) or by emotional or psychological pressure (for this also is a form of abuse). We are not to be domineering, to insist on our rights, let alone that we should have the more interesting, the less demanding or the more highly praised lives. If a

---

80. In the discussion that follows I am indebted to Barth, *CD* III/4:176–181.

husband understands the nature of Christlike headship in marriage and his wife does not share this understanding, it will be difficult for him to fulfil it. But he is not to insist that their marriage should conform to his understanding. He is to love sacrificially, to treat his wife with honour, to learn to understand and care for her. Even if she will not allow him to give a lead in other ways, he is not to seek to enforce this. He will always remember that it is God, not the husband, who calls the wife to Christian submission; it will never be his demand.

b. The compliant wife

It is sadly possible (and all too common) for a wife to cooperate with her husband's tyranny. She chooses the paradoxical security of placing herself as a passive, infinitely pliable and biddable 'doormat' under his feet. She allows his peacock behaviour to impress and please her. She becomes infinitely flexible and compliant, waiting on her tyrant's moods. She is 'his pliable kitten, his flattering mirror. In pleasing him, she thus pleases herself' (Barth, CD III/4:178).

Such a woman may live in a kind of peace with such a man, but it is a false peace. To adopt this demeanour is not consistent with the calling and dignity of woman in the Bible, for she abdicates her responsibility to be the helper of Genesis 2:18. She places herself on the level of a tame animal, who might do Adam's bidding but who could never be the helper suitable for him that he so needed for the undertaking of God's task. The positive portrayals of the virtuous wife of Proverbs 31, or of David's wife Abigail (1 Sam. 25), or of Priscilla with Aquila (Acts 18, Rom. 16) are utterly inconsistent with the wife who is passive, a mere cipher for her husband's will. To live with wisdom, dignity and energy, to be a source of wise counsel, to be a valued partner, these are God's calling to the wife.

c. The rebellious wife

We have seen that the most natural exegesis of the headship/submission texts leaves a close correlation between headship and authority (under the authority of God), even an uncomfortably close overlap of language between submission and obedience (subject to the prior obedience to God). Further, we have seen that the apostles Paul and Peter appear to see a lasting theological rationale behind a cleansed and redeemed order of the husband's headship and the wife's submission. The order supported by this rationale is not the fallen disorder of male oppression, but nor is it the all-encompassing egalitarianism of function and role which is the dogmatic orthodoxy of contemporary culture.

If this reading of the texts and their theology is correct, the Christian wife will need to decide how she will respond to this word of God. The word of God gives her the dignity and honour of being created from man and for the sake of man, to be his partner – equal in value and dignity – helping and supporting him in the task of obeying and loving God in his world. This help involves encouraging her husband to be to her a Christlike head, and it involves dignified voluntary Christian submission.

d. The abdicator husband

The most common way in which God's order is subverted in contemporary Western society is by none of the three above. Rather, it is the husband who abdicates his God-given responsibility to give Christlike sacrificial headship in his marriage. For all manner of reasons (perhaps including the pyrrhic 'victories' of secular feminism) the man fights shy of the sphere of home. Either this is no longer a place where he has a clear masculine role or responsibility, or it is a place he has responsibilities he fears and wishes to avoid, because they are so costly. So he deserts this sphere (whenever he can) for the much safer and more affirming sphere perhaps of the workplace or the sports club. He 'works' long hours not because he really has to but as an escape. In may be the workplace is the arena of *technē*, control, achievement, doing things and getting things done; in some ways this is so much simpler than the demanding home with its responsibility to love and cherish his wife 'according to knowledge' and to discipline and nurture children.

Paradoxically, it may not be the challenges of secular feminism that pose the greatest threat to God's order of marriage, but the pathetic abdications of sinful males who will not take upon ourselves our God-given responsibility to exercise headship in our marriages and our homes.

15. THE HEART OF MARRIAGE – FAITHFULNESS

Marriage is
the voluntary sexual and public social union
of one man and one woman
from different families.
This union is patterned upon the union of God with his people his bride,
the Christ with his church.
Intrinsic to this union is God's calling to lifelong exclusive sexual faithfulness.

The heart of marriage is better expressed as faithfulness than love. The word 'love' on its own is too elastic in contemporary usage to serve as the fundamental virtue of marriage. Faithfulness is the foundation, or perhaps we may say faithful love.

I have argued in Chapters 6 – 10 that the definition of marriage is arbitrary unless we first understand something of its purpose in the mind of the Creator. Once we grant that marriage *is* (it has an objective existence in the order placed in creation, see Part One), and we gain some understanding of *why* marriage is (see Part Two), then we may approach the question of *what* marriage is (its shape and its limits, see Part Three) with some hope of discerning a coherent structure. All the elements of definition we have explored in Chapters 11 – 14 are important, but to study them is like walking around the moat and walls rather than exploring the glories of the castle itself. If marriage is to serve the purposes of God in his world, then it must be at its heart a sexual relationship characterized by faithfulness, for faithful love is what

characterizes the Creator in his relationship with his world. This is the fundamental moral obligation of a husband towards his wife and a wife towards her
husband from the day they are married.

From the moment a man and a woman enter marriage God calls them
steadily and persistently to faithfulness until death tears them apart. This
unchanging divine call may be drowned out by the morally undemanding
clamour of other voices, but yet he calls. And if we who are married are to
fulfil God's purpose we must hear and heed his call, for as he calls, marriage
becomes the theatre in which faithfulness is learned, even for some the fire in
which it is forged.

There are two seminal ways in which Scripture presses home to us the
steady call to faithfulness: marriage is a covenant to which God is witness; and
marriage is a joining in which God enacts the union. We consider these before
we study the necessary but negative prohibition of adultery.

Marriage is a covenant to which God is witness

God has a marriage with his people, his bride. The redemption of the created
order is often spoken of in terms of the struggles and finally the consummation of this divine betrothal, which is often spoken of in terms of covenant.
But human marriage is also spoken of as covenant, and in particular as a covenant witnessed (and therefore buttressed) by God. The clearest explicit
example of this is Malachi 2:14.

Malachi 2:14

'. . . the LORD was a witness between you and the wife of your youth, to whom
you have been faithless, though she is your companion and your wife by covenant.' At one level a marriage is simply a human agreement or contract,
between two people or two families. 'Marriage in the Pentateuch is a contract
between two families and between two individuals. This contract was often
recorded in a document that included the financial arrangements, the stipula-
tions which could lead to divorce if the contract was broken, and the financial
arrangements in the event of divorce' (Instone Brewer 2002:19).

When Scripture describes marriage as a covenant, however, something
more is meant, for the sanctions following breach of covenant are not merely
human but divine. In marriage a man and a woman make a public agreement
(or covenant) to live together in a sexual and social union until death parts
them. To this agreement God stands witness. He is present when the covenant is made (and this has nothing to do with whether or not there is any
ecclesiastical context for the vows, for this is irrelevant). His presence at all

marriages means that he will hold each party accountable to him for the keeping of these vows. He places the whole weight of divine presence in support of the vows and in judgment on any who threaten or break them. This gives to faithfulness an inescapable dimension of ethical seriousness.

In his significant study *Marriage as a Covenant*, Gordon Hugenberger suggests that Malachi 2:14 is a 'reverse application' of the divine marriage analogy in which, 'while the marriage analogy was originally intended to elucidate Yahweh's relationship to Israel, it is now being reapplied to serve as a paradigm for marriage itself' (Hugenberger 1994:295, n.58). Not all agree that Malachi 2:14 does mean this. Malachi 2:10–16 contains an unusual concentration of textual and exegetical difficulties (see Hugenberger 1994; Fuller 1991) and we need to defend our interpretation that verse 14 speaks of human marriage as a covenant between man and wife witnessed by the Lord. (We shall also return to the passage in Chapter 13 when we consider the bearing of verse 16 on the ethics of divorce.)

Verse 14 addresses the people's complaint (v. 13) that the Lord no longer accepts their offerings with favour. When they ask why they no longer experience his blessing, the prophet answers,

> Because the LORD was a witness [*hēʿîd*]
> between you and the wife of your youth [*ʾēšet nᵉʿôrêkā*]
> to whom you have been faithless
> though she is your companion [*ḥăbertᵉkā*, from verb √*ḥbr*, to join,
>   unite][1]
> and your wife by covenant [*wᵉʾēšet bᵉrîtekā*].[2]

Since the usual meaning of 'covenant' is the Lord's covenant with his people (and therefore only applicable metaphorically to marriage), and this is the use in verse 10 ('the covenant of our ancestors'), on what basis may we claim that it refers in verse 14 to the human marriage agreement between husband and wife?

We do need to be careful. In other contexts the metaphorical and the literal intermingle in such a way as to encourage caution. For example, in Ezekiel 16 the divine husband says to the young woman 'Jerusalem' (v. 3), 'I pledged myself to you and entered into a covenant with you . . . and you became mine'

---

1. The masculine form *ḥābēr* occurs fifteen times in the Old Testament, usually meaning 'companion' or the adjective 'united to', 'associated with'. This is the only Old Testament occurrence of the feminine form. BDB suggests 'consort, i.e. wife'.

2. LXX *gynē diathēkēs sou*.

(v. 8; cf. vv. 59, 60, 62). It would be precarious to conclude from this covenant language in a metaphorical text that human marriage is also considered to be a covenant (Hugenberger 1994:302–309).

In Malachi 2:14, however, there is good reason to understand the covenant to be the human one between man and wife. If it is a metaphorical one, we meet insuperable exegetical problems. The husband is here being unfaithful, whereas in all the metaphorical uses of covenant for the divine marriage, the husband is the faithful Yahweh (and it is unthinkable in prophetic imagery to cast Yahweh as the wronged wife). Other attempts to understand covenant here metaphorically are unconvincing (outlined and answered in Hugenberger 1994: esp. 32f.).

The expression 'the wife of your youth' echoes Proverbs 5:18, where it refers to a human woman. The idea that 'wife by covenant' means that the woman was a fellow member of the covenant community (the covenant being that between Israel and the Lord) relies on understanding 'covenant' (*berît*) in a lexically forced sense (van der Woude answered by Hugenberger 1994:32f.) and neglects the indicator in verse 13 ('as well') that a new and distinct accusation is being made, over and beyond that of faithlessness to the divine covenant by intermarriage with foreigners (vv. 10–12).

It is altogether more natural to understand that Malachi teaches that human marriage is a covenant of which husband and wife are the parties and to which the Lord is witness (though not a third party to a three-way covenant, *pace* Storkey 1996:40). The judicial and moral authority of the Lord stand behind the marriage covenant. As witness, the Lord stands ready to judge anyone who breaks this covenant. The idea is paralleled in Genesis 31:50, where Laban says to Jacob about their agreement, '. . . though no one else is with us, remember that God is witness between you and me' (Hugenberger 1994:28). The burden of Malachi 2:14 is therefore that the casual readiness of the Israelite men to divorce their wives was a breach of divinely witnessed covenant and brought God's judgment on their land.

It is worth noting that it is not 'covenant' that distinguishes marriage from other human relationships in Scripture. Marriage is not defined by the concept of covenant, but rather (as we have argued) from the order of creation. In Scripture covenant is not confined to the divine marriage and human marriage. The loyal friendship between David and Jonathan (as much a political alliance as an affectionate friendship, Ackroyd 1975; Thompson 1974) is described by David in 1 Samuel 20:8 as 'a covenant of the LORD' (*berît yhwh*). Although the divine covenant expressed in the language of the divine marriage sheds light on the human covenant of marriage, it cannot be the concept of covenant *per se* which marks out human marriage from other human alliances and friendships. Furthermore, we must beware of using 'covenant' as more or less a synonym for 'interpersonal relationship', since the two concepts are distinct (Hugenberger 1994:4, n.26).

In a careful study of the vast scholarly literature surrounding the concept of covenant (*b'rît*) Hugenberger concludes, 'The predominant sense of (*b'rît*) in Biblical Hebrew is an elected, as opposed to natural, relationship of obligation established under divine sanction' (Hugenberger 1994:171). In the marriage covenant it is the divine witness and hence sanction that presses on us the call to faithfulness, and that distinguishes marriage from simply a relationship chosen by the man and the woman.

Proverbs 2:16f.

A second possible reference to human marriage as a covenant occurs in Proverbs 2:16f (see Hugenberger 1994:296–302).[3] The young man who follows wisdom,

> . . . will be saved from the loose woman ['*iššâ zārâ*],
> from the adulteress with her smooth words,
> who forsakes the partner of her youth ['*allûp n'ûrêhā*]
> and forgets her sacred covenant [lit. 'the covenant of her God'].

It is likely that the phrase 'the covenant of her God' refers here to the marriage covenant, made by the adulteress with her husband, to which God was witness. She does not simply forget the covenant of Israel with the Lord (by sin, which in her case happens to be sexual),[4] but specifically her marriage covenant with her husband (by adultery, the explicit context of the saying and putting 'forgets' in close parallel with 'forsakes'; she forsakes her husband,[5] which is to forget her marriage covenant).

That the god in mind is the true God seems clear. Although Boström argues it is her pagan deity to whom she is bound, it seems very unlikely the proverb would condemn her for breaking that kind of covenant (Hugenberger 1994:297f.).

To interpret the covenant as that of marriage also makes sense of the unusual expression 'covenant of *her* God' (*b'rît 'elōhêhā*). This draws attention

---

3. Cf. Camp 1985:235–237, 269–271, draws attention to the many similarities both of vocabulary and sentiment between Prov. 2:16f. and Mal. 2:14.

4. So, e.g. A. Cohen, referring back to the seventh commandment, and Kidner (see Hugenberger 1994:298f.)

5. Cf. similar phrases involving 'youth' used of husbands in Jer. 3:4; Prov. 5:18; Joel 1:8; Mal. 2:14f.

to something personal to her which fits her (particular) marriage better than her (shared and corporate) belonging to Israel.

The idea that 'the covenant of her God' refers to the marriage covenant as witnessed by her God (as in Mal. 2:14) is supported by other human agreements made before God in Scripture. In Ezekiel 17:16–20 Zedekiah is condemned for breaking his covenant (i.e. pledged alliance) with Nebuchadnezzar. Although Zedekiah and Nebuchadnezzar are clearly the parties to the covenant, in verse 19 the Lord describes it as '*my* covenant' (*b^erîtî*), the breach of which is 'treason . . . committed against *me*' (v. 20). In Jeremiah 34:8 Zedekiah makes a covenant with the people that they will proclaim liberty to Hebrew slaves. When they go back on this it is described by the Lord as a transgression of '*my* covenant' (v. 18). We have already seen that the covenant between David and Jonathan is called 'a covenant of Yahweh' (1 Sam. 20:8). To refer to a covenant as 'God's covenant' does not imply that God must be a party to it; rather, it reminds us that God is witness to it, so that those who break it come under his judgment. The covenant of marriage broken by the loose woman is 'the covenant of her God' because the Lord is witness.

In Proverbs 2:16f. it is the wife who breaks her marriage covenant; in Malachi 2:14 it is the husband. In both cases equally this is viewed with the utmost seriousness because the Lord is witness. The divine witness calls each married person to the strong moral obligation of lifelong exclusive faithfulness.

Marriage is a joining by God

Jesus expresses the moral obligation to faithfulness even more strongly than the texts we have just considered. He speaks of marriage as a union in which God is not merely the witness but also the agent who makes the bond. '. . . the two shall become one flesh. So they are no longer two, but one flesh. Therefore what God has joined together, let no one separate' (Mark 10:8f.; cf. Matt. 19:5f.). This is a crucial saying for the ethics of marriage. It is important for us to be clear about what it means.

Every married couple is joined by God
Probably the most profoundly wrong treatment of this theme is to be found in Barth's *Church Dogmatics* (III/4:207–213). Because Barth roots his ethics radically in the (arbitrary and absolute) command of God rather than in creation order, he understands the joining by God to be predicated on God's particular command that this shall be so for a particular couple; and therefore that when God has so commanded for a particular couple, there must (by virtue of the sovereignty of God) attach to their marriage a character of

indissolubility. 'The door (sc. out of this marriage) thus closed cannot be opened again' (*CD* III/4:207).

However, argues Barth, no couple on earth may claim that this is definitely true for their marriage, no matter how much they may hope or indeed be encouraged to think it may be so. 'By no means every human striving, coming and being together of two partners in love and marriage automatically implies and indicates that God has joined them together and that permanence and indissolubility attach to their union.' For, he claims, to believe this 'is tantamount to a conviction that in their own strength they have rendered and still render the obedience which the divine command requires' (*CD* III/4:207). Of course no couple may know this; if it is true, it will be hidden from them and neither any amount of ongoing erotic passion nor the public pledge of union in marriage nor sexual consummation can 'guarantee that they are joined together by God' (*CD* III/4:208). Indeed, in time some couples will reluctantly come to the conclusion that their marriage was not a joining by God and in some extreme cases *ought* to be dissolved, 'because it is not in the judgment of God a tenable marriage' (*CD* III/4:211). And 'what is called and has the appearance of marriage may really be no marriage' (*CD* III/4:213).

The focus of Barth on the 'inner genesis' of marriage, which is free and mutual love, means also that a relationship may grow into becoming real marriage even if it did not begin this way. 'What was not marriage can later become marriage.' Marriage 'becomes and is and remains true marriage primarily and directly in virtue of its inner genesis' (*CD* III/4:215f.).

From a very different standpoint, the liberal Protestant William Countryman uses a similar argument. Countryman regards marriage as essentially a property transaction in which there ought to be an exchange of 'goods'; these goods in our society are no longer exterior (sexual union to procreate children, property and so on) but interior (to do with the giving of subjective personhood). But, he argues, these interior goods are developed within a marriage rather than brought to it at the beginning. Therefore we may never be sure to what extent this essential personality property transaction has really taken place, for 'not every external marriage in our own experience constitutes a real marriage in the more interior sense demanded in our society'. Countryman develops what we may call a liberal Protestant doctrine of annulment: 'We must therefore be prepared to consider the possibility that what some divorces – perhaps a large percentage of them – do is not to end an existing marriage but to announce that, despite whatever efforts were made and ceremonies performed, no marriage has in fact taken place' (Countryman 1989:262).

With characteristic caution the Anglican scholar Anthony Harvey argues that the injunction not to put asunder what God has joined may mean something along the lines of, 'Don't divorce, because it *may* be that your marriage was "made in heaven" and so you take the risk of breaking up something God has joined together' (Harvey 1994:26). (One is reminded of Pascal's wager.)

Such arguments suggest that in the traditional marriage ceremony we should replace the inappropriately confident quotation of Jesus' words ('those whom God has joined let no man put asunder'), or 'I therefore declare that you are man and wife', with something like, 'I therefore pronounce that you may or may not grow into becoming man and wife and it may or may not prove in due course that you have been joined by God.' Indeed, Countryman follows this logic and suggests that the church would do better to bless unions only retrospectively when it becomes clearer that it looks like 'the real thing' (Countryman 1989:263).

These misunderstandings of the joining of God are perverse in their exegetical character and catastrophic in their pastoral consequences. In the context of the debate with the Pharisees over divorce, the moral thrust of Jesus' saying is forceful and entirely one-sided against initiating or causing divorce. 'That which God has joined *let no man put asunder.*' The force of this argument relies entirely on the necessity that a married couple may know by virtue of being married that they are joined by God and therefore that they have a strong moral obligation not to separate.

This obligation only makes sense if (a) they may objectively know that they have been joined by God, and (b) they understand that it is possible but impermissible for either of them to break their marriage. Were it impossible, there would be no need for the moral injunction not to do this. The tragedy and paradox of marriage is precisely that in his sovereignty God joins in such a way that human beings can break, though they may not do so.

It is necessary for the integrity and force of Jesus' argument with the Pharisees that marriage should be an objective visible and verifiable joining by God, that when a couple are validly married the reality of God's joining does not depend on some hidden and mystical obedience of the will but on their public pledge. The moment we allow Barth's argument to hold sway we pull the rug from under Jesus' feet, for naturally those who contemplate divorce will persuade themselves that in their particular marriages there was no joining by God.

What Barth has done is to bring back in by the subjective experiential back door the abuse of nullity that the Reformers so vigorously expelled by the front. Whereas in the late Middle Ages a person seeking to divorce his or her spouse sought grounds for nullity, to prove that they were never 'really' married, now the Barthian seeking to divorce claims interior grounds that they were never 'really' married. And just as the medieval church allowed (re)marriage under the name of marriage after nullification of a previous marriage, so Barth advocates (re)marriage after the spiritual annulment of a previous marriage (*CD* III/4:213). This point is recognized by Thatcher (1999:34–37), who none the less explicitly views marriage as a process in which indissolubility may gradually be conferred, whatever that might mean (Thatcher 1999:279–285).

The traditional understanding relies on the barriers to valid marriage being in principle objective, not subjective, and therefore verifiable rather than known only to God. The fear that a marriage will be annulled ought only to be the fear that some previously hidden barrier may come to light (such as an existing marriage). To allow one partner to claim retrospectively that the quality of relationship shows it is not a 'real' marriage introduces into marriage a terrible instability. For Jesus' saying to have the moral force he intended, it must be possible for a married couple to know that simply by virtue of being validly married they are joined together by God.

The 'one flesh' union means marriage (no more, no less)

The contention above that God joins *all* married couples is often disputed in the context of discussion about what 'one flesh' union means. The simplest and most exegetically sound answer is that it means quite simply what marriage means, which is what Genesis 2:24 suggests and Paul clearly assumes when he quotes this in Ephesians 5:31. 'One flesh' is neither less than marriage in its essential meaning, nor is it more than marriage (such that a marriage merely strives towards it as a goal).

One flesh is a public family bond

In our study of incest (Chapter 13) we rejected the view that Leviticus 18 implies that ties of affinity are strictly on a par with ties of kinship, that marriage creates a tie as unbreakable as one of blood. We must recognize, however, that the language of 'one flesh' in Scripture strongly suggests a bond which is public and familial, and therefore *comparable* to ties of blood. It is the creation not merely of a sexual union but also of a public social unit. A new family unit is created by marriage. The Hebrew word 'flesh' (*bāśār*) is also used for a clan or family group (Skinner 1930:70). It is used in Genesis 29:14; 37:27; 2 Samuel 5:1 and Isaiah 58:7 of family belonging and loyalty. Gordon Hugenberger argues persuasively that 'one flesh' in Genesis 2 speaks of the creation of a new family (Hugenberger 1994:162f.).

In view of this we must also conclude the following.

One flesh is more than sexual intercourse (though it is not less)

The strongly physical and bodily context of Genesis 2:18–25 would make it very odd to interpret 'one flesh' as anything less than sexual intercourse

(Gundry 1976:64). Paul's reference to 'one flesh' in the context of the men of Corinth going to prostitutes is entirely in accord with this (1 Cor. 6:16).

We cannot accept, however, that 'one flesh' refers to sexual union alone. Rather, the context of leaving parents in Genesis 2:24 together with the associations of 'flesh' with family bonds (noted above) strongly suggest a union which is both sexual and public. The fact that Paul wants the men of Corinth to break off their prostitute unions rather than maintain them (as might be expected if they were indissoluble) suggests that there is something contradictory about a sexual union that is not marriage. It flies in the face of the order of creation, which is why his reference to Genesis 2 is so pertinent.

One flesh is less than 'full personal union'

If we must not allow 'one flesh' to be devalued into *just* sex, neither must we allow it to be falsely inflated into a union which goes beyond the institution and status of marriage. For, in a characteristically modern way of thought, 'one flesh' is sometimes referred to the idea that sexual union is (or ought to be) 'full' or 'total' personal union.

Since we have already argued that 'one flesh' goes beyond sex and takes in a public social union, we may readily agree with all who stress the personal nature of proper sexual union. Human sex is more than the satiation of an impersonal animal appetite. In the language of the Greek loves, Eros involves interpersonal desire and 'personalises appetite' (Meilander 1995:74). In his secular defence of traditional sexual ethics Roger Scruton argues cogently that interpersonal intentionality is intrinsic to *all* sexual union (Scruton 1986: chs. 2 and 4). We must distinguish undifferentiated sexual hunger, as when a sailor goes on shore 'wanting a woman', from the directed and interpersonal desire when a particular man meets a particular woman and wants *her*. The former is not so much a desire as 'a desire to desire'. An orgasm cannot properly be the object of interpersonal desire. This would be like saying it does not matter whether one is 'turned on' by someone of the opposite sex, or the same sex, or ice-cream cartons (Scruton 1986:74–76).

This is why the face matters so much, because 'the face is the primary expression of consciousness' (Scruton 1986:23), and why a loving glance between two persons each aware of the other is to be distinguished from what Robert Grant has eloquently called the 'orthodontic grimace' of a Miss World (quoted in Scruton 1986:28), or for that matter the 'come on' in the face in the pornographic image. This is why we consider the sexual organs as inseparable from the person. As Scruton puts it very bluntly, 'To be penetrated by a man's penis is to be penetrated by *him* (to be enclosed by a woman's vagina is to be enclosed by *her*)' (Scruton 1986:28). Scruton sums up his argument by saying,

> Sexual arousal has . . . an epistemic intentionality: it is a response to another
> individual, based on revelation and discovery, and involving a reciprocal and
> cooperative heightening of the common experience of embodiment. It is not
> directed beyond that individual, to the world at large, and it is not transferable to
> another, who 'might do just as well'.
> (Scruton 1986:30)

Whereas Kant argued for an intrinsic dualism in which the animal desire for sex needs to have love combined with it to rescue us from bestiality, Scruton argues that sexual desire is in its nature an interpersonal longing. We must not dissolve desire (which is interpersonal) into appetite (which is not).

C. S. Lewis likewise argues for the proper personal dimension to sexual union. He distinguishes what he calls 'Venus' (the carnal or animal sexual element within Eros) from Eros itself which is personal. He illustrates this by quoting Orwell's 'dreadful' hero Winston in *Nineteen Eighty-Four* asking the heroine Julia before having sex with her, 'You like doing this? I don't mean simply me; I mean the thing in itself.' He is not satisfied till he gets the answer, 'I adore it.' 'That was above all what he wanted to hear. Not merely the love of one person but the animal instinct, the simple *undifferentiated* desire: that was the force that would tear the Party to pieces' (Orwell 1954:103, quoted in Lewis 1960: ch. 5, my italics). Lewis comments, 'Sexual desire, without Eros, wants it, the thing in itself; Eros wants the Beloved. The thing is a sensory pleasure.' When we say a lustful prowler 'wants a woman', we actually mean that a woman is 'just what he does not want. He wants a pleasure for which a woman happens to be the necessary piece of apparatus. How much he cares about the woman as such may be gauged by his attitude to her five minutes after fruition (one does not keep the carton after one has smoked the cigarettes). Now Eros makes a man really want, not a woman, but one particular woman' (Lewis 1960:87).

Barth likewise argues that sexual activity cannot be divorced from the person who engages in the activity, so that for the integrity of the whole person the 'one flesh' or 'one body' union must engage the whole person, so that 'coitus without co-existence is demonic' (*CD* III/4:133, and see all of 129–139).

Bailey also notes that coitus cannot be 'merely a detached and (as it were) peripheral venereal function involving no more than an appropriate exercise of the genital organs' (Bailey 1959:10).

We may agree with all those who thus emphasize the properly personal nature of sex. Yet we must be suspicious when Bailey goes on to claim that in 1 Corinthians 6:12–20 Paul 'insists that [sexual union] is an act which, by reason of its very nature, engages and expresses *the whole personality* in such a way as to constitute an unique mode of self-disclosure and self-commitment' (Bailey 1959:10, my italics). This emphasis on *total* personal disclosure burdens sex with an obligation to express and reveal 'the whole person' in a manner it cannot do.

The same kind of inadequately guarded language sometimes creeps in to the perceptive works of Jack Dominian (cf. the critique in Moore 1992: ch. 6). For example, when he writes that the deficiency in sexual relationships outside marriage 'is to be found in the fact that these encounters engage *less than the whole person*' (Dominian 1981:95, my italics), we need to ask what is meant by 'the whole person'. It is not clear from Scripture that sexual union has been charged by the Creator with this role or meaning.

No couple experience total personal union in sex; always there is a frustrating incompleteness, however strong the desire or wonderful the sex. C. S. Lewis writes movingly about this frustration as he watched his wife suffer and die of cancer.

> It is incredible how much happiness . . . we sometimes had together after all hope was gone. How long, how tranquilly, how nourishingly, we talked together that last night! And yet, not quite together. There's a limit to the 'one flesh'. You can't really share someone else's weakness, or fear or pain. What you feel may be bad. It might conceivably be as bad as what the other felt, though I should distrust anyone who claimed that it was. But it would still be quite different . . . The mind can sympathize; the body, less. In one way the bodies of lovers can do it least. All their love passages have trained them to have, not identical, but complementary, correlative, even opposite, feelings about one another.
> (Lewis 1961a:14)

Lewis refers elsewhere to Milton's fancy of angelic creatures who can achieve 'total interpenetration instead of our mere embraces' (Lewis 1960:88f.).

We may contrast this fancy with the reality eloquently expressed in Dryden's translation of a poem by Lucretius (which Roger Scruton calls 'the finest description of sexual intercourse in the [English] language').

> So Love with fantomes cheats our longing eyes . . .

There follows a description of 'the raging foam of full desire . . .'

> They grip, they squeeze, their humid tongues they dart,
> As each wou'd force their way to t'other's heart:
> In vain; they only cruze about the coast,
> For bodies cannot pierce, nor be in bodies lost . . .

The poem describes how after sexual satisfaction desire reawakens:

> A pause ensues; and Nature nods a while,
> Till with recruited rage new spirits boil;
> And then the same vain violence returns,
> With flames renewed the erected furnace burns.
> Agen they in each other wou'd be lost,
> But still by adamantine bars are crossed;
> All wayes they try, successless all they prove,
> To cure the secret sore of lingring love.
> (quoted from Scruton 1986:94f.)

This eloquent frustration (crossed by 'adamantine bars') encapsulates the paradox that even the most fulfilled sexual union is ultimately unfulfilled in its longing for full personal union.

Excursus: 1 Corinthians 6:12–20

One of the reasons commentators have spoken of sexual union as in some unique way revealing the whole person is their reading of 1 Corinthians 6:18. 'Every sin that a person commits is outside the body; but the fornicator sins against the body itself [*eis to idion sōma*].' In this passage Paul appears to give to sexual sin a unique personal seriousness (as self-harm at a uniquely deep level), which would be consonant with giving to sexual union a unique inter-personal significance.

I think this reading of verse 18 may be mistaken. Although this passage 'is widely acknowledged to be one of the most difficult in the Pauline corpus' (Rosner 1998:336),[6] we must try to see what light it sheds on the 'one flesh' union. Since the work of Robinson it has been almost a truism to assert that the concept of *sōma* is holistic, 'the nearest equivalent to our word "personality"' (Robinson 1952:28). He firmly distinguishes the Pauline use of 'flesh' (*sarx*) from that of *sōma*, so that, 'While *sarx* stands for man, in the solidarity of creation, in his distance from God, *sōma* stands for man, in the solidarity of creation, as made for God' (Robinson 1952:31).[7] A sin 'against the body itself' is therefore a sin against the person. Those who expound this passage on

---

6. For fuller discussion and a variety of influential views see Fee 1987, ad loc.; Robinson 1952; Bultmann 1952 (vol. 2):194ff.; Jewett 1971; Gundry 1976; Murphy O'Connor 1978; Byrne 1983; Best 1955; Rosner 1998. See also Rosner 1994: ch. 5.

7. This in spite of Paul's using *sōma* and *sarx* in strict parallelism in v. 16 (albeit the latter is from a LXX quotation).

Robinsonian lines say that the problem with prostitute sex is that it falls short of full personal union.

The problem – on this understanding – lies with the shallowness and superficiality of the sex these men were having. 'The deficiency of all other relationships (sc. outside marriage) is to be found in the fact that these encounters engage less than the whole person' (Dominian 1981:95). There is an immediate pragmatic problem (which Dominian admits) that even in marriage sexual acts fall short of engaging the whole person.

There is also a hermeneutical problem with Robinson's paradigm. If (following Robinson 1952 and later Bailey 1959:10ff.) we see the problem as sex involving less than full personal (i.e. somatic) union, it is hard to avoid the objection that an even fuller personal union (i.e. marriage) would contradict union with Christ even more radically than the fleeting (and therefore less deep and threatening) union with the prostitute. Paul's theological problem in this passage is the incompatibility of the man's 'one flesh' union with the prostitute with his 'one spirit' union with Christ (v. 17). To move from a shallow union with a prostitute to a deep union in marriage would seem to pose a worse threat to union with Christ, if both unions are regarded as comparable (i.e. interpersonal).

Robinson's holistic understanding has been convincingly challenged by Gundry, who argues that *sōma* is (as had generally previously been thought) physical rather than holistic; it does indeed mean 'body' rather than 'person'. Man is indeed a unity, argues Gundry, but

> a unity of parts, inner and outer, rather than a monadic unity . . . The *soma* may *represent* the whole person simply because the *soma* lives in union with the soul/spirit. But *soma* does not *mean* 'whole person', because its use is designed to call attention to the physical object which is the body of the person rather than the whole personality. Where used of whole people, *soma* directs attention to their bodies, not to the wholeness of their being. (Gundry 1976:79f.)

The point about Paul speaking of sex as somatic union here is not that it must be fully or totally personal, but that it is precisely physical and – unlike the Corinthians – Paul insists that what we do in our bodies (our *sōmata*) is of enduring ethical significance. The resurrection is in the forefront of Paul's mind (v. 14) and will be not 'spiritual' in some sense of strict discontinuity with the created order, but somatic (chapter 15).

It is sometimes assumed that when Paul says (or quotes them as saying),[8]

---

8. See the commentaries for discussion of how far the quotation goes, if it is a quotation.

'Food is meant for the stomach and the stomach for food, and God will destroy both one and the other' (v. 13), he accepts that what we eat does not have ethical significance; he therefore contrasts this with sexual union, which is personal whereas 'union' with food is not.

However, (a) it is unlikely Paul thought of a resurrection body without a stomach (cf. Luke 24:36–43), and (b) in chapters 8 and 9 he quite clearly sees decisions about food as having ethical significance; he does not argue that sex decisions matter because they are interpersonal, whereas food decisions do not because they are not. The Corinthians may well have claimed that food decisions had no ethical significance because God would destroy the stomach, but Paul does not agree. What we do with our stomachs matters just as what we do with our sexual organs matters, since we look forward to a somatic resurrection. We must not allow a strict dualism between the matters of the 'spirit' and matters of the 'body' or 'flesh'.

In verses 13b–15 he stresses the fundamental union of the believer's *body* with Christ; the former will be raised, the latter has been. Because of this continuity (guaranteed by the Spirit, v. 19) between our present bodies (with all their physical sexuality) and the resurrection body, it is unthinkable to take the 'members of Christ' and make them 'members of a prostitute'. The reason is not that the union with the prostitute is inadequately or incompletely personal; it is not the fact of a competing 'union' which is the problem (for that would rule out marriage), but rather specifically the union *with a prostitute*.

The reason is simply that such a union is immoral. Although chapter 7 begins a new section (v. 1, 'concerning the things about which you wrote'), we need not assume a complete caesura in Paul's thought. In 7:2 he affirms that 'because of cases of sexual immorality [*tas porneias*] each man should have his own wife and each woman her own husband'. The contrast between immorality and marriage has nothing to do with the completeness or otherwise of the interpersonal union, but rather and quite simply to do with one man having one woman and one woman one man. The problem with the union with the prostitute (*pornē*) in chapter 6 correlates precisely with Paul's remedy for immorality (*porneia*) in chapter 7: faithfulness within marriage. The focus is not (*pace* Barth and many twentieth-century commentators) the interior qualities of a sexual relationship, but simply the public external requirement that one man should have one woman and one woman one man. This is the pattern for marriage instituted in creation; the only sexual behaviour that glorifies God the Creator (v. 20) is within this simple framework.

We ought therefore to understand verse 18 as follows. After Paul's strong injunction to 'Shun fornication [*porneia*]!' there is a quotation. 'You say, "Every sin that a person commits is outside the body"' [in other words, you claim that sin is a 'spiritual' (in your sense of the word) affair, affecting the spirit in *contrast* to the body]. But [and here Paul contradicts their general statement and focuses specifically on sexual sin since this is his subject] the fornicator [*ho porneuōn*] sins against the body itself.' Paul is not here assigning a unique seriousness to sexual sin, but rather using sexual sin (his current topic) to make the point that sexual sin, because it is against the body (which will be raised), is a serious matter. In other contexts he might have said the same about other very evidently harmful bodily sins such as drunkenness, gluttony, substance abuse or suicide.

By contrast, if we see in verse 18 an affirmation of the unique seriousness of sexual sin we run into a raft of difficulties (Rosner 1998:143f.). Nowhere else in Scripture is sexual immorality called unique among sins, and it was not the prototypical sin of Adam and Eve.

When Byrne asserts that 'there is something about fornication that strikes at one's own "body" in some particularly direct way, in comparison with which other sins are somehow "outside" the body' (Byrne 1983:613), it is hard to see how heroin addiction (for example) fits in without importing a strange dualism by which sex gets to the soul but substance abuse only affects the 'outer' person. And we are still left with the problem of sins of the mind, such as pride.

Godet argues that the uniqueness of sexual sin is that it is a sin against 'the body in the body', the 'living and life-giving organism' rather than just the 'external and purely physical organism'. 'It is to this inner organism that he sins, while other sins only reach its wrapping, the external body' (Godet 1898:312). This convoluted exegesis ought to alert us to a better way. It is more in harmony with the wider context and the rest of Scripture to understand Paul's assertion in verse 18b as merely one example (the issue to hand) of the moral seriousness of all somatic actions, in contrast to the Corinthian claim that somatic actions lack moral significance.

The moral resources of God are therefore available in support of marriage, just as the moral sanctions of God oppose its dissolution

We return to our theme of the consequences of marriage being a joining by God. The third major consequence is a strong encouragement. If God is *against* any who break a marriage, he is also *for* the actions of maintaining and strengthening marriage. Since he calls to faithfulness, he will himself offer his moral and spiritual resources to sustain faithfulness. What God has joined God upholds. The moral resources of God are turned towards the support and maintenance of marriage and never towards its fracture. This may seem obvious, but because it ought to be obvious it is infrequently stated.

That God has joined a married couple has profound implications for the availability of moral resources. David Atkinson eloquently calls marriage 'a calling lived before God, *open to the resources of his grace and forgiveness*' (Atkinson

1994:86, my italics). Precisely in the gospel there is a dynamic that makes forgiveness, forbearance, perseverance and patience possible. Any married couple may know that as and when they act and will towards the maintenance of faithfulness in marriage their wills are aligned (in this respect) with God's will. There is no need to pray, 'If it be your will' when praying for the upholding of a marriage: we know this is his will. This knowledge removes a hugely unsettling moral uncertainty which inheres in all Barthian views of marriages as 'maybe made in heaven but we can't be sure until later'.

Faithfulness excludes rivals (the prohibition of adultery)

We have seen that marriage is a union to which God is witness and of which God himself is the agent, joining each married couple in a bond that ought not to be broken. We turn our attention now to the consequences of this for marital faithfulness.

'Of all the behaviour that can be construed as an attack on marriage, infidelity is the one recognized by almost everyone as the most serious' (Dominian 1984:132). We may distinguish two facets of the moral obligation to faithfulness. On the one hand, faithfulness excludes rivals; on the other, it perseveres over time. The exclusive and the enduring aspects of faithfulness enjoy a deep coherence, but they are not identical.

We focus first on exclusivity. Marriage in its nature excludes the possibility of sexual union with anyone other than the pledged marriage partner. Indeed, the very exclusivity of marriage distinguishes it from the inclusivity of friendships (in which three is not a crowd and four is better still, Lewis 1960:59, 63f.). This reinforces our conclusion that marriage is not in principle the Creator's remedy for human aloneness.

The scriptural term for a sexual union that breaks a marriage bond is adultery.

Adultery in the Old Testament

The Old Testament verb 'to commit adultery' is *nā'ap* (or, rarely, its derivatives *nā'ªpūp* or *nî'ūp*).[9] While the concept of adultery is not restricted to occurrences of this word group,[10] it is theologically instructive to consider some of the contexts in which it occurs.

---

9. See the useful summary article in *TDOT* IX: 113ff.

10. For example, the word group is not present in Deut. 22:22 or in the episode of David and Bathsheba in 2 Sam. 11.

Adultery is prohibited crisply in the seventh commandment (Exod. 20:14 and Deut. 5:18). There are allusions to the wrongness of literal adultery in connection with other Decalogue-related sins, in a number of places in the prophets Hosea (4:2; perhaps 7:4), Jeremiah (7:9; 9:2; 23:10, 14; 29:23), Ezekiel (16:38; 18:6, 11, 15; 22:11; 33:26) and Malachi (3:5). In Leviticus 20:10 (echoed in 22:22) adultery was a capital offence for both adulterer and adulteress (assuming consent).

Adultery is sin against God

Adultery is not simply an offence against a human being but more deeply a sin against God. We see this in Joseph's protestations to Potiphar's wife, in which after a strong appeal to the trust Potiphar has placed in him (Gen. 39:8,9a) we might expect him to continue by expressing horror at doing 'this great wickedness, and sin against *Potiphar*'. Instead he calls it sin 'against *God*' (v. 9). The same priority is evident even more strongly in David's confession in Psalm 51 after his adultery with Bathsheba and conspiracy to kill Uriah: 'Against you, you only, have I sinned . . .' (Ps. 51:4). The reason adultery is a sin against God is that it contravenes the order the Creator has placed in this world. To break his order is to insult him.

Old Testament adultery law does not assume wives were their husbands' property

It is sometimes claimed that the Old Testament ethic of adultery assumes that the wife is the property of the husband (e.g. Avis 1989:105; Countryman 1989: chs. 2, 8 and repeatedly; cf. Wright 1990:183f.). It is often claimed that a married man may have sexual relations with an unmarried woman without infringing on his own marriage. So Hauck claims, 'Unconditional fidelity is demanded only of the woman, who in marriage becomes the possession of her husband' (*TDNT* IV:730). Phillips claims that until the Deuteronomic reforms, women 'had no legal status, being the personal property first of their fathers and then of their husbands' (Phillips 1970:15).

This claim has been comprehensively refuted by C. J. H. Wright (1990:90–92 and ch. 6). Amongst other arguments, Wright points out that the 'chattel' view rests on a gross oversimplification of the meaning of 'property' and a confusion between the categories of property and authority. If property is in any sense appropriate it is in terms of the wife's sexuality, and even then this 'belonged' to the husband 'only for the purposes which marriage exists to serve, and not just as an object among his possessions' (Wright 1990:188). The *mōhar* (bride-price) was not a payment for property transferred (cf. Hugenberger 1994:243–247) but a compensation for the surrender of authority, and also an important provision for the well-being of the wife (including sometimes provision for her needs if widowed or divorced). To be under the authority of a father or husband does not in any way diminish personhood or reduce a person to the category of chattel. It is true that in Exodus 20:17 the same verb (*ḥāmad*) is used of coveting the house, wife, slave, ox or donkey, but to argue that this places the wife in the same category as the house is as absurd as to imply that oxen and donkeys are considered to be inanimate because houses are.

The theological character of adultery in the Old Testament

Adultery (along with prostitution, √*znh*) is often used metaphorically in the prophets, of the people's unfaithfulness to Yahweh. It is sometimes difficult to distinguish this metaphorical use from a literal use in view of the background of cultic prostitution in the Canaanite cults (see Chapter 8).

We note here five suggestive theological characteristics of adultery.

(i) Adultery is a turning away from a pledge

Adultery is in its genesis a turning away or an abandonment of one to whom we ought to be devoted. This is clear, for example, by the use of the root *šûb* (to turn) in Jeremiah 3:9 (NRSV 'that *faithless* one, Israel') and by the use of *'āzab* (to forsake) in Jeremiah 5:7 ('. . . *forsaken* me'). Although the adulterer feels he is being driven by attraction (to the new woman), and may indeed by intoxicated by her charms, in its essence what he is doing is turning away from the one to whom he owes faithfulness. In its inner nature adultery is an aberration.

Although it might seem (and often does in people's hopes) to be a turning away from one partner to *one* other partner, nevertheless because it is fundamentally a turning *from* rather than a turning *to*, it introduces into life not a replacement loyalty so much as a terrible plurality, instability and dissipation. This tragic theme is laden with theological meaning and pastoral significance: sexual immorality tends towards plurality, dissipation and disintegration, whereas the faithfulness of one man and one woman has an inner integrity and singularity of focus which promotes and sustains order and life.

At its simplest and most extreme this is illustrated by the image of the young man dissipating his wealth and strength (and his family's wealth, cf. Luke 15:30) amongst prostitutes. We see this in the warnings of Proverbs 5:15ff. and 29:3. This theme underlies warnings such as that of King Lemuel (Prov. 31) including (v. 3), 'Do not give your strength to women, your ways to those who destroy kings,' which is immediately followed by a warning about the dissipation of strong drink. Here is a picture of a ruler whose judgment is clouded by a myriad of competing affections and whose strength is sapped by being pulled in many directions. The simple ethic of one man being loyal to one woman and one woman to one man for life images with limpid clarity the singularity of focus that ought to characterize the moral life of humankind.

(ii) Adultery is inherently secretive

Adultery, because it is a breach of faith, has an inherent tendency towards secrecy and deceit; it shrinks from the public realm. We see this in the language of darkness in a section of Job's speech in Job 24:13–17. Just as the murderer and thief have a preference for darkness (v. 14), so the adulterer 'waits for the twilight, saying, "No eye will see me"; and he disguises his face.' Just as we have argued that marriage is inherently a public institution, so adultery is addictively private. It may not be successfully private, but in its intention and its conduct it will aim at privacy. News of a marriage is broadcast with joy by invitations and announcements; news of an adultery, if it breaks at all, comes out by rumour and leak or under pressure of resented enquiry. It comes with openness only in the context of confession, repentance and renunciation.

(iii) Adultery is self-destructive

Adultery (like all sin) has an inherent dynamic towards self-justification. We noted in Chapter 2 how past sexual sin (if unrepented) contributes to our prejudice in the assessment of sexual ethics (cf. Prov. 30:20). The conscience is seared by this private breach of public pledge; a fissure is opened between the private and public realms in the individuals concerned, integrity is compromised and the moral fabric of those involved is deeply scarred.

(iv) Adultery is socially destructive

Adultery is not only inwardly destructive; it is also socially destructive. In his work on 'seriousness' of offence in biblical law, Burnside has pointed out that 'the impact of a crime in Biblical law is felt more widely than just its immediate victims. All offences are regarded as crimes against YHWH . . .' and therefore adversely affecting the whole land and people. By contrast, 'some offences that warranted the death penalty in Biblical law (e.g. false worship, dishonouring parents and promiscuity) would today be regarded as "victimless" crimes'; they are not, for they scar the social fabric (Burnside 2000a/2000b).

In the case of adultery the causal chain that leads to social destruction is traceable in terms of the passions and jealousies it arouses. It arises out of passionate and seemingly uncontrollable desire, as the imagery of the 'heated oven' that needs no stoking in Hosea 7:4–7 so vividly portrays. But although the passions that fuel adultery may seem to be life-enhancing to the adulterers, they ignite other passions that are deeply destructive.

This is the point of the wisdom writer's argument in Proverbs 6:32–35. The reason why 'he who commits adultery has no sense' is that adultery is self-destructive. The adulterer 'will get wounds and dishonour, and . . . disgrace' because he will stir up a husband's jealous fury and provoke revenge. But we

may broaden the focus of this argument. Not only does adultery destroy relationships on a small scale, but when it becomes endemic in the structure of
society it is deeply destructive of the social fabric on a much larger scale.

In this connection we should note the far-reaching social implications of
the warning in Proverbs 2:16–19 and chapter 5 (cf. 22:14; 23:27) that a man
should avoid sexual liaison with 'the loose woman'. C. J. H. Wright
(1990:92–97) has argued convincingly that the woman is 'strange' and 'foreign'
in the sense that by her repudiation of her own marriage (2:17 forsaking the
marriage covenant) she has placed herself 'out of her family'. She is an 'out of
family' woman. Not that she has been divorced and expelled from the family
home, for in chapter 7 she is portrayed as seducing the unwary using her
marital home as a base, but figuratively and spiritually she has become a
stranger to her own household. Wright suggests that the danger of a liaison
with such a woman is not just the husband's jealousy thus aroused, but that it
is a liaison with someone who has placed herself outside the covenant community and therefore outside the whole sphere of blessing and secure relationship with Yahweh (hence the very relevant warnings of 2:20–22).
Although at one level this is relevant only to ancient Israel, the link between
adultery and social breakdown leading to social curse is fraught with warning
today. A loose attitude to marriage is infectious, as implied in Psalm 50:18 (the
wicked who 'keep company with adulterers').

When Jeremiah laments (23:10) that 'the land is full of adulterers', he goes on
to observe that 'because of the curse the land mourns, and the pastures of the
wilderness are dried up'. The context is primarily spiritual adultery, forsaking
the Lord; the curse upon the land is the judgment on this spiritual unfaithfulness. Nevertheless, I do not think we are reading too much into this to observe
that part of the observable process of sin and judgment is physical adultery
(perhaps the meaning of the plural in v. 10) leading to social disintegration and
contributing to the tragedy of a cursed land. This vicious dynamic is evident in
Western societies today.

(v) Adultery damages children

More tentatively, we note the repeated association of adultery with violence
against children. In a few places in the Prophets and the Law we find prohibition or condemnation of sexual sin side by side with prohibition or horror
expressed at the giving of children for sacrifice or to Molech (e.g. Lev. 18:21;
20:2–5; Ezek. 16:20f., 38; 23:37–39, 43–49; Is. 57:1–6). Since the nature religions involved 'sacred' prostitution, 'It is quite possible that the children sacrificed were the very children begotten in cultic intercourse' (*TDOT*:117).

Maybe the association of child sacrifice with adultery and prostitution is
purely accidental, a cultural coincidence in Canaanite religion, but I suspect

there is a deeper, theological, connection. We have seen that the purpose of marriage includes the conception, birth and godly nurture of the next generation to care for God's world. These children are to be born in the context of marital faithfulness and to learn from their parents what it is to be faithful, so that they themselves may mirror the faithfulness of the Creator in caring for his world. When this secure fabric of faithfulness is torn by adultery and a loose attitude to sexual liaisons, it is not surprising that children are also cut loose from the framework of creation order and purpose. The way in which parents then begin to think of children is now open for fragmented reinvention. Some regard children in sentimental terms, as 'sweet', others for their economic usefulness, yet others as an inconvenience, an unwelcome intrusion into personal 'freedom'. In all of these the value of children, the 'good' of nurturing children, is removed and children become vulnerable to the changing whims of cultural fashion. In one breath they may be treasured for sentimental reasons, in the next rejected as 'unwanted'. The way the 'unwanted' child is treated may not be so very different from being given over to Molech. This is a theme that could be further explored.

The Old Testament concept of adultery has about it a deep and multifaceted disastrous character. To breach a marriage by adultery is a turning away from faithfulness; it removes a relationship from the openness and potential for usefulness of the public realm; it sears the conscience; it fractures the fabric of society; and it has disastrous implications for the security and nurture of the next generation.

Adultery in the New Testament

The New Testament's teaching about adultery is fundamentally the same as that of the Old. The word group in both New Testament and LXX is from the root *moich-* and has five members: *moichalis* (used both for the adjective 'adulterous' and the feminine 'adulteress'), *moichaō* ('to commit adultery', also in the middle form *moichaomai*), *moicheuō* (also 'to commit adultery'), *moicheia* (adultery), and *moichos* (adulterer). In the LXX this word group is the usual translation of *nā'ap*.

The Old Testament metaphorical use of the concept is continued (though less frequently), to convey with horror the turning away of people from the true God. So in Matthew 12:39 and 16:4 (cf. Mark 8:38) Jesus speaks of an 'evil and adulterous generation'. When James calls his readers *moichalides* he makes it clear that he means this metaphorically because they are flirting with 'friendship with the world' (Jas. 4:4). It is likely that those who 'commit adultery' with the false prophet Jezebel in Thyatira (Rev. 2:20–23) are also doing so in the spiritual sense of following her teachings, although here (as with so many of the Old Testament occurrences in connection with the Canaanite cults) we cannot be confident that physical sexual misconduct is not an integral part of this spiritual apostasy (note the word *porneusai*, 'to practise fornication', alongside the presumably physical eating of food sacrificed to idols in v. 20).

Mostly, however, adultery is referred to in a physical sense. There are references to the seventh commandment alongside other commandments (Mark 10:19; Rom. 2:22; 13:9; Jas. 2:11; Matt. 5:27f.) or in sin lists (Matt. 7:22; Luke 18:11; 1 Cor. 6:9). In John 7:53–8:11 we have the famous incident of the woman caught in the act of adultery.[11] These texts place the commandment in varied contexts and draw out different aspects of law and gospel. For example, the reference to this sin by the Pharisee in Luke 18:11, by the young ruler in Mark 10:19 and by James in James 2:11 draw attention to the dangers of moral complacency and self-righteousness, and the episode in John 8 of the woman caught in adultery likewise warns against a self-righteous judgmentalism. But all these allusions to and quotations of the seventh commandment assume its enduring validity and in this respect stand in strong continuity to Old Testament sexual ethics.

As with the Old Testament, so in the New adultery is a turning *away*, which leads to instability. In its most visible form we see this disintegration and dissolution in the polemic against drunkenness, orgies and the like, for example in Romans 13:11–14, 1 Peter 4:3 or in the abandonment of Ephesians 4:19. Dissipation is the opposite of integrity, which is expressed in self-control. We see this in 2 Peter 1:4–6. On the one hand (v. 4) there is overwhelming passionate lust, on the other (v. 6) self-control. Later 2 Peter 2:12–16 paints in primary colours lives out of control, in which moral dissolution reduces a human being to the level of an animal (v. 12).

There is an analogy here with the move from true worship to idolatry. The single-hearted worship of the one true God brings to the human heart integrity, coherence and peace. It is not possible to turn away to *one* alternative loyalty, for intrinsic to idolatry is competition and plurality. It is the same with marriage. Marital loyalty is single and promotes integrity in the heart. To turn away introduces competition and plurality, and carries with it a terrible tendency to further turnings away. It is not difficult to see this theological theme evidenced in the sequential breakdowns in the sexual integrities of men and women in whom the first unfaithfulness is so often not the last.

---

11. The textual history of this Gospel pericope is complex and it is far from certain that it originally belonged to John's Gospel, or this point in the Gospel. But it is generally regarded as going back to authentic Jesus tradition. See Metzger 1971 for the textual issues.

Adultery, the heart and the eye

Important New Testament texts press the prohibition of adultery to its source in the human heart *and its expression by the human eye*. These texts implicitly link the seventh commandment to the tenth. In Mark 7:22 Jesus teaches that adultery (along with other sins) has its genesis in the human heart. And in two further places the New Testament moves this from the heart to the *eye*. In Matthew 5:27–28 Jesus presses home the radicalizing effect of the tenth commandment on the seventh when he teaches that 'everyone who looks at a woman [*ho blepōn gunaika*] in order to lust after her [*pros to epithumēsai autēn*] has already committed adultery with her in his heart'. In 2 Peter 2:14 the false teachers (2:1) are described as having 'eyes full of adultery [*ophthalmous . . . mestous moichalidos*]'; cf. 1 John 2:16 'the lust of the eyes'.

The expression of adulterous desire in the eye and the look is, however, not simply another way of speaking of the desire of the heart. The eye is an external organ and a look is a part of our external behaviour. Peter did not need supernatural insight to know that the false teachers had *eyes* full of adultery (2 Pet. 2:14); this was evident to any observant bystander at their meetings.

The verb *epithumeō* (to desire) is a strong word referring to a serious desire which will (unless it is prevented) lead to action. The lustful look (which we hope will be reciprocated as the woman in question catches our eye and returns our meaningful look with interest and encouragement) is the beginning of a sequence of actions. Although in the mercy of God many social constraints usually prevent the desire being taken any further, the look is the external evidence of a heart in which adultery dwells. Adultery may begin with the repeated flirtatious glance answered in kind. We must not speak (as is often loosely done) as if the heart were some separate sphere of ethics, as though there were sins of thought that were in a separate moral compartment from sins of deed. On the contrary, the heart 'is precisely the source of action. If it is in your heart to do it, then you do it, unless you are prevented from doing it' (Moore 1992:19 and all of ch. 2). We see this process very clearly in the narrative of 2 Samuel 11. In verse 2 David *saw* a woman bathing and looked for long enough to observe that she was 'very beautiful'. And *because he was king* (note the reminder in v. 2a that he was 'walking about on the roof of the king's house') no constraint prevented him doing what was in his heart and had been expressed with his eye. So he did it.

It is important to be clear that the look to which Jesus refers and the uses of the eye to which Peter refers are not sinful *per se*. There is nothing in biblical perspective wrong with a man looking with sexual desire upon a woman. Indeed, this is presumably at least part of the poetic delight of Genesis 2:23; it is certainly evident in the Song of Songs. In Genesis 29:17b Rachel is described literally as 'beautiful in form and beautiful to look at'; we might say that she had a good figure and Jacob liked what he saw (cf. Rebekah in Gen. 24:16, who was 'fair to see'). Jacob wants to marry Rachel at least partly because he is physically attracted to her. This is part and parcel of normal life and has no moral disapprobation attached to it. The reason why the looks described by Jesus, Peter and the narrator of 2 Samuel 11 are condemned is that they are directed either from a married man to a woman other than his wife or to a woman already married to someone other than himself. It is not the sexual desire that is sinful, but the *adulterous* desire.

Hebrews 13:4

Hebrews 13:4 is a brief but theologically important statement about marriage and adultery. 'Let marriage be held in honour by all, and let the marriage bed be kept undefiled; for God will judge fornicators and adulterers.'

In the context of the pursuit of holiness, the writer begins with two parallel injunctions. First, marriage (here regarded as an institution, the ongoing married life of couples) must be held in honour by all. Marriage is a public institution to be publicly supported and protected. Second, 'the marriage bed' (the sexual dimension of married life) must be 'undefiled', kept pure and unadulterated. Sexual exclusivity is central to the integrity of marriage. A sexually 'open' marriage is a contradiction in terms. Sexual unfaithfulness (adultery) breaks the heart of marriage like nothing else.

Faithfulness is for life

We are not simply human beings who live in the present. We are men and women in whom personhood involves continuity; we are people with stories. We live with recollections and regrets from the past and longings and fears for the future as well as experience of the present. One of the deepest prophetic themes that relate to marriage and permanence is that of remembered love (e.g. Jer. 2:1f., 32; Ezek. 16:22, 43, 60f.). If adultery in its primary sense is a breach of marriage in the present tense, we need also to explore the dimension of faithfulness through time. We must be clear on the nature and reason for the call to faithfulness through time.

The moral call to stay married

When a man and woman are married, each *ought* to be faithful to the other for life. Marriage carries with it the moral obligation of, and divine calling to, faithfulness, persevering faithful love towards husband or wife. There are two sides to this. On the one hand, it means giving to the other what is promised or implied in marriage – sexual love and faithfulness (where 'sexual' is interpreted in its widest sense including all the practical, emotional and wider caring dimensions associated with the physical relationship). On the other hand, it means being forgiving and patient and showing forbearance towards the other when they fail to give to us what is promised or implied in marriage. Marriage is about both obligation and grace, giving and forgiving.

The moral call to support the marriages of others

Further, we all have a wider moral obligation to support the marriages of others. The maintenance of a marriage is not the private concern of a couple alone. There are many wider influences that support or weaken marriage. At a personal level, each of us is under obligation to do nothing that will weaken or break the marriage of another. At a church level, we need to be very careful that our testimony and our teaching support marriage. At a political level, we must be aware of the influence of law, custom, taxation, and the example of the famous, on marriage.

Marriage and permanence

Attacks are sometimes made in principle on the connection between marriage and permanence. Clearly marriages do break down. But some suggest that a time-limited marriage commitment ought in principle to be considered.

> Greater economic equality has helped to modernize marriage – serial monogamy is likely to become the norm, according to forecasting group the Henley Centre. With greater economic autonomy there is simply no need for 'till death us do part'. The 'partner for life' is going the way of 'the job for life'. Hence the call by the independent think-tank Demos for 10-year marriage contracts as a more realistic and flexible form of the institutions for the future.
>
> (*Observer*, 25 October 1998, p. 15)

A time-limited commitment cannot be marriage. This is not an arbitrary claim. The calling to lifelong faithfulness is not a heteronomous command which comes to us from outside and with no rationale. The commitment to permanence inheres in marriage as ordered in creation. It does so because it inheres in the character of the Creator and how he relates to his creation.

The calling to faithfulness is rooted in the faithful love of God for the people he has made. Permanence is rooted in biblical theology and anthropology. The Creator God is himself unchangeably faithful and utterly trustworthy in his eternity, both in what we may call his intratrinitarian relationships and in all his dealings with his creatures. His eternity and his faithfulness are inseparable. Were he to change with time in his commitments, his perfection would be destroyed and the moral fabric of the cosmos would disintegrate.

This eternity, this longing for permanence, is written deep in the human heart (cf. Eccles. 3:11). We long for a relationship that goes beyond the temporary comradeship of a shared task or a common enemy to a commitment that outlives changing circumstances. It follows that the quality of a personal relationship and its durability are as inseparable as are God's perfection and his eternity.

Whatever critics may say, the evidence from literature, poetry and lyrics of love cannot but illustrate this longing for permanence. When did a love song declare, 'I love you passionately, totally, you alone, *until further notice*'? The whole tragedy of broken love is that we hoped it would last 'for ever'.

This tendency to permanence has deep pastoral implications. A 'trial' or time-limited commitment has about it an inherent superficiality and triviality. Although Barth argues for permanence finally on the grounds of God's arbitrary command rather than creation order, he recognizes the link with anthropological reality when he argues passionately that only when this 'ruling tendency to permanence' is recognized can a sexual relationship have true 'seriousness'. In a so-called 'trial marriage', 'Love would . . . be replaced by what is essentially a constant playing at love, and the full and exclusive life-partnership of marriage by a flabby and non-binding experimentation which dispenses with all real discipline . . .' (Barth, *CD* III/4:206).

We must beware the devaluation of 'faithfulness' that excises the element of duration over time. For example, when John Shelby Spong advocates 'betrothal' as a form of moral living together, he describes it as 'a relationship that is *faithful*, committed, and public, but not legal or *necessarily for a lifetime*' (Spong 1988:177, my italics). He has thereby devalued faithfulness to mean simply the exclusion *in the present* of a rival party.

Scruton makes a similar point when he distinguishes the 'minimal self' (who understands 'I/me' and can speak of his own mental state) from the mature human who has moved from present self-awareness to moral intention towards the future and moral responsibility for the past. The 'maximal self' projects forward and backward in time, and 'lives according to the logic of a human biography' (Scruton 1986:331f.).

In a penetrating discussion of the distinction between marriage and sub-marital relationships, Clapp makes the following point:

Covenantal fidelity is intimacy with a particular story or history, the story of a specific woman and man who share a growing list of joys, who have endured trials and sufferings unique to their marriage, their life together. The past matters. In fact, any one marriage or intimacy *is* its unique history, and so an intimacy that can be understood and told only as a story. Contractual fidelity, on the other hand, is intimacy with no particular story or history. It is concerned with satisfaction or

fulfilment from moment to moment. Guaranteed by no past promise and assured of no future, it lives only in the present and wants no story, no account of where it has been or where it is going.
(Clapp 1993:130)

Not only is a trial or time-limited commitment superficial, it is also, and as a consequence, terribly fragile. The faithfulness of God is the foundation of all human security. Because he does not change we are not destroyed (cf. Mal. 3:6, and the covenant of Gen. 9). Faithfulness is the foundation of security and is to be greatly valued. As the wisdom writer observes in Proverbs 20:6, 'Many proclaim themselves loyal [ḥeseḏ], but who can find one worthy of trust?' There is a difference between the profession of loyalty (ḥeseḏ) and the proof in long-term trustworthiness. The wise man also sees the disastrous effects of the absence of faithfulness: 'Like a bad tooth or a lame foot is trust in a faithless person [bôḡēḏ] in time of trouble' (Prov. 25:19). It is precisely in 'time of trouble' that faithfulness proves to be the core virtue of marriage, and it is because of times of trouble that we need the security of the public marriage pledge.

It is against this theological and anthropological background that we may appreciate the perceptive work of Jack Dominian in drawing out the sustaining and healing power for human personhood of an enduring marriage. 'At the very centre of permanence is a precious truth, that continuity spares as much as possible the discarding of human beings, the partner as an object that can no longer be loved because we can no longer make sense of them' (Dominian 1981:85f., and see all of chs. 4 – 7).

Conclusion

We conclude that faithfulness is the heart of marriage and its core virtue. God is witness to every marriage and he joins every married couple; every married man and woman may therefore know the call of God upon their lives as married people to show faithfulness to husband or wife both in the present and so long as they both live.

CONCLUSION

It is a matter of some frustration for a pastor-teacher to write a book of theological foundations, for all my instincts are to build pastoral practice upon these foundations. Such building is vital. The detailed work of re-examining Scripture and revisiting the theology of marriage is fruitless until it is translated into the patient work of marriage preparation, marriage nurture and marriage healing. And yet firm attachment to foundations is essential. As I myself know from painful experience, when we practise pastoral work with an unsure grasp of foundations, we are pastoral jerry-builders.

I have argued in Part One that marriage exists as an objective entity, instituted by the Creator God as a part of the order he has graciously placed in his world. It will be there for our blessing so long as this age continues, and in the age to come all the blessing of human marriages will be gathered up and distilled into the ecstatic consummation of the Lover God's great marriage with his people. Marriage exists, and marriage is enduringly significant. This was the argument of Part One.

In Part Three I argued that the traditional biblical definition of marriage is both simple and deeply demanding. It is simple, for it is the voluntary sexual and public social union of one man and one woman from different families, patterned on the marriage of God with his people his bride, the Christ with his church. But it is also deeply demanding, for it carries with it, as a covenant to which God is witness and a union which God himself joins, God's calling to lifelong exclusive faithfulness.

Such faithfulness is sometimes easy and delightful, sometimes hard. It needs to be supported in at least two ways. First, it must be public, for a private or ambiguous arrangement is deeply fragile. Second, in Part Two I have argued that one of the keys to building a good marriage is a clear answer to the question 'Why?' What is the point of marriage? We do not have within ourselves the moral resources such that by gazing into one another's eyes we can summon up the quality of lifelong faithfulness. Such an introspective concept of 'coupledom' is paradoxically deeply destructive of the intimacy it seeks. Every married couple need a sense of calling from beyond themselves. God has given to human beings the unique dignity that in responsible relationship to him they may exercise stewardship over his world, and he has instituted marriage in the context of that responsible dignity and task. There is work to be done, a garden to be tended, order to be maintained and fruitfulness to be fostered. When a married couple can hear this personal calling by a loving God who has for them a part in a glorious purpose, their faithfulness can be imbued with vision for a shared usefulness. They work together to build a marriage in which faithful love overflows in fruitfulness beyond the borders of themselves as a couple alone. As they do so, their story of marriage (in all its ordinariness) may be gathered up into the great story of God's marriage against the ecstatic intensity of whose consummation the greatest sex within human marriage will seem tame and dilute.

The theology of marriage is shot through with the Christian gospel, which is both the blessing of law and the wonder of grace. The church has no need to defend marriage as if its very existence were under threat. We may teach marriage and practise marriage with confidence, warmth and joy, for it is both as safe and as good as the great story of God's marriage, which is the gospel.

That great story of God's marriage also has a place for the very many who are unmarried for any or all of this life. But that must be the subject of another study.

BIBLIOGRAPHY

Achtemeier, P. J. (1996), *1 Peter*, Hermeneia Commentaries, Minneapolis: Fortress Press.

Ackroyd, P. R. (1975), 'The Verb Love – *'āhēb* in the David-Jonathan Narratives – A Footnote', *VT* 25:213f.

Adams, J. E. (1980), *Marriage, Divorce and Remarriage in the Bible*, Grand Rapids, Michigan: Zondervan.

Alexander, P. S. (1988), 'Jewish Aramaic Translations of Hebrew Scriptures', in M. J. Mulder (ed.), *Mikra*, chapter 7, Philadelphia: Fortress Press.

Allen, L. C. (1976), *Joel, Obadiah, Jonah and Micah*, NICOT, Grand Rapids: Eerdmans.

Anderson, A. A. (1988), 'Law in Old Israel: Laws Concerning Adultery', in B. Lindars (ed.), *Law and Religion: Essays on the Place of the Law in Israel and Early Christianity*, London: James Clarke.

Aquinas, T. (Summa III), *Summa Theologica*, Part III, 1926 ed., London: Burns Oates & Washbourne.

ASB (1980), *Alternative Service Book*, London: Hodder and Stoughton.

Atkinson, D. (1979), *To Have and to Hold*, London: Collins.

— (1994), *Pastoral Ethics*, Oxford: Lynx Communications.

Augustine (City of God), *The City of God against the Pagans*, Loeb Classical Library, Vol. 4, London: Heinemann.

— (On the Good of Marriage), *On the Good of Marriage*, in *A Select Library of the Nicene and Post-Nicene Fathers*, Vol. III, 399–413, repr. Grand Rapids: Eerdmans, 1980.

— (On Original Sin), *On Original Sin*, in *A Select Library of the Nicene and Post-Nicene Fathers*, Vol. V, 237–255, repr. Grand Rapids: Eerdmans, 1980.

— (On Marriage), *On Marriage and Concupiscence*, in *A Select Library of the Nicene and Post-Nicene Fathers*, Vol. V, 257–308, repr. Grand Rapids: Eerdmans, 1980.

Aune, D. E. (1997), *Revelation 1–5*, Dallas, Texas: Word Biblical Commentary.

Austen, J. (1813), *Pride and Prejudice*, repr. London: Chatto & Windus, 1946.

Avis, P. (1989), *Eros and the Sacred*, London: SPCK.

Babylonian Talmud, *Babylonian Talmud*, The Schottenstein Edition, New York: Mesorah Publications, 1995.

Baelz, P. (1977), *Ethics and Belief*, London: Sheldon Press.

Bailey, D. S. (1952), *The Mystery of Love and Marriage*, London: SCM.

— (1955), *Homosexuality and the Western Christian Tradition*, London: Longmans.

— (1959), *The Man-Woman Relation in Christian Thought*, London: Longmans.

Balch, D. J. (1981), *Let Wives be Submissive: The Domestic Code in 1 Peter*, SBL Monograph Series, Chico, California: Scholars Press.

Banner, M. (1992), 'Directions and Misdirections in Christian Sexual Ethics', *Epworth Review* 19:95–108.

— (1993), 'Five Churches in Search of Sexual Ethics: A short commentary on a statement from the House of Bishops and some other recent reports', *Theology*, July 1993.

— (1996), '"Who are my mother and my brothers?": Marx, Bonhoeffer and Benedict and the Redemption of the Family', in *Studies in Christian Ethics* 9.1:1–22, Edinburgh: T. and T. Clark.

— (1999), *Christian Ethics and Contemporary Moral Problems*, Cambridge: University Press.

Barrett, C. K. (1965), 'Things Sacrificed to Idols', *NTS* xi:138–153.

— (1968), *The First Epistle to the Corinthians*, London: A. and C. Black.

— (1987), 'The Apostolic Decree of Acts 15:29', *Australian Biblical Review* 35:50–59.

Barth, K. (CD), *Church Dogmatics*, ET Edinburgh: T. and T. Clark, 1958.

Barton, C. (1985), *Cohabitation Contracts: extra-marital partnerships and law reform*, Aldershot: Gower Press.

Barton, G. A. (1934), 'A Liturgy for the Celebration of the Spring Festival at Jerusalem in the age of Abraham and Melchizedek', *JBL* LIII:61ff.

Barton, J. (1998), *Ethics and the Old Testament*, London: SCM.

Barton, S. C. (2001), *Life Together: Family, Sexuality and Community in the New Testament and Today*, Edinburgh: T. and T. Clark.

Baugh, S. M. (1995), 'A Foreign World: Ephesus in the First Century', in Kostenberger and others (eds.), *Women in the Church*, 13–52, Grand Rapids: Baker Books.

Beckwith, R. T. (1988), 'Formation of the Hebrew Bible', in M. J. Mulder (ed.), *Mikra*, 61–73, Philadelphia: Fortress Press.

Bedale, S. (1954), 'The Meaning of *kephalē* in the Pauline Epistles', *JTS* 5:211–215.

Bellah, R. (1985), *Habits of the Heart*, Berkeley and Los Angeles: University of California Press.

Berger, B. and P. (1984), *The War Over the Family: Capturing the Middle Ground*, Harmondsworth: Penguin Books.

Berger, P. (1974), 'Cakes for the Queen of Heaven: 2500 years of Religious Ecstasy', *The Christian Century*, Vol. XCI, no. 45.

Bernard, J. H. (1907), 'The Connexion Between the Fifth and Sixth Chapters of 1 Corinthians', *The Expositor*, Series 7, Vol. 3:433–443.

Best, E. (1955), *One Body in Christ: A study in the relationship of the Church to Christ in the Epistles of the Apostle Paul*, London: SPCK.

— (1998), *Ephesians, ICC*, Edinburgh: T. and T. Clark.

Bilezikian, G. (1985), *Beyond Sex Roles*, Grand Rapids: Baker.

Birch, B. C., and L. Rasmussen (1976), *Bible and Ethics in the Christian Life*, Minnesota: Augsburg.

— (1988), 'Old Testament Narrative and Moral Address', in Tucker, Petersen, and Wilson (eds.), *Canon, Theology and Old Testament Interpretation (Festschrift for B. S. Childs)*, 75–91, Philadelphia: Fortress Press.

Blaine Smith, M. (2000), *Should I get married?*, Downers Grove, Illinois: IVP.

Bloch, A. and C. Block (1998), *The Song of Songs*, California: University of California Press.

Block, D. I. (1997), *Ezekiel 1 – 24*, NICOT, Grand Rapids, Michigan: Eerdmans.

Bockmuehl, M. (1995a), 'The Noachide Commandments and New Testament Ethics, with special reference to Acts 15 and Pauline Halakhah', *Revue Biblique* No. 1:72–101.

— (1995b), 'Natural Law in Second Temple Judaism', *VT* XLV,1:17–44.

— (1997), '"The Form of God" (Phil. 2:6) Variations on a Theme of Jewish Mysticism', *JTS* 48:1–23.

— (2000), *Jewish Law in Gentile Churches*, Edinburgh: T. and T. Clark.

Boswell, J. (1980), *Christianity, Social Tolerance and Homosexuality*, Chicago: University of Chicago Press.

Bradshaw, T. (ed.) (1997), *The Way Forward? Christian Voices on Homosexuality and the Church*, London: Hodder and Stoughton.

Bray, G. (1996), *Biblical Interpretation Past and Present*, Leicester: Apollos.

Brenner, A. (1989), *The Song of Songs*, Old Testament Guides, Sheffield: Academic Press.

Bridger, F. (1995), *Celebrating the Family*, Nottingham: Grove Ethics booklet no. 99a.

Bright, J. (1965), *Jeremiah*, Anchor Bible, New York: Doubleday.

Bromiley, G. W. (1980), *God and Marriage*, Grand Rapids: Eerdmans.

Brooke, C. (1989), *The Medieval Idea of Marriage*, Oxford: University Press.

Brooks, B. A. (1941), 'Fertility Cult Functionaries in the Old Testament', *JBL* 60:227–253.

Brown, D. (1983), *Choices: Ethics and the Christian*, Oxford: Basil Blackwell.

Brown, P. (1989), *The Body and Society: Men, Women and Sexual Renunciation in Early Christianity*, London: Faber.

Browning, D. S., and others (1997), *From Culture Wars to Common Ground: Religion and the American Family Debate*, The Family, Religion and Culture Series, Louisville, Kentucky: Westminster, John Knox Press.

Bruce, F. F. (1968), *Ephesians*, London: Pickering & Inglis (first published 1961).

— (1990), *The Acts of the Apostles: Greek Text with Introduction and Commentary*, 3rd ed., Leicester: Apollos.

Brundage, J. (1987), *Law, Sex, and Christian Society in Medieval Europe*, Chicago: University of Chicago Press.

— (1993), 'Implied Consent to Intercourse', in *Consent and Coercion to Sex and Marriage in Ancient and Medieval Societies*, 245–256, Washington DC: Dumbarton Oaks.

Bucer, M. (De Regno Christi), *De Regno Christi*, Library of Christian Classics XIX, ET London: SCM, 1969.

— (Marriage), *Marriage, Divorce and Celibacy*, in *Common Places of Martin Bucer*, Courtenay Library of Reformation Classics, 1972, trans. and ed. D. F. Wright, 403–428, ET Sutton Courtenay: Sutton Courtenay Press.

Budd, P. J. (1984), *Numbers*, Waco, Texas: Word Biblical Commentary.

Bultmann, R. (1952), *Theology of the New Testament*, 2 vols., ET London: SCM.

Burnside, J. (2000a), 'A Truly Serious Offence? Modern Law and the Problem of "Seriousness"', Whitefield Briefing 5.1.

— (2000b), 'Justice, Seriousness and Relationships', in P. Beaumont and K. Wotherspoon (eds.), *Law and Relationism*, Carlisle: Paternoster.

Byrne, B. (1983), 'Sinning against One's Own Body. Paul's Understanding of the Sexual Relationship in 1 Corinthians 6:18', *CBQ* 45:608–616.

Callan, T. (1993), 'The Background to the Apostolic Decree', *CBQ* 55:284–297.

Calvin, J. (Genesis), *Commentary on Genesis*, repr. Grand Rapids: Baker, 1993.

— (Harmony), *Commentary on the four last books of Moses, arranged in the form of a harmony*, Vol. 2, repr. Grand Rapids: Baker, 1993.

— (1–2 Cor), *The Epistles of Paul the Apostle to the Corinthians*, repr. Grand Rapids: Baker, 1993.

Camp, C. V. (1985), *Wisdom and the Feminine in the book of Proverbs*, Sheffield: Almond Press.

Carrington, P. (1940), *The Primitive Christian Catechism: A Study in the Epistles*, Cambridge: University Press.

Carroll, R. P. (1986), *Jeremiah*, London: SCM.

Carson, D. A. (1991), 'Silent in the Churches', in Piper and Grudem (eds.), *Recovering Biblical Manhood and Womanhood*, 140–153, Wheaton, Illinois: Crossway Books.

Cassuto, U. (1967), *A Commentary on the Book of Exodus*, ET Jerusalem: The Magnes Press (Hebrew University).

Charlesworth, J. H. (ed.) (1983, 1985), *The Old Testament Pseudepigrapha*, 2 vols., New York: Doubleday.

Church of England (1935), *The Church and Marriage*, London: SPCK.

— (1940), *Kindred and Affinity as Impediments to Marriage*, London: SPCK.

— (1955), *The Church and the Law of Nullity of Marriage*, London: SPCK.

— (1958), *The Family in Contemporary Society*, London: SPCK.

— (1971), *Marriage, Divorce and the Church* (Root Report), London: SPCK.

— (1978), *Marriage and the Church's Task* (Lichfield Report), London: CIO.

— (1984), *No Just Cause: The Law of Affinity in England and Wales: Some Suggestions for Change*, London: CIO.

— (1988), *An Honourable Estate: The Doctrine of Marriage according to English law and the obligation of the Church to marry all parishioners who are not divorced*, London: CIO.

— (1991), *Issues in Human Sexuality: A Statement by the House of Bishops*, London: Church House Publishing.

— (1995), *Something to Celebrate – Valuing Families in Church and Society*, Church of England

Board of Social Responsibility Working Party Report, London: Church House Publishing.

Clapp, R. (1993), *Families at the Crossroads: Beyond Traditional and Modern Options*, Leicester/ Downers Grove: IVP.

Clark, S. (1999), *Putting Asunder*, Bridgend: Bryntirion Press.

Clark, S. B. (1980), *Man and Woman in Christ*, Ann Arbor, Michigan: Servant Books.

Clifford, P. (1987), *Divorced Christians and the Love of God*, London: SPCK/Triangle.

Clines, D. J. A. (1968), 'The Image of God in Man', *TB* 19:53–103.

— (1990), *What does Eve do to help?*, JSOT Supplement 94), Sheffield: Academic Press.

Clulow, C. (ed.) (1995), *Women, Men and Marriage*, London: Sheldon Press.

— (1996), *Partners Becoming Parents: Talks from the Tavistock Marital Studies Institute*, London: Sheldon Press.

Collingwood, J. (1994), *Common Law Marriage: The Case for a Change in the Law*, Nottingham: Grove Ethical Studies no. 93.

Collins, R. F. (1992), *Divorce in the New Testament*, Collegeville, Minnesota: The Liturgical Press.

— (1999), *First Corinthians*, Collegeville, Minnesota: The Liturgical Press.

Connolly, C. (ed.) (1987), *New Life: Church Teaching on Technology and Fertilization*, Belfast: Four Courts Press.

Conzelmann, H. (1975), *A Commentary on the First Epistle to the Corinthians*, ET Philadephia: Fortress Press (German edition, 1969).

Cooper-White, P. (1995), *The Cry of Tamar: Violence Against Women and the Church's Response*, Minneapolis: Fortress Press.

Cornes, A. (1993), *Divorce and Remarriage*, London: Hodder and Stoughton.

Cotterell, P. and M. Turner (1989), *Linguistics and Biblical Interpretation*, London: SPCK.

Countryman, L. W. (1989), *Dirt, Greed and Sex: Sexual Ethics in the New Testament and their Implications for Today*, London: SCM.

Coupland, D. (1992), *Generation X*, London: Abacus.

Craigie, P. C. (1985), *Twelve Prophets*, Edinburgh: St Andrew Press, Daily Study Guides.

— (1991), *Jeremiah*, Dallas: Word Biblical Commentary.

Cudmore, L. (1996), 'Infertility and the Couple', in C. Clulow, *Partners becoming Parents*, 55–65, London: Sheldon Press.

Cyprian (Epistles), *Letters of Cyprian*, in *The Ante-Nicene Fathers*, Vol. V, repr. Grand Rapids, Michigan: Eerdmans, 1990.

Davies, E. W. (1981), 'Inheritance Rights and the Hebrew Levirate Marriage', *VT* 31:138–144, 257–268.

Davies, J. (1997), 'Sex These Days, Sex Those Days: Will it Ever End?', in Davies and Loughlin, *Sex these days*, 18–34, Sheffield: Academic Press.

Davies, J. (ed.) (1993), *The Family: Is it Just Another Lifestyle Choice?*, London: IEA Health and Welfare Unit.

Davies, J. and G. Loughlin (eds.) (1997), *Sex these days: Essays on theology, sexuality and society*, Sheffield: Academic Press.

Davies, W. D. (1970), *Paul and Rabbinic Judaism*, 3rd ed., London: SPCK.

Dawes, G. W. (1998), *The Body in question: metaphor and meaning in the interpretation of Ephesians 5:21–33*, Leiden: Brill.

Day, J. (2000), *Yahweh and the gods and goddesses of Canaan*, Sheffield: Academic Press.

de Vaux, R. (1973), *Ancient Israel: Its Life and Institutions*, ET London: Darton, Longman & Todd.

Delitzsch, F. (1888), *New Commentary on Genesis*, Vol. I, ET Edinburgh: T. and T. Clark.

Delling, G. (1972), '*tassō etc*', *TDNT*, Vol. 8:27–48, repr. Grand Rapids: Eerdmans, 1988.

Deming, W. (1995), *Paul on marriage and celibacy: The Hellenistic background of 1 Corinthians 7*, Cambridge: Cambridge University Press.

Dennis, N. (1995), *Family Disintegration and The Retreat From Common Sense*, Newcastle: The Christian Institute.

Dennis, N. and G. Erdos (1993), *Families without Fatherhood*, 2nd ed., London: IEA Health and Welfare Unit.

Dickson, G. and A. (1997), 'Childlessness', in D. W. Torrance (ed.), *God, Family and Sexuality*, 79–94, Carberry, Scotland: The Handsel Press.

Dixon, P. (1995), *The Rising Price of Love: The True Cost of the Sexual Revolution*, London: Hodder and Stoughton.

Dominian, J. (1967), *Christian Marriage*, London: Darton, Longman & Todd.

— (1971), *The Church and the Sexual Revolution*, London: Darton, Longman & Todd.

— (1975), *Cycles of Affirmation: Psychological Essays in Christian Living*, London: Darton, Longman & Todd.

— (1977), *Proposals for a New Sexual Ethic*, London: Darton, Longman & Todd.

— (1981), *Marriage, Faith and Love*, London: Darton, Longman & Todd.

— (1984), *Make or Break: An Introduction to Marriage Counselling*, New Library of Pastoral Care, London: SPCK.

— (1987), *Sexual Integrity*, London: Darton, Longman & Todd.

— (1991), *Passionate and Compassionate Love*, London: Darton, Longman & Todd.

— (2001), *Let's Make Love: The Meaning of Sexual Intercourse*, London: Darton, Longman & Todd.

Dominian, J. and H. Montefiore (1989), *God, Sex and Love*, London: SCM.

Dormor, D. (1992), *The Relationship Revolution*, London: One plus One.

Douglas, M. (1966/1984), *Purity and Danger*, London: Routledge & Kegan Paul (1984 edition also quoted).

Driver, S. R. (1902), *Deuteronomy, ICC*, Edinburgh: T. and T. Clark.

Dunn, J. (1996), 'The Household Rules in the New Testament', in S. C. Barton (ed.), *The Family in Theological Perspective*, 43–64, Edinburgh: T. and T. Clark.

Durham, J. I. (1987), *Exodus*, Waco, Texas: Word Biblical Commentary.

C. Dyer and M. Berlins (1982), *Living Together*, London: Hamlyn.

Emmerson, G. I. (1989), 'Women in Ancient Israel', in R. E. Clements (ed.), *The World of Ancient Israel: Sociological, Anthropological and Political Perspectives*, 371–394, Cambridge: Cambridge University Press.

Evans, G. R. (1987), *Bernard of Clairvaux: Selected Works*, New York: Paulist Press.

Fee, G. D. (1987), *The First Epistle to the Corinthians*, Grand Rapids: Eerdmans.

Fiorenza, E. S., and M. S. Copeland (eds.) (1994), *Violence Against Women*, London: SCM.

Fitzmyer, J. A. (1957/8), 'A Feature of Qumran Angelology and the Angels of 1 Corinthians XI.10', *NTS* IV:48–58.

— (1993), '*Kephalē* in 1 Corinthians 11:3', *Interpretation* 47:52–59.

Forster, G. (1988), *Marriage before Marriage? The moral validity of 'common law' marriage*, Nottingham: Grove Ethical Studies no.69.

Forster, G. (1994), *Cohabitation and Marriage: a Pastoral Response*, London: Marshall Pickering.

— (1995), *Healing Love's Wounds: a pastoral approach to divorce and to remarriage*, London: Marshall Pickering.

Foucault, M. (1978), *The History of Sexuality*, 3 vols., ET London: Penguin Books.

Frye, N. (1982), *The Great Code: The Bible and Literature*, London: Routledge and Kegan Paul.

Fuller, R. (1991), 'Text-Critical Problems in Malachi 2:10–16', *JBL* 110:47–57.

Fung, R. Y. K (1988), *Galatians*, Grand Rapids: Eerdmans.

Gadamer, H.-G. (1975), *Truth and Method*, ET London: Sheed and Ward.

Gagnon, R. A. J. (2001), *The Bible and Homosexual Practice*, Nashville: Abingdon Press.

Gaster, T. H. (1941), 'Ezekiel and the Mysteries', *JBL* LX:289–310.

Genesis Rabbah (1985), *Genesis Rabbah: The Judaic Commentary to the Book of Genesis, A New American Translation*, Jacob Neusner, Atlanta, Georgia: Scholars Press.

Ghee, C. (2001), 'Population Review of 2000: England and Wales', in *Population Trends* 106 (Winter 2001), 7–14, London: Office of National Statistics.

Giddens, A. (1992), *The Transformation of Intimacy: Sexuality, Love and Eroticism in Modern Societies*, Cambridge: Polity Press.

Gillis, J. (1988), *For Better, For Worse: British Marriages, 1600 to the Present*, Oxford: Oxford University Press.

Gledhill, T. (1994), *The Message of the Song of Songs*, Bible Speaks Today series, Leicester: IVP.

Godet, F. (1898), *1 Corinthians*, ET Edinburgh: T. and T. Clark.

Gray, J. (1962), 'Ashtoreth', in *Interpreter's Dictionary of the Bible*, Vol. I:255f., New York: Nashville.

Gray, J. (1993), *Men are from Mars, Women are from Venus: a practical guide to getting what you want in your relationships*, repr. London: Thorsons, 1997.

Green, J. T. (1992), *Balaam and His Interpreters: A Hermeneutical History of the Balaam Traditions*, Atlanta, Georgia: Scholars Press.

Greenberg, M. (1983), *Ezekiel 1 – 20*, Anchor Bible, New York: Doubleday.

Greene, G. (1938), *Brighton Rock*, repr. London: Heinemann-Octopus, 1981.

— (1951), *The End of the Affair*, repr. London: Heinemann-Octopus, 1981.

Greer, G. (1985), *Sex and Destiny: the politics of human fertility*, London: Picador.

Grenz, S. J. (1997a), *Sexual Ethics: An Evangelical Perspective*, Louisville, Kentucky: Westminster, John Knox Press.

— (1997b), *The Moral Quest: Foundations of Christian Ethics*, Leicester: Apollos.

— (1998), *Welcoming But Not Affirming: An Evangelical Response to Homosexuality*, Louisville, Kentucky: Westminster, John Knox Press.

Grudem, W. (1985), 'Does kefalh ("Head") Mean "Source" or "Authority over" in Greek Literature? A Survey of 2,336 Examples', *Trinity Journal* 6:38–59.

Gundry, R. H. (1976), *SOMA in Biblical Theology with emphasis on Pauline Anthropology*, SNTS Monograph Supplement 29, Cambridge: University Press.

Gurney, O. R. (1962), 'Tammuz Reconsidered: Some Recent Developments', *JSS* 7.2:147–160.

Guroian, V. (1987), 'An Ethic of Marriage and Family', in *Incarnate Love: Essays in Orthodox Ethics*, 79–114, Notre-Dame: Notre-Dame University Press.

Halperin, D. J. (1993), *Seeking Ezekiel: Text and Psychology*, University Park, Pennsylvania: Pennsylvania State University Press.

Hampson, D. (1990), *Theology and Feminism*, Oxford: Blackwell.

Hardy, T. (1874), *Far from the Madding Crowd*, repr. London: Penguin Popular Classics, 1994.

Hartley, J. E. (1992), *Leviticus*, Dallas: Word Biblical Commentary.

Harvey, A. E. (1993), 'Marriage, Sex and the Bible', *Theology* XCVI:364–372, 461–468.

— (1994), *Promise or Pretence: A Christian's Guide to Sexual Morals*, London: SCM.

Haskey, J. (1992), 'Pre-marital Cohabitation and the Probability of Subsequent Divorce: Analyses Using New Data from the General Household Survey', in *Population Trends* 68, London: HMSO.

— (1999), 'Cohabitational and Marital Histories of Adults in Great Britain', in *Population Trends 96* (Summer 1999), 13–24, London: Office of National Statistics.

— (2001a), 'Cohabitation in Great Britain: past, present and future trends and attitudes', in *Population Trends 103* (Spring 2001), London: Office of National Statistics.

— (2001b), 'Cohabiting couples in Great Britain: accommodation sharing, tenure and property owning', in *Population Trends 103* (Spring 2001), London: Office of National Statistics.

Hauck, F. and S. Schultz (1968), '*pornē etc*', in *TDNT* Vol. 6:579–595, Grand Rapids: Eerdmans.

Hauerwas, S. (1981), *A Community of Character: Towards a Constructive Christian Social Ethic*, London/Notre Dame: University of Notre Dame Press.

— (1991), *After Christendom?*, Nashville: Abingdon Press.

Haw, R. (1952), *The State of Matrimony*, London: SPCK.

Hayman, S. (1994), *Other People's Children*, London: Penguin Books.

Hays, R. B. (1986), 'Relations Natural and Unnatural: A Response to John Boswell's Exegesis of Romans 1', *JRE* 14:184.

— (1996), *The Moral Vision of the New Testament*, Edinburgh: T. and T. Clark.

— (1997), *1 Corinthians*, Louisville: John Knox Press.

Hebblethwaite, B. (1981), *The Adequacy of Christian Ethics*, London: Marshall, Morgan and Scott.

Hemer, C. J. (1986), *The Letters to the Seven Churches of Asia in their Local Setting, JSNT Supplement* 11, Sheffield: JSOT Press.

Heth, W. A., and G. J. Wenham (1984), *Jesus and Divorce*, London: Hodder and Stoughton.

Hill, C. (1986), *Society and Puritanism in Pre-Revolutionary England*, Harmondsworth: Penguin Books.

Hill, M. (1977), 'Paul's Concept of "Encrateia"', *Reformed Theological Review* 36:70–78.

— (1994), 'Homosexuality and Ethics', in *Theological and Pastoral Responses to Homosexuality*, Moore Theological College Explorations 8, Adelaide: Open Book Publishers.

Holladay, W. L. (1986), *Jeremiah 1 – 25*, Philadelphia: Fortress Press.

Hooker, M. (1963), 'Authority on her head: an examination of 1 Corinthians XI.10', *NTS* X:410–416.

Hove, R. (1999), *Equality in Christ? Galatians 3:28 and the Gender Dispute*, Wheaton, Illinois: Crossway Books.

Hudson Taylor, J. (1967), *Union and Communion*, London: Overseas Missionary Fellowship.

Hudson, N. and K. Warrington (1994), 'Cohabitation and the Church', *EPTA Bulletin* 13:63–73.

Hugenberger, G. P. (1994), *Marriage as a Covenant: A study of Biblical Law and Ethics governing Marriage developing from the perspective of Malachi, VT* Supplement LII, Leiden: Brill.

Hunkin, W. (1925), 'The Prohibitions of the Council of Jerusalem (Acts xv.28–29)', *JTS* 27:272–283.

Hurley, J. B. (1981), *Man and Woman in Biblical Perspective*, Leicester: IVP.

Instone Brewer, D. (2002), *Divorce and Remarriage in the Bible*, Grand Rapids, Michigan: Eerdmans.

Jacobsen, T. (1976), *The Treasures of Darkness: A History of Mesopotamian Religion*, Yale: University Press.

James, P. D. (1992), *Children of Men*, London: Penguin Books.

Jenkins, G. J. (1993), *Cohabitation: A Biblical Perspective*, Nottingham: Grove Ethical Studies no. 84.

— (1995), 'Cohabitation', in *New Dictionary of Christian Ethics and Pastoral Theology*, Leicester: IVP.

Jensen, J. (1978), 'Does Porneia mean Fornication? A Critique of Bruce Malina', *NT* 20:161–184.

Jenson, R. W. (1999), 'The Religious Power of Scripture', in *Scottish Journal of Theology* 52.1:89–105.

Jewett, P. K. (1975), *MAN as male and female*, Grand Rapids: Eerdmans.

Jewett, R. (1971), *Paul's Anthropological Terms*, Leiden: Brill.

Johnson, L. T. (1981), *Sharing Possessions*, Philadelphia: Fortress Press.

Joint Liturgical Group of Great Britain (1999), *An Order of Marriage: For Christians from Different Churches*, Norwich: Canterbury Press.

Jones, D. R. (1992), *Jeremiah*, New Century Bible, London: Marshall Pickering.

Josephus (Antiquities), *The Antiquities of the Jews*, ET London: Heinemann, Loeb Classical Library.

Joy, D. (1986), *Rebonding*, Waco, Texas: Word Books.

Kaiser, W. (1983), *Toward Old Testament Ethics*, Grand Rapids, Michigan: Zondervan.

Kasper, W. (1980), *Theology of Christian Marriage*, London: Burns and Oates.

Kass (1992), 'Regarding Daughters and Sisters: The Rape of Dinah', *Commentary* 93:29–38.

Keener, C. S. (1992), *Paul, Women and Wives: Marriage and Women's Ministry in the Letters of Paul*, Peabody, Mass.: Hendrickson.

Kidner, D. (1967), *Genesis*, London: Tyndale Press.

Kiernan, K. (1999), 'Cohabitation in Western Europe', in *Population Trends 96* (Summer 1999), 25–32, London: Office of National Statistics.

Kline, M. G. (1961), 'Divine Kingship and Genesis 6:1–4', *Westminster Theological Journal* 24:187–204.

Knight, G. W. (1991), 'Husbands and Wives as analogues of Christ and the Church', in Piper and Grudem (eds.), *Recovering Biblical Manhood and Womanhood*, ch. 8, Wheaton, Illinois: Crossway Books.

Kostenberger, A. J., T. R. Schreiner, and H. Scott Baldwin (eds.) (1995), *Women in the Church: a fresh analysis of 1 Timothy 2:9–15*, Grand Rapids: Baker.

Kroeger, C. C., and J. R. Beck (eds.) (1996), *Women, Abuse and the Bible: How Scripture Can Be Used to Hurt or to Heal*, Grand Rapids: Baker.

Kroeger, C. C. (1987), 'The Classical Concept of Head as "Source"', in G. G. Hull, *Equal to Serve*, 267–283, London: Scripture Union.

Laetsch, T. (1952), *Jeremiah*, St. Louis: Concordia Publishing House.

Laiou, A. E. (ed.) (1993), *Consent and Coercion to Sex and Marriage in Ancient and Medieval Societies*, Washington DC: Dumbarton Oaks.

Landy, F. (1983), *Paradoxes of Paradise*, Sheffield: Almond Press.

Lash, J. (1998), *Blood Ties*, London: Bloomsbury.

Lawson, M. (1998), *The Better Marriage Guide: Achieve a happy and more fulfilling relationship*, London: Hodder and Stoughton.

Levine, B. A. (1989), *Leviticus*, JPS Torah Commentary Series, Philadelphia: Jewish Publication Society.

Lewis, C. S. (1960), *The Four Loves*, repr. London: Fount, 1977.

— (1961a), *A Grief Observed*, London: Faber.

— (1961b), *Reflections on the Psalms*, repr. London: Fount, 1977.

Lincoln, A. (1990), *Ephesians*, Waco, Texas: Word Biblical Commentary.

Lion (1985), *Isaac finds a wife*, Lion Story Bible Vol. 5, Tring, England: Lion.

Loane, M. (1968), *The Hope of Glory*, London: Hodder and Stoughton.

Longenecker, R. (1984), *New Testament Social Ethics for Today*, Grand Rapids: Eerdmans.

— (1986), 'Authority, Hierarchy and Leadership Patterns in the Bible', in A. Mickelsen (ed.), *Women, Authority and the Bible*, 66–85, Downers Grove, Illinois: IVP.

— (1990), *Galatians*, Dallas, Texas: Word Biblical Commentary.

Louth, A. (1997), 'The body in Western Catholic Christianity', in S. Coakley (ed.), *Religion and the Body*, 111–130, Cambridge: University Press.

Luther, M. (Babylonian), *On the Babylonian Captivity of the Church*, in *Luther's Primary Works*, London: Hodder and Stoughton, 1896.

Lycett, A. (1999), *Rudyard Kipling*, London: Weidenfeld and Nicholson.

MacIntyre, A. (1981), *After Virtue*, London: Duckworth.

Macquarrie, J. (1975), 'The Nature of the Marriage Bond', *Theology LXXVIII*:230–236.

Maier, W. A. (1986), *'ašerah: Extrabiblical Evidence*, Harvard Semitic Monographs 37, Atlanta, Georgia: Scholars Press.

Malina, B. (1972), 'Does Porneia mean Fornication?', *NT* 14:10–17.

Martin, R. P. (1991), *Ephesians, Colossians, and Philemon*, Atlanta: John Knox Press.

Mayes, A. D. H. (1979), *Deuteronomy*, New Century Bible, London: Oliphants.

McAllister, F. (ed.) (1995), *Marital Breakdown and the Health of the Nation*, 2nd ed., London: One plus One.

McEwan, I. (2001), *Atonement*, London: Jonathan Cape.

McEwen, B. C. (1997), 'Fertility, Contraception and the Family', in D. W. Torrance (ed.), *God, Family and Sexuality*, 120–128, Carberry, Scotland: The Handsel Press.

McKane, W. (1986), *Jeremiah*, 2 vols., Edinburgh: T. and T. Clark.

McKeating, H. (1979), 'Sanctions against Adultery in ancient Israelite Society, with some reflections on methodology in the study of Old Testament ethics', *JSOT* 11:57–72.

McLaren, A. S. (1992), *A History of Contraception: from antiquity to the present day*, Oxford: Blackwell.

Meeks, W. A. (1974), 'The Image of the Androgyne: Some Uses of a Symbol in Earliest Christianity', *History of Religions* 13.3:165–208.

— (1983), *The First Urban Christians (the Social World of the Apostle Paul)*, Yale: University Press.

— (1987), *The Moral World of the First Christians*, London: SPCK.

— (1993), *The Origins of Christian Morality*, Yale: University Press.

Meilander, G. C. (1995), 'Sexuality', in *New Dictionary of Christian Ethics and Pastoral Theology*, 71–78, Leicester: IVP.

Mellor, P. A. and C. Shilling (1997), 'Confluent Love and the Cult of the Dyad', in Davies and Loughlin, *Sex these days*, 51–78, Sheffield: Academic Press.

Mendenhall, G. E. (1973), *The Tenth Generation*, Baltimore and London: The John Hopkins University Press.

Metzger, B. M. (1971), *A Textual Commentary on the Greek New Testament*, Stuttgart, Germany: United Bible Societies.

Meyers, C. (1997), 'The Family in Early Israel', in L. Perdue, and others, *Families in Ancient Israel*, 1–47, Louisville, Kentucky: John Knox Press.

Michaels, J. (1988), *1 Peter*, Waco, Texas: Word Biblical Commentary.

Mickey, P. A. (1995), 'Prostitution', in *New Dictionary of Christian Ethics and Pastoral Theology*, 701f., Leicester: IVP.

Mishnah (1988), *The Mishnah, a New Translation by Jacob Neusner*, New Haven and London: Yale University Press.

Moore, G. (1992), *The Body in Context: Sex and Catholicism*, London: SCM.

Moore, G. F. (1927), *Judaism in the First Centuries of the Christian Era: the age of the Tannaim*, Cambridge, Mass.: Harvard University Press.

Morgan, P. (2000), *Marriage-Lite: The Rise of Cohabitation and its Consequences*, London: Institute for the Study of Civil Society.

Mounce, W. D. (2000), *The Pastoral Epistles*, Nashville: Thomas Nelson, Word Biblical Commentary.

Murphy-O'Connor, J. (1976), 'The non-Pauline character of 1 Corinthians 11:2–16', *JBL* 45:615–627.

— (1978), 'Corinthian Slogans in 1 Corinthians 6:12–20', *CBQ* 40:391–396.

— (1983), *St Paul's Corinth: Texts and Archaeology*, Delaware: Michael Glazier.

Murray, J. (1957), *Principles of Conduct*, London: Tyndale Press.

Nelson, J. B. (1979), *Embodiment: An Approach to Sexuality and Christian Theology*, London: SPCK.

— (1983), *Between Two Gardens: Reflections on Sexuality and Religious Experience*, New York: Pilgrim Press.

Neuer, W. (1990), *Man and Woman in Christian Perspective*, ET London: Hodder and Stoughton.

Nineham, D. (1976), *The Use and Abuse of the Bible*, London: Macmillan.

Noonan, J. T. (1986), *Contraception: A History of Its Treatment by the Catholic Theologians and Canonists*, Cambridge, Mass.: Harvard University Press.

Nygren, A. (1982), *Agape and Eros*, ET London: SPCK.

O'Brien, P. (1982), *Colossians and Philemon*, Waco, Texas: Word Biblical Commentary.

— (1999), *The Letter to the Ephesians*, Leicester: Apollos.

— (1978), *Marriage and Permanence*, Nottingham: Grove Ethical Booklets, no. 26.

— (1982), 'Usus and Fruitio in Augustine', *JTS* 33:361–397.

— (1994), *Resurrection and Moral Order: An Outline for Evangelical Ethics*, 2nd ed., Leicester: IVP.

Olyan, S. M. (1988), *Asherah and the Cult of Yahweh in Israel*, SBL Monograph Series, Atlanta, Georgia: Scholars Press.

Oppenheimer, H. (1990), *Marriage*, London: Mowbrays.

Ortlund, R. C. (1996), *Whoredom: God's Unfaithful Wife in Biblical Theology*, New Studies in Biblical Theology 2, Leicester: Apollos.

Orwell, G. (1954), *Nineteen Eighty-Four*, London: Penguin Books.

Osiek, C and D. L. Balch (1997), *Families in the New Testament World*, Louisville, Kentucky: Westminster John Knox Press.

Outhwaite, R. B. (1995), *Clandestine Marriage in England, 1500–1850*, London: Hambledon Press.

Parker, S. (1990), *Informal Marriage, Cohabitation and the Law 1750–1989*, London: Macmillan.

Peck, S. (1978), *The Road Less Travelled*, New York: Simon & Schuster.

Perdue, L. G., J. Blenkinsopp, J. J. Collins and C. Meyers (1997), *Families in Ancient Israel*, Louisville, Kentucky: Westminster John Knox Press.

Perriman, A. (1998), *Speaking of Women*, Leicester: Apollos.

Phillips, A. C. J. (1970), *Ancient Israel's Criminal Law: A New Approach to the Decalogue*, Oxford: Oxford University Press.

— (1980), 'Uncovering the father's skirt', *VT* 30:38–43.

— (1983), 'The Decalogue – ancient Israel's criminal law', *JJS* 34:1–20.

— (1973), 'Some Aspects of Family Law in Pre-Exilic Israel', *VT* 23:349–361.

— (1981), 'Another Look at Adultery', *JSOT* 20:3–25.

— (1982), 'A Response to Dr McKeating', *JSOT* 22:142–143.

Phipps, W. E. (1982), 'Is Paul's Attitude towards Sexual Relations Contained in 1 Corinthians 7:1?', *NTS* 28:129–130.

Phypers, D. (1985), *Christian Marriage in Crisis*, Bromley, Kent: MARC Europe.

Piper, J. and W. Grudem (eds.) (1991), *Recovering Biblical Manhood and Womanhood: a response to evangelical feminism*, Wheaton, Illinois: Crossway Books.

Plato (Symposium), *The Symposium of Plato*, London: Penguin Classics, 1951.

Pope, M. H. (1977), *Song of Songs*, Anchor Bible, New York: Doubleday.

Population Trends 106 (2001), 'Annual Update', in *Population Trends 106* (Winter 2001), 69–72, London: Office of National Statistics.

Pratt, E. (1994), *Living in Sin?*, enlarged ed., Southsea: St Simon's Church.

Pritchard, J. B. (1954), *The Ancient Near East in Pictures*, Princeton: University Press.

Ramsay, W. M. (1907), *The Cities of St Paul*, Minneapolis: James Family Christian Publications.

Ramsey, P. (1975), *One Flesh: A Christian View of Sex within, outside and before Marriage*, Nottingham: Grove Ethical Booklets no. 8; first published in *Journal of Religion*, 1965.

Reed, W. L. (1962), 'Asherah', in *Interpreter's Dictionary of the Bible* 1:250, New York: Nashville.

Reif, S. C. (1971), 'What enraged Phinehas? A Study of Numbers 25:8', *JBL* 90:200–206.

Richards, M. (1995), 'The Companionship Trap', in C. Clulow (ed.), *Women, Men and Marriage*, 55–64, London: Sheldon Press.

Richardson, J. (1995), *God, Sex and Marriage*, St Matthias Press/MPA Publications.

Ringgren, H. (1973), *Religions of the Ancient Near East*, London: SPCK.

Robertson and Plummer (1911), *First Epistle of St Paul to the Corinthians, ICC*, Edinburgh: T. and T. Clark.

Robinson, J. A. T. (1952), *The Body. A Study in Pauline Theology*, London: SCM.

Rofe, A. (1987), 'Family and Sex Laws in Deuteronomy', *Henoch* 19:131–159.

Rosner, B. S. (1994), *Paul, Scripture and Ethics: a study of 1 Corinthians 5–7*, Leiden: Brill.

— (1998), 'Temple Prostitution in 1 Corinthians 6:12–20', *NT* 40.4:336–351.

— (1999), 'The Concept of Idolatry', *Themelios* 24.3:21–30.

— (forthcoming), *Greed, the Second Idolatry: The Origin and Meaning of a Pauline Metaphor*, Tübingen: Mohr.

Rowley, H. H. (1965), 'The Interpretation of the Song of Songs', in *The Servant of the Lord and Other Essays on the Old Testament*, 197–245, Oxford: Basil Blackwell.

Sampley, J. P. (1971), *'And the Two Shall Become One Flesh': A Study of Traditions in Ephesians 5:21–33*, Cambridge: Cambridge University Press.

Sarna, N. M. (1989), *Genesis*, JPS Torah Commentary Series, Philadelphia: Jewish Publication Society.

Scase, R. (2000), *Britain in 2010*, Oxford: Capstone Publishing.

Schillebeeckx, E. (1965), *Marriage: Human Reality and Saving Mystery*, London: Sheed and Ward.

Schluter, M. and D. Lee (1993), *The R Factor*, London: Hodder and Stoughton.

Schmidt, T. E. (1995), *Straight and Narrow? (Compassion and Clarity in the homosexuality debate)*, Leicester: IVP.

Schrage, W. (1988), *The Ethics of the New Testament*, ET Edinburgh: T. and T. Clark.

Schreiner, T. R. (1991), 'Head Coverings, Prophecy and the Trinity', in Piper and Grudem (eds.), *Recovering Biblical Manhood and Womanhood*, ch. 5, Wheaton, Illinois: Crossway Books.

Schüssler Fiorenza, E. (1983), *In Memory of Her: A Feminist Theological Reconstruction of Christian Origins*, London: SCM.

Scruton, R. (1986), *Sexual Desire: A Philosophical Investigation*, London: Weidenfeld & Nicholson.

Selwyn, E. G. (1947), *The First Epistle of St Peter*, London: Macmillan.

Shaw, G. (1983), *The Cost of Authority: manipulation and freedom in the New Testament*, London: SCM.

Simon, M. (1981), 'The Apostolic Decree and its Setting in the Ancient Church', in *Le Christianisme antique et son contexte religieux: Scripta Varia*, WUNT 23:414–437, Tübingen: Mohr.

Skinner, J. (1930), *Genesis*, *ICC*, Edinburgh: T. and T. Clark.

Snodgrass, K. R. (1986), 'Galatians 3:28: Conundrum or Solution?' in A. Mickelsen (ed.), *Women, Authority and the Bible*, 161–181, Downers Grove, Illinois: IVP.

Social Trends 31 (2001), *Social Trends 31*, London: Office of National Statistics.

Soskice, J. M. (1985), *Metaphor and Religious Language*, Oxford: Clarendon Press.

Spong, J. S. (1988), *Living in Sin? A Bishop Rethinks Human Sexuality*, San Francisco: Harper and Row.

Stackhouse, M. L. (1997), *Covenant and Commitments: Faith, Family and Economic Life*, Louisville, Kentucky: Westminster, John Knox Press.

Stafford, T. (1993), *Sexual Chaos*, rev. ed., Downers Grove: IVP.

Stark, R. (1996), *The Rise of Christianity*, Princeton: University Press.

Stendahl, K. (1966), *The Bible and the Role of Women*, trans. E. T. Sanders, ET Philadelphia: Fortress Press.

Sternberg, M. (1985), *The Poetics of Biblical Narrative*, Bloomington: Indiana University Press.

Stone, L. (1979), *The Family, Sex and Marriage in England 1500–1800*, abridged ed., London: Pelican Books.

Storkey, A. (1994), *The Meanings of Love*, Leicester: IVP.

— (1996), *Marriage and its Modern Crisis*, London: Hodder and Stoughton.

Storkey, E. (1985), *What's right with feminism*, London: SPCK.

— (1995), *The Search for Intimacy*, Hodder and Stoughton.

— (1997), 'Spirituality and Sexuality' in D. W. Torrance (ed.), *God, Family and Sexuality*, ch. 10, Carberry, Scotland: Handsel Press.

— (2000), *Men and Women: Created or Constructed? The Great Gender Debate*, Carlisle: Paternoster Press.

Stott, J. R. W. (1991), *The Message of Thessalonians*, Bible Speaks Today series, Leicester: IVP.

Strabo (Geography), *Strabo's Geography*, 8 vols., Cambridge, Mass.: Harvard University Press, Loeb Classical Library.

Taylor, L. and M. Taylor (2001), 'What are Children For?' in *Prospect*, June 2001, 22–26.

Taylor, P. (1998), *For Better or Worse: Marriage and Cohabitation Compared*, London: CARE.

TDNT (1964–), *Theological Dictionary of the New Testament*, Grand Rapids: Eerdmans.

Tertullian (Fasting), *On Fasting*, in *Library of Ante-Nicene Fathers IV*, repr. Grand Rapids: Eerdmans, 1989.

Thatcher, A. (1993), *Liberating Sex – A Christian Sexual Theology*, London: SPCK.

— (1999), *Marriage after Modernity: Christian Marriage in Postmodern Times*, Sheffield: Academic Press.

— (2002), *Living together and Christian ethics*, Cambridge: Cambridge University Press.

Thielicke, H. (1979), *The Ethics of Sex*, ET London: James Clarke (first published in German as Vol. 3 of *Theological Ethics*).

Thiselton, A. (1997), 'Can Hermeneutics Ease the Deadlock?', in T. Bradshaw (ed.), *The Way Forward? Christian Voices on Homosexuality and the Church*, 145–196, London: Hodder and Stoughton.

Thompson, J. A. (1974), 'The Significance of the verb love in the David-Jonathan Narratives in 1 Samuel', *VT* 24:334–338.

Tigay, J. H. (1996), *Deuteronomy*, JPS Torah Commentary, Philadelphia: Jewish Publication Society.

Toffler, A. (1971), *Future Shock*, New York: Bantam Books.

Tomlin, G. (1999), *The Power of the Cross*, Carlisle: Paternoster.

Torrance, D. W. (1997), 'Marriage in the Light of Scripture', in D. W. Torrance (ed.), *God, Family and Sexuality*, 31–47, Carberry, Scotland: The Handsel Press.

Tosato, A. (1984), 'The Law of Leviticus 18:18: A Reexamination', *CBQ* 46:199–214.

Tosefta (1981), *The Tosefta*, translated from the Hebrew, Fourth Division, by Jacob Neusner, New York: Ktav Publishing House.

Trible, P. (1978), *God and the Rhetoric of Sexuality*, Philadelphia: Fortress Press.

Tsumura, D. T. (1989), *The Earth and the Waters in Genesis 1 and 2, JSOT* Supplement 83, Sheffield: JSOT Press.

Vermes, G. (1961), *Scripture and Tradition in Judaism: Haggadic Studies*, Leiden: Brill.

Von Rad, G. (1972a), *Wisdom in Israel*, ET London: SCM.

— (1972b), *Genesis*, ET London: SCM.

Walsh, J. T. (1977), 'Genesis 2:4b–3:24: A Synchronic Approach', *JBL* XCVI:161–177.

Ware, K. (1997), '"My helper and my enemy": the body in Greek Christianity', in S. Coakley (ed.), *Religion and the Body*, 90–110, Cambridge: Cambridge University Press.

Webb, B. G. (ed.) (1994), *Theological and Pastoral Responses to Homosexuality*, Adelaide: Openbook.

Weinfeld, M. (1972), *Deuteronomy and the Deuteronomic School*, Oxford: Oxford University Press.

Wenham, G. (1972), '"Betulah" A Girl of Marriageable Age', *VT* 22:326–348.

— (1979a), *Leviticus*, NICOT, Grand Rapids: Eerdmans.

— (1979b), 'The Restoration of Marriage Reconsidered', *JJS* 30:36–40.

— (1987), *Genesis 1– 15*, Dallas, Texas: Word Biblical Commentary.

Westermann, C. (1987), *Genesis*, Grand Rapids: Eerdmans.

Williams, S. (1993), 'I will: the Debate about Cohabitation', *Anvil* 10.3:209–224.

Winter, B. (1994), *Seek the Welfare of the City: Christians as benefactors and citizens*, Grand Rapids: Eerdmans.

— (2000), 'The "New" Roman Wife and 1 Timothy 2:9–15: The Search for a Sitz im Leben', *TB* 51.2:285–294.

— (2001), *After Paul left Corinth*, Grand Rapids: Eerdmans.

Wire, A. C. (1990), *The Corinthian Women Prophets*, Minneapolis: Fortress Press.

Witherington, B. (1980), 'Rite and Rights for Women – Galatians 3:28', *NTS* 27:593–604.

— (1988), *Women in the earliest churches*, Cambridge: Cambridge University Press.

— (1995), *Conflict and Community in Corinth: A Socio-Rhetorical Commentary on 1 & 2 Corinthians*, Grand Rapids: Eerdmans.

Witte, J. (1997), *From Sacrament to Contract: Marriage, Religion and Law in the Western Tradition*, Louisville, Kentucky: Westminster, John Knox Press.

Wolff, H. W. (1974), *Hosea*, ET Philadelphia: Fortress Press.

Woodhead, L. (1996), 'Christianity For and Against the Family: a Response to Nicholas Peter Harvey', in *Studies in Christian Ethics* 9.1: 40–46, Edinburgh: T. and T. Clark.

— (1997), 'Sex in a wider context', in Davies and Loughlin, *Sex these days*, 98–120, Sheffield: Academic Press.

Wright, C. J. H. (1983), *Living as the People of God: The Relevance of Old Testament Ethics*, Leicester: IVP.

— (1990), *God's People in God's Land*, Grand Rapids: Eerdmans.

Wright, D. (1994), *The Christian Faith and Homosexuality*, Edinburgh: Rutherford House.

Wright, G. E. (1962), *Biblical Archaeology*, Philadelphia: Westminster.

Yamauchi, E. M. (1965), 'Tammuz and the Bible', *JBL* 84:283–290.

Yarbrough, O. L. (1985), *Not Like the Gentiles: Marriage Rules in the Letters of Paul*, Chico: Scholars Press.

Zimmerli, W. (1979), *Ezekiel 1 – 24*, Philadelphia: Fortress Press.

SCRIPTURE INDEX

Genesis
1 – 2 150, 254
1:1 – 2:3 65f., 112–114
1 – 11 90
1:26–28 107, 158, 178,
  274, 277, 284, 293, 318
2:4–25 115–122, 158, 274,
  304
2:16 90
2:18 107, 116–122, 168,
  338
2:18–25 110, 197
2:23 49, 363
2:24 88f., 237, 252, 325,
  348f.
3:9–19 277–279
3:16 80, 159
3:17 80, 159
4:19–24 249
5 88, 171, 244
5:1–5 114, 159
6:1–4 159, 249, 297
9 91, 367
9:1–7 92, 97, 107, 114,
  159
9:22f. 236
9:31 88
10 172, 244
11 159, 171, 244, 255
12:1–3 130, 160, 187
12:10–20 186
13:17 262
15:5 160
16 249
17:5f. 160

17:17 137
18:12f. 137, 330
18:15 137, 330
18:19 163
19:14 137
19:30–38 218, 260
20 226, 236
20:4 258
20:12 260
21:6 137
21:9 137
23:1f. 186
24:16 213, 364
24:67 186
26:8 137, 186
26:34f. 166f.
28 166f.
29:14 348f.
29:17 348f.
29:20 186
29:21–30 263
29:22 234
31:50 343
34 237f.
35:22 153, 259
36 172
37:27 348
38 212–214, 218, 251,
  261–263
38:11–13 29
38:15 291
39:8 357
39:9 357
39:14 137
39:17 137

41:50ff. 167
42:9 236
42:12 236
48:7 186
49:4 259
49:21 186
49:25 161

Exodus
1 – 2 160, 172
3:15 174
6:20 261
10:12 164
12:26f. 164
13:14 164
18:4 277
20:12 334
20:14 264, 357
20:17 153, 358
20:26 206, 235
21:10f. 250f.
22:16f. 216, 222
23:26 161
28:42 235
32:6 135f.
34:13 143
34:14 147
38:8 149

Leviticus
12:7 263
15:20 263
17 95, 97
17:7 134
18 91f., 95f., 257–266

Leviticus (continued)
18 – 20   235, 257
18:6   268
18:18   250f.
18:21   360
19:18   324, 326
19:29   213
20:1–6   134, 264, 360
20:10   357
20:10–21   259–264
21:7   213
21:9   213
21:14   213
22:22   357
26:9   160
26:22   160

Numbers
11:34   135f.
12:1f.   167
15:37–40   134
14:1–38   135f.
16:41   135f.
21:4–9   135f.
22 – 25   137–142
25:1ff.   135f.
27:8   263
31:1–18   138f.

Deuteronomy
1:10   160
4:3f.   138
4:9   164
4:16   147
5:2f.   78
5:18   264, 357
5:21   153
6:4–9   165
6:20–25   165
7:3–5   166
7:5   143
7:13   160
10:22   160
11:18–21   164
12:3   143
13:6   186
13:17   160
16:21   144

18:10   264
20:7   162
21:15–17   250f.
21:18–21   336
22:13–21   184, 213
22:14   258
22:22   356
22:23–29   216, 222, 228
23:3–6   138f.
23:17f.   212
23:18   149
24:1–4   251
24:5   162
25:5–10   218, 251, 257, 261f.
27:15–26   80, 257
27:20   259
27:21   264
27:22   260
27:23   263
28:30   161
28:54   186
31:16   134
32:20f.   134

Joshua
2 & 6   213f.
4:4–7   164
6:22   142
14:21f.   164
15:16   230
22:17   138
23:12   166

Judges
2:10   165
2:13   145
2:16f.   134
3:7   143
6:25–30   143
8:27   134
8:33   134
9:25   289
9:36   289
10:6   145
11:1   213
11:34–40   161
13   172
16:1   213

16:25   137
19 – 21   216
19:2   214
19:12   31
21:25   165

Ruth
1 – 4   29, 166
4   262
4:6   251
4:13ff.   172

1 Samuel
1   172, 181, 249
1:5–8   186
2:22   149, 212
7:3f.   145
12:10   145
18 – 20   118
20:8   343, 345
25   168, 338
31:10   145

2 Samuel
1:26   116
3   230
3:15f.   186
5:1   348
7   172
7:14   284
11   356, 363f.
11 – 12   29
11 – 13   31
12:8   250
12:11   250
13   237
13:13   260
13:14   216
13:15   182
15:16   259
16:21   259
20:3   259
22:44   290
24:1   250

1 Kings
1   29, 190

2:22 259
3:1 166
3:16 213
7:8 166
7:16 289
7:41 289
8:8 289
9:24 166
11:1–13 166f.
11:5 145
11:33 145
14:15 143f.
14:21 167
14:23 143f.
14:24 212
14:31 167
15:1f. 167
15:10 167
15:12 212
15:13 143f.
16:31ff. 143f., 166
18:19 143f.
21:12 290
21:25 167
22:42 167
22:47 212
23:38 213

2 Kings
8:18 166
8:25–27 167f.
11 167
12:1 167
13:6 143
14:1ff. 167f.
15:1ff. 167f.
15:32ff. 167f.
16:3 264
17:10 143f.
17:16 143f.
18:1ff. 168
18:4 143
21:1 250
21:1ff. 168
21:3 143f.
21:7 143f., 147
21:19 168
22:1f. 168

23:4–15 143f.
23:6 147
23:7 212
23:10 264
23:13 145
23:31 168
23:36 168
24:8 168
24:15 168
24:18 168

1 Chronicles
1–9 172, 243
5:1 259
16:15 174

2 Chronicles
13:1f. 168
13:21 250
15:16 144f.
20:31f. 168
21:13 134
22:1–3 168
24:1–3 252
25:1 168
26:3 168
27:1f. 168
29:1f. 168
33:7 147
33:15 147

Ezra
9–10 166

Nehemiah
9:21 167
10:30 166f.
13:1–3 167
13:2 138f.
13:23–27 166f.

Esther
1–10 249
1:5 234
2:18 234
6:12 291
9:22 234

Job
24:13–17 359
31:1 206
31:9–12 80
36:14 212

Psalms
8 69, 84, 131, 159, 313, 318
15:4 220
18:43 290
19 93
19:5 186
22:9f. 165f.
22:30 165
34:11 165
37 81
42:1 118
45 118
45:11 186
48:12–14 165
49 81
50:18 360
51 29
51:4 357
68:6 118
70:5 277
73 80f.
78 135f., 165
78:63 186
84:2 118
100:3 67
103:5 118
105:24 160
106 135f.
106:28–31 138, 141
119:9 31, 206
127 162
127:3–5 161
128:3 161
135:15–19 127
138:1 297

Proverbs
1:8 163
2:16f. 344–353, 360
3:19 66
3:25 331

Proverbs (continued)
5 – 7   213
5:15ff.   358, 360
5:18f.   186, 193, 343f.
6:20–35   80, 110, 359
11:22   168
12:4   293
13:12   118
13:19   118
19:13   168
20:6   367
21:9   168
22:14   360
23:27   214, 360
25:19   367
25:22   317
25:24   168
26:21   168
27:15f.   168
29:3   219, 358
30:15   125
30:18f.   22
30:20   25, 359
31:3   358
31:10–31   168f., 338
31:12   293
31:23   293

Ecclesiastes
1:12 – 2:26   129
3:5   171
3:11   366
4:9f.   120
7:10   19
7:26   213
9:9   186
12:5   190

Song of. Songs
1 – 8   49, 86, 110,
  192–198, 363
2:5   186
2:7   196
2:10   197
2:10–13   198
2:16   196
3:5   196
3:6–11   195, 199

4:12 – 5:1   198
5:1   195–197
5:8   186
5:8f.   196
5:12   195
5:16   196
6:1   196
6:2   198
6:11   198
7:1–10   196
7:12   198
8:8f.   196

Isaiah
1:21   134
1:29   143
3:16 – 4:1   168
3:18–24   329
4:4   29
6:2   291
7:14   172
17:8   143
23:15–18   218
25:6   194
27:6   160
27:9   143
30:33   264
40:10   278
42:1–4   30
43:6   284
47:3   235
48:18f.   160
49:2   162
50:1   89
51:1f.   160, 330
54:1–10   89, 160
56:5   171
57:1–6   360
57:3–10   143
58:7   348
61:10   186
62:4f.   89, 122, 186, 192
65:17   85
65:17–25   162
66:22   85

Jeremiah
2 – 4   89

2:1f.   364
3:1   218
3:4   344
3:6   143
3:6–13   250
3:9   358
5:7f.   142f., 358
7:9   357
7:17f.   146
7:34   186
9:2   357
13:26f.   143
16:1–4   174
16:9   186
17:2   143f.
23:10   357, 360
23:13f.   134
23:14   357
25:10   186
29:6   174
29:23   357
31:21f.   134
33:11   186
34:8   345
44:15–25   146
49:4   134

Lamentations
1:2   134
1:8   235
5:11   216

Ezekiel
6:9   134
6:13   143
8   147–149
11:18–21   148
14:7f.   97
14:13   134
16   22, 89, 212, 342f., 364
16:1–14   323
16:8   236
16:20f.   360
16:36   204
16:38   357, 360
17:16–20   345
18:6   263f., 357
18:11   264, 357

18:15   264, 357
20:27–31   143
20:31   214
22:10   259, 263
22:11   260f., 264, 357
23   22, 89, 212, 250
23:10   235
23:18   206, 235
23:29   235
23:36–49   92
23:37–39   264, 360
23:43–49   360
24:15ff.   186
33:23–26   92
33:25   266
33:26   357
37:15–28   243
43:7–9   134

Daniel
5:2   249
5:23   249

Hosea
1 – 3   89
2:9–11   235
4:2   357
4:14   143, 212
7:4–7   357–359
9:10–13   138f., 141
9:14   161
14:5–8   86
14:9   78

Joel
1:3   165
1:8   346
2:25   30
2:28f.   284
3:3   213

Amos
1 – 2   92
1:13   161
2:7   259
2:15   216
4:1   169

5:2   134
7:17   213
8:13   186
9:11f.   94

Micah
1:7   134
5:2–5   172
5:13   143
6:5   138f.
6:6f.   264

Nahum
3:4   134

Zechariah
8:2   134
8:5   174
14:2   216

Malachi
2:14   238, 341–344
2:14f.   344
2:15   159
2:16   245
3:5   357
3:6   367
4:5f.   164
4:6   245

Matthew
1:1–17   29, 171
1:18–25   223
5:16   306
5:27–30   206
5:27f.   362f.
5:32   96, 215
5:46   198
6:24   154
7:1f.   29
7:22   362
7:24–27   81
9:10–13   30
9:12f.   28
9:14f.   89
10:28   331
11:29   30

12:20   30
12:30   243
12:39   134, 361
14:3f.   257
15:19   215
16:4   134, 361
18:15   328
19:4f.   112
19:5   252
19:5f.   345
19:9   96, 215
21:31f.   30, 214
22:1–14   89
22:2ff.   234
22:23–32   158
22:24ff.   257
22:29f.   87
22:34–40   28
23:4   30, 94
24:19   161
24:37   186
25:1–13   89
25:10   234

Mark
1:15   24
2:27   188
7:21   215
7:22   363
8:38   361
10:2–12   128
10:6f.   112
10:8   252
10:8f.   345
10:19   362
12:24f.   87
12:28–33   28

Luke
1:5–38   172
1:8   312
2:21–40   172
2:40–52   164
2:51   315, 334
3:23–38   171
5:30   30
6:32   123, 199
7:34   30

Luke (continued)
7:36–50   30
10:17   313
10:20   313
10:25–28   28
11:46   30
12:36   234
13:16   330
14:8   234
15:2   30
15:30   214
16:13   154
16:22   87
16:27f.   123
18:9–14   29
18:11   362
20:27ff.   158
20:36   174

John
1:18   117
2:1–11   186, 234
4:1–42   29f.
4:34   128
8:1–11   30, 362
8:11   32
8:41   214
9:1ff.   31
10:16   243
13 – 16   118
13:14f.   309
15:30   358
19:11   335
20:34–36   87f.
24:36–43   354

Acts
2:25   326
5:1–11   123
9:15   333
9:36ff.   131
10:2   91
10:22   91
10:35   91
11:27–30   93
13:16   91
13.26   91
13:36   104

13:50   91
14:2   328
15   93–99, 141, 215
15:19f.   152
15:28f.   152
15:29   136
16:1   166
16:14   91
17:4   91
17:6   19, 57
18:6   291
18:7   91
18:18ff.   328
19:9   328
21:25   152
24:18   285

Romans
1:16   19
1:18   29
1:21   254
1:23–25   152
1:26f.   298
2:1f.   29
2:6   220
2:22   29, 362
3:19f.   28
3:21–26   29
4:5   29
5:13f.   28
5:20   28
7:18f.   32
7:22   335
8:7   314, 334
8:18–27   31
8:19   85
8:19–21   131
8:20   78, 313
8:29   30
10:3   314, 334
10:12f.   280
11:13–32   305
12:20   317
13:1–7   304, 314, 334
13:8–10   28
13:9   362
13:11–14   362

14:4   175f.
15:31   328
16:3–5   131, 338

1 Corinthians
1:18 – 2:5   19, 70
4:5   29
4:9   297
5:1   96, 214, 257, 259
5:9–11   215
6:9–11   28, 31, 152, 215, 362
6:12–20   214f., 350–355
6:16   112, 325, 345
7:1f.   354
7:1–6   188–192, 204f., 216, 294
7:2   110, 173, 215
7:3f.   228
7:4   328
7:5   333
7:12–16   327
7:17–24   282
7:21–24   285
7:23   335
7:29   87
7:36–38   232
8:4   127
8:4–6   133
9:19–22   328
10:1–13   78, 135–142
10:8   215
10:14–22   133
11:2–16   273, 286–302, 317
11:3   318
11:7f.   277
11:8   304
12:13   282
12:21   317
13   118
14:33–36   302–305
14:34   316
14:40   312
15:24–28   313
15:27f.   290, 318
15:35ff.   85
16:3   166
16:15f.   315

2 Corinthians
4:2 70
4:5 308
4:7 333
6:6 332
6:16–18 284
9:13 309, 312
10:3–5 70
11:1–3 89, 134, 323
12:21 215

Galatians
1 – 2 93f.
2:4 297
2:5 309, 312
3:15–22 172, 255
3:16 171
3:24 28
3:26–29 273, 280–286, 305
4:6 284
4:21 – 5:1 330
5:19 215
5:19–21 152

Ephesians
1:9f. 84, 325
1:22f. 313f., 317–319
2:20f. 319
3:3 325
3:4 325
3:9 325
3:17 319
3:19 319
4:1 86
4:7–21 319
4:15f. 317f.
4:19 362
4:28 169
5:2 319
5:3 22
5:3–5 153–155, 215
5:10 319
5:17 319
5:19 319
5:21 319
5:21–33 89, 110, 273, 285, 307–327
5:21 – 6:9 304

5:22–24 290, 328
5:25 169
5:31 112, 252, 348
6:1 315f.
6:1–4 164
6:5 315
6:19 325

Philippians
2:3–8 308f.
2:5–11 230
3:21 313

Colossians
1:15–20 84
1:18 317f.
2:5 312
2:9f. 317f.
3:5 153–155, 215
3:11 282
3:18f. 273, 285, 307–327
3:18 – 4:1 304
3:20 315f.
3:22 315f.
4:5 306

1 Thessalonians
1:10 195
2:6–8 117f.
2:7 325
4:1 32, 94
4:1ff. 86
4:1–8 173, 215
4:4 333
4:6 111
4:12 306

1 Timothy
1:8–11 28
1:10 215
2:2–4 306
2:8–15 280
2:9 329
2:11 309, 312, 316
2:13f. 277, 293, 304
2:15 166
3:2 252
3:4 164, 309, 312, 315f.

3:12 164
3:15 269
4:3f. 155
5:2 31, 269
5:9 252
5:11–15 205
5:21 297
6:1f. 303, 315
6:17 193

2 Timothy
1:5 166
2:2 166
2:22 31
3:10 31
3:15 166

Titus
1:6 164, 252
2:1–10 304
2:3–5 280, 294f.
2:4 299, 325
2:4f. 320
2:5 316, 328
2:6 31
2:9 315
2:11–14 30f.
3:1 315

Philemon
116

Hebrews
2:5–9 84, 313, 318
2:8f. 131
3:7 88
3:16 88
4:1–11 89
5:6 312
5:10 312
6:20 312
7:11 312
7:17 312
11:31 214
12:9 314, 316
12:16 215
13:4 215, 234, 264, 364
13:17 315

James
1:13f.   32
2:10f.   29
2:11   362
2:25   214
3:1f.   22
4:4   134, 361
4:7   314, 334
5:16   309f.

1 Peter
1:3   83f.
1:4f.   85
1:17   329
2:12   306, 320
2:13   315, 335
2:13–17   334
2:13 – 3:7   230, 304
2:16   335
2:18   315, 329
2:18–25   334
2:19   335
2:21–23   327

3:1–7   273, 327–336
3:1, 6   316
3:3ff.   168
3:6   316
3:7   286
3:15f.   320
3:20   166
3:22   313
4:3   362
4:4   306
5:3–5   308f., 315

2 Peter
1:4–6   362
1:5   332
2:12–16   138f., 362f.
3:7–13   83, 85f.

1 John
2:13f.   31
2:16   363
3:2   29f.
4:7–21   117

Jude
7   212
11   138f.

Revelation
2:14   98, 136, 138f., 152
2:20   98, 136, 138, 141, 152
2:20–23   361
9:20f.   98, 152, 215
12:1 – 13:1   172
14:8   134, 214
17:1 – 19:10   134, 214
18   134
18 – 22   89
18:23   186
19:7   234
19:9   234
21 – 22   85
21:8   98, 215
22:15   152, 215